Divine Ministry–
The First Gospel

Jesus Among the Nephites

~

by

Monte Nyman

Distributed by:

Granite Publishing and Distribution, LLC
868 North 1430 West
Orem, Utah 84057
(801) 229-9023 • Toll Free (800) 574-5779
Fax (801) 229-1924

Page Layout & Design by Myrna Varga, The Office Connection, Inc.
Cover Design by Steve Gray

"Jesus Christ Visits the Nephites" by John Scott
© by Intellectual Reserve, Inc.

Library of Congress Control Number: 2002116838
ISBN: 1-930980-96-5

Printed in the United States of America

10 9 8 7 6 5 4 3 2 1

Contents

∿

Introduction

∿

A study of the Life of Christ, or of the New Testament Gospels, would be incomplete if it did not include the contribution of the Book of Mormon. President Ezra Taft Benson gave the following counsel to the members of the Church:

> The Book of Mormon is the instrument that God designed to "sweep the earth as with a flood, to gather out [His] elect" (Moses 7:62). This sacred volume of scripture needs to become more central in our preaching, our teaching, and our missionary work.
>
> At present, the Book of Mormon is studied in our Sunday School and seminary classes every fourth year. This four-year pattern, however, must not be followed by the Church members in their personal and family study. We need to read daily from the pages of the book that will get a man "nearer to God by abiding by its precepts, than by any other book." (History of the Church, 4:461)
>
> And when we are called upon to study or teach other scriptures, we need to strengthen that undertaking by frequent reference to the additional insights which the Book of Mormon may provide on the subject. (See 1 Nephi 13:40; 2 Nephi 3:12) [CR, October 1988, 3.]

Third Nephi, the account of Jesus' ministry to the Nephites, especially provides extensive additional insights to an understanding of the teachings of our resurrected Lord and Savior.

Jesus ministered for three years among the people of Palestine as a mortal being. This will be referred to as his "mortal ministry" in this work. His ministry in the Americas following his resurrection in Jerusalem will be referred to as his "divine ministry." He ministered for just three days as a divine, resurrected being among the more righteous of the Nephites who were spared from the destruction at the time of his crucifixion. Although Mormon, the abridger of the records tells us, "there cannot be written in this book even a hundredth part of the things which Jesus did truly teach unto the people" (3 Nephi 26:6),[1] what is provided gives us a basis of understanding the four New Testament Gospels.

As pointed out by President N. Eldon Tanner, "Third Nephi gives us additional information in more detail than the four Gospels in the New Testament, and preserves the doctrines, teachings, and compassion of the Lord. For this reason there are many who refer to Third Nephi as the fifth Gospel" (CR, April 1975, 52). Acknowledging the insight of those who call it the fifth Gospel, Third Nephi would more accurately be viewed as the first and foremost Gospel of Jesus Christ. Based upon the theories of the world it was written before the New Testament Gospels,[2] but more importantly, it defines and explains the gospel per se, as well as many other teachings of the Savior.

In addition to defining the gospel,[3] Third Nephi interprets and clarifies many New Testament teachings, which further justifies desig-

---

[1] The writer of the Gospel of John made a similar statement: "And there are also many other things which Jesus did, the which, if they should be written every one, I suppose that even the world itself could not contain the books that should be written. Amen" (John 21:25).

[2] Although there is a wide variance among scholars in the dating of the writing of the New Testament Gospels, the traditional dates of the four Gospels being written are about: Mark A.D. 65–70.; Matthew A.D. 75–80; Luke A.D. 80–85; John A.D. 95–100. However, 1 Nephi 13:24 indicates the records were written much earlier than the traditional dates, probably during and following Jesus' ministry. The Nephite account of his ministry, from which Mormon made his abridgment, was also made at the time of the Nephite ministry (see 3 Nephi 26:7–8).

[3] The gospel is defined in 3 Nephi 27:13–22. We will discuss the definition given there in chapter 14 of this work.

nating it as the first Gospel. Third Nephi 8 through 28:12 and Moroni 2–6 (an appendage of the Savior's teachings to the Nephites added by Moroni) contains as much information about Jesus' teachings as there is in any of the four New Testament accounts. The information in Third Nephi is also of a higher quality. President, J. Reuben Clark made this observation several years ago:

> I reflected a bit on where might I go to find the real words of the Savior. I knew I could not go to the Bible. We do not believe the Bible is absolutely correct. Students tell us there are 4500 different manuscripts of the Bible, and a few years ago it was estimated that there were 120,000 variations. Then it came to me almost as a revelation: Why do you not go to the Book of Mormon? So I took Third Nephi. I went over it with great care. I parallel-columned it with the parts of the New Testament concerning the Sermon on the Mount and the Sermon on the Plain. In the Old Testament I noted the instructions to Malachi as they were repeated by the Savior, because they had no record of Malachi, who lived after they left Jerusalem.
>
> I found some differences, some omissions from the word that he was recorded as having spoken in Palestine. But I resorted to the Book of Mormon and to Third Nephi with the feeling that I was getting really what the Savior said. I commend an equal study by you brethren of those great books of the Book of Mormon and so far as the Savior's immediate mission was concerned, Third Nephi. There we may believe we have the true teachings, for the record was made by inspired men, abridged by another inspired man, and translated through the inspiration and revelation of the Lord himself. Brethren, I commend that to you, study it, if you never have done so, you will find great joy in the doing [CR, April 1960, 43].

Jesus was limited in what he could teach among the people of Palestine because of their lack of faith. To the Nephite disciples, on the second day of his ministry among them, he said:

"So great faith have I never seen among all the Jews; wherefore I could not show unto them so great miracles, because of their unbelief" (3 Nephi 19:35). He even taught many things that were not recorded because of our lack of faith in the day when the Book of Mormon was to come forth. If we faithfully study and follow the Book of Mormon teachings, these unrecorded things are promised to be given to us (see 3 Nephi 26:9–10, discussed in chapter 13).

In a general conference of the Church, President Gordon B. Hinckley declared the importance of studying the accounts of Jesus.

> Let us establish in our lives the habit of reading those things which will strengthen our faith in the Lord Jesus Christ, the Savior of the world. He is the pivotal figure of our theology and our faith. Every Latter-day Saint has the responsibility to know for himself or herself with a certainty beyond doubt that Jesus is the resurrected, living son of the living God. The Brethren of the Council of the Twelve are advocating that we read a chapter a day of the Gospels—that is, Matthew, Mark, Luke, and John in the Bible; and Third Nephi in the Book of Mormon, particularly beginning with the eleventh chapter of Third Nephi where is found the account of Christ's visit among the Nephites in this hemisphere. I should like to endorse this program and commend it to you and urge you to follow it [CR, April 1983, 110].

More recently President Benson has said: "Third Nephi is a book that should be read and read again. Its testimony of the resurrected Christ in America is given in purity and beauty."[4] A study of Third Nephi should give us a solid foundation for understanding the gospel of the Lord Jesus Christ as well as the accounts of his teachings in the New Testament. For this reason, this study incorporates the concepts and principles of the New Testament Gospels within the chronology of the Third Nephi record, and in as far as it seems appropriate, provides parallel accounts of Third Nephi and the New Testament Gospels. The study of Third Nephi as an additional gospel has usually been done as an appendage to the other gospels, probably because it was an extension of his mortal ministry.[5] The course pursued is optional, but the Book of Third Nephi is the primary source for gaining insight into the teachings of Jesus Christ, the Son of God, and is therefore considered the First Gospel.

---

[4] Ezra Taft Benson. *A Witness and a Warning*, (Deseret Book Company: Salt Lake City, 1988) p. 43.

[5] See J. Reuben Clark, Jr. *Our Lord of the Gospels,* (Deseret Book: Salt Lake City, 1954) or James E. Talmage, (Deseret Book: Salt Lake City, 1951).

The New Testament contains four separate accounts of Jesus Christ's life and mission, which are called the Gospels. They were written by Matthew, Mark, Luke, and John; apostles of Jesus Christ, and eyewitnesses of his ministry. The Prophet Joseph Smith was called to write a revelatory translation of the Bible. The Lord promised that " the scriptures shall be given, even as they are in mine own bosom, to the plain and precious parts that had been lost from it hundreds of years before.[6] This work is called the Joseph Smith Translation (hereafter the JST). In his work, the Prophet changed the title of these four records from "Gospels" to "Testimonies" of Matthew, Mark, Luke, and John, showing that they are more correctly the written testimonies of these disciples about the life and ministry of Jesus of Nazareth. Matthew, Mark, and Luke are called the synoptic [synonymous] Gospels because they concentrate primarily on a general survey of Jesus' ministry. Matthew begins with the genealogy and birth of Jesus Christ, and places emphasis on the fulfillment of

---

[6] The angel also told Nephi: "Behold it proceedeth out of the mouth of a Jew. And I, Nephi, beheld it; and he said unto me: The book that thou beholdest is a record of the Jews, which contains the covenants of the Lord, which he hath made unto the house of Israel; and it also containeth many of the prophecies of the holy prophets; and it is a record like unto the engravings which are upon the plates of brass, save there are not so many; nevertheless, they contain the covenants of the Lord, which he hath made unto the house of Israel; wherefore, they are of great worth unto the Gentiles.

24 And the angel of the Lord said unto me: Thou hast beheld that the book proceeded forth from the mouth of a Jew; and when it proceeded forth from the mouth of a Jew it contained the fulness of the gospel of the Lord, of whom the twelve apostles bear record; and they bear record according to the truth which is in the Lamb of God.

25 Wherefore, these things go forth from the Jews in purity unto the Gentiles, according to the truth which is in God.

26 And after they go forth by the hand of the twelve apostles of the Lamb, from the Jews unto the Gentiles, thou seest the formation of that great and abominable church, which is most abominable above all other churches; for behold, they have taken away from the gospel of the Lamb many parts which are plain and most precious; and also many covenants of the Lord have they taken away.

27 And all this have they done that they might pervert the right ways of the Lord, that they might blind the eyes and harden the hearts of the children of men." 1 Nephi 13:23–27

Old Testament prophecies. Mark begins with John the Baptist's preparatory ministry before the ministry of Jesus, and although he has longer, more detailed accounts than the other gospels, he does not include many events that are in the others, making it the shortest record. Luke begins with the births of John the Baptist and Jesus, and is much more comprehensive, being written to the larger gentile audience. John's testimony begins with a discussion of the pre-mortal Messiah, a brief witness of Christ as the light of the world, and John the Baptist's witness of him. His account is more doctrinal, giving a spiritual dimension to the life of Christ. The majority of the record of all four testimonies concerns the three-year ministry of Jesus as the Christ. Each testimony adds a unique contribution to our knowledge of his sojourn on earth.

Because of its unique contribution to an understanding of the birth and the ministry of Jesus, Third Nephi must be considered as yet another Gospel or Testimony. Furthermore, it confirms and clarifies many of the doctrines and principles taught in the four New Testament Gospels. It is indeed "Another Testament of Jesus Christ," as stated in the subtitle of the Book of Mormon.[7] While the subtitle appropriately refers to the whole book, it is specifically true of Third Nephi, which covers the time period in America that parallels the Savior living in the flesh upon the earth. Throughout this book, the whole Book of Mormon will be used as a second witness of the Christ, but the primary emphasis will be upon the account in Third Nephi.

The Pre-Mortal Life of Jesus Christ

As noted above, the Gospel of John begins with an account of the pre-mortal Messiah. The JST Testimony of John makes some significant changes in the Gospel of John. The Lord gave a revelation to the Prophet Joseph Smith that further confirms the role of Jesus Christ prior to his coming to the earth in mortality. The three accounts are listed below in parallel columns for easier comparison.

---

[7] The subtitle was added in 1982 (see Packer, Elder Boyd K. CR Oct. 1982, p. 75).

From the JST and the Doctrine and Covenants we learn that Jesus was already a God in the pre-mortal life, that he was the administrator of the gospel there, that he was a creator, and that the gospel was the life and light of men.

John 1	JST John 1	Doctrine and Covenants Section 93
1 In the beginning was the Word, and the Word was with God, and the **Word** was God.	2 In the beginning was **the gospel preached through the Son. And the gospel was the word, and the word was** with **the Son, and the Son was** with God, and the **Son** was **of** God. . . .	8 Therefore, in the beginning the Word was, for he was the Word, even the messenger of salvation—
2 The same was in the beginning with God.		9 The light and the Redeemer of the world; the Spirit of truth, who came into the world, because the world was made by him, and in him was the life of men and the light of men. (See also D&C 34:2)
3 All things were made by him; and without him was not any thing made **that** was made.	3 All things were made by him; and without him was not anything made **which** was made.	
4 In him was **life**; and the life was the light of men.	4 In him was **the gospel, and the gospel was the life**, and the life was the light of men;	
5 And the light shineth in **darkness**; and the **darkness comprehended** it not.	5 And the light shineth in **the world**, and the **world perceiveth** it not.	

The Book of Mormon verifies all of the JST and Doctrine and Covenants contributions.

In about 124 B.C., an angel told King Benjamin, "For behold, the time cometh, and is not far distant, that with power, the Lord Omnipotent who reigneth, who was, and is from all eternity to all eternity, shall come down from heaven among the children of men" (Mosiah 3:5). Christ reigned as a God from eternity (before mortality) to eternity (after mortality). About 600 B.C. he appeared to Lehi,[8] and later Nephi "did cry unto the Lord; and behold he did visit me" (1 Nephi 2:16). Lehi said to Jacob: "And thou hast beheld in thy youth his glory" (2 Nephi 2:4). Nephi recorded: "And my brother, Jacob, also has seen [Christ] as I have seen him" (2 Nephi 11:3). "A voice came unto [Enos], saying: thy sins are forgiven thee" (Enos 1:5): and still later "the voice of the Lord came to [Alma]" (Mosiah 26:20). Nephi bore testimony: "But there is a God, and he is Christ, and he cometh in the fullness of his own time" (2 Nephi 11:7). Nephi quoted the Lord God, saying:

> Know ye not that there are more nations than one? Know ye not that I, the Lord your God, have created all men, and that I remember those who are upon the isles of the sea; and that I rule in the heavens above and in the earth beneath; and I bring forth my word unto the children of men, yea, even upon all the nations of the earth? [2 Nephi 29:7]

Jesus Christ was also the God of the Jaredites.[9] He identified himself to the brother of Jared, "Behold, I am he who was prepared from the foundation of the world to redeem my people. Behold, I am Jesus Christ" (Ether 3:14). "[Christ] ministered unto [the brother of Jared] even as he ministered unto the Nephites; and all this, that this man might know that he was God" (Ether 3:18). Other evidences of his pre-mortal ministry will be given as his resurrected ministry among the Nephites is analyzed.

THE PROPHECIED BIRTH OF CHRIST

The Testimony of Matthew records, "Now *as it is written* the birth of Jesus Christ was on this wise" and explains the espousal of Mary

---

[8] [Lehi] ". . . saw One descending out of the midst of heaven, and he beheld that his luster was above that of the sun at noon-day.

And he also saw twelve others following him, and their brightness did exceed that of the stars in the firmament." (1 Nephi 1:9–10)

[9] The traditional date of the Jaredites is about 2200 B.C., but an exact date is not known.

to Joseph, and her being with child through the power of the Holy Ghost (JST Matthew 2:1; italics added). The Testimony of Luke records the visit of the angel Gabriel to Mary. He said: "Hail, thou *Virgin, who* art highly favored of the Lord. The Lord is with thee, *for thou art chosen and blessed* among women. And when she saw *the angel,* she was troubled at his saying, and *pondered* in her mind what manner of salutation this should be." Gabriel went on to explain that her conception would be "Of the Holy Ghost and the power of the Highest. Therefore also, that holy *child that* shall be born of thee shall be called the Son of God" (JST Luke 1:28–29, 35; italics added). The Book of Mormon prophets had previously been shown, and had recorded their testimonies, that Jesus was to be born of the Virgin Mary as the Son of the Eternal Father. Nephi, son of Lehi, was shown in the city of Nazareth "a virgin most beautiful and fair above all other virgins" (1 Nephi 11:13–15), and was told by an angel:

> Behold, the virgin whom thou seest is the mother of the Son of God, after the manner of flesh. And it came to pass that I beheld that she was carried away in the Spirit; and after she had been carried away in the Spirit for the space of time the angel spake unto me saying: Look! And I looked and beheld the virgin again, bearing a child in her arms. And the angel said unto me: Behold the Lamb of God, yea, even the Son of the Eternal Father! [1 Nephi 11:18–21]

The angel's words to Nephi were an explanation to Nephi of "the condescension of God" (1 Nephi 11:16). Our Father in Heaven (Elohim) had condescended or come down from his exalted place of residence, and his exalted and glorified state, to be the father of the Son through a mortal woman. The Spirit told Alma:

> Repent ye, and prepare the way of the Lord, and walk in his paths, which are straight; for behold, the kingdom of heaven is at hand, and the Son of God cometh upon the face of the earth. And behold, he shall be born of Mary, at Jerusalem which is the land of our forefathers, she being a virgin, a precious and chosen vessel, who shall be overshadowed and conceive by the power of the Holy Ghost, and bring forth a son, yea, even the Son of God. [Alma 7:9–10]

We know no more, nor do we need to know more, of how Mary

conceived. We do know, through the Book of Mormon and JST, that Mary was able to endure the presence of the Father through the power of the Holy Ghost that came upon her, and that Jesus was the Son of the Eternal Father. We also know and appreciate the greatness of Mary as the foreordained, "chosen" woman in the pre-mortal life, and "blessed" to be the mother of the Son of God. Certainly she was the only woman given this high and holy calling.

DEFINITION OF TERMS AND IDENTIFICATION OF NAMES
(Unfamiliar to Those Not Members of
The Church of Jesus Christ of Latter-day Saints)

Joseph Smith: The Prophet and founder of The Church of Jesus Christ of Latter-day Saints, on April 6, 1830, and the person responsible for bringing forth the Book of Mormon as told below in his own words.

The Angel Moroni:

On the evening of the above-mentioned twenty-first of September, (1823) after I had retired to my bed for the night, I betook myself to prayer and supplication to Almighty God for forgiveness of all my sins and follies, and also for a manifestation to me, that I might know of my state and standing before him; for I had full confidence in obtaining a divine manifestation, as I previously had one.

30 While I was thus in the act of calling upon God, I discovered a light appearing in my room, which continued to increase until the room was lighter than at noonday, when immediately a personage appeared at my bedside, standing in the air, for his feet did not touch the floor.

33 He called me by name, and said unto me that he was a messenger sent from the presence of God to me, and that his name was Moroni; that God had a work for me to do; and that my name should be had for good and evil among all nations, kindreds, and tongues, or that it should be both good and evil spoken of among all people. [Joseph Smith—History 1:29–30, 33]

The Book of Mormon:

34 He said there was a book deposited, written upon gold plates, giving an account of the former inhabitants of this continent, and the source from whence they sprang. He also said that the fulness of the everlasting Gospel was contained in it, as delivered by the Savior to the ancient inhabitants;

35 Also, that there were two stones in silver bows—and these stones, fastened to a breastplate, constituted what is called the Urim and Thummin—deposited with the plates; and the possession and use of these stones were what constituted "seers" in ancient or former times; and that

God had prepared them for the purpose of translating the book. [Joseph Smith— History 1:34–35]

Joseph translated the ancient record and it was first published to the world in the year 1830 as the Book of Mormon.

Lehi and Nephi: The first prophet of the Book of Mormon record which began in 600 B.C. Nephi was his youngest son at the time. After Lehi's death, about thirty years later, the people of Lehi separated into two groups; Nephi being the leader and prophet of the righteous known as Nephites, and the other group followed Lehi's oldest son Laman and were known as Lamanites.

Third Nephi: The eleventh book of fifteen books designated by the name of its principle author. The first two books were authored by Nephi, Son of Lehi, and are called "The First Book of Nephi, and The Second Book of Nephi. Just prior to the birth of Jesus Christ, nearly six hundred years later, another prophet named Nephi kept the record, which is called Third Nephi.

The Joseph Smith Translation: The revelation received by the Prophet Joseph made clear that the King James Version, great as it was, did not contain all that the ancient manuscripts had once contained. Many plain and precious things had been lost (see I Nephi 13). Being more than just a matter of translation of languages, the problem centered around a faulty transmission of the text. The King James Version is thus a remarkable vestige of an even more remarkable record of the gospel that was preached anciently.

With the Restoration, another revision of the English Bible was in order, not by a scholar but by a prophet. And it would come, not from an ancient manuscript, but from direct revelation of the same Lord from whom the Bible had originated. It was to be done at the Lord's commission rather than at the request of an earthly monarch or pope. This revision was to be an inspired version of the King James Bible, a divine restoration of ancient biblical knowledge. It is known today as the Inspired Version or, more properly, as the Joseph Smith Translation of the Bible. It should be seen, in perspective, as another step in the struggle to give mankind a Bible that, not only can be read, but also can be understood. The Prophet Joseph Smith made his translation during the years 1830–1844.[10]

---

[10] The explanation of *The Joseph Translation* was taken from: Matthews, Robert J. Selected Writings of, Gospel Scholars Series, p. 10, Deseret Book Company, Salt Lake City, Utah, 1999 .

PART 1

The Birth of Christ to A.D. 34

~

Thirty-four years of the Nephite record are covered in the first
seven chapters of Third Nephi. The first year, which was the
ninety-first year of the reign of the judges, was the year before
Christ's birth. It was the year that Mary conceived as recorded in the
first chapters of Matthew and Luke. The next thirty-three years begin
shortly before the sign of Christ's birth. Thus these chapters of Third
Nephi are parallel years to the mortal life of Jesus of Nazareth. Christ
spoke to Nephi just prior to his birth, verifying his pre-mortal life
spoken of in John chapter one. Twenty-five of the thirty-four years
are covered in the first four chapters plus eight verses of chapter 5 (the
remaining nineteen verses of chapter 5 contain an editorial comment
by Mormon after he had abridged that part of the Nephite record).
These twenty-five years parallel the Savior's growing-up years in
Egypt and Nazareth, of which the New Testament gives very little
information. Similarly, only three of these years are commented on
by Mormon in any length: the ninety-second year of the reign of the
judges, or the year of Christ's birth (see 3 Nephi 1:4–26); the sixteenth
year after Christ's birth (see 3 Nephi 3:1–21); and the twenty-fourth
year (see 3 Nephi 4:16–5:6).

When Nephi, the writer of the first two books of the Book of
Mormon, turned the responsibility of keeping the records over to his
brother Jacob, he commanded him to "write upon these plates a few
of the things which [he] considered to be most precious; that [he]

should not touch, save it were lightly, concerning the history of this people" (Jacob 1:2). As Mormon abridged the records into what is called Third Nephi, he followed these same instructions. His light touch of history was merely a framework for the precious signs of Christ's birth given to the Nephites, the gathering of the faithful in anticipation of further fulfillment of prophecy, and Satan's opposition that followed. It is assumed that similar things were happening in Jerusalem.

Third Nephi 6 and 7 cover the last eight years (A.D. 26–33) before Christ's visit to America. Mormon's abridgement concentrates on two of these years (A.D. 30–31) wherein he again inserted selective editorial comments. The Book of Mormon's overall description of the period explains the wickedness prior to the destruction of the Nephite cities in A.D. 34.

These two sections of 3 Nephi, the first twenty-five years and the next eight, that parallel the life of Christ, are discussed in the two chapters that follow. Mormon's extensive comments made at the end of Chapter Five, is the natural division for these two chapters.

Chapter 1

The Birth of Jesus Christ and the Gathering of Israel

3 Nephi 1–5

Third Nephi opens just prior to the time of the fulfillment of the prophecies of both Old Testament and Book of Mormon prophets. The first five chapters are outlined below as an overview of the reading. The outline is an extension of the italicized headings at the beginning of each chapter. These headings were not translated from the Book of Mormon plates, but were written by various modern-day apostles who were appointed to do so. New headings were written periodically as new editions of the Book of Mormon were printed. The present headings may be sufficient for many readers, but the extended outline is presented to give more detail and provide an overview in preparation for a deeper study of the text. Each chapter of this work will outline a part of the Book of Mormon for this purpose. Some may choose to skip the reading of the outline. Chapter one contains the longest segment in the book because more of the Book of Mormon text is discussed (about eleven of the fifty-eight pages of Third Nephi).

OUTLINE • 1 NEPHI 1–5

Superscription: Helaman was the son of Helaman, a son of Alma, son of Alma, being a descendant of Nephi and Lehi, who came out of Jerusalem in the first year of the reign of Zedekiah, king of Judah.

➤ 1:1–3   The ninety-first year (of the reign of the judges) had passed away, and six hundred years had passed away since Lehi had left Jerusalem.

     a. Lachoneus was the chief judge and the governor over the land. v. 1

     b. Nephi, son of Helaman, gave his son Nephi charge of all the records and other sacred things, and departed out of the land of Zarahemla. v. 2

     c. Where he went no man knows. v. 3

➤ 1:4–26   In the ninety-second year, the prophecies of the prophets began to be fulfilled more fully, for greater signs and wonders were wrought among the people.

     a. Some said the time was past when Samuel the Lamanite's prophecies were to be fulfilled. vv. 5–8

        1. Some rejoiced saying; those who had faith in Christ being born was in vain.

        2. The believers were sorrowful lest the prophecies should not be fulfilled.

        3. They did watch for the day and the night and the day that would be as one day.

     b. A day was set apart for all the believers to be put to death unless the sign came to pass. vv. 9–14

        1. Nephi cried mightily unto the Lord all that day, in behalf of those who were about to be destroyed.

        2. The Lord's voice came: This night shall the sign be given, on the morrow come I into the world.

        3. I came unto my own (Judah) to fulfill all things made known from the foundation of the world.

    4. I do the will of the Father and the Son, the Father because of me, the Son because of my flesh.

  c. The words of the Lord to Nephi were fulfilled, there was no darkness at the going down of the sun, and the people were astonished. vv. 15–18

    1. Many unbelievers fell as if dead, knowing their plan to destroy the believers was frustrated.

    2. All the people in the whole [land] began to know that the Son of God must shortly appear.

    3. They knew the prophets had testified, the sign was at hand, and they feared because of their iniquity and unbelief.

  d. There was no darkness that night, the sun arose in the morning, and they knew it was the day the Lord should be born. The sign had come to pass. A new star did appear. vv. 19–21

  e. Satan began to send forth lyings to harden the people's hearts that they might not believe the signs and wonders, but the more part did believe and were converted unto the Lord. v. 22

  f. Nephi and others went among the people baptizing unto repentance, and there was a great remission of sins, bringing peace into the land again. vv. 23–25

    1. There were no contentions except a few endeavoring to prove by the scriptures that it was no more expedient to observe the law of Moses, not understanding the scriptures.

    2. They were soon convinced of their error, knowing the law must be fulfilled, every jot and tittle.

  g. The year passed away bringing glad tidings because of the sign and prophecies being fulfilled. v. 26

➢ 1:27–30   The next year passed in peace, but Gadianton robbers dwelt in the mountains and infested the land.

  a. Their secret places were strong, they could not be taken, and they committed many murders. v. 27

           b. In the ninety-fourth year, they increased greatly through Nephite dissenters. v. 28

           c. There was great sorrow among the Lamanites because many children were led away by the lyings and flattery of some Zoramites, and joined the Gadianton robbers. v. 29

           d. The Lamanites decreased in righteousness because of wickedness in the rising generation. v. 30

➢ 2:1–10   The ninety-fifth year passed away and the people began to forget the signs and wonders they had had, and were less astonished at current ones, disbelieving all they had heard and seen.

           a. Vain things were wrought by men, or the power of the devil, to lead away the people. vv. 2–3

              1. Satan possessed their hearts again, and led them to believe the doctrine of Christ was foolish.

              2. Wickedness and abominations were prevalent; they did not believe in future signs and wonders.

           b. The ninety-sixth through the hundredth year passed away. vv. 4–5

           c. Six hundred and nine years passed since Lehi left Jerusalem, and nine years since the sign of Christ's birth was given. vv. 6–9

              1. The people began to reckon their time from this period, or from the coming Christ

              2. Nephi, the father of Nephi did not return to Zarahemla, and could not be found in all the land.

           d. The ninth through the eleventh year passed away in iniquity (there is no record of year twelve). v. 10

➢ 2:11–19   In the thirteenth year there began to be wars and contention throughout the land.

           a. The Gadianton robbers were so numerous, and spread such death and carnage, that both the Nephites and Lamanites took up arms against them. v. 11

    b. The converted Lamanites united with the Nephites, and were compelled to take up arms for their safety, and to maintain the church and their liberty. v. 12

    c. The Nephites were threatened with utter destruction. v. 13

    d. The Lamanites united with and were numbered with the Nephites. vv. 14–16

        1. The curse was taken from them, and their skins also became white.

        2. Their young men and daughters became exceedingly fair and were called Nephites.

    e. In the fourteenth year, the war became exceedingly sore, but the Nephites did gain some advantage of the robbers. v. 17

    f. By the fifteenth year's end, because of wickedness and contentions, the robbers gained advantage, and the sword of destruction hung over the Nephites. v. 19

➢ 3:1–10   An epistle from the leader and governor of the band of robbers to Lachoneus , the governor of the land, in the sixteenth year from the coming of Christ.

    a. I praise you and your people for firmness in what you suppose is your right and liberty. vv. 2–5

        1. Ye stand as if supported by God in defense in what you call your liberty, property, and country.

        2. It seems a pity that you are so foolish and vain to suppose you can stand against my brave men who are anxious to destroy the Nephites.

        3. I know of their unconquerable spirit, having proved them in battle, and of their hatred because of the many wrongs you have done unto them.

        4. I have written this epistle, feeling for your welfare, because of your belief in what ye believe to be right, and your noble spirit in battle.

    b. I desire you yield up your people, cities, lands, and possessions, rather than be destroyed. vv. 6–8

       1. Unite with us and become acquainted with our secret works, be brethren, not our slaves, and partners of our substance.

       2. I swear an oath, if you will do this we will not destroy you, but if not, on the morrow we will come and not spare you until you are extinct.

  c. I am Giddianhi, governor of the secret society of Gadianton, that is good, and has been handed down from ancient date. vv. 9–10

       1. Deliver yourselves without shedding of blood, that my people regain their rights and government.

       2. Except they do this, I will avenge their wrongs.

➤ 3:11–21 Lachoneus was astonished at Giddianhi's boldness, but was a just man and was not frightened by him.

  a. He caused his people to cry unto the Lord for strength against the robbers. v. 12

  b. He sent a proclamation to gather women, children, animals, and substance to one place vv. 13–15

       1. He built fortifications and caused armies of both Nephites and Lamanites to guard them.

       2. He said that except they repent of their iniquities, they wouldn't be delivered.

  c. So great were the words and prophecies of Lachoneus that the people feared and exerted themselves to do according to his words. v. 16

  d. Lachoneus appointed chief captains to command his armies. vv. 17–19

       1. The chief and great commander of all the armies was Gidgiddoni.

       2. The custom was to appoint those who had the spirit of revelation, and the spirit of prophecy, except in times of wickedness.

       3. Gidgiddoni was a great prophet, as was the chief judge (Lachoneus).

e. The people asked Gidgiddoni to pray, and go into the wilderness and destroy the robbers (vv. 20–21).

1. He said if they did, the lord would deliver us into their hands.

2. We will prepare ourselves in the center of the land, and wait until they come against us, and the Lord will deliver them into our hands.

➤ 3:22–26   The latter end of the seventeenth year, they had gathered to the place appointed to defend themselves.

a. They gathered to the land of Zarahemla, and the land between there and Bountiful, and the line between the lands of Bountiful and Desolation. vv. 23–24

1. A great many thousands of Nephites gathered.

2. They gathered in the land southward because the land northward had a great curse upon it.

b. They fortified themselves, and dwelt in one body. vv. 25–26

1. They repented of their sins, and prayed for the Lord God to deliver them.

2. They were sorrowful because of their enemies.

3. Gidgiddoni caused them to make weapons of war.

➤ 4:1–4   The end of the eighteenth year, the robbers took possession of the lands deserted by the Nephites.

a. There were no wild beasts or game for the robbers except in the wilderness. vv. 2–3

1. The robbers could only exist in the wilderness.

2. The Nephites had left their lands desolate.

b. The robbers could only plunder and obtain food by coming to battle with the Nephites. v. 4

1. The Nephites had provisions for seven years.

2. They hoped to destroy the robbers in that time.

➤ 4:5–15   The Nineteenth year, Giddianhi came to battle for they could not subsist except to rob and murder.

a. They feared to raise grain lest the Nephites come and slay them. v. 6

     b. They came in the sixth month, and it was a great and terrible day. v. 7

        1. They girded their loins with lambskin, dyed in blood, with heads shorn and head plates.

        2. Great and terrible was the appearance of their enemies.

     c. The Nephites saw their appearance, and fell to the earth, crying to the Lord to deliver them. vv. 8–12

        1. The robbers thought the Nephites had fallen in fear and rushed upon them.

        2. The Nephites received them in the strength of the Lord.

        3. Great and terrible was the slaughter, none so great since Lehi left Jerusalem.

        4. In spite of Giddianhi's oath, the Nephites beat them, and they fell back.

     d. Gidgiddoni pursued them to the borders of the wilderness. vv. 13–15

        1. Giddianhi was slain in battle, and the Nephites returned to their places.

        2. The robbers did not come up again, in this year or the twentieth year.

➤ 4:16–33   The twenty-first year, the robbers attempted to cut off the Nephite's outward privileges.

     a. Zemnarihah was their new leader, and originator of this plan. vv. 17–23

        1. The Nephites had an advantage because of their much provisions.

        2. The robbers had only wild game found in the wilderness and were about to perish.

        3. The Nephites were cutting them off by thousands and ten thousands.

        4. Zemnarihah commanded his people to withdraw to the land northward.

    b. Gidgiddoni, knowing their design, sent his armies in the night-time to cut off their retreat. vv. 24–27

        1. The robbers were met by the Nephites, both in the front and rear, and cut off their place of retreat.

        2. Thousands yielded themselves up as prisoners, and the remainder were slain.

    c. Zemnarihah was hanged from the top of a tree until he was dead. vv. 28–29

        1. They felled the tree and cried with a loud voice:

        2. May the Lord preserve his people in righteousness, and may those who seek to slay them by power and secret combinations be felled as this man.

    d. May the God of Abraham, Isaac, and Jacob preserve this people in righteousness. vv. 30–33

        1. They broke forth as one, singing and praising God for their being preserved.

        2. Their hearts were swollen with joy, gushing out many tears.

        3. They knew they had been delivered because of their repentance and humility.

➤ 5:1–7   There was not one soul among the Nephites who doubted the words of all the holy prophets.

    a. They knew Christ had come because of the many signs given. vv. 2–3

        1. They knew all things spoken would come to pass.

        2. They forsook their sins, and served God diligently day and night.

    b. They preached the word of God to the prisoners they had taken. vv. 4–6

        1. As many as repented, and would enter into a covenant to murder no more, were set at liberty.

        2. Those who would not enter into a covenant, and continued in their secret works, were condemned and punished according to the law, and an end came to the abominable combination.

c. The twenty-second through the twenty-fifth year passed away. v. 7

➤ 5:8–26   Mormon comments on his abridging, and prophesies.

a. This book cannot contain even a hundredth part of what was done in the space of twenty-five years. vv. 8–11

1. There are other records, a shorter but true account given by Nephi, from which I take my record.

2. Nephi engraved on the plates of Nephi; I make my record on plates I made with my own hand.

b. I am Mormon, called after the land where Alma established the first church. vv. 12–13

1. I am a disciple of Jesus Christ, the Son of God.

2. I have been called of him to declare his word, that the people may have everlasting life.

c. It is expedient of God for me to make this record, that the prayers of the holy ones who were before me should be fulfilled according to their faith. vv. 14–19

1. It is a small record from the time Lehi left Jerusalem unto the present time.

2. My record is from the accounts of those before me, and what I have seen with my own eyes.

3. My record is just and true, but many things, according to our language, we are unable to write.

d. I am a pure descendant of Lehi, and bless my God and my Savior Jesus Christ, that he brought our fathers out of Jerusalem. v. 20

e. Christ has blessed the house of Jacob, and has been merciful to the seed of Joseph. vv. 21–26

1. As the children of Lehi have kept the commandments, he has blessed them.

2. He shall again bring a remnant of Joseph to the knowledge of the Lord, and gather all his seed.

3. His covenant with the house of Joseph shall be fulfilled in the Lord's due time.

4. All the house of Jacob shall be restored to the knowledge of the covenant made to them.

5. They shall know their Redeemer, who is Jesus Christ, and be gathered to their own lands.

NOTES AND COMMENTARY

1 Now it came to pass that the ninety and first year had passed away and it was six hundred years from the time that Lehi left Jerusalem; and it was in the year that Lachoneus was the chief judge and the governor over the land.

2 And Nephi, the son of Helaman, had departed out of the land of Zarahemla, giving charge unto his son Nephi, who was his eldest son, concerning the plates of brass, and all the records which had been kept, and all those things which had been kept sacred from the departure of Lehi out of Jerusalem.

3 Then he departed out of the land, and whither he went, no man knoweth; and his son Nephi did keep the records in his stead, yea, the record of this people. [3 Nephi 1:1–3]

The first three verses are a summary of what happened in the year before Jesus was born. The book of Helaman ends with the ninetieth year, and so this is all that was recorded about this year. A new prophet leader had been appointed who is responsible for the old records and other sacred objects kept over the years. He is also the writer of this book we now know as Third Nephi. His name is Nephi, the same as his father of whom more will be said later.

The Book of Mormon prophets, Lehi and Nephi, had foretold Jesus' birth six hundred years from the time Lehi, Nephi's father, left Jerusalem (see 1 Nephi 10:4; 19:8; 2 Nephi 25:19). That his name would be called Christ or Jesus Christ was made known to Jacob and Nephi, Lehi's sons, and to King Benjamin (2 Nephi 10:3; 25:19; Mosiah 3:8). Nephi, son of Lehi, had prophesied that signs would be given unto his people of the birth of the Messiah (2 Nephi 26:3). Samuel, a Lamanite prophet, had prophesied five years before of the time of the Savior's birth, and had given signs whereby the people in

America might know that this blessed event had taken place in Jerusalem (Helaman 14:1–8). Those times had now come.

> 4 And it came to pass that in the commencement of the ninety and second year, behold, the prophecies of the prophets began to be fulfilled more fully; for there began to be greater signs and greater miracles wrought among the people.
>
> 5 But there were some who began to say that the time was past for the words to be fulfilled, which were spoken by Samuel, the Lamanite.
>
> 6 And they began to rejoice over their brethren, saying: Behold the time is past, and the words of Samuel are not fulfilled; therefore, your joy and your faith concerning this thing hath been vain.
>
> 7 And it came to pass that they did make a great uproar throughout the land; and the people who believed began to be very sorrowful, lest by any means those things which had been spoken might not come to pass.
>
> 8 But behold, they did watch steadfastly for that day and that night and that day which should be as one day as if there were no night, that they might know that their faith had not been vain.
>
> 9 Now it came to pass that there was a day set apart by the unbelievers, that all those who believed in those traditions should be put to death except the sign should come to pass, which had been given by Samuel the prophet. [3 Nephi 1:4–9][1]

The skepticism and threatened violence regarding the prophesied time of Christ's birth being past shows the influence and power of Satan that existed in the land. His influence was also in the land of Jerusalem. When the wise men from the east came seeking "he that is born king of the Jews," Herod the king "was troubled, and all Jerusalem with him" (Matthew 2:2–3). After Herod learned that Christ was to be born in Bethlehem, he sent them there and said, "When ye have found him, bring me word again, that I may come and worship him also." The wise men, having found the Christ child, were "warned of God in a dream that they should not return to Herod." An

---

[1] Nephi's departure out of the land has led to the speculation that he was translated at this time. While this may be true, there is no scriptural support that he was translated (see also 3 Nephi 2:9).

angel of the Lord appeared to Joseph, husband of Mary, "in a dream, saying, Arise, and take the young child and his mother, and flee into Egypt, . . . for Herod will seek the young child to destroy him" (Matthew 2:8–13). These Satanic incidents verify what the Prophet Joseph taught: "In relation to the kingdom of God, the devil always sets up his kingdom at the same time in opposition to God" (TPJS 365).

In this dispensation, the power of Satan came upon Joseph Smith as he prayed in what we now call the Sacred Grove. "He was seized upon by some power which entirely overcame [him], . . . as if [he] were doomed to sudden destruction. But, exerting all [his] powers to call upon God to deliver [him] out of the power of this enemy" he was delivered by the greater power of God (Joseph Smith—History 1:15–16). The Devil knew that the dispensation of the fullness of times was about to be ushered in. He did all in his power to stop it, but could not.

Amidst scornful rejoicing by the unbelievers, and steadfast faithful watching by the believers, the time was at hand for the sign of Jesus Christ's birth in the land of Jerusalem.[2]

> 10 Now it came to pass that when Nephi, the son of Nephi, saw this wickedness of his people, his heart was exceedingly sorrowful.
>
> 11 And it came to pass that he went out and bowed himself down upon the earth, and cried mightily to his God in behalf of his people, yea, those who were about to be destroyed because of their faith in the tradition of their fathers.
>
> 12 And it came to pass that he cried mightily unto the Lord all that day; and behold, the voice of the Lord came unto him, saying: [3 Nephi 1:10-12]

---

[2] Alma's prophecy (Alma 7:10) says Jesus would be born at Jerusalem, the land of our forefathers. Some critics want to discredit the Book of Mormon because of Alma's statement and the fact that Jesus was born in Bethlehem. The designation "land of Jerusalem" commonly referred to the entire region and would have included Bethlehem. See Hugh Nibley, *An Approach to the Book of Mormon,* 3rd ed. (Salt Lake City: Deseret Book, 1988) 100–102.

A righteous man is always concerned for his people. Lehi prayed "with all his heart in behalf of his people" when Jerusalem was threatened to be destroyed (1 Nephi 1:5). Furthermore, the Lord will always answer the prayers of a righteous man, but in different ways. Nephi, son of Nephi, the current prophet, prayed in behalf of his people "who were about to be destroyed because of their faith" (v. 11). In response to Nephi's pleas, the voice of the Lord came to him, saying:

> 13 Lift up your head and be of good cheer; for behold, the time is at hand, and on this night shall the sign be given, and on the morrow come I into the world, to show unto the world that I will fulfil all that which I have caused to be spoken by the mouth of my holy prophets.
>
> 14 Behold, I come unto my own, to fulfil all things which I have made known unto the children of men from the foundation of the world, and to do the will, both of the Father and of the Son—of the Father because of me, and of the Son because of my flesh. And behold, the time is at hand, and this night shall the sign be given. [3 Nephi 1:13–14][3]

The fulfillment of the sign of Samuel the Lamanite followed. As Jesus taught; "signs follow them that believe" (Mark 16:17; Mormon 9:24).

> 15 And it came to pass that the words which came unto Nephi were fulfilled, according as they had been spoken; for behold, at the going down of the sun there was no darkness; and the people began to be astonished because there was no darkness when the night came.
>
> 16 And there were many, who had not believed the words of the prophets, who fell to the earth and became as if they were dead, for they knew that the great plan of destruction which they had laid for those who

---

[3] Jesus speaking to Nephi before he was born is another evidence of the pre-mortal Messiah. The designation of him as the Father and the Son is consistent with the Book of Mormon and the Gospel of John (see Mosiah 15:1–4; Alma 11:26–39; Ether 3:14; John 14:8–12; see also D&C 93:3–4). By divine investiture of authority, he represents the Father upon the earth. For a detailed explanation of Jesus fulfilling the role of the Father and the Son, see "The Father and the Son: A Doctrinal Exposition by the First Presidency and the Twelve," in James R. Clark, comp., *Messages of the First Presidency of The Church of Jesus Christ of Latter-day Saints,* 6 vols. (Salt Lake City: Bookcraft, 1971), 5:23–34; also reprinted in James E. Talmage, *The Articles of Faith,* 42nd ed. (Salt Lake City: Deseret Book, 1982), 466–73.

believed in the words of the prophets had been frustrated; for the sign which had been given was already at hand.

17 And they began to know that the Son of God must shortly appear; yea, in fine, all the people upon the face of the whole earth from the west to the east, both in the land north and in the land south, were so exceedingly astonished that they fell to the earth.

18 For they knew that the prophets had testified of these things for many years, and that the sign which had been given was already at hand; and they began to fear because of their iniquity and their unbelief.

19 And it came to pass that there was no darkness in all that night, but it was as light as though it was mid-day. And it came to pass that the sun did rise in the morning again, according to its proper order; and they knew that it was the day that the Lord should be born, because of the sign which had been given.

20 And it had come to pass, yea, all things, every whit, according to the words of the prophets.

21 And it came to pass also that a new star did appear, according to the word. [3 Nephi 1:5–21]

The time for the Lord to intervene was at hand; he had spoken to another prophet, Nephi, son of Nephi. His words were fulfilled as was the prophecy of Samuel the Lamanite. A part of the latter's prophecy, that is not always recognized, is the falling to the earth of all the people (v. 17; see Helaman 14:7). The Lord's words are fulfilled, "every whit" (v. 20).

The wise men from the east followed "his star" to find "the child that is born, the Messiah of the Jews" (JST Matthew 2:2). The new star that appeared (v. 21) fulfilled the prophecy of Samuel the Lamanite; "there shall a new star arise," and "shall be a sign unto you" (Helaman 14:5). The same sign had apparently also been prophesied in the east. Thus, the birth of Jesus Christ had been confirmed on the western continent as well as on the eastern continent. Therefore, 3 Nephi 1:15–21 is another testimony of the birth of Jesus Christ.

The Boyhood of Jesus

The ministry of Jesus did not begin for another thirty years, and his visit to America was thirty-three years later. The New Testament gospels tell us little about the thirty-year period before his ministry began. His childhood was described in one verse by Luke, "And the child grew, and waxed strong in spirit, filled with wisdom: and the grace of God was upon him" (Luke 2:40). We have one incident at the age of twelve, of him teaching the learned doctors in the temple "and they were hearing him, and asking him questions" (JST Luke 2:46). This incident sustains a prophecy of Isaiah also quoted in the Book of Mormon. "For [Jesus] shall grow up before [Elohim] as a tender plant, and as a root out of a dry ground: he hath no form nor comeliness; and when we shall see him, there is no beauty that we should desire him." (Isaiah 53:2, Mosiah 14:2). That Isaiah was foretelling Jesus being taught by his Heavenly Father, as interpreted above, is confirmed by Jesus' response to his earthly parents when they found him with the learned doctors.

> 48 And when they saw him, they were amazed: and his mother said unto him, Son, why hast thou thus dealt with us? Behold, thy father and I have sought thee sorrowing.
>
> 49 And he said unto them, How is it that ye sought me? Wist ye not that I must be about my Father's business?
>
> 50 And they understood not the saying which he spake unto them. [Luke 2:48–50]

All we know of the Savior's life from twelve to thirty is: "And Jesus increased in wisdom and stature, and in favour with God and man." (Luke 2:52). He grew and developed in all four areas of life: mental, physical, spiritual, and social. The Book of Mormon tells us much more about this time period, but nothing about the life of Christ. Third Nephi 1–5 covers the period of the first twenty-five years of his life (A.D. 1–25). Many of these years are brushed over lightly: five years in four verses—3 Nephi 2:1–4; with three years in one-third of a verse—3 Nephi 2:10; and four years in yet another verse—3 Nephi 5:7.

> 22 And it came to pass that from this time forth there began to be lyings sent forth among the people, by Satan, to harden their hearts, to the intent that they might not believe in those signs and wonders which they had seen; but notwithstanding these lyings and deceivings the more part of the people did believe, and were converted unto the Lord.

> 23 And it came to pass that Nephi went forth among the people, and also many others, baptizing unto repentance, in the which there was a great remission of sins. And thus the people began again to have peace in the land.

> 24 And there were no contentions, save it were a few that began to preach, endeavoring to prove by the scriptures that it was no more expedient to observe the law of Moses. Now in this thing they did err, having not understood the scriptures.

> 25 But it came to pass that they soon became converted, and were convinced of the error which they were in, for it was made known unto them that the law was not yet fulfilled, and that it must be fulfilled in every whit; yea, the word came unto them that it must be fulfilled; yea, that one jot or tittle should not pass away till it should all be fulfilled; therefore in this same year were they brought to a knowledge of their error and did confess their faults.

> 26 And thus the ninety and second year did pass away, bringing glad tidings unto the people because of the signs which did come to pass, according to the words of the prophecy of all the holy prophets. [3 Nephi 1:22–26]

As the Nephites gathered together to protect themselves, and prepare for the time prophesied by Nephi, son of Lehi, "after Christ shall have risen from the dead he shall show himself unto you" (2 Nephi 26:1), Satan also gathered his forces to counteract the work of God. We assume similar things were happening in Jerusalem prior to the ministry of John the Baptist. Although the testimony of Third Nephi adds little to our knowledge of the life of Christ, it serves another important purpose. Today we are living in a similar time period prior to the Second Coming of Christ. Although Mormon does not include "even a hundredth part of what was done among so many people in the space of twenty and five years" (3 Nephi 5:8), he does give us some guidelines and some warnings to prepare us for Christ's Second Coming, and he prophesies of the gathering of Israel in the latter days. The lessons we learn from both the righteous efforts of the Nephites, and those of Satan in opposing the prophets of the Lord, should help us as we prepare for Christ's coming millennial reign. As President Ezra Taft Benson has said:

> In the Book of Mormon we find a pattern for preparing for the Second Coming. A major portion of the book centers on the few decades just prior to Christ's coming to America. By careful study of that time period, we can determine why some were destroyed in the terrible judgments that preceded His coming and what brought others to stand at the temple in the land of Bountiful and thrust their hands into the wounds of His hands and feet [CR, October 1986, 5].

The gathering of Israel was taught throughout the Old Testament period. Jesus Christ was the instigator of the gathering of Israel throughout that era (see Matthew 23:37). As Jesus ministered to the Jews and the Nephites, he also foretold the gathering of Israel in the latter days in preparation for his Second Coming.

The gospel was restored in these latter days to prepare for the Second Coming.

> 12 Prepare ye, prepare ye for that which is to come, for the Lord is nigh;
>
> 13 And the anger of the Lord is kindled, and his sword is bathed in heaven, and it shall fall upon the inhabitants of the earth.
>
> 14 And the arm of the Lord shall be revealed; and the day cometh that they who will not hear the voice of the Lord, neither the voice of his servants, neither give heed to the words of the prophets and apostles, shall be cut off from among the people. [D&C 1:12–14]

The members of the Church "are called to bring to pass the gathering of mine elect; for mine elect hear my voice and harden not their hearts;

> 8 Wherefore the decree hath gone forth from the Father that they shall be gathered in unto one place upon the face of this land, to prepare their

hearts and be prepared in all things against the day when tribulation and desolation are sent forth upon the wicked.

9 For the hour is nigh and the day soon at hand when the earth is ripe; and all the proud and they that do wickedly shall be as stubble; and I will burn them up, saith the Lord of Hosts, that wickedness shall not be upon the earth." [D&C 29:7–9]

The first five chapters of 3 Nephi illustrate the principles that gathered the Nephites before Christ came among them in A.D. 34, and that are included in the principles that will be followed in the latter-day gathering of Israel.

Principles of the Gathering of Israel

Joseph Smith taught that "one of the most important points in the faith of the Church of the Latter-day Saints through the fullness of the everlasting gospel is the gathering of Israel" (TPJS 92). Joseph also taught that "the 13th chapter of His Gospel according to St. Matthew, which in my mind, afforded us as clear an understanding upon the important subject of the gathering, as anything recorded in the Bible" (TPJS 94). Although Joseph explained the eight parables that are contained in that chapter of Matthew, and their latter-day fulfillment in the gathering of Israel (TPJS 94–102), we will here quote only a few verses as examples of the latter-day gathering.

Let both grow together until the harvest, and in the time of harvest, I will say to the reapers, Gather ye together first the wheat into my barn; and the tares are bound in bundles to be burned.[JST Matthew 13:29; cp. Matthew 13:40]

48 Again, the kingdom of heaven is like unto a net that was cast into the sea, and gathered of every kind, which, when it was full, they drew to shore, and sat down, and gathered the good into vessels; but cast the bad away.

49 So shall it be at the end of the world.

50 And the world is the children of the wicked.

51 The angels shall come forth, and sever the wicked from among the just, and shall cast them out into the world to be burned. There shall be

wailing and gnashing of teeth. [JST Matthew 13:48–51; cp. Matthew 19:47–50]

John the Baptist predicted the gathering of Israel as part of the mission of Jesus: "For behold, and lo, he shall come, as it is written in the book of the prophets, to take away the sins of the world, and to bring salvation unto the heathen nations, to gather together those who are lost, who are of the sheepfold of Israel;" (JST Luke 3:5). In the Christian world, the concept of Israel being gathered is rarely talked about, and when it is, it is in reference to the Jews gathering to Jerusalem. The gathering of Israel is much broader and rightly includes all twelve tribes of Israel, not just Judah. Today, Israel has begun to gather. However, as in the days of Nephi, son of Nephi, the prophecies of the prophets are being fulfilled and most people fail to recognize them.

As the ninety-second year commenced, the first year of the life of Christ (A.D. 1), Mormon's abridgment reads, "Behold, the prophecies of the prophets began to be fulfilled more fully; for there began to be greater signs and greater miracles wrought among the people" (3 Nephi 1:4). Some days later in that same year, the Savior appeared to Nephi and declared that "on the morrow come I into the world, to show unto the world that I will fulfill all that which I have caused to be spoken by the mouth of my holy prophets" (3 Nephi 1:13).

When the angel Moroni appeared to Joseph Smith on the morning of September 22, 1823, he "commenced quoting the prophecies of the Old Testament" (JS–History 1:36). "In addition to [Malachi 3&4], he quoted the eleventh chapter of Isaiah, saying that it was about to be fulfilled" (JS–History 1:40). The eleventh verse of that chapter speaks of the Lord setting "his hand again the second time to recover the remnant of his people." This is quoted several times in the Book of Mormon in the context of the latter days (see 2 Nephi 25:17; 29:1; Jacob 6:2).

Another latter-day gathering prophecy quoted by Moroni was Jeremiah.

14 Therefore, behold, the days come, saith the LORD, that it shall no more be said, The LORD liveth, that brought up the children of Israel out of the land of Egypt;

15 But, The LORD liveth, that brought up the children of Israel from the land of the north, and from all the lands whither he had driven them: and I will bring them again into their land that I gave unto their fathers.

16 Behold, I will send for many fishers, saith the LORD, and they shall fish them; and after will I send for many hunters, and they shall hunt them from every mountain, and from every hill, and out of the holes of the rocks. [Jeremiah 16:14–16]

This prophecy of a gathering of Israel greater than the one out of Egypt will be from all the lands into which the Lord had driven the house of Israel. They will return unto the lands he gave to their fathers.[4] America "is the land of [the remnant of Joseph]; and the Father hath given it unto [them]" (3 Nephi 15:13).

The first principle of the gathering of Israel is that it will always be foretold by the prophets. The Church of Jesus Christ of Latter-day Saints bears solemn testimony to the world that the gathering spoken of by Isaiah and Jeremiah is well underway. The people who have gathered to the restored Church since 1830 are primarily those who are descendants of Ephraim, son of Joseph who was sold into Egypt, and whose fathers were driven out of Palestine and scattered "among all nations" of the earth (Amos 9:9). "They are the ten thousands of Ephraim" that Moses said "shall push the people together to the ends of the earth" (Deuteronomy 33:13–17). The Lord confirmed in a revelation in August 1831, that "the residue of the elders of my church . . . shall push the people together from the ends of the earth"

---

[4] Jeremiah 16:14–16 is not mentioned in the JS–H although Joseph does acknowledge that Moroni quoted many other scriptures. According to Oliver Cowdery writing in the *Messenger and Advocate* in April 1835, p. 109–10, Jeremiah 16:16 was quoted by Moroni as one to soon be fulfilled.

(D&C 58:44–45).[5] Thus the prophecies regarding the latter-day gathering of Israel began to be fulfilled in 1830, just as they did among the Nephites in A.D. 1. The wheat and the tares are being gathered "together until the harvest" when the good are gathered "into vessels, but cast the bad away . . . at the end of the world" (Matthew 13:30, 48–49).

A second principle of the gathering is the restoring of the knowledge of God's true nature. Conversely, one major sign of an apostasy is the loss of the correct understanding about God.[6] Jesus implied that the Jews had lost their understanding of God when he testified that they had "never heard his voice at any time, nor seen his shape. For ye have not his word abiding in you" (JST John 5:38–39). Christ's declaration that "on the morrow come I into the world, . . . to do the will, both of the Father and of the Son" (3 Nephi 1:13–14) revealed to Nephi a correct understanding of the position of Jesus Christ as the Father by divine investiture of authority. Unbelievers of that day probably did not understand this concept just as it is not understood by people other than the Latter-day Saints today. An explanation of this concept will not be given here, but it is taught in modern scripture (see footnote 3 in this chapter). Through Joseph Smith's experience in the sacred grove in New York when the Father

---

[5] For more evidence that the people of The Church of Jesus Christ of Latter-day Saints are literal descendants of the house of Israel, Joseph and Ephraim specifically, see Monte S. Nyman, "The Second Gathering of the Literal Seed," in *Doctrines for Exaltation*, (Salt Lake City: Deseret Book: 1989), 186–200.

[6] Moses had prophesied: "the LORD shall scatter you [Israel] among the nations, and ye shall be left few in number among the heathen, whither the LORD shall lead you.

And there ye shall serve gods, the work of men's hands, wood and stone, which neither see, nor hear, nor eat, nor smell" (Deuteronomy 4:27–28). Paul called to the men of Athens attention to "an altar with this inscription, TO THE UNKNOWN GOD. Whom therefore ye ignorantly worship" (Acts 17:23). Alma told of the apostate Zoramites, who believed that God "wast a spirit, and that thou art a spirit, and that thou wilt be a spirit forever" (Alma 31:15).

and the Son appeared to him (JS–H 1:17; cp. D&C 130:22), Joseph came to understand the truth about the Godhead. He knew they were "two Personages." He learned that the Father delegated or invested his divine authority in the Son; "One of them spake unto [Joseph], calling [him] by name and said, pointing to the other—*This is My Beloved Son. Hear Him!*" However, Satan actively opposed the knowledge that had been restored both among the Nephites in A.D. 1 and to Joseph Smith in 1820.

Satan opposed Jesus' preparation for the ministry. After being "led up of the Spirit, into the wilderness," . . . fasting "for forty days and forty nights, and had communed with God," Satan came to him and tempted him, saying, "If thou be the Son of God, command that these stones be made bread," thus representing a temptation of the appetites and passions. He also tempted Jesus, "If thou be the Son of God, cast thyself down" from the pinnacle of the temple, and the angels "shall bear thee up," an appeal to yield to the pride and recognition of the world. Finally, Satan offered Christ "all the kingdoms of the world and the glory of them, if thou wilt fall down and worship me," something that was already his. This was a temptation of the riches and power of the world (JST Matthew 4:1–11). President David O. McKay taught that "nearly every temptation that comes to you and me comes in one of these forms."[7] Satan continued to tempt Jesus during the following three years. Those who followed Satan were similarly tempted. Those who remained faithful were appointed a kingdom (see Luke 22:28).

Satan also sent lyings among the people of Nephi "to harden their hearts," so that they "might not believe in those signs and wonders" among them. However, "the more part of the people did believe, and were converted unto the Lord." These believers were baptized and gathered into the Church, thus bringing "peace to the land" (3 Nephi 1:22–23). Opposition from Satan also came to the boy prophet, Joseph

---

[7] McKay, David O. "Gospel Ideals" The Improvement Era Publication, Salt Lake City, Utah, 1953, pp. 154–155.

Smith, as he testified of his sacred experience in the grove in New York.

21 Some few days after I had this vision, I happened to be in company with one of the Methodist preachers, who was very active in the before mentioned religious excitement; and, conversing with him on the subject of religion, I took occasion to give him an account of the vision which I had had. I was greatly surprised at his behavior; he treated my communication not only lightly, but with great contempt, saying it was all of the devil, that there were no such things as visions or revelations in these days; that all such things had ceased with the apostles, and that there would never be any more of them.

22 I soon found, however, that my telling the story had excited a great deal of prejudice against me among professors of religion, and was the cause of great persecution, which continued to increase; and though I was an obscure boy, only between fourteen and fifteen years of age, and my circumstances in life such as to make a boy of no consequence in the world, yet men of high standing would take notice sufficient to excite the public mind against me, and create a bitter persecution; and this was common among all the sects—all united to persecute me.

23 It caused me serious reflection then, and often has since, how very strange it was that an obscure boy, of a little over fourteen years of age, and one, too, who was doomed to the necessity of obtaining a scanty maintenance by his daily labor, should be thought a character of sufficient importance to attract the attention of the great ones of the most popular sects of the day, and in a manner to create in them a spirit of the most bitter persecution and reviling. But strange or not, so it was, and it was often the cause of great sorrow to myself.

25 So it was with me. I had actually seen a light, and in the midst of that light I saw two Personages, and they did in reality speak to me; and though I was hated and persecuted for saying that I had seen a vision, yet it was true; and while they were persecuting me, reviling me, and speaking all manner of evil against me falsely for so saying, I was led to say in my heart: Why persecute me for telling the truth? I have actually seen a vision; and who am I that I can withstand God, or why does the world think to make me deny what I have actually seen? For I had seen a vision; I knew it, and I knew that God knew it, and I could not deny it, neither dared I do it; at least I knew that by so doing I would offend God, and come under condemnation. [Joseph Smith—History 1:21–23, 25]

Those who believed the Prophet Joseph were later given the opportunity to be baptized and were organized into the Church of Jesus Christ.[8] The time period between the people being baptized and the Church being organized was longer in Joseph Smith's day than in the time of the ministry of Jesus or in the days of Christ's visit to the Nephities. The shorter time period was apparently because Jesus' ministry was only three years, and the Church and the authority to baptize was already among the Nephites when Christ visited them. However, the same results were obtained. Through the gatherings, people are able to overcome the influence of the devil and find internal peace. This is the third principle of the gathering.

Jesus admonished the Jews to "Search the scriptures; for in them ye think ye have eternal life: and they are they which testify of me" (John 5:39). He also chastised the Sadducees because they did "err, not knowing the scriptures, nor the power of God" (Matthew 22:29). Among the Nephites, contentions arose over misunderstanding the scriptures. Through the wisdom and revelation that came to those gathered together, false doctrine and other errors were corrected (3 Nephi 1:24–25 quoted above). Similar contentions arose in the Church in the 1830 era, but were resolved through revelation and the wisdom of Joseph Smith.[9] Therefore, a fourth benefit that comes to those who are gathered is that they overcome false doctrines and concepts

---

[8] Revelation through Joseph Smith, April 1830. *History of the Church* 1:64–70.

1 The rise of the Church of Christ in these last days, being one thousand eight hundred and thirty years since the coming of our Lord and Savior Jesus Christ in the flesh, it being regularly organized and established agreeable to the laws of our country, by the will and commandments of God, in the fourth month, and on the sixth day of the month which is called April—

2 Which commandments were given to Joseph Smith, Jun., who was called of God, and ordained an apostle of Jesus Christ, to be the first elder of this church; [D&C 20:1–2]

[9] A difference of opinion arising between [Joseph and Oliver Cowdery] about the account of John the Apostle, mentioned in the New Testament, as to whether he died or continued to live, we mutually agreed to settle it by the Urim and Thummim and the following is the word which we received: (D&C section 7) HC 1:35–36

through scripture study, and personal revelation. All four of these principles of gathering, as illustrated above among the Nephites, were evidenced in the first year after the birth of Christ (the ninety-second year of the judges). The lessons continued in the succeeding years.

> 27 And it came to pass that the ninety and third year did also pass away in peace, save it were for the Gadianton robbers, who dwelt upon the mountains, who did infest the land; for so strong were their holds and their secret places that the people could not overpower them; therefore they did commit many murders, and did do much slaughter among the people.
>
> 28 And it came to pass that in the ninety and fourth year they began to increase in a great degree, because there were many dissenters of the Nephites who did flee unto them, which did cause much sorrow unto those Nephites who did remain in the land.
>
> 29 And there was also a cause of much sorrow among the Lamanites; for behold, they had many children who did grow up and began to wax strong in years, that they became for themselves, and were led away by some who were Zoramites, by their lyings and their flattering words, to join those Gadianton robbers.
>
> 30 And thus were the Lamanites afflicted also, and began to decrease as to their faith and righteousness, because of the wickedness of the rising generation. [3 Nephi 1:27–30]

Satan does not sit idly by while the Church is progressing. The children of the rising Lamanite generation joining with the Gadianton band caused great sorrow among the Lamanites (vv. 29–30). In Jerusalem Jesus warned against offending "one of these little ones which believe in me" (Matthew 18:6). The estrangement that often comes between parents and children is called the generation gap. As the Saints gather, they can more easily overcome the generation gap because of the influence of the gospel and the righteous examples of other friends, families and associates. This is a fifth principle of the gathering. Modern-day revelation warns parents "that teach them [their children] not to understand the doctrine of repentance, faith in Christ the Son of the living God, and of baptism and the gift of the Holy Ghost by the laying on of hands, when eight years old, the sin be upon the heads of the parents" (D&C 68:25). The generation gap narrows when both parents and children understand the gospel.

> 1 And it came to pass that thus passed away the ninety and fifth year also, and the people began to forget those signs and wonders which they had heard, and began to be less and less astonished at a sign or a wonder from heaven, insomuch that they began to be hard in their hearts, and blind in their minds, and began to disbelieve all which they had heard and seen—

> 2 Imagining up some vain thing in their hearts, that it was wrought by men and by the power of the devil, to lead away and deceive the hearts of the people; and thus did Satan get possession of the hearts of the people again, insomuch that he did blind their eyes and lead them away to believe that the doctrine of Christ was a foolish and a vain thing.

> 3 And it came to pass that the people began to wax strong in wickedness and abominations; and they did not believe that there should be any more signs or wonders given; and Satan did go about, leading away the hearts of the people, tempting them and causing them that they should do great wickedness in the land. [3 Nephi 2:1–3]

As time passed, signs and wonders were forgotten and man-made explanations, influenced by Satan, replaced some people's belief in the gospel miracles. In Jerusalem, Jesus told a certain nobleman "Except ye see signs and wonders, ye will not believe" (John 4:48). This he spoke of that generation, not of the nobleman himself. Undoubtedly many others, in both Jerusalem and among the Nephites, were secure in the faith because of the proper partaking of the sacrament. The sacrament will be discussed more fully in a later chapter, but suffice it to say here that, as we gather weekly to partake of the bread and water in remembrance of our blessings and covenants related to the Resurrection and the Atonement, we are more apt to remain faithful in the Church.[10] Thus, a sixth principle is: by gathering together we are strengthened through the partaking of the sacrament and participating in other ordinances and teachings that strengthen us.

---

[10] I am indebted to my friend and colleague, Robert J. Parsons, for this concept.

The Nephites instituted a new reckoning of time in the one hundredth year of the reign of the judges and made their new system retroactive to the year of the sign of the birth of Christ, nine years earlier.

> 4 And thus did pass away the ninety and sixth year; and also the ninety and seventh year; and also the ninety and eighth year; and also the ninety and ninth year;
>
> 5 And also an hundred years had passed away since the days of Mosiah, who was king over the people of the Nephites.
>
> 6 And six hundred and nine years had passed away since Lehi left Jerusalem.
>
> 7 And nine years had passed away from the time when the sign was given, which was spoken of by the prophets, that Christ should come into the world.
>
> 8 Now the Nephites began to reckon their time from this period when the sign was given, or from the coming of Christ; therefore, nine years had passed away.
>
> 9 And Nephi, who was the father of Nephi, who had the charge of the records, did not return to the land of Zarahemla, and could nowhere be found in all the land. [3 Nephi 2:4–9]

This was the third dating system used in the Book of Mormon. The first was measured "from the time that [Lehi] left Jerusalem" (1 Nephi 10:4). The second began with the appointment of Alma as the first chief judge, and was called "the reign of the judges" (Mosiah 29:44; Alma 1:1). The last one, from the time of the birth of Christ, was used to the end of the Book of Mormon record.

> 10 And it came to pass that the people did still remain in wickedness, notwithstanding the much preaching and prophesying which was sent among them; and thus passed away the tenth year also; and the eleventh year also passed away in iniquity.
>
> 11 And it came to pass in the thirteenth year there began to be wars and contentions throughout all the land; for the Gadianton robbers had become so numerous, and did slay so many of the people, and did lay waste so many cities, and did spread so much death and carnage throughout the land, that it became expedient that all the people, both the Nephites and the Lamanites, should take up arms against them.

> 12 Therefore, all the Lamanites who had become converted unto the Lord did unite with their brethren, the Nephites, and were compelled, for the safety of their lives and their women and their children, to take up arms against those Gadianton robbers, yea, and also to maintain their rights, and the privileges of their church and of their worship, and their freedom and their liberty. [3 Nephi 2:10–12]

This nearly four year period, the ninth through the twelfth (there is no record of the twelfth year, but it must have been the same as the previous three), is a polarization of the righteous and the wicked. We have no record of the New Testament parallel time period, but the Lord foretold a similar grouping to evolve in the time period leading up to his Second Coming. He said that "peace shall be taken from the earth, and the devil shall have power over his own dominion. And also the Lord shall have power over his saints, and shall reign in their midst, and shall come down in judgment upon Idumea, or the world" (D&C 1:35–36). While these verses seem to describe the time immediately before his Second Coming, the gradual buildup will and has begun as it did among the Nephites before his first coming. Quite obviously, peace has been taken from the earth today, but the time has not yet come "when no man will have any peace but in Zion and her stakes" (TPJS 161). As the Prophet Joseph also said, "We ought to have the building up of Zion as our greatest object. When wars come we shall have to flee to Zion" [and her stakes], (TPJS 160 see also D&C 45:68–75; 115:4–6; Isaiah 4:5–6; 2 Nephi 14:5–6).

In the thirteenth year, as many of the Lamanites were converted to the Lord, they united with the Nephites for their protection, and to maintain their God-given freedoms and liberty (v. 12). The seventh principle of the gathering of the righteous among the Nephites is here illustrated: the maintaining of the freedoms that God had given them. As Jesus said: "Ye shall know the truth, and the truth shall make you free" (John 8:32). The Nephites had been taught to "stand fast in that liberty wherewith God has made them free" (Alma 58:40; see also Alma 43:45–48; 61:9). This principle had also been taught to other dispensations. Paul taught the Galatians: "Stand fast therefore in the liberty wherefore Christ has made us free" (Galatians 5:1). More importantly to the Saints of this generation, the Lord said: "Abide ye in the liberty wherewith ye are made free; entangle not yourselves in sin, but let your hands be clean, until the Lord comes" (D&C 88:86; see also 98:4–10). It is a principle that is desired and followed wherever the Lord's children are gathered together in righteousness.

13 And it came to pass that before this thirteenth year had passed away the Nephites were threatened with utter destruction because of this war, which had become exceedingly sore.

14 And it came to pass that those Lamanites who had united with the Nephites were numbered among the Nephites;

15 And their curse was taken from them, and their skin became white like unto the Nephites;

16 And their young men and their daughters became exceedingly fair, and they were numbered among the Nephites, and were called Nephites. And thus ended the thirteenth year. [3 Nephi 2:13–16]

The eighth principle of the gathering is the overcoming of the cultural barrier. The Lamanites overcame their curse, and their children were blessed. Jesus proclaimed: "In the world ye shall have tribulation: but be of good cheer; I have overcome the world" (John 16:33). The Lord's will is for his people in this generation to "overcome the world" (D&C 64:1–2). The Apostle John declared: For whatsoever is born of God overcometh the world: and this is the victory that overcometh the world, *even* our faith. Who is he that overcometh the world, but he that believeth that Jesus is the Son of God? (1 John 5:4–5).

The Saints should develop their own gospel culture. He revealed in 1832 that Church members were under condemnation for not using the Book of Mormon as they should.

57 And they shall remain under this condemnation until they repent and remember the new covenant, even the Book of Mormon and the former commandments which I have given them, not only to say, but to do according to that which I have written—

58 That they may bring forth fruit meet for their Father's kingdom; otherwise there remaineth a scourge and judgment to be poured out upon the children of Zion. [D&C 84:57–58]

President Ezra Taft Benson reemphasized this warning and scourge that was still upon us after more than 150 years later.[11] This scourge seems to be the Gentile culture that we live among. The Prophet Joseph interpreted Isaiah 52:2 to be: "The bands of her neck are the curses of God upon her, or the remnants of Israel in their scattered condition among the Gentiles" (D&C 113:10). Church members are being affected by the Gentile culture. Through gathering together, we should have the courage and the strength to set our own cultural patterns as dictated by the Lord.

> 17 And it came to pass in the commencement of the fourteenth year, the war between the robbers and the people of Nephi did continue and did become exceedingly sore; nevertheless, the people of Nephi did gain some advantage of the robbers, insomuch that they did drive them back out of their lands into the mountains and into their secret places.
>
> 18 And thus ended the fourteenth year. And in the fifteenth year they did come forth against the people of Nephi; and because of the wickedness of the people of Nephi, and their many contentions and dissensions, the Gadianton robbers did gain many advantages over them.
>
> 19 And thus ended the fifteenth year, and thus were the people in a state of many afflictions; and the sword of destruction did hang over them, insomuch that they were about to be smitten down by it, and this because of their iniquity. [3 Nephi 2:17–19]

A complete change took place among the Nephites in just a fifteen-year period. The Nephite society went from the more part of the people being converted unto the Lord, and peace being established (3 Nephi 1:22–26 quoted above); to the sword of destruction hanging over their heads because of iniquity (3 Nephi 2:19). The cost of wickedness is high.

> 1 And now it came to pass that in the sixteenth year from the coming of Christ, Lachoneus, the governor of the land, received an epistle from the leader and the governor of this band of robbers; and these were the words which were written, saying:

---

[11] CR, April 1986, p. 100.

2 Lachoneus, most noble and chief governor of the land, behold, I write this epistle unto you, and do give unto you exceedingly great praise because of your firmness, and also the firmness of your people, in maintaining that which ye suppose to be your right and liberty; yea, ye do stand well, as if ye were supported by the hand of a god, in the defense of your liberty, and your property, and your country, or that which ye do call so.

3 And it seemeth a pity unto me, most noble Lachoneus, that ye should be so foolish and vain as to suppose that ye can stand against so many brave men who are at my command, who do now at this time stand in their arms, and do await with great anxiety for the word—Go down upon the Nephites and destroy them.

4 And I, knowing of their unconquerable spirit, having proved them in the field of battle, and knowing of their everlasting hatred towards you because of the many wrongs which ye have done unto them, therefore if they should come down against you they would visit you with utter destruction.

5 Therefore I have written this epistle, sealing it with mine own hand, feeling for your welfare, because of your firmness in that which ye believe to be right, and your noble spirit in the field of battle.

6 Therefore I write unto you, desiring that ye would yield up unto this my people, your cities, your lands, and your possessions, rather than that they should visit you with the sword and that destruction should come upon you.

7 Or in other words, yield yourselves up unto us, and unite with us and become acquainted with our secret works, and become our brethren that ye may be like unto us—not our slaves, but our brethren and partners of all our substance.

8 And behold, I swear unto you, if ye will do this, with an oath, ye shall not be destroyed; but if ye will not do this, I swear unto you with an oath, that on the morrow month I will command that my armies shall come down against you, and they shall not stay their hand and shall spare not, but shall slay you, and shall let fall the sword upon you even until ye shall become extinct.

9 And behold, I am Giddianhi; and I am the governor of this the secret society of Gadianton; which society and the works thereof I know to be good; and they are of ancient date and they have been handed down unto us.

10 And I write this epistle unto you, Lachoneus, and I hope that ye will deliver up your lands and your possessions, without the shedding of blood, that this my people may recover their rights and government, who have dissented away from you because of your wickedness in retaining from them their rights of government, and except ye do this, I will avenge their wrongs. I am Giddianhi. [3 Nephi 3:1–10]

This epistle from the governor of the Gadianton secret society is a masterpiece of flattery, belittlement, ridicule, bluff, lying, and threat. Verse two uses flattery, in verse three he belittles and ridicules, in verse four he bluffs, and in verse five he outright lies. The sixth and seventh verses disclose his real objective, the obtaining of the Nephite property. The eighth verse uses a threat. Had it gone to someone of lesser character than Lachoneus, it might have been effective. However, due to his great and marvelous leadership, the Nephites were able to withstand the efforts of Giddianhi and the Gadianton band.

11 And now it came to pass when Lachoneus received this epistle he was exceedingly astonished, because of the boldness of Giddianhi demanding the possession of the land of the Nephites, and also of threatening the people and avenging the wrongs of those that had received no wrong, save it were they had wronged themselves by dissenting away unto those wicked and abominable robbers.

12 Now behold, this Lachoneus, the governor, was a just man, and could not be frightened by the demands and the threatenings of a robber; therefore he did not hearken to the epistle of Giddianhi, the governor of the robbers, but he did cause that his people should cry unto the Lord for strength against the time that the robbers should come down against them.

13 Yea, he sent a proclamation among all the people, that they should gather together their women, and their children, their flocks and their herds, and all their substance, save it were their land, unto one place.

14 And he caused that fortifications should be built round about them, and the strength thereof should be exceedingly great. And he caused that armies, both of the Nephites and of the Lamanites, or of all them who were numbered among the Nephites, should be placed as guards round about to watch them, and to guard them from the robbers day and night.

15 Yea, he said unto them: As the Lord liveth, except ye repent of all your iniquities, and cry unto the Lord, ye will in no wise be delivered out of the hands of those Gadianton robbers.

16 And so great and marvelous were the words and prophecies of Lachoneus that they did cause fear to come upon all the people; and they did exert themselves in their might to do according to the words of Lachoneus. [3 Nephi 3:11–16]

Lachoneus was the political leader of the people and a man of God, the type of man that the Lord has directed us to choose and uphold as political leaders; "honest men and wise men should be sought for diligently, and good men and wise ye should observe to uphold" (D&C 98:10). As George Washington and our founding fathers were "wise men whom [God] raised up" to establish the U.S. Constitution (D&C 101:80), Lachoneus had undoubtedly been raised up to preserve the Nephites in that age.

17 And it came to pass that Lachoneus did appoint chief captains over all the armies of the Nephites, to command them at the time that the robbers should come down out of the wilderness against them.

18 Now the chiefest among all the chief captains and the great commander of all the armies of the Nephites was appointed, and his name was Gidgiddoni.

19 Now it was the custom among all the Nephites to appoint for their chief captains, (save it were in their times of wickedness) some one that had the spirit of revelation and also prophecy; therefore, this Gidgiddoni was a great prophet among them, as also was the chief judge.

20 Now the people said unto Gidgiddoni: Pray unto the Lord, and let us go up upon the mountains and into the wilderness, that we may fall upon the robbers and destroy them in their own lands.

21 But Gidgiddoni saith unto them: The Lord forbid; for if we should go up against them the Lord would deliver us into their hands; therefore we will prepare ourselves in the center of our lands, and we will gather all our armies together, and we will not go against them, but we will wait till they shall come against us; therefore as the Lord liveth, if we do this he will deliver them into our hands. [3 Nephi 3:17–21]

Lachoneus chose other men of God to assist him, a pattern that should be followed today rather than following a pattern of political appointments to reward financial or other forms of support. Those chosen to be chief captains had the spirit of prophecy, which is "the testimony of Jesus" (Revelation 19:10), and of revelation, or being told "in your mind and in your heart, by the Holy Ghost" (D&C 8:2–3). The chiefest of these captains, one Gidgiddoni, led them according to the commandments of God, refusing to take the offensive in war but willing to defend his people (v. 21). This policy was according to the law of war: "the Nephites were taught to defend themselves against their enemies, even to shedding of blood if it were necessary; yea, and they were also taught never to give an offense" (Alma 48:14; see also 43:46–47; D&C 98:33–38). Later, when the Nephites took the offensive, "they began to be smitten; for were it not for that, the Lamanites could have had no power over them (see Mormon 4:4).

The examples of men like Lachoneus and Gidgiddoni show the ninth principle of gathering. The Lord provides inspired leadership to protect and guide those who are gathered. The Lord has provided similar leadership for the Church to follow in these latter days. The Nauvoo Legion and the Utah War are good examples. Men such as Daniel Wells, Porter Rockwell, and Lott Smith were men of God, and defended the saints and their prophet.

> 22 And it came to pass in the seventeenth year, in the latter end of the year, the proclamation of Lachoneus had gone forth throughout all the face of the land, and they had taken their horses, and their chariots, and their cattle, and all their flocks, and their herds, and their grain, and all their substance, and did march forth by thousands and by tens of thousands, until they had all gone forth to the place which had been appointed that they should gather themselves together, to defend themselves against their enemies.
>
> 23 And the land which was appointed was the land of Zarahemla, and the land which was between the land Zarahemla and the land Bountiful, yea, to the line which was between the land Bountiful and the land Desolation.
>
> 24 And there were a great many thousand people who were called Nephites, who did gather themselves together in this land. Now Lachoneus did cause that they should gather themselves together in the

land southward, because of the great curse which was upon the land northward.

25 And they did fortify themselves against their enemies; and they did dwell in one land, and in one body, and they did fear the words which had been spoken by Lachoneus, insomuch that they did repent of all their sins; and they did put up their prayers unto the Lord their God, that he would deliver them in the time that their enemies should come down against them to battle.

26 And they were exceedingly sorrowful because of their enemies. And Gidgiddoni did cause that they should make weapons of war of every kind, and they should be strong with armor, and with shields, and with bucklers, after the manner of his instruction. [3 Nephi 3:22–26]

The Book of Mormon teaches us an important lesson for defending ourselves. We must prepare physically and spiritually. The Nephites used their best physical efforts, but also put their lives in order with the Lord and prayed for him to deliver them.

1 And it came to pass that in the latter end of the eighteenth year those armies of robbers had prepared for battle, and began to come down and to sally forth from the hills, and out of the mountains, and the wilderness, and their strongholds, and their secret places, and began to take possession of the lands, both which were in the land south and which were in the land north, and began to take possession of all the lands which had been deserted by the Nephites, and the cities which had been left desolate.

2 But behold, there were no wild beasts nor game in those lands which had been deserted by the Nephites, and there was no game for the robbers save it were in the wilderness.

3 And the robbers could not exist save it were in the wilderness, for the want of food; for the Nephites had left their lands desolate, and had gathered their flocks and their herds and all their substance, and they were in one body.

4 Therefore, there was no chance for the robbers to plunder and to obtain food, save it were to come up in open battle against the Nephites; and the Nephites being in one body, and having so great a number, and having reserved for themselves provisions, and horses and cattle, and flocks of every kind, that they might subsist for the space of seven years, in the which time they did hope to destroy the robbers from off the face of the land; and thus the eighteenth year did pass away. [3 Nephi 4:1–4]

The foresight of Lachoneus in gathering his people and storing food for seven years paid off. Why he advocated a period of seven years is not stated, but it reminds us of Joseph of Egypt interpreting the Pharaoh's dream to store up food for the same time period (Genesis 41). Since Joseph's account was on the plates of brass, it may have been an influence. It takes planning and organization to have the right kinds of food, and knowledge and wisdom to know how to store it and preserve it without losing its food value. Apparently, the Nephites had done this. Our inspired leaders have admonished us to have a one year supply. The example of the Nephites should encourage us to follow them.

5 And it came to pass that in the nineteenth year Giddianhi found that it was expedient that he should go up to battle against the Nephites, for there was no way that they could subsist save it were to plunder and rob and murder.

6 And they durst not spread themselves upon the face of the land insomuch that they could raise grain, lest the Nephites should come upon them and slay them; therefore Giddianhi gave commandment unto his armies that in this year they should go up to battle against the Nephites.

7 And it came to pass that they did come up to battle; and it was in the sixth month; and behold, great and terrible was the day that they did come up to battle; and they were girded about after the manner of robbers; and they had a lamb-skin about their loins, and they were dyed in blood, and their heads were shorn, and they had head-plates upon them; and great and terrible was the appearance of the armies of Giddianhi, because of their armor, and because of their being dyed in blood.

8 And it came to pass that the armies of the Nephites, when they saw the appearance of the army of Giddianhi, had all fallen to the earth, and did lift their cries to the Lord their God, that he would spare them and deliver them out of the hands of their enemies.

9 And it came to pass that when the armies of Giddianhi saw this they began to shout with a loud voice, because of their joy, for they had supposed that the Nephites had fallen with fear because of the terror of their armies.

10 But in this thing they were disappointed, for the Nephites did not fear them; but they did fear their God and did supplicate him for protection; therefore, when the armies of Giddianhi did rush upon them they were prepared to meet them; yea, in the strength of the Lord they did receive them.

11 And the battle commenced in this the sixth month; and great and terrible was the battle thereof, yea, great and terrible was the slaughter thereof, insomuch that there never was known so great a slaughter among all the people of Lehi since he left Jerusalem.

12 And notwithstanding the threatenings and the oaths which Giddianhi had made, behold, the Nephites did beat them, insomuch that they did fall back from before them.

13 And it came to pass that Gidgiddoni commanded that his armies should pursue them as far as the borders of the wilderness, and that they should not spare any that should fall into their hands by the way; and thus they did pursue them and did slay them, to the borders of the wilderness, even until they had fulfilled the commandment of Gidgiddoni.

14 And it came to pass that Giddianhi, who had stood and fought with boldness, was pursued as he fled; and being weary because of his much fighting he was overtaken and slain. And thus was the end of Giddianhi the robber. [3 Nephi 4:5–14]

The teachings of Gidgiddoni were verified. The robbers did come up against them, and the Lord did deliver them into the Nephites' hands (3 Nephi 3:21). The dress of the armies of Giddianhi followed the pattern of the Lamanites and apostate Nephites who "marked themselves with red in their foreheads after the manner of the Lamanites" (Alma 3:4–5,13–14; see also Enos 1:20; Mosiah 10:8; Alma 43:20). We cannot help but surmise that, had the robbers had the Spirit of the Lord with them, or had they been led by inspired leaders, they would not have supposed that the Nephites had fallen in fear at the sight of the armies of Giddianhi. The Nephites fought with the strength of the Lord and were able to starve out and defeat the Gadianton robbers. Gathering together gave them a combined physical strength, but also the strength of the Lord beyond their own. This illustrates collectively what the Lord taught to his New Testament disciples, and revealed anew to Oliver Cowdery.

32 Verily, verily, I say unto you, as I said unto my disciples, where two or three are gathered together in my name, as touching one thing, behold, there will I be in the midst of them—even so am I in the midst of you. [D&C 6:32; see also Matthew 18:20.]

The new leader of the Gadianton robbers, Zemnarihah, came up with a new plan to conquer the Nephites.

15 And it came to pass that the armies of the Nephites did return again to their place of security. And it came to pass that this nineteenth year did pass away, and the robbers did not come again to battle; neither did they come again in the twentieth year.

16 And in the twenty and first year they did not come up to battle, but they came up on all sides to lay siege round about the people of Nephi; for they did suppose that if they should cut off the people of Nephi from their lands, and should hem them in on every side, and if they should cut them off from all their outward privileges, that they could cause them to yield themselves up according to their wishes.

17 Now they had appointed unto themselves another leader, whose name was Zemnarihah; therefore it was Zemnarihah that did cause that this siege should take place.

18 But behold, this was an advantage to the Nephites; for it was impossible for the robbers to lay siege sufficiently long to have any effect upon the Nephites, because of their much provision which they had laid up in store,

19 And because of the scantiness of provisions among the robbers; for behold, they had nothing save it were meat for their subsistence, which meat they did obtain in the wilderness;

20 And it came to pass that the wild game became scarce in the wilderness insomuch that the robbers were about to perish with hunger.

21 And the Nephites were continually marching out by day and by night, and falling upon their armies, and cutting them off by thousands and by tens of thousands.

22 And thus it became the desire of the people of Zemnarihah to withdraw from their design, because of the great destruction which came upon them by night and by day. [3 Nephi 4:15–22]

The plan failed because of the preparation that the Nephites had made. Zemnarihah's people became discouraged because of the

destruction they were experiencing. This failure caused him to withdraw his troops to the land northward.

> 23 And it came to pass that Zemnarihah did give command unto his
> people that they should withdraw themselves from the siege, and march
> into the furthermost parts of the land northward.
>
> 24 And now, Gidgiddoni being aware of their design, and knowing
> of their weakness because of the want of food, and the great slaughter
> which had been made among them, therefore he did send out his armies
> in the night-time, and did cut off the way of their retreat, and did place
> his armies in the way of their retreat.
>
> 25 And this did they do in the night-time, and got on their march
> beyond the robbers, so that on the morrow, when the robbers began their
> march, they were met by the armies of the Nephites both in their front
> and in their rear.
>
> 26 And the robbers who were on the south were also cut off in their
> places of retreat. And all these things were done by command of
> Gidgiddoni.
>
> 27 And there were many thousands who did yield themselves up
> prisoners unto the Nephites, and the remainder of them were slain.
>
> 28 And their leader, Zemnarihah, was taken and hanged upon a tree,
> yea, even upon the top thereof until he was dead. And when they had
> hanged him until he was dead they did fell the tree to the earth, and did
> cry with a loud voice, saying:
>
> 29 May the Lord preserve his people in righteousness and in holiness
> of heart, that they may cause to be felled to the earth all who shall seek
> to slay them because of power and secret combinations, even as this man
> hath been felled to the earth. [3 Nephi 4:23–29]

Again Gidgiddoni was able to spoil their plans. The text implies he
was directed of the Lord, but is not definite. The hanging of Zemnarihah, then cutting the tree down, was a practice carried out under the
law of Moses.[12]

---

[12] Under the law of Moses, if a man was hanged upon a tree, the tree was felled
after his death (see Deuteronomy 21:22–23; Joshua 8:29). This is another evidence that
the Nephites came from the Mideast culture.

The Nephite people acknowledged and rejoiced in their God, who was the God of Abraham, Isaac, and Jacob, and the Lord God Almighty, the Most High God.

> 30 And they did rejoice and cry again with one voice, saying: May the God of Abraham, and the God of Isaac, and the God of Jacob, protect this people in righteousness, so long as they shall call on the name of their God for protection.

> 31 And it came to pass that they did break forth, all as one, in singing, and praising their God for the great thing which he had done for them, in preserving them from falling into the hands of their enemies.

> 32 Yea, they did cry: Hosanna to the Most High God. And they did cry: Blessed be the name of the Lord God Almighty, the Most High God.

> 33 And their hearts were swollen with joy, unto the gushing out of many tears, because of the great goodness of God in delivering them out of the hands of their enemies; and they knew it was because of their repentance and their humility that they had been delivered from an everlasting destruction. [3 Nephi 4:30–33]

They did not "offend God." They did acknowledge and confess "his hand in all things" in their victory over the Gadianton robbers (D&C 59:21). Certainly, they were a people gathered of the Lord.

> 1 And now behold, there was not a living soul among all the people of the Nephites who did doubt in the least the words of all the holy prophets who had spoken; for they knew that it must needs be that they must be fulfilled.

> 2 And they knew that it must be expedient that Christ had come, because of the many signs which had been given, according to the words of the prophets; and because of the things which had come to pass already they knew that it must needs be that all things should come to pass according to that which had been spoken.

> 3 Therefore they did forsake all their sins, and their abominations, and their whoredoms, and did serve God with all diligence day and night.

> 4 And now it came to pass that when they had taken all the robbers prisoners, insomuch that none did escape who were not slain, they did cast their prisoners into prison, and did cause the word of God to be preached unto them; and as many as would repent of their sins and enter into a covenant that they would murder no more were set at liberty.

5 But as many as there were who did not enter into a covenant, and who did still continue to have those secret murders in their hearts, yea, as many as were found breathing out threatenings against their brethren were condemned and punished according to the law.

6 And thus they did put an end to all those wicked, and secret, and abominable combinations, in the which there was so much wickedness, and so many murders committed. [3 Nephi 5:1–6]

The Nephites had been blessed for their faith in Christ, but those blessings had also increased their faith in him who was to come. It also caused them to forsake their sins, thus improving their lives. Their being blessed again is what King Benjamin called being "eternally indebted to your heavenly Father," because when you keep the commandments you will prosper in the land. "All that [God] requires of you is to keep his commandments," and then "he doth immediately bless you; and therefore he hath paid you. And ye are still indebted unto him," and are thus "eternally indebted to your heavenly Father" (Mosiah 2:22, 24, 34). Jesus taught similarly, "If ye keep my commandments, ye shall abide in my love" (John 15:10).

Previously, the converted Lamanites had preached the word of God to the Gadianton robbers, and they were "utterly destroyed from among" them (Helaman 6:37). Perhaps the Nephites learned to preach to their prisoners from those Lamanites. The word of God, as Alma taught, "had more powerful effect upon the minds of the people than the sword, or anything else" (Alma 31:5; see also 61:14).

The work of preaching to the prisoners and eliminating the secret combinations took place for another four years. During this period, the Nephites experienced many great and marvelous things that Mormon did not record, but were recorded elsewhere, and if Mormon's record is believed, "then shall the greater things be made manifest" (3 Nephi 26:9).

7 And thus had the twenty and second year passed away, and the twenty and third year also, and the twenty and fourth, and the twenty and fifth; and thus had twenty and five years passed away.

8 And there had many things transpired which, in the eyes of some, would be great and marvelous; nevertheless, they cannot all be written in this book; yea, this book cannot contain even a hundredth part of what was done among so many people in the space of twenty and five years;

9 But behold there are records which do contain all the proceedings of this people; and a shorter but true account was given by Nephi.

10 Therefore I have made my record of these things according to the record of Nephi, which was engraven on the plates which were called the plates of Nephi. [3 Nephi 5:7–10]

In the brief account that was abridged, Mormon has shown the advantages and blessings of the righteous Nephites gathering together as the people of the Lord. We have shown that those same principles were taught by the Savior, and will assist the Latter-day Saints in preparing for the Second Coming of Christ. By way of review, a list of the ten principles of gathering that are shown in this account are summarized at the end of the chapter. While there are other principles that could be added to the list, these ten are taught in 3 Nephi 1–5. The gathering of Israel is indeed one of the most important points of the faith of The Church of Jesus Christ of Latter-day Saints (TPJS, 92). As the Second Coming gets closer, these principles will become more and more important to the faithful members of the Church, as Satan increases his efforts to destroy them.

Prophecies of the Gathering of Israel

Mormon was apparently so impressed with the record he had abridged that he added some of his own prophecies. He laid a foundation for his prophecies by declaring his qualifications to prophesy.

11 And behold, I do make the record on plates which I have made with mine own hands.

12 And behold, I am called Mormon, being called after the land of Mormon, the land in which Alma did establish the church among the people, yea, the first church which was established among them after their transgression.

13 Behold, I am a disciple of Jesus Christ, the Son of God. I have been called of him to declare his word among his people, that they might have everlasting life. [3 Nephi 5:11–13]

Nephi also abridged his father's record "upon plates which I have made with mine own hands," (1 Nephi 1:17), and Jacob recorded on plates "made by the hand of Nephi" (Jacob 3:14). Because of the plate's special need for endurability, the Lord may have revealed a special formula to Nephi, who passed it on to others or the formula was revealed anew when needed.

"Now it was the custom of the people of Nephi to call their lands, and their cities, and their villages, yea, even all their small villages, after the name of him who first possessed them" (Alma 8:7). Mormon's "father's name was Mormon" (Mormon 1:5), and so the land had probably been named after his father, or another ancestor. However, Mormon equates his name with the land of Mormon where Alma had established the first Church "after their transgressions" (v. 12).[13] The name Mormon was sacred to the Nephites, and "how beautiful are they to the eyes of them who there came to the knowledge of their Redeemer" (Mosiah 18:30). Mormon possibly gave the association of his name to this sacred place to bring the mission of Christ to their attention.

A major purpose of the gathering of Israel is to establish the Church. Mormon declared that he was a disciple of Jesus Christ (v. 13), or an apostle, and thus the Nephites were "built upon the foundation of the apostles and prophets" (Ephesians 2:19–22). That Mormon was an apostle is drawn from a statement by Joseph Smith. He taught that Christ "planted the gospel here in all its fullness, and richness, and power, and blessing; that they had Apostles, Prophets, Pastors, Teachers, and Evangelists; the same order, the same priest-

---

[13] The first church after their transgression probably refers to the transgression of Noah and his people. There was a prophet, seer, and revelator in the Land of Zarahemla at the time of Alma (Mosiah 8:13–17). Therefore, Alma was not the first to establish a church among the Nephites in the Americas, but was the first to do so in the land of Lehi-Nephi.

hood, the same ordinances, gifts, powers, and blessings, as were enjoyed on the eastern continent" (HC 4:538). Mormon's declaration that he was a disciple, and had been called of Jesus Christ strongly supports the inference of his apostleship. Having been called as a special witness, he was qualified to prophesy.

Mormon had also, under the command of God, abridged the records of previous prophets in addition to making a record of the things that he had seen with his own eyes.

> 14 And it hath become expedient that I, according to the will of God, that the prayers of those who have gone hence, who were the holy ones, should be fulfilled according to their faith, should make a record of these things which have been done—
>
> 15 Yea, a small record of that which hath taken place from the time that Lehi left Jerusalem, even down until the present time.
>
> 16 Therefore I do make my record from the accounts which have been given by those who were before me, until the commencement of my day;
>
> 17 And then I do make a record of the things which I have seen with mine own eyes.
>
> 18 And I know the record which I make to be a just and a true record; nevertheless there are many things which, according to our language, we are not able to write. [3 Nephi 5:14–18]

His record was just (accurate) and true (v. 18). Although he did not record all things, the background of what he had abridged and seen was definitely a qualifier for his prophecies. He was also an eyewitness of many of the events he recorded, however, in a different sense than the New Testament authors.

> 19 And now I make an end of my saying, which is of myself, and proceed to give my account of the things which have been before me.
>
> 20 I am Mormon, and a pure descendant of Lehi. I have reason to bless my God and my Savior Jesus Christ, that he brought our fathers out of the land of Jerusalem, (and no one knew it save it were himself and those whom he brought out of that land) and that he hath given me and my people so much knowledge unto the salvation of our souls.
>
> 21 Surely he hath blessed the house of Jacob, and hath been merciful unto the seed of Joseph.

22 And insomuch as the children of Lehi have kept his commandments he hath blessed them and prospered them according to his word. [3 Nephi 5:19–22]

The knowledge of Lehi and his party leaving Jerusalem was kept secret "lest [the Jews] should pursue us and destroy us" (1 Nephi 4:36).

Mormon began his prophecies by acknowledging the greatness of his Savior Jesus Christ and the blessings that were prophesied to the house of Jacob (Israel), and especially to the seed of Joseph, of whom Lehi was a descendant. Mormon was a pure descendant of Lehi, and therefore, a recipient of these blessings. The promise frequently mentioned throughout the Book of Mormon that if they, as Joseph's posterity, kept the commandments they would prosper in the land had been fulfilled to Lehi and his children (v. 22; cp. Genesis 49:22–26). Based upon these qualifications and experiences, Mormon gives three prophecies, all of which are being fulfilled in our day.

22 And insomuch as the children of Lehi have kept his commandments he hath blessed them and prospered them according to his word.

23 Yea, and surely shall he again bring a remnant of the seed of Joseph to the knowledge of the Lord their God.

24 And as surely as the Lord liveth, will he gather in from the four quarters of the earth all the remnant of the seed of Jacob, who are scattered abroad upon all the face of the earth.

25 And as he hath covenanted with all the house of Jacob, even so shall the covenant wherewith he hath covenanted with the house of Jacob be fulfilled in his own due time, unto the restoring all the house of Jacob unto the knowledge of the covenant that he hath covenanted with them.

26 And then shall they know their Redeemer, who is Jesus Christ, the Son of God; and then shall they be gathered in from the four quarters of the earth unto their own lands, from whence they have been dispersed; yea, as the Lord liveth so shall it be. Amen. [3 Nephi 5:22–26]

The first prophecy was that "a remnant of the seed Joseph" would again be brought "to the knowledge of the Lord their God" (v. 23). The fulfillment of this prophecy began with the First Vision when the

Father and the Son appeared to Joseph Smith (JS–H 1:17 quoted above). Joseph Smith was a descendant "of Ephraim, or of the house of Joseph, on whom was laid much power," and "unto whom rightly belongs the priesthood, and the keys of the kingdom" (D&C 113:4–6). Brigham Young described him as a "pure Ephraimite.[14] His father Joseph, Sr., as the patriarch of the Church, was "the oldest man of the blood of Joseph or of the seed of Abraham" then upon the earth (TPJS, 151). The knowledge of his descendancy was given him by blessing, "holding the keys of the patriarchal priesthood over the kingdom of God on the earth" as was also his right as shown through the same calling, as patriarch, being given to his son Hyrum "by his father, by blessing and also by right" after the death of Joseph, Sr. (D&C 124:91). As the Prophet Joseph taught the truth about God that he had learned in the First Vision, that knowledge was extended to others of the remnant of Joseph and to the whole world. Those who accept these truths will gather together as part of the fulfillment of the other prophecies of Mormon.

Mormon's second prophecy was that the Lord would "gather in from the four quarters of the earth all the remnant of the seed of Jacob, who are scattered abroad upon all the face of the earth" (v. 24). Joseph Smith was given the keys "for the gathering of my people in the last days" (D&C 113:6). He initiated the gathering that has thus far brought in millions of the seed of Ephraim and Manasseh. More will be said of this in a later chapter.

Mormon's third prophecy was concerning "the restoring all the house of Jacob unto the knowledge of the covenant" that God had made with them (v. 25). Since Joseph's remnant was to be gathered first, the rest of the tribes of Jacob would follow. According to the allegory of the house of Israel foretold through the ancient prophet Zenos, there are three groups of these tribes: the lost ten tribes, the

---

[14] JD 2:268–69. Being a pure Ephraimite does not mean that he had only the blood of Ephraim in his veins, but that he was a literal descendant. Therefore, Brigham Young's statement does not contradict D&C 113:1–6 that Joseph also was a descendant of Jesse (Judah).

Jews, and the Lamanites. These are to be restored or grafted back into the mother trunk of Israel so that they "begin at the last that they may be first, and that the first may be last." Therefore, the order will be the Lamanites, the Jews, and the ten tribes (Jacob 5:63). We see this now beginning to be fulfilled. As the remnant of Joseph is firmly established, the Lord "will graft in unto them the branches of their mother tree" (Jacob 5:54–56). Thus, Jacob's comment on the allegory that God "remembereth the house of Israel, both roots and branches" (Jacob 6:4), is coming to pass. The roots of the house of Israel gathered to establish the mother tree are "the remnant of the seed of Joseph (3 Nephi 5:23). They were gathered from among the nations of the Gentiles. The branches of Israel to be grafted into Joseph's trunk are the other tribes of Israel mentioned above that have retained their identity as a people. All of Israel, Joseph's remnants and the other tribes, shall come to "know their Redeemer who is Jesus Christ, the Son of God; and then shall they be gathered in from the four quarters of the earth unto their own lands, from whence they have been dispersed; yea, as the Lord liveth so shall it be. Amen" (3 Nephi 5:26). Mormon was as sure of these prophecies as he was of the truth of the record he had kept.

There is one more important element of the gathering of Israel that Joseph Smith taught that needs to be confirmed. Said Joseph: "The object of the gathering of the Jews, or the people of God in any age of the world . . . was to build unto the Lord a house whereby He could reveal unto His people the ordinances of His house and the glories of His kingdom, and teach the people the way of salvation; for there are certain ordinances and principles that, when they are taught and practiced, must be done in a place or house built for that purpose" (TPJS 307–308). The remnant of Joseph has been gathering for over 170 years (see D&C 58:44–45; Deuteronomy 33:13–17; quoted above and D&C 96:7), and have dotted the land with the temples of God as the gathering has progressed. President Howard W. Hunter, at the time of his ordination to be the President of the Church, June 6, 1994, gave this admonition to the members of The Church of Jesus Christ of Latter-day Saints:

I also invite the members of the Church to establish the temple of the Lord as the great symbol of their membership and the supernal setting for their most sacred covenants. It would be the deepest desire of my heart to have every member of the Church temple worthy. I would hope that every adult member would be worthy of—and carry—a current temple recommend, even if proximity to a temple does not allow immediate or frequent use of it.

Let us be a temple-attending and a temple-loving people. Let us hasten to the temple as frequently as time and means and personal circumstances allow. Let us go not only for our kindred dead, but let us also go for the personal blessing of temple worship, for the sanctity and safety which is provided within these hallowed and consecrated walls. The temple is a place of beauty, it is a place of revelation, it is a place of peace. It is the house of the Lord. It is holy unto the Lord. It should be holy unto us. [From the full text of President Hunter's statement to the news media June 6, 1994, Church News June 11, 1994, p. 14; see also CR Oct. 94, 8.]

As the time of the Second Coming of the Lord approaches, Mormon's three prophecies are well on their way to being fulfilled.

The first five chapters of Third Nephi add a unique contribution to our understanding of the first twenty-five years of the life of Christ through its testimony of the birth of Christ occurring in the land of Jerusalem. They also verify the opposition of Satan to the work of the Lord, and the principles of the gathering of Israel that precede both comings of Jesus Christ. Once more, we note that the book of Third Nephi qualifies as another gospel or testimony of Christ.

TEN PRINCIPLES OF THE GATHERING OF ISRAEL

1. **The Fulfillment of the Prophecies of the Prophet**
   3 Nephi 1:4.

2. **A Restoration of the True Knowledge of God**
   3 Nephi 1:13–14.

3. **The Overcoming of the Influence of Satan**
   3 Nephi 1:22–23.

4. **False Doctrines and Other Errors are Corrected**
   3 Nephi 1:24.

5. **Help in Overcoming the Generation Gap is Obtained**
   3 Nephi 1:29.

6. **Strengthened Through the Sacrament and Other Ordinances**
   3 Nephi 2:1–3.

7. **Being Able to Stand Fast in the Liberty God has Given**
   3 Nephi 2:12.

8. **Help in Overcoming the Cultural Gap**
   3 Nephi 2:14–16.

9. **Inspired Leadership is Provided**
   3 Nephi 3:16.

10. **United in the Strength of the Lord**
    3 Nephi 4:8–10.

Chapter 2

Nephite Parallel Years to the Jerusalem Ministry

3 Nephi 6:1–8:4 (A.D. 26–33)

We learn from the Gospel of Luke that Jesus Christ began his ministry when he was "about thirty years of age" (Luke 3:23). From John's Gospel we learn that it commenced when "the Jews' Passover was at hand" (John 2:13), and that it was finished three years later at the fourth Passover of his ministry. "Now before the feast of the Passover, when Jesus knew that his hour was come that he should depart out of this world unto the Father, having loved his own which were in the world, he loved them unto the end." (John 13:1) The Lord offered himself as the paschal sacrifice at this Passover. John also identifies the other two passovers (see John 5:1; 6:4). The book of John, which is entirely set in Palestine, gives a wonderful commentary of these miraculous events.

It is during this same time period that we pick up the story in the New World. The sixth and seventh chapters of Third Nephi show us the events among the Nephites that parallel the Lord's ministry in Jerusalem. Although those events cover more than twice the length of the three years (A.D. 26–33), most of the detail is found in two specific years—the thirty and thirty-first years after the signs were given on the American continent concerning the Lord's birth. These two years are the year before and the year that Christ began his ministry. There is no record of the previous years in the New Testament.

As we read these Book of Mormon chapters, one thing that immediately strikes our attention is Satan's opposition to the Church at this time. It is apparent that Satan knew of the coming of the greatest era of this earth's mortal existence, when the Savior would atone for the sins of mankind, and that he (Satan) was aware of the eventual resurrection of all men if the Lord prevailed. An outline giving an overview of these two chapters follows.

Outline • 3 Nephi 6:1–8:4

➤ 6:1–9   In the twenty-sixth year, the Nephites returned with their families, animals, and belongings, to both the lands northward and southward.

    a. They took what provisions they had not devoured with them. v. 2

    b. The robbers who had covenanted to keep peace, and desired to remain Lamanites, were granted land upon which they could subsist. v. 3

    c. The people began to prosper and wax great as the next two years passed away, and there was great order due to the laws of equity and justice. vv. 4–8

        1. Nothing but transgression could hinder them from prospering.

        2. Their leaders, Gidgiddoni and Lachoneus, had established this great peace.

        3. Many cities were built, and many highways and roads were made.

    d. The twentieth-eighth year, also passed away in continual peace. v. 9

➤ 6:10–18   The twenty-ninth year, saw some disputings, and some lifted up in pride, boasting of their riches.

    a. There were many merchants, lawyers, and officers in the land. vv. 11–13

1. The people began to be distinguished by ranks, according to their riches and chances for learning.

2. Some were ignorant because of their poverty, and others were learned because of their riches.

3. Some were lifted up in pride, and some were humble.

4. Some returned railing for railing, and others were persecuted and afflicted without reviling, but were humble and penitent before God.

b. The thirtieth year, great inequality caused the church to be broken up, save among a few of the Lamanites who were converted to the true faith. vv. 14–18

1. Satan's power caused this inequality, stirring up the people to iniquity and pride.

2. He tempted them to seek for power and authority, riches, and the vain things of the world.

3. They had enjoyed peace for only a few years, and were in an awful state of wickedness.

4. They did not sin ignorantly; they had been taught and knew the will of God, and wilfully rebelled.

c. Lachoneus, son of Lachoneus, governed that year in the place of his father. vv. 19–20

1. Men inspired from heaven went among the people, preaching and testifying boldly of their sins.

2. They testified boldly of the redemption of Christ, his death, and his resurrection.

d. Many were angry because the inspired men testified of these things. vv. 21–24

1. They were mainly the chief priests, those who had been high priests, and the lawyers.

2. No lawyer, judge, or high priest had the power to condemn anyone to death save the governor.

3. Many of the testifiers were secretly put to death by the judges without the governor's knowledge.

  e. A complaint came to the governor and the wicked judges were taken and judged by the law. vv. 25–29

    1. Almost all the lawyers and high priests united with the kindred of those being judged.

    2. They entered into a covenant of old, administered by the devil, to combine against all righteousness.

    3. They covenanted to destroy the Lord's people, and deliver the murderers from justice.

  f. They set at defiance the law and the rights of their country, and covenanted to destroy the governor, and establish a king over the land. v. 30

➢ 7:1–8 They did not establish a king, but in the thirtieth year they murdered the chief judge.

  a. The people separated into tribes, of family, kindred, and friends, destroying the government. vv. 2–4

    1. Every tribe appointed a chief, and they became tribes and leaders of tribes.

    2. Each tribe was numerous, having much family, kindred, and friends.

  b. There were no wars, but iniquity came because of yielding to the power of Satan. vv. 5–8

    1. The regulations of the government were destroyed because of the secret combinations.

    2. The great contention in the land caused nearly all the more righteous to become wicked.

    3. In six years, the people had turned like a dog to its vomit.

➢ 7:9–14 The secret combinations gathered and appointed a man called Jacob as king.

  a. He was one of the chiefest against the prophets who testified against Jesus. vv. 10–11

    1. They were not as numerous as the tribes of the people.

    2. The tribes of the people were united in hatred of those who covenanted to destroy the government.

    b. Jacob commanded his people to flee northward, and build up a kingdom. vv. 12–13

        1. He flattered them to believe there would be sufficient dissenters to contend with the tribes.

        2. They fled speedily, and could not be impeded before they were out of reach.

    c. The thirty-first year, the tribes were not united, but covenanted to not go against each other. v. 14

        1. They had strict laws to not trespass against each other and had a degree of peace.

        2. Their hearts were turned from the Lord and they stoned and cast out the prophets.

➤ 7:15–20   Nephi was visited daily by angels and by the voice of the Lord, and had power given him to know of the ministry of Christ. He was also an eyewitness of their quick return from righteousness to wickedness.

    a. He testified boldly of repentance and remission of sins through faith on the Lord. vv. 16

    b. He ministered with power and authority many things that cannot be written in this book. vv. 17–20

        1. The people were angry because Nephi had greater power, and it was impossible to not believe.

        2. In the name of Jesus Christ, he cast out devils and unclean spirits.

        3. He raised from death his brother, who had been stoned by the people.

        4. They were angry because of his power, and many more miracles did he do.

    c. The thirty-first year passed away, and few were converted unto the Lord. vv. 21–22

        1. The converted did truly signify that they had been visited by the power and Spirit of God.

        2. Those who had devils cast out, manifested that they had been healed by the Spirit of God.

    d. The next two years (A.D. 32–33), Nephi preached repentance and remission of sins. vv. 23–26

        1. Those brought to repentance were baptized, and Nephi ordained men to the ministry.

        2. Many were baptized as a witness and a testimony before God, and unto the people, that they had repented and received a remission of their sins.

➤ 8:1–4   According to our record, which we know to be true, the thirty-third year passed away.

    a. A just man kept the record, who truly did many miracles in the name of the Lord. v. 1

    b. No man could do a miracle unless cleansed every whit from his iniquity. v. 1

    c. The people began to look for signs given by Samuel the Lamanite. vv. 3–4

        1. There was to be darkness over the land for three days.

        2. There began to be doubtings and disputations among the people.

NOTES AND COMMENTARY

1 And now it came to pass that the people of the Nephites did all return to their own lands in the twenty and sixth year, every man, with his family, his flocks and his herds, his horses and his cattle, and all things whatsoever did belong unto them.

2 And it came to pass that they had not eaten up all their provisions; therefore they did take with them all that they had not devoured, of all their grain of every kind, and their gold, and their silver, and all their precious things, and they did return to their own lands and their possessions, both on the north and on the south, both on the land northward and on the land southward.

3 And they granted unto those robbers who had entered into a covenant to keep the peace of the land, who were desirous to remain Lamanites, lands, according to their numbers, that they might have, with their labors, wherewith to subsist upon; and thus they did establish peace in all the land.

4 And they began again to prosper and to wax great; and the twenty and sixth and seventh years passed away, and there was great order in the land; and they had formed their laws according to equity and justice.

5 And now there was nothing in all the land to hinder the people from prospering continually, except they should fall into transgression.

6 And now it was Gidgiddoni, and the judge, Lachoneus, and those who had been appointed leaders, who had established this great peace in the land.

7 And it came to pass that there were many cities built anew, and there were many old cities repaired.

8 And there were many highways cast up, and many roads made, which led from city to city, and from land to land, and from place to place.

9 And thus passed away the twenty and eighth year, and the people had continual peace. [3 Nephi 6:1–9]

The Nephites returned to their own lands with their families, animals, and possessions. Once there, they restored the old cities and built new ones, established order, and for the next two years (A.D. 27–28), maintained continual peace (vv. 1–9). In Mormon's words, "there was nothing in all the land to hinder the people from prospering continually, except they should fall into transgression" (v. 5). However, the established peace and order was short-lived.

10 But it came to pass in the twenty and ninth year there began to be some disputings among the people; and some were lifted up unto pride and boastings because of their exceedingly great riches, yea, even unto great persecutions;

11 For there were many merchants in the land, and also many lawyers, and many officers.

12 And the people began to be distinguished by ranks, according to their riches and their chances for learning; yea, some were ignorant because of their poverty, and others did receive great learning because of their riches.

13 Some were lifted up in pride, and others were exceedingly humble; some did return railing for railing, while others would receive railing and persecution and all manner of afflictions, and would not turn and revile again, but were humble and penitent before God.

14 And thus there became a great inequality in all the land, insomuch that the church began to be broken up; yea, insomuch that in the thirtieth year the church was broken up in all the land save it were among a few of the Lamanites who were converted unto the true faith; and they would not depart from it, for they were firm, and steadfast, and immovable, willing with all diligence to keep the commandments of the Lord. [3 Nephi 6:10–14]

The cycle from peace to posterity to pride began again among them. Mormon attributes the changes to "many merchants, many lawyers," and "many officers." The people once again "began to be distinguished by ranks, according to their riches and their chances for learning" (vv. 10–12). As this great inequality spread through all the land, it resulted in the break-up of the Church in the thirtieth year. Finally, the only people who were not affected were "a few of the Lamanites who were converted unto the true faith" (v. 14). These converts were like unto the original Lamanite converts who "called their names Anti-Nephi-Lehies" (Alma 23:17). Mormon said of these people, "When these Lamanites were brought to believe and to know the truth, they were firm, and would suffer even unto death rather than commit sin; and thus we see that they buried their weapons of peace, or they buried the weapons of war, for peace" (Alma 24:19).

15 Now the cause of this iniquity of the people was this—Satan had great power, unto the stirring up of the people to do all manner of iniquity, and to the puffing them up with pride, tempting them to seek for power, and authority, and riches, and the vain things of the world.

16 And thus Satan did lead away the hearts of the people to do all manner of iniquity; therefore they had enjoyed peace but a few years.

17 And thus, in the commencement of the thirtieth year—the people having been delivered up for the space of a long time to be carried about by the temptations of the devil whithersoever he desired to carry them, and to do whatsoever iniquity he desired they should—and thus in the commencement of this, the thirtieth year, they were in a state of awful wickedness.

18 Now they did not sin ignorantly, for they knew the will of God concerning them, for it had been taught unto them; therefore they did wilfully rebel against God. [3 Nephi 6:15–18]

Mormon attributes "this iniquity of the people" to Satan's great power to puff the people up with pride, and to tempt them "to seek for power, and authority, and riches, and the vain things of the world." He describes their condition as an "awful state of wickedness." His reason for such a description was not just because of what they were doing, but also because of their attitudes. Satan had a great hold on the hearts of the people (vv. 15–17). Mormon records, "Now they did not sin ignorantly, for they knew the will of God concerning them, for it had been taught unto them; therefore they did wilfully rebel against God" (v. 18).

Pride vs. Prophets

The thirtieth year was similar upon both continents. In Jerusalem, John the Baptist was calling the people to repentance, and fulfilling his prophesied mission to "prepare ye the way of the Lord" (Isaiah 40:3). Jesus was preparing to begin his mortal ministry. The Book of Mormon prophets had also foretold the ministry of John:

JST John 1	Mark 1	1 Nephi 10
6 There was a man sent from God, Whose name was John. a prophet who should come 7 The same came **into the world** for a witness, to bear witness of the light, **to bear record of the gospel through the Son, unto all,** that through him **men** might believe. ye the way of the Lord, and make 8 He was not that light, but came to bear witness of that light, ye know not; and he is mightier 9 **Which** was the true light, which lighteth every man **who** cometh into the world; (see also Luke 3:2–4)	The beginning of the gospel of Jesus Christ, the Son of God; 2 As it is written in the prophets, Behold, I send my messenger before thy face, which shall prepare thy way before thee. 3 The voice of one crying in the wilderness, Prepare ye the way of the Lord, make his paths straight. 4 John did baptize in the wilderness, and preach baptism of repentance for the remission of sins. (see also Matthew 3:1–3; Luke 3:2–4)	7 And he spake also concerning a prophet who should come before the Messiah, to prepare the way of the Lord— 8 Yea, even he should go forth and cry in the wilderness: Prepare ye the way of the Lord, and make his paths straight; for there standeth one among you whom ye know not; and he is mightier than I, whose shoe's latchet I am not worthy to unloose.

In the Americas, an "awful state of wickedness" prevailed, but there were men sent among them similar to John the Baptist.

> 19 And now it was in the days of Lachoneus, the son of Lachoneus, for Lachoneus did fill the seat of his father and did govern the people that year.
>
> 20 And there began to be men inspired from heaven and sent forth, standing among the people in all the land, preaching and testifying boldly of the sins and iniquities of the people, and testifying unto them concerning the redemption which the Lord would make for his people, or in other words, the resurrection of Christ; and they did testify boldly of his death and sufferings. [3 Nephi 6:19–20]

Mormon's description further equates them with John the Baptist. They were "inspired from heaven ... preaching and testifying boldly of the sins and iniquities of the people, and ... the redemption which the Lord would make for his people," (v. 20). The people in their pride were being left without excuse, and were thus fully accountable for their actions. The problem of pride was also prevalent in Palestine as evidenced by the reaction of many to John's message:

> But when he saw many of the Pharisees and Sadducees come to his baptism, he said unto them, O, generation of vipers! who hath warned you to flee from the wrath to come? Why is it that ye receive not the preaching of him whom God hath sent? If ye receive not this in your hearts, ye receive not me; and if ye receive not me, ye receive not him of whom I am sent to bear record; and for your sins ye have no cloak. Repent, therefore, and bring forth fruits meet for repentance; And think not to say within yourselves, We are the children of Abraham, and we only have power to bring seed unto our father Abraham; for I say unto you that God is able of these stones to raise up children into Abraham. [JST Matthew 3:33–36, see also Matthew 3:7–9]

There are many parallels between our time period and the one in which the Savior lived. Our society is experiencing a similar problem with pride and boasting because of riches. There are also many merchants, lawyers, and officers in government that tend to be bureaucratic. The Book of Mormon previously warned: "because some of you have obtained [riches] more abundantly than that of your brethren ye are lifted up in the pride of your heart" (Jacob 2:13); and "the people of the church began to wax proud, because of their exceeding riches" (Alma 4:6). People also tend to distinguish themselves by rank, according to "their riches, and chances for learning" (3 Nephi 6:12). The Lord has begun to warn us through his prophets. We have been specifically warned by President Ezra Taft Benson to beware of pride:

> The Doctrine and Covenants tells us that the Book of Mormon is the "record of a fallen people" (D&C 20:9). Why did they fall? This is one of the major messages of the Book of Mormon. Mormon gives the answer in the closing chapters of the book in these words: "Behold, the pride of this nation, or the people of the Nephites, hath proven their destruction" (Moroni 8:27). And then, lest we miss that momentous Book of Mormon message from that fallen people, the Lord warns us in the Doctrine and Covenants, "Beware of pride, lest ye become as the Nephites of old" [D&C 38:39].
>
> . . .It was essentially the sin of pride that kept us from establishing Zion in the days of the Prophet Joseph Smith. It was the same sin of pride that brought consecration to an end among the Nephites (see 4 Nephi 1:24–25).
>
> Pride is the great stumbling block to Zion. I repeat: Pride is the great stumbling block to Zion.
>
> We must cleanse the inner vessel by conquering pride (see Alma 6:2–4; Matthew 23:25–26).
>
> We must yield 'to the enticings of the Holy Spirit,' put off the prideful 'natural man,' become 'a saint through the atonement of Christ the Lord,' and become' as a child, submissive, meek, humble' (Mosiah 3:19; see also Alma 13:28) [CR, April 1989, 3 and 7].

President Gordon B. Hinckley, and Elder Dallin H. Oaks have warned us about the dangers of litigation:

> We live in an environment where there is much of litigation and conflict, of suing and countersuing. Even here (Christ's) powers of healing may be invoked (instead of litigation) [Hinckley, Gordon B., Ensign, November 1988, p. 54].
>
> Persons who prosecute frivolous lawsuits do not measure up to (the Lord's) high standard. Groundless litigation rewards some plaintiffs

handsomely, but it injures everyone else by raising the price of products and services [Oaks, Dallin H., CR, October 1986 p. 26].

Elder Boyd K. Packer has admonished the faculty and students of Brigham Young University to maintain a blend of reason and revelation in order to maintain the proper balance of learning in education:

> Each of us must accommodate the mixture of reason and revelation in our lives. The gospel not only permits but requires it. An individual who concentrates on either side solely and alone will lose both balance and perspective. History confirms that the university environment always favors reason; with the workings of the Spirit made to feel uncomfortable. I know of no examples to the contrary.
>
> Spirituality, while consummately strong, reacts to very delicate changes in its environment. To have it present at all and to keep it in some degree of purity, requires a commitment and a watch-care which can admit to no embarrassment when compared with what the scholarly world is about.
>
> The moral and spiritual capacity of the faculty and what they shall give, and the spiritual atmosphere in which students are to learn and what they receive will not emerge spontaneously! They happen only if they are caused to happen and thereafter maintained with unwavering determination. We at BYU can be competent in both, and at once merit the respect of those charged with the accreditation of institutions of higher learning.
>
> . . .The fusion of reason and revelation will produce a man and woman of imperishable worth.
>
> On the one hand is reason: the thinking, the figuring things out, the research, the pure joy of discovery and the academic degrees which man bestows to honor that process. On the other is revelation with the very private and very personal, the very individual confirmation of truth. The combining of them is THE test of mortal life! [BYU Devotional, February 12, 1991; pp. 11–13].

The warning of pride in the Book of Mormon is of great significance to us. By examining how the Lord has previously attended to his people, we can become better prepared to accept his counsel and to obey his commandments today.

21 Now there were many of the people who were exceedingly angry because of those who testified of these things; and those who were angry were chiefly the chief judges, and they who had been high priests and lawyers; yea, all those who were lawyers were angry with those who testified of these things.

22 Now there was no lawyer nor judge nor high priest that could have power to condemn any one to death save their condemnation was signed by the governor of the land.

23 Now there were many of those who testified of the things pertaining to Christ who testified boldly, who were taken and put to death secretly by the judges, that the knowledge of their death came not unto the governor of the land until after their death.

24 Now behold, this was contrary to the laws of the land, that any man should be put to death except they had power from the governor of the land— [3 Nephi 6:21–24]

The reaction of many of the Nephites also serves as a warning to us. They were exceedingly angry with those who testified of these things as well as by what they said (v. 21). Did they indeed know that the prophets were correct? Since the people were willfully sinning, it would seem that they did know the truth of the message of the prophets. The critics were the lawyers and judges and those who had been high priests and lawyers" (v. 21). What is the significance of the words "who had been"? Were those "who had been" high priests former members of the Church who had left the Church or had been excommunicated? Were those "who had been" lawyers now occupying the offices of judges? Although we must wait for the unabridged records to fully answer these questions, such seems to be the case. The corrupt judges were secretly putting to death the prophets, contrary to the law of the land.

25 Therefore a complaint came up unto the land of Zarahemla, to the governor of the land, against these judges who had condemned the prophets of the Lord unto death, not according to the law.

26 Now it came to pass that they were taken and brought up before the judge, to be judged of the crime which they had done, according to the law which had been given by the people.

27 Now it came to pass that those judges had many friends and kindreds; and the remainder, yea, even almost all the lawyers and the high priests, did gather themselves together, and unite with the kindreds of those judges who were to be tried according to the law.

28 And they did enter into a covenant one with another, yea, even into that covenant which was given by them of old, which covenant was given and administered by the devil, to combine against all righteousness.

29 Therefore they did combine against the people of the Lord, and enter into a covenant to destroy them, and to deliver those who were guilty of murder from the grasp of justice, which was about to be administered according to the law.

30 And they did set at defiance the law and the rights of their country; and they did covenant one with another to destroy the governor, and to establish a king over the land, that the land should no more be at liberty but should be subject unto kings. [3 Nephi 6:25–30]

The judges who were brought before the governor for their illegal actions against the prophets were able to rally their "many friends and kindreds," and "almost all the lawyers and the high priests" in their defense. They organized themselves through covenants with each other, even as the secret combinations of old that were administered by the devil. Their purpose was "to combine against all righteousness" (vv. 25–29). There seem to be similar efforts combining today against things in our society that are righteous.

Are the precious freedoms of the United States Constitution being "set at defiance" today? President Ezra Taft Benson, in speaking of the two hundredth anniversary of the Constitution stated:

At this bicentennial celebration we must, with sadness, say that we have not been wise in keeping the trust of our Founding Fathers. For the past two centuries, those who do not prize freedom have chipped away at every major clause of our Constitution until today we face a crisis of great dimensions.[1]

President Benson has continually urged the members of the Church to do as the Lord commanded, and support and befriend the Constitution. A revelation to Joseph Smith justified the "brethren of my church, in befriending that law which is the constitutional law of the land" (D&C 98:6; see also 101:77–80 partially quoted in chapter one). It is our responsibility to preserve constitutional principles so that this nation does not fail, as did the Nephite government.

1 Now behold, I will show unto you that they did not establish a king over the land; but in this same year, yea, the thirtieth year, they did destroy upon the judgment-seat, yea, did murder the chief judge of the land.

2 And the people were divided one against another; and they did separate one from another into tribes, every man according to his family and his kindred and friends; and thus they did destroy the government of the land.

3 And every tribe did appoint a chief or a leader over them; and thus they became tribes and leaders of tribes.

4 Now behold, there was no man among them save he had much family and many kindreds and friends; therefore their tribes became exceedingly great.

5 Now all this was done, and there were no wars as yet among them; and all this iniquity had come upon the people because they did yield themselves unto the power of Satan.

6 And the regulations of the government were destroyed, because of the secret combination of the friends and kindreds of those who murdered the prophets.

---

[1] Ezra Taft Benson, *The Constitution: A Heavenly Banner* (Salt Lake City: Deseret Book, 1986), 24–25; also in Ezra Taft Benson, *The Teachings of Ezra Taft Benson* (Salt Lake City: Bookcraft, 1988), 612; see pages 593–625 for other statements regarding the Constitution).

7 And they did cause a great contention in the land, insomuch that the more righteous part of the people had nearly all become wicked; yea, there were but few righteous men among them. [3 Nephi 7:1–7]

Although the secret band did not accomplish their goal of having a king, they did murder the chief judge of the land. They also destroyed the government of the land and instituted a tribal system of government (vv. 1–4). All of this was done internally. There were no wars or open fighting, but the gradual erosion of the laws and government of the people occurred "because they did yield themselves unto the power of Satan," who led them to organize into secret combinations, until "the more righteous part of the people had nearly all become wicked; yea, there were but few righteous men among them" (vv. 6–7). Is our society following a similar internal decay?

Having fulfilled his intent of showing the government's downfall, Mormon inserts a conclusion regarding the past six years of the Nephite people: "the more part of the people had turned from their righteousness, like the dog to his vomit, or like the sow to her wallowing in the mire" (vv. 6–8). Mormon's conclusion is a sad commentary on the reality of Satan and his influence. By contrast, ten years earlier (A.D. 21), Mormon had commented: "there was not a living soul among all the people of the Nephites who did doubt in the least the words of all the holy prophets. . . ; for they knew . . . they must be fulfilled (3 Nephi 5:1). Because of this conviction in the hearts of the Nephite people, they had put "an end to all those wicked, and secret, and abominable combinations" (3 Nephi 5:6). This cleansing of the land apparently took them five years. Mormon spoke of putting an end to the wicked and secret and abominable combinations in the twenty-first year, but then quickly speaks of the next four years (A.D. 22–25) passing away (3 Nephi 5:7). The six years to which Mormon refers would be the four years of continual peace (A.D. 25–28), and the beginning of pride in the twenty-ninth year until the "state of awful wickedness" in the thirtieth year (v. 6–17). The change from total dedication and commitment to anarchy was, therefore, really done in a two-year period, but Mormon's six years were from putting an end to the secret combinations to their again obtaining a firm grasp in the society. Satan does not sit idly by. How rapidly can a people change? Those who lived in the 1960s did not see a total change equal to the Nephite period here described, but they did witness a change from peace and order to an internal revolution in the country in a few short years. There are interesting parallels between our day and the days of the Nephites. Although the New Testament record is silent on the parallel years in the land of Palestine, there were probably similar happenings there.

> 9 Now this secret combination, which had brought so great iniquity upon the people, did gather themselves together, and did place at their head a man whom they did call Jacob;
>
> 10 And they did call him their king; therefore he became a king over this wicked band; and he was one of the chiefest who had given his voice against the prophets who testified of Jesus.
>
> 11 And it came to pass that they were not so strong in number as the tribes of the people, who were united together save it were their leaders did establish their laws, every one according to his tribe; nevertheless they were enemies; notwithstanding they were not a righteous people, yet they were united in the hatred of those who had entered into a covenant to destroy the government.
>
> 12 Therefore, Jacob seeing that their enemies were more numerous than they, he being the king of the band, therefore he commanded his people that they should take their flight into the northernmost part of the land, and there build up unto themselves a kingdom, until they were joined by dissenters, (for he flattered them that there would be many dissenters) and they become sufficiently strong to contend with the tribes of the people; and they did so.
>
> 13 And so speedy was their march that it could not be impeded until they had gone forth out of the reach of the people. And thus ended the thirtieth year; and thus were the affairs of the people of Nephi. [3 Nephi 7:9–13]

The secret band appointed their own king, a man named Jacob. Also, the central government's failure had led to the establishment of tribal units, many of which were enemies to each other; nonetheless, they were sufficiently united to hate and oppose the people governed by Jacob who sought to destroy the Nephite government. Therefore, Jacob took his people into the northernmost part of the land and built up his own kingdom. Through flattery he persuaded many to dissent from the other tribal units and join him in the north as the thirtieth year ended (vv. 9–13). The multiplicity of governing bodies among the Nephites, reminds us of the rulers in Palestine at this time, controlled by Rome with a procurator governing in the land, but with the high priest and the San Hedrin having some power among the Jews. More about this will be said later.

The Three Years of Christ's Jerusalem Ministry

The thirty-first year of the Nephite calendar was the year Jesus' ministry began in Palestine. The preparatory ministry of John the Baptist resulted in his imprisonment and eventual death. "But Herod the tetrarch, being reproved by him for Herodias his brother Philip's wife, and for all the evils which Herod had done, Added yet this above all, that he shut up John in prison" (Luke 3:19–20). Among the Nephites, the tribal units of family, kindred, and friends agreed to not war with each other.

14 And it came to pass in the thirty and first year that they were divided into tribes, every man according to his family, kindred and friends; nevertheless they had come to an agreement that they would not go to war one with another; but they were not united as to their laws, and their manner of government, for they were established according to the minds of those who were their chiefs and their leaders. But they did establish very strict laws that one tribe should not trespass against another, insomuch that in some degree they had peace in the land; nevertheless, their hearts were turned from the Lord their God, and they did stone the prophets and did cast them out from among them.

15 And it came to pass that Nephi—having been visited by angels and also the voice of the Lord, therefore having seen angels, and being eye-witness, and having had power given unto him that he might know concerning the ministry of Christ, and also being eye-witness to their quick return from righteousness unto their wickedness and abominations;

16 Therefore, being grieved for the hardness of their hearts and the blindness of their minds—went forth among them in that same year, and

began to testify, boldly, repentance and remission of sins through faith on the Lord Jesus Christ.

17 And he did minister many things unto them; and all of them cannot be written, and a part of them would not suffice, therefore they are not written in this book. And Nephi did minister with power and with great authority. [3 Nephi 7:14–17]

Although the Nephites differed in their manner of government, they strictly adhered to the laws for individual tribal government and thus retained some degree of peace. They did not, however, respect religious freedom, for they stoned the prophets and cast them out (v. 14). One cannot help but think that the teachings of the Church concerning individual families were a big help in establishing at least some of the tribal units to some degree of righteousness. Certainly "The Proclamation of the Family" announced by The First Presidency and the Council of the Twelve Apostles in September 1995 has already had a tremendous effect on the Church and in some of the world, and will continue to have an effect in our day as the Second Coming approaches.

While in this Nephite time period, the lives of prophets were taken and others were cast out, there was one prophet upon whom they had no power. Nephi, son of Nephi, because of his righteousness, was "visited by angels and also the voice of the Lord." There is also a unique statement made by Mormon that might easily be overlooked: Nephi "being [an] eyewitness, and having had power given unto him that he might know concerning the ministry of Christ" (v. 15) strongly suggests that Nephi was shown Jesus' Palestine ministry in vision. Did Nephi see events such as Christ's baptism, his gathering of disciples from whom the Twelve were selected, his miracle of changing water to wine and others? Nephi, son of Lehi, in about 600 B.C. had seen in vision that, "The Lamb of God went forth and was baptized of [John]; and after he was baptized, I beheld the heavens open, and the multitudes were gathered together to hear him; and I beheld that they cast him out from among them" (1 Nephi 11:27). Certainly the Lord could have shown Nephi, son of Nephi, as well.

Apparently space would not permit Nephi to give a full account, but someday we will have a full record of his "eyewitness" account (v. 17). Whatever he was shown, he clearly became a special witness of Christ's ministry and testified of it to the Nephite people. With such sure knowledge, it is no wonder that Nephi was able to testify boldly of "repentance and remission of sins through faith on the Lord Jesus Christ" (v. 16).

> 18 And it came to pass that they were angry with him, even because he had greater power than they, for it were not possible that they could disbelieve his words, for so great was his faith on the Lord Jesus Christ that angels did minister unto him daily.
>
> 19 And in the name of Jesus did he cast out devils and unclean spirits; and even his brother did he raise from the dead, after he had been stoned and suffered death by the people.
>
> 20 And the people saw it, and did witness of it, and were angry with him because of his power; and he did also do many more miracles, in the sight of the people, in the name of Jesus.
>
> 21 And it came to pass that the thirty and first year did pass away, and there were but few who were converted unto the Lord; but as many as were converted did truly signify unto the people that they had been visited by the power and Spirit of God, which was in Jesus Christ, in whom they believed.
>
> 22 And as many as had devils cast out from them, and were healed of their sicknesses and their infirmities, did truly manifest unto the people that they had been wrought upon by the Spirit of God, and had been healed; and they did show forth signs also and did do some miracles among the people. [3 Nephi 7:18–22]

Nephi had such great faith that his testimony was bolstered daily by the visit of angels. His great faith empowered him to perform great miracles in the name of Jesus, even to the raising of his brother Timothy from the dead. This great power angered the people because they could not disbelieve his words.

The words Nephi taught and the miracles he performed were a witness of Christ to the Nephites. Though few hearts were converted, those who were converted had great manifestations given to them, and they in turn manifested that power to others (vv. 18–22). This year of Nephi's ministry had some similarities to Jesus' ministry in Jerusalem. In the first year and just before, Jesus had commanded "water [and it] was made wine" (John 2:1–11); healed the nobleman's son "at the same hour, in which Jesus said unto him [at Cana], Thy son liveth [in Capernaum]" (John 4:46–54); "with authority commanded he even the unclean spirits, and they do obey him [cast them out]" (Mark 1:21–26); healed "all manner of sickness, and all manner of disease among the people" (Matthew 4:23), and many other great miracles. At the first passover "he drove [the money changers] all out of the temple" (John 2:13–16). He had greater power than they did. In the second year, "there was a dead man carried out [of Nain], the only son of his mother, and she was a widow; ... And when the Lord saw her, he had compassion on her, and said unto her, Weep not. And he came and touched the bier: and they that bare *him* stood still. And he said, Young man, I say unto thee, Arise. And he that was dead sat up, and began to speak. And he delivered him to his mother," (Luke 7:11–15). The daughter of Jairus was also raised from the dead.

> 49 While he yet spake, there cometh one from the ruler of the synagogue's *house,* saying to him, Thy daughter is dead; trouble not the Master.
>
> 50 But when Jesus heard *it,* he answered him, saying, Fear not: believe only, and she shall be made whole.
>
> 51 And when he came into the house, he suffered no man to go in, save Peter, and James, and John, and the father and the mother of the maiden.
>
> 52 And all wept, and bewailed her: but he said, Weep not; she is not dead, but sleepeth.
>
> 53 And they laughed him to scorn, knowing that she was dead.
>
> 54 And he put them all out, and took her by the hand, and called, saying, Maid, arise.
>
> 55 And her spirit came again, and she arose straightway: and he commanded to give her meat.
>
> 56 And her parents were astonished: but he charged them that they should tell no man what was done. [Luke 8:49–56]

Those on both continents certainly witnessed the power of God among them.

> 23 Thus passed away the thirty and second year also. And Nephi did cry unto the people in the commencement of the thirty and third year; and he did preach unto them repentance and remission of sins.
>
> 24 Now I would have you to remember also, that there were none who were brought unto repentance who were not baptized with water.
>
> 25 Therefore, there were ordained of Nephi, men unto this ministry, that all such as should come unto them should be baptized with water, and this as a witness and a testimony before God, and unto the people, that they had repented and received a remission of their sins.
>
> 26 And there were many in the commencement of this year that were baptized unto repentance; and thus the more part of the year did pass away. [3 Nephi 7:23–26]

There is no specific record of the second or third Nephite parallel years of Jesus' ministry. The general description mentioned above is all that the Book of Mormon provides regarding those years (v. 23). Mormon affirms that all who were brought to repentance were baptized with water, and that men were ordained to the ministry to baptize those who were converted (vv. 24–25).

Mormon concludes the account of the thirty-third year with a testimony of the truth of the Nephite record, and of the character of Nephi, the keeper of the record.

> 1 And now it came to pass that according to our record, and we know our record to be true, for behold, it was a just man who did keep the record—for he truly did many miracles in the name of Jesus; and there was not any man who could do a miracle in the name of Jesus save he were cleansed every whit from his iniquity—
>
> 2 And now it came to pass, if there was no mistake made by this man in the reckoning of our time, the thirty and third year had passed away;
>
> 3 And the people began to look with great earnestness for the sign which had been given by the prophet Samuel, the Lamanite, yea, for the time that there should be darkness for the space of three days over the face of the land.

4 And there began to be great doubtings and disputations among the people, notwithstanding so many signs had been given. [3 Nephi 8:1–4]

Based upon the miracles that Nephi performed, Mormon testified that neither Nephi nor any other man could perform "a miracle in the name of Jesus save he was cleansed every whit from his iniquity" (v. 1). This reminds us of Jesus' response to his disciples' inability to cure a lunatic: "This kind goeth not out but by prayer and fasting" (Matthew 17:14–21). Prayer and fasting would cleanse them of their iniquity and enable them to perform the miracle of healing the lunatic. Such a testimony should also remind us of the requirements needed to perform miracles in our day, and of the advantage of having good men appointed as the keepers of our records. Furthermore, the record of Third Nephi is indeed another gospel, or the testimony of Nephi, a true disciple of Christ, that is comparable to Matthew, Mark, Luke, and John.

The three years of the Nephite record paralleling the three-year ministry of Jesus Christ in Jerusalem is sparse in detail, but it is rich in testimony of the power attained by the faithful. It further should whet our anticipation of the coming forth of the full account on the large plates of Nephi. From it we may gain greater knowledge of what was shown to Nephi, and the specific events that happened among the Nephite people. It was indeed an eventful three years among the Nephites in America. The New Testament is likewise an incomplete record. "And there are also many other things which Jesus did, the which, if they should be written every one, I suppose that even the world itself could not contain the books that should be written. Amen" (John 21:25). Someday we will learn more of what Jesus did, and probably see many more parallels.

A final summation of the eight years covered in chapters six and seven of Third Nephi shows a people who had lived in a peaceful, prosperous society turn to wickedness and chaos. During the chaotic era, the righteous became stable and more righteous, and the wicked became unstable and more wicked. The same pattern will follow in the period prior to the Second Coming: "peace shall be taken from the earth, and the devil shall have power over his own dominion. And also the Lord shall have power over his saints, and shall reign in their midst, and shall come down in judgment upon Idumea, or the world" (D&C 1:35–36). Our challenge is to so live that we may be among the Saints now, and at the time of the Second Coming.

PART 2

The Crucifixion of Christ—The Beginning of A.D. 34

3 Nephi 8:5–10:17

The thirty-fourth year since the sign of the birth of Christ to the Nephites began with their expectation of the sign of three days' darkness coming upon the land as prophesied by Samuel the Lamanite. On the fourth day of the first month, "arose a great storm, such an one as never had been known in all the land" (3 Nephi 8:5). This was followed by the anticipated three days of darkness (3 Nephi 10:9).

The first week of the thirty-fourth year is described in 3 Nephi 8–10. There were three days before the storm, then three days of darkness, and on the seventh day the darkness dispersed. Most of these three chapters consist of words spoken by the Savior at the end of the three days of darkness. The end of chapter 10 is a fairly lengthy commentary by Mormon. The storm, Jesus' words, and Mormon's commentary are analyzed in the following chapter.

Chapter 3

The Higher Law of Sacrifice

3 Nephi 8:5–10:17

The religious sacrifice of animals in Old Testament times was a type and shadow of the coming sacrifice of Jesus Christ by the shedding of his blood, which was to bring "a stop to the shedding of blood; then shall the law of Moses be fulfilled" . . . the "great and last sacrifice will be the Son of God" (Alma 34:13–14). A new type of sacrifice was instituted under Christ's higher law. This he explained to the Nephites when he visited them following his crucifixion. His words are recorded in the three chapters of Third Nephi under consideration.

The law of Moses was not fulfilled until "the Lamb of God, which taketh away the sin of the world" was crucified (John 1:29). The Passover Lamb was symbolic of "the precious blood of Christ, as of a lamb without blemish and without spot" (1 Peter 1:19; see also Exodus 12:3–5). In the time period of these Book of Mormon chapters the sacrifice of Christ was at hand. The Nephites' failure to collectively accept the purpose of the law of Moses, "our schoolmaster to bring us unto Christ" (Galatians 3:24; 2 Nephi 25:24–25), had resulted in other kinds of sacrifices among them. A sacrifice is something that is willingly offered. Because of "a great inequality in all the land, . . . the church began to be broken up" among the Nephites," (3 Nephi 6:14). Because of Satan's power and influence, the people "did not sin ignorantly, for they knew the will of God . . . therefore they did wilfully rebel against God" (3 Nephi 6:18), and thus sacrificed the Church. The Nephites' central government had similarly been sacrificed through the willful, destructive covenants of the wicked judges, high priests, and lawyers "to combine against all righteousness" (3 Nephi 6:28). This also was because of Satan's power. A system of tribal units replaced the God-inspired government and "did destroy the government of the land" (3 Nephi 7:2). Many of those prophets who were "inspired from heaven and sent forth" had boldly testified of Christ, but were stoned "and [the people] did cast them out from among them" (3 Nephi 6:20; 7:14). Thus, they were likewise sacrificed. Those who sinned were also willingly sacrificing their opportunity to receive miracles in their behalf; "there was not any man who could do a miracle in the name of Jesus save he were cleansed every whit from his iniquity" (3 Nephi 8:1). Thus, the wicked Nephites had chosen to sacrifice the blessings of the Church and the gospel in exchange for the destructive influence of the devil.

The iniquity and the abominations of the Nephites caused many cities and their inhabitants to be sunk, buried, burned, or sacrificed (3 Nephi 9:2–10). The destructive sacrifice of these cities and inhabitants in the Americas was one inaugurated by Jesus Christ and not by Satan. The destruction was an act of judgment and illustrates the principle taught by Jesus in his mortal ministry: "For the Father judgeth no man, but hath committed all judgment unto the Son" (John 5:22). An outline of the chapters in Third Nephi discussed in this chapter follows as an overview to prepare for a deeper study of the text.

Outline • 3 Nephi 8:5–10:17

➤ 8:5–18   On the thirty-fourth year, first month, fourth day, there arose a great storm as never known before.

      a.   The city of Zarahemla took fire; Moroni sank into the sea, drowning its inhabitants; and Moronihah had earth carried upon it, becoming a mountain. vv. 8–10

       b. There was great destruction in the land southward, but greater in the land northward. vv. 11–16

          1. The whole face of the land was changed by the storm, and the great quaking of the earth.

          2. Highways were broken up, level roads spoiled, and smooth places became rough.

          3. Many cities were sunk and burned, buildings shaken to the earth, the inhabitants slain, and left desolate.

          4. Many cities remained, but were greatly damaged, and many people were slain.

          5. Some inhabitants were carried away in the whirlwind to unknown places.

       c. The whole earth was deformed; rocks were rent in twain, and broken fragments were found in seams and cracks upon all the earth. vv. 17–18

➤ 8:19–25   The storm and quaking ceased after three hours, and then darkness was upon the earth for three days.

       a. The darkness was thick; the inhabitants could feel the vapor of darkness. vv. 20–22

          1. There could be no light at all; neither candles, torches, or fire kindled.

          2. There was no light from the sun, moon, or stars.

       b. There was great mourning, howling, and weeping among the people; saying: vv. 23–25

          1. If they had repented, our brethren in Zarahemla would not have been burned.

          2. If we had not stoned the prophets, and cast them out, our mothers and fair daughters, and children would not have been buried in Moronihah.

➤ 9:1–12   A voice was heard by all the people saying wo shall come except they repent. The devil laughs, and his angels rejoice because of their sins, the blood of the prophets, and the saints.

a. It is because of their iniquity and abominations that they are slain. vv. 1–8

   1. I caused Zarahemla to be burned, Moroni sunk, Moronihah buried, and their inhabitants slain, to hide their iniquities from me, that the blood of the prophets and the saints shall come no more to me.

   2. The cities and the inhabitants of Gilgal, Onihah, Mocum, and Jerusalem were also sunk.

   3. The cities and the inhabitants of Gadiandi, Gadiomnah, Jacob, and Gimgimno were also buried.

b. The city of Jacobugath, inhabited by the people of king Jacob, I caused to be burned because of their sins, the blood of the prophets, and the saints. v. 9

   1. Their wickedness was above all that of the earth because of their secret murders and combinations.

   2. They destroyed the peace of my people and the government.

c. The cities of Laman, Gosh, Gad, and Kishkumen, I caused to be burned because they cast out the prophets and stoned them. vv. 10–11

   1. I sent them to declare their wickedness and abominations.

   2. There were no righteous remaining among them.

d. Many great destructions have I caused because of the people's wickedness and abominations. v. 12

➤ 9:13–22   The voice continued to all who were spared because they were more righteous than those destroyed.

a. Return unto me, repent of your sins and be converted, that I may heal you. vv. 13–14

   1. Come unto me and ye shall have eternal life.

   2. My arm of mercy is extended, and you will be blessed.

b. I am Jesus Christ, the Son of God. vv. 15–22

1. I created the heavens and the earth and all things therein.
2. I was with the Father from the beginning, and am in the Father and the Father in me.
3. In me hath the Father glorified his name.
4. I came unto my own, they received me not, and the scriptures about my coming are fulfilled.
5. As many as received me have become the sons of God, as many as will believe on my name shall be redeemed, and in me is the law of Moses fulfilled
6. I am the light and the life of the world; Alpha and Omega, the beginning and the end.
7. You shall no more offer sacrifices of blood and burnt offerings, for I will not receive them.
8. You shall offer a sacrifice of a broken heart and a contrite spirit.
9. Those who so offer will be baptized with fire and the Holy Ghost, even as the Lamanites, because of their faith in me at the time of their conversion, and they knew it not.
10. I came into the world to bring redemption, and to save the world from sin.
11. Whosoever comes unto me as a little child, I will receive, for of such is the kingdom of God.
12. For such I have laid down my life, and taken it up again.
13. Come unto me ye ends of the earth, and be saved.

➤ 10:1–8   All the people heard Christ; many hours of silence followed, as lamenting over their dead ceased.

     a. A voice came again that all the people heard. vv. 3–7

         1. Ye house of Israel, how oft have I gathered you and nourished you?

         2. How oft would I have gathered you as a hen gathers her chicks; ye in Jerusalem, as ye that are fallen, but ye would not.

       3. How oft will I gather you, if you will repent and return to me.

       4. If not, your dwellings shall remain desolate until the covenant made to the fathers is fulfilled.

  b. The people began again to weep and wail for the loss of their kindred and friends. v. 8

➤ 10:9–17   Three days passed, the darkness dispersed, the earth ceased to tremble, the groans and noises ceased.

  a. Those alive ceased to mourn, and they began to give praises and thanks to Jesus Christ. vv. 10–14

       1. Thus far were the scriptures fulfilled as spoken by the prophets.

       2. The more righteous part of the people were saved; those who received the prophets, and those who had not shed the blood of the saints.

       3. They were not buried, or drowned, or burned, or crushed, or carried away, or overpowered.

       4. The readers are to understand that the destructions were fulfilling the words of the prophets.

  b. Many testified of these things at the time of Christ's coming, and were slain. vv. 15–17

       1. Zenos and Zenoch testified particularly concerning us, who are remnants of their seed.

       2. Our father Jacob testified of us, a remnant of Joseph, and were written upon the plates of brass.

NOTES AND COMMENTARY

5 And it came to pass in the thirty and fourth year, in the first month, on the fourth day of the month, there arose a great storm, such an one as never had been known in all the land.

6 And there was also a great and terrible tempest; and there was terrible thunder, insomuch that it did shake the whole earth as if it was about to divide asunder.

7 And there were exceedingly sharp lightnings, such as never had been known in all the land.

8 And the city of Zarahemla did take fire.

9 And the city of Moroni did sink into the depths of the sea, and the inhabitants thereof were drowned.

10 And the earth was carried up upon the city of Moronihah, that in the place of the city there became a great mountain.

11 And there was a great and terrible destruction in the land southward.

12 But behold, there was a more great and terrible destruction in the land northward; for behold, the whole face of the land was changed, because of the tempest and the whirlwinds, and the thunderings and the lightnings, and the exceedingly great quaking of the whole earth;

13 And the highways were broken up, and the level roads were spoiled, and many smooth places became rough.

14 And many great and notable cities were sunk, and many were burned, and many were shaken till the buildings thereof had fallen to the earth, and the inhabitants thereof were slain, and the places were left desolate.

15 And there were some cities which remained; but the damage thereof was exceedingly great, and there were many in them who were slain.

16 And there were some who were carried away in the whirlwind; and whither they went no man knoweth, save they know that they were carried away.

17 And thus the face of the whole earth became deformed, because of the tempests, and the thunderings, and the lightnings, and the quaking of the earth.

18 And behold, the rocks were rent in twain; they were broken up upon the face of the whole earth, insomuch that they were found in broken fragments, and in seams and in cracks, upon all the face of the land. [3 Nephi 8:5–18]

The three days of darkness were preceded by a destructive storm that lasted for "about the space of three hours" (3 Nephi 8:19). The storm was so severe that it shook the whole earth such as "never had been known in all the land" (vv. 5–7). The area southward and northward saw such terrible destruction that the whole face of the land was changed (vv. 8–12). Highways were broken up, many people were slain or carried away in a whirlwind, and the earth and the people were destroyed just as Samuel the Lamanite had foretold (vv. 13–19; see Helaman 14:20–24).

In Jerusalem, "from the sixth hour there was darkness over all the land unto the ninth hour . . . and the earth did quake, and the rocks rent" (Matthew 27:45,51). Although there was a three-hour darkness and a storm in both the Old and New World, the storm apparently was not as destructive in Jerusalem as in America. "The veil of the temple was rent in twain from the top to the bottom" (Matthew 27:51), but no destruction was recorded by the Gospel writers.

The storm in the Americas was followed by a sign given to the Nephites. Zenos, an Old Testament prophet whose record has been removed from the Bible, foretold "the three days of darkness, which should be a sign given of [Christ's] death unto those who should inhabit the isles of the sea, more especially given unto those who are of the house of Israel." (1 Nephi 19:10). However, the storm may also be a parallel of what will take place at the time of the Second Coming. In 1832, the Lord instructed Bishop Newell K. Whitney to warn the cities of New York, Albany, and Boston "of the desolation and utter abolishment which await them if they reject [the gospel]" (D&C 84:114).

The broken fragments of rocks that "were found . . . in seams and cracks, upon all the face of the land" (v. 18) should be a challenge to LDS scientists and explorers. Samuel the Lamanite had prophesied that these would be found "both above the earth and beneath." He also said that the more part of it was known to be one solid mass before the storm (Helaman 4:21–22). The finding and dating of such evidence would be most interesting.

> 19 And it came to pass that when the thunderings, and the lightnings, and the storm, and the tempest, and the quakings of the earth did cease—for behold, they did last for about the space of three hours; and it was said by some that the time was greater; nevertheless, all these great and terrible things were done in about the space of three hours—and then behold, there was darkness upon the face of the land.

20 And it came to pass that there was thick darkness upon all the face of the land, insomuch that the inhabitants thereof who had not fallen could feel the vapor of darkness;

21 And there could be no light, because of the darkness, neither candles, neither torches; neither could there be fire kindled with their fine and exceedingly dry wood, so that there could not be any light at all;

22 And there was not any light seen, neither fire, nor glimmer, neither the sun, nor the moon, nor the stars, for so great were the mists of darkness which were upon the face of the land.

23 And it came to pass that it did last for the space of three days that there was no light seen; and there was great mourning and howling and weeping among all the people continually; yea, great were the groanings of the people, because of the darkness and the great destruction which had come upon them. [3 Nephi 8:19–23]

Another sacrifice had taken place. The light of the sun had been sacrificed for total darkness. While this darkness was a physical thing, for those inhabitants that were killed, it was a sacrifice of the light of Christ and his gospel in exchange for the darkness of the spirit prison of hell. Because they had willfully chosen evil works rather than good, they would have "no part nor portion of the Spirit of the Lord . . . the spirit of the devil did enter into them, and take possession of their house" (Alma 40:13). Hopefully, the light of the gospel will penetrate many of their hearts as they dwell in the spirit prison, and are given the opportunity to accept or reject the truth. The more righteous, who were spared, recognized that they had made foolish sacrifices.

24 And in one place they were heard to cry, saying: O that we had repented before this great and terrible day, and then would our brethren have been spared, and they would not have been burned in that great city Zarahemla.

25 And in another place they were heard to cry and mourn, saying: O that we had repented before this great and terrible day, and had not killed and stoned the prophets, and cast them out; then would our mothers and our fair daughters, and our children have been spared, and not have been buried up in that great city Moronihah. And thus were the howlings of the people great and terrible. [3 Nephi 8:24–25]

They lamented over having not repented, which would have caused their cities, their prophets, and various family members to have been spared (vv. 23–25). As these Nephites recognized, in a symbolic sense, hell is a knowledge of opportunity lost.

Assumably, though the text is not specific, during these three days of darkness all the inhabitants of the land of the Nephites heard a voice.

> 1 And it came to pass that there was a voice heard among all the inhabitants of the earth, upon all the face of this land, crying:
>
> 2 Wo, wo, wo unto this people; wo unto the inhabitants of the whole earth except they shall repent; for the devil laugheth, and his angels rejoice, because of the slain of the fair sons and daughters of my people; and it is because of their iniquity and abominations that they are fallen! [3 Nephi 9:1–2]

Some may have not understood the voice. There is a difference between "a voice was heard *among* all the inhabitants," and "*all* the inhabitants hearing the voice." Perhaps only the more righteous heard the voice, and they informed the others. Nonetheless, the Savior taught many great truths to his captive audience. The first three truths were in regard to the destruction that had just taken place. The first truth was that the devil laughed, and his angels rejoiced over the number of those who had been slain among the sons and daughters of Israel, the Lord's people (v. 2). Father Lehi had learned from the plates of brass that, because the devil "had fallen from heaven, and had become miserable forever, he sought also the misery of all mankind" (2 Nephi 2:18). The devil had laughed because he had been so successful in destroying, both temporally and spiritually, a great number of Nephites and Lamanites at this time. They had become miserable as well.

The second truth was that Jesus Christ was the engineer of this great destruction. He was the one who caused the various cities to be burned, sunk, and buried in the earth.

3 Behold, that great city Zarahemla have I burned with fire, and the inhabitants thereof.

4 And behold, that great city Moroni have I caused to be sunk in the depths of the sea, and the inhabitants thereof to be drowned.

5 And behold, that great city Moronihah have I covered with earth, and the inhabitants thereof, to hide their iniquities and their abominations from before my face, that the blood of the prophets and the saints shall not come any more unto me against them.

6 And behold, the city of Gilgal have I caused to be sunk, and the inhabitants thereof to be buried up in the depths of the earth;

7 Yea, and the city of Onihah and the inhabitants thereof, and the city of Mocum and the inhabitants thereof, and the city of Jerusalem and the inhabitants thereof; and waters have I caused to come up in the stead thereof, to hide their wickedness and abominations from before my face, that the blood of the prophets and the saints shall not come up any more unto me against them.

8 And behold, the city of Gadiandi, and the city of Gadiomnah, and the city of Jacob, and the city of Gimgimno, all these have I caused to be sunk, and made hills and valleys in the places thereof; and the inhabitants thereof have I buried up in the depths of the earth, to hide their wickedness and abominations from before my face, that the blood of the prophets and the saints should not come up any more unto me against them.

9 And behold, that great city Jacobugath, which was inhabited by the people of king Jacob, have I caused to be burned with fire because of their sins and their wickedness, which was above all the wickedness of the whole earth, because of their secret murders and combinations; for it was they that did destroy the peace of my people and the government of the land; therefore I did cause them to be burned, to destroy them from before my face, that the blood of the prophets and the saints should not come up unto me any more against them.

10 And behold, the city of Laman, and the city of Josh, and the city of Gad, and the city of Kishkumen, have I caused to be burned with fire, and the inhabitants thereof, because of their wickedness in casting out the prophets, and stoning those whom I did send to declare unto them concerning their wickedness and their abominations. [3 Nephi 9:3–10]

Christ is the governing God of this earth. He reigns "with almighty power, according to the will of the Father" (D&C 20:24).

When a people "are ripe in iniquity," he destroys them (1 Nephi 17:35–37). The Amorites were not destroyed because their iniquity "is not yet full" (Genesis 15:16). Christ had visited the Nephite portion of the house of Israel with "thunderings and the lightnings of his power, by tempest, by fire, by smoke, and vapor of darkness, and by the opening of the earth, and by mountains which shall be carried up." These things had undoubtedly caused "many of the kings of the isles of the sea [to be] wrought upon by the Spirit of God to exclaim: The God of nature suffers" as the prophet Zenos had foretold (1 Nephi 19:11–12). Since the kings' exclamation was inspired by the Spirit of God, it is certainly authentic. The prophecy of Zenos was fulfilled, and Christ had demonstrated that he was the God of Nature.

The third truth revealed regarding the destruction was its cause. The general cause was the "iniquity and abominations" and wickedness of the people.

> 11 And because they did cast them all out, that there were none righteous among them, I did send down fire and destroy them, that their wickedness and abominations might be hid from before my face, that the blood of the prophets and the saints whom I sent among them might not cry unto me from the ground against them.
>
> 12 And many great destructions have I caused to come upon this land, and upon this people, because of their wickedness and their abominations. [3 Nephi 9:11–12]

Specifically, the shedding of the blood of the Saints and of the prophets had brought forth the destructive power of the justice of God (vv. 5, 7–9). The wickedness of the secret murders and combinations had destroyed the peace of the Lord's people and the government of the land (v. 9); and the casting out of the prophets, and stoning them, and casting out all of the righteous had brought down fire from heaven (vv. 10–11). When a people become ripened in iniquity, their next stage is rottenness; therefore, the Lord destroys them as stated above. However, "never hath any of them been destroyed save it were foretold them by the prophets of the Lord" (2 Nephi 25:9). The Lord had sent his prophets among the Nephites, and they had rejected those prophets by killing them or casting them out. Meanwhile, the people had ripened in iniquity.

Instructions to the More Righteous

13 O all ye that are spared because ye were more righteous than they, will ye not now return unto me, and repent of your sins, and be converted, that I may heal you?

14 Yea, verily I say unto you, if ye will come unto me ye shall have eternal life. Behold, mine arm of mercy is extended towards you, and whosoever will come, him will I receive; and blessed are those who come unto me. [3 Nephi 9:13–14]

The prophet Zenos had also prophesied that the Lord God would "surely visit all the house of Israel at that day, some with his voice, because of their righteousness, unto their great joy and salvation" (1 Nephi 19:11). This prophecy was also fulfilled in this interim period as Jesus addressed the more righteous who were spared. Even though they were spared, they still had need to repent. While being spoken to must have caused "great joy," the Savior's more significant call to repentance was to bring about their "salvation." He invited them to "be converted, that I may heal you" (v. 13). The healing was a spiritual one.

Jesus invited the Nephite survivors to come unto him in order to obtain eternal life (v. 14). In other words, he invited them to be baptized (3 Nephi 12:1–2). Since a new dispensation was being introduced, this applied to all people even though they had been previously baptized under the Mosaic dispensation as will be discussed in a later chapter. As Nephi taught, baptism places a person on the path to eternal life, but that person "must press forward with a steadfastness in Christ" to obtain eternal life (2 Nephi 31:17–20). The Lord promised to receive those who entered on this path and bless them in their endeavors (v. 14).

15 Behold, I am Jesus Christ the Son of God. I created the heavens and the earth, and all things that in them are. I was with the Father from the beginning. I am in the Father, and the Father in me; and in me hath the Father glorified his name. [3 Nephi 9:15]

He identified himself as Jesus Christ, the Son of God. The people had probably already assumed that it was either the Father or the Son who had spoken to them. How much of the information that followed was known beforehand and how much was new can only be surmised. Some of the people were probably already aware of his role with the Father as a premortal God, but most likely the majority had not comprehended his status. While his position and mission had been taught among the Nephites, it should be remembered that there had been much wickedness and apostasy during the past generation. Although the ones spared were the more righteous, many of those would have been honorable people of the earth, but not necessarily spiritually attuned to the gospel truths that were now to be enumerated.

Jesus informed the Nephites that he was the creator of this earth and also of the heavens and all things therein (v. 15). The "creator of the heavens" has reference to the other earths or planets of which he was the creator. This is consistent with New Testament teachings. Paul wrote; "For by him were all things created, that are heaven, and that are in the earth" (Colossians 1:16). He also spoke of God's Son "by whom also he made the worlds [plural] (Hebrews 1:2). Christ told the Nephites that he "was with the Father from the beginning" (v. 15). In the Testimony of John, we read: "In the beginning was the gospel preached through the Son. And the gospel was the word, and the word was with the Son, and the Son was with God, and the Son was of God. The same was in the beginning with God. All things were made by him; and without him was not anything made which was made" (JST John 1:1–3).

By divine investiture of authority, he represented the Father in bringing "to pass the immortality and eternal life of man" (Moses 1:39). Therefore, he was "in the Father, and the Father in [him]; and in [Christ] hath the Father glorified his name" (v. 15). Jesus did not introduce himself as directly during his mortal ministry as he did to the Nephites, although he repeatedly bore witness of being the Messiah. When he did announce his Messiahship in Nazareth; they "rose up, and thrust him out of the city, and led him unto the brow of the hill whereon their city was built, that they might cast him down headlong. But he passing through the midst of them went his way" (Luke 4:29–30). In Jerusalem, after declaring he was "I Am" [Jehovah],[1] "Then took they up stones to cast at him: but Jesus hid himself, and went out of the temple, going through the midst of them, and so passed by" (John 8:59–60). He was "the God of Abraham, and of Isaac, and the God of Jacob" (1 Nephi 19:10).

> 16 I came unto my own, and my own received me not. And the scriptures concerning my coming are fulfilled.
>
> 17 And as many as have received me, to them have I given to become the sons of God; and even so will I to as many as shall believe on my name, for behold, by me redemption cometh, and in me is the law of Moses fulfilled. [3 Nephi 9:16–17]

John's gospel also taught that "He came unto his own, and his own received him not" (John 1:11). Jesus was born into the lineage of David, and his ministry in Palestine gave the tribe of Judah the opportunity to accept Christ and his gospel. His advent to the earth had been foretold by the prophets; thus, the "scriptures concerning [Christ's] coming are fulfilled" (v. 16). While the majority of the people of Palestine had rejected Christ, many had not. Those who "received [him], to them [had he] given to become the sons of God" (v. 17). Again John's gospel gives the identical message (John 1:12). A person becomes a son or daughter of God through being born again, which is a spiritual adoption. King Benjamin taught his subjects:

> 7 And now, because of the covenant which ye have made ye shall be called the children of Christ, his sons, and his daughters; for behold, this day he hath spiritually begotten you; for ye say that your hearts are changed through faith on his name; therefore, ye are born of him and have become his sons and his daughters. [Mosiah 5:7]

---

[1] In Exodus 3:14, God told Moses to tell the children of Israel that "I AM hath sent me unto you." Thus, the Jews stoned him for saying he was Jehovah, the God of the Old Testament.

Once more the New Testament teachings are the same.

14 For as many as are led by the Spirit of God, they are the sons of God.

15 For ye have not received the spirit of bondage again to fear; but ye have received the Spirit of adoption, whereby we cry, Abba, Father.

16 The Spirit itself beareth witness with our spirit, that we are the children of God:

17 And if children, then heirs; heirs of God, and joint-heirs with Christ; if so be that we suffer with *him,* that we may be also glorified together. [Romans 8:14–17]

The invitation to be spiritually adopted through believing in Christ and being born again was now extended to those Nephites, who had not previously had this experience. The law of Moses was now fulfilled, and the plan of salvation offered redemption through the higher law of Christ (v. 17).

The Savior further identified himself : "I am the light and the life of the world. I am Alpha and Omega, the beginning and the end" (3 Nephi 9:18). Every man and woman is born into the world with the light, or spirit, of Christ that enables him or her to judge between good and evil. Mormon taught: "the Spirit of Christ is given to every man, that he may know good from evil; wherefore, I show unto you the way to judge; for every thing which inviteth to do good, and to persuade to believe in Christ, is sent forth by the power and gift of Christ; wherefore ye may know with a perfect knowledge it is of God." (Moroni 7:16). The gospel of John also teaches that "[Christ] was the true Light, which lighteth every man that cometh into the world" (John 1:9).

The light of Christ "giveth life to all things," and "is the law by which all things are governed" (D&C 88:13). Thus, Christ is not only the creator, but also the source of enlightening the inhabitants of the earth, and the governing power to maintain the earth as a place of habitation. Paul taught similar doctrine on Mars Hill: "For in him we live, and move, and have our being; as certain also of your own poets have said, For we are also his offspring" (Acts 17:28).

Jesus' concluding point of identification was that he was "Alpha and Omega, the beginning and the end" (v. 18). Alpha and Omega represent the first and the last letters of the Greek alphabet. The words refer to Christ as the creator of the earth in the beginning, and also the finisher or holder of its final destiny, and of the inhabitants who reside upon it. Paul and Moroni both call him "the author and finisher of our faith" (Hebrews 12:2; Moroni 6:4). Both men may be quoting from another source. The source may have been what Jesus taught but was not recorded (see John 21:25), or from the Old Testament but has since been lost. Under the administration of Jesus Christ, the earth will fulfill the measure of its creation, and be inhabited eternally by those who qualify as celestial beings.

> 17 And the redemption of the soul is through him that quickeneth all things, in whose bosom it is decreed that the poor and the meek of the earth shall inherit it.
>
> 18 Therefore, it must needs be sanctified from all unrighteousness, that it may be prepared for the celestial glory;
>
> 19 For after it hath filled the measure of its creation, it shall be crowned with glory, even with the presence of God the Father;
>
> 20 That bodies who are of the celestial kingdom may possess it forever and ever; for, for this intent was it made and created, and for this intent are they sanctified. [D&C 88:17–20]

He is the finisher of our faith.

Having outlined his qualifications, Jesus gave the formula to obtain an eternal home upon the earth. The formula was based upon the principle of sacrifice. The fulfillment of the law of Moses had come, bringing an end to the need for the shedding of sacrificial blood (see Alma 34:13–14 quoted above). Upon the cross, when Jesus uttered, "It is finished," and gave up the ghost (John 19:30), the pascal lamb was sacrificed and the law of Moses was fulfilled. Jesus confirmed to the Nephites that their sacrifices according to the law of

Moses would no longer be acceptable. Another sacrifice was now required.

> 19 And ye shall offer up unto me no more the shedding of blood; yea, your sacrifices and your burnt offerings shall be done away, for I will accept none of your sacrifices and your burnt offerings.
>
> 20 And ye shall offer for a sacrifice unto me a broken heart and a contrite spirit. And whoso cometh unto me with a broken heart and a contrite spirit, him will I baptize with fire and with the Holy Ghost, even as the Lamanites, because of their faith in me at the time of their conversion, were baptized with fire and with the Holy Ghost, and they knew it not. [3 Nephi 9:19–20]

A sacrifice, as before stated, means that one thing is given up willingly for something else. To offer a broken heart is to give up the pride of your heart, and to recognize that your sins contributed to the suffering of Jesus Christ in the garden of Gethsemane. This knowledge should break your heart.

To offer a contrite spirit is to give up the arrogance of self-conceit, and to acknowledge that the source of all intelligence is the light of Christ.

> 11 And the light which shineth, which giveth you light, is through him who enlighteneth your eyes, which is the same light that quickeneth your understandings;
>
> 12 Which light proceedeth forth from the presence of God to fill the immensity of space—
>
> 13 The light which is in all things, which giveth life to all things, which is the law by which all things are governed, even the power of God who sitteth upon his throne, who is in the bosom of eternity, who is in the midst of all things. [D&C 88:11–13)

The converted person is thereby teachable through the Spirit. As a horse is broken to be ridden, or to work, he submits himself (heart) to his master. The converted human being submits himself or herself (heart) to the will of the Savior in recognition of his or her dependence upon Christ.

Those who sacrifice their heart and spirit to Christ will, in return, receive a baptism of fire and of the Holy Ghost (v. 20). The word baptize means to immerse. Therefore, the promised baptism by fire is an immersion in the Holy Ghost. As taught here by the Savior, this experience can take place without a person knowing it. The example Jesus used to illustrate this was the baptism of the Lamanites, "and they knew it not" (v. 20). The incident to which Jesus referred was probably the three hundred Lamanites who were, in about 30 BC, "encircled about, yea every soul, by a pillar of fire . . . And behold, the Holy Spirit of God did come down from heaven, and did enter into their hearts" (Helaman 5:43–49). Although they didn't know they had been baptized with the Holy Ghost, they certainly knew that something spiritual had happened to them. Their baptism was a spiritual experience. What was told Enos was applicable to all of them, "thy sins are forgiven thee, and thou shalt be blessed" (Enos 1:5).

> 21 Behold, I have come unto the world to bring redemption unto the world, to save the world from sin.
>
> 22 Therefore, whoso repenteth and cometh unto me as a little child, him will I receive, for of such is the kingdom of God. Behold, for such I have laid down my life, and have taken it up again; therefore repent, and come unto me ye ends of the earth, and be saved. [3 Nephi 9:21–22]

As a resurrected being, Christ had completed his atonement "to bring about the plan of mercy, to appease the demands of justice, that God might be a perfect, just God, and a merciful God also" (Alma 42:15). Through his mercy, "the truly penitent are saved" (Alma 42:24). Those who repented and came unto him "as a little child" would be received into the kingdom of God. His coming into the world, and laying down his life and taking it up again, was for this purpose. He now personally extended this plan of mercy to the surviving Nephites (v. 22).

Chastisement and Warning

How long Jesus spoke to the humbled Nephi audience is not stated, but it was probably only a matter of several minutes based upon the length of time it takes to read the recorded message (3 Nephi 9). It seems to be a verbatim quote, although who recorded it and how he did so is not explained. In any case, Jesus' words were extremely powerful.

> 1 And now behold, it came to pass that all the people of the land did hear these sayings, and did witness of it. And after these sayings there was silence in the land for the space of many hours;
>
> 2 For so great was the astonishment of the people that they did cease lamenting and howling for the loss of their kindred which had been slain; therefore there was silence in all the land for the space of many hours.
>
> 3 And it came to pass that there came a voice again unto the people, and all the people did hear, and did witness of it, saying: [3 Nephi 10:1–3]

The people ceased lamenting and were silent, but what were their thoughts? They must have sat pondering over the message they had been given. Perhaps the words were so indelibly engraved upon their hearts, after several hours of rehearsal in their minds, that at least some were able to record them later. Nonetheless, after a period of silent pondering, another message was given for all to hear (v. 3). Once more the message was short and to the point. It was, at least in part, like the message given to the Jews as Jesus entered the city of Jerusalem on the last week of his mortal ministry, "how often would I [Jesus, the God of the Old Testament] have gathered thy children together, even as a hen gathereth her chickens under her wings, and ye would not" (Matthew 23:37). The Nephite message contains two more dimensions than the message given to the Jews, at least as presently recorded.

> 4 O ye people of these great cities which have fallen, who are descendants of Jacob, yea, who are of the house of Israel, how oft have I gathered you as a hen gathereth her chickens under her wings, and have nourished you.

5 And again, how oft would I have gathered you as a hen gathereth her chickens under her wings, yea, O ye people of the house of Israel, who have fallen; yea, O ye people of the house of Israel, ye that dwell at Jerusalem, as ye that have fallen; yea, how oft would I have gathered you as a hen gathereth her chickens, and ye would not.

6 O ye house of Israel whom I have spared, how oft will I gather you as a hen gathereth her chickens under her wings, if ye will repent and return unto me with full purpose of heart.

7 But if not, O house of Israel, the places of your dwellings shall become desolate until the time of the fulfilling of the covenant to your fathers. [3 Nephi 10:4–7]

Both the Old and the New World accounts speak of how oft Jesus—as the God of Abraham, Isaac, and Jacob—had gathered his people. Israel's many gatherings are best exemplified in the book of Judges where, periodically, for several hundred years, the Lord raised up leaders to gather his people out of bondage. The Nephite account refers to many other times when he would have gathered his people of Israel, but they did not respond. Those among the Nephites to whom he spoke, were "spared because ye were more righteous than they [who were destroyed]" (3 Nephi 9:13). The other times when Jesus would have gathered them were not recorded since the people had not gathered.

It is interesting that Jesus addresses the people who "dwell at Jerusalem" (v. 5) when speaking to the Nephites. Had those in Jerusalem also heard him declare that he would have gathered them? Had it once been included in the message recorded in the testimony of Matthew? Only as the plain and precious parts that were lost are restored, will the answers to these questions be known, or as it may be revealed anew to latter-day prophets.

The third dimension of the message to the Nephites was a declaration for many future gatherings, and an invitation for those who had been spared to gather. It also included a warning of desolation, or scattering of Israel, until the covenant made with their fathers was fulfilled (v. 7). The fathers to whom the covenants were made were Abraham (Genesis 12:1–3), Isaac (Genesis 22:15–18), and Jacob

(Genesis 28:13–15). The total fulfillment of those covenants would be in the latter days, "when the Gentiles shall sin against my gospel, and shall reject the fulness of my gospel . . . then will I remember my covenant which I have made unto my people, O house of Israel" (3 Nephi 16:10–12).

The warning of desolation and scattering of Israel was yet another example of the principle of sacrifice. Due to the wickedness of the children of Israel, the blessings of gathering that centered around the building of a temple would be sacrificed. Temples were built to "reveal unto His people the ordinances of His house and the glories of His kingdom, and teach the people the way of salvation" (TPJS, 307–8). These ordinances would be sacrificed for a destruction and scattering among the nations of the earth, and thus a loss of these sacred blessings. A warning of "instead of gathering you, except ye repent behold, he shall scatter you" had been given earlier by Nephi, son of Helaman, about 20 B.C. (Helaman 7:19). It had also been fulfilled in the recent destruction of the Nephite cities, and was reiterated by the Savior to these surviving Nephites. Their gathering had been sacrificed for a destruction and scattering, but they were now offered the blessings of the gathering again if they would repent and come unto Christ.

> 8 And now it came to pass that after the people had heard these words, behold, they began to weep and howl again because of the loss of their kindred and friends.
>
> 9 And it came to pass that thus did the three days pass away. And it was in the morning, and the darkness dispersed from off the face of the land, and the earth did cease to tremble, and the rocks did cease to rend, and the dreadful groanings did cease, and all the tumultuous noises did pass away.
>
> 10 And the earth did cleave together again, that it stood; and the mourning, and the weeping, and the wailing of the people who were spared alive did cease; and their mourning was turned into joy, and their lamentations into the praise and thanksgiving unto the Lord Jesus Christ, their Redeemer. [3 Nephi 10:8–10]

The first message above was one of condolence and hope, the second message was one of chastisement and warning. The people, therefore, returned to their weeping and howling (v. 8). This lamentation lasted until the three days of darkness ended. As the darkness dispersed, the mourning and weeping and wailing was turned into joy and "praise and thanksgiving unto the Lord Jesus Christ their Redeemer" (vv. 9–10).

All of these terrible and wonderful things had happened among the Nephites in just three days: the fourth, fifth, and sixth days of the beginning of the thirty-fourth year since the birth of Jesus Christ in Jerusalem. His speaking to them was during the three days that his body was lying in the sepulchre in Jerusalem. While his body lay there, his spirit had visited and spoken to the Nephites for a few precious minutes, although his spirit body was not seen. At other times during these same three days he had ministered in the world of spirits, where "from among the righteous, he organized his forces" for the gospel to be "preached to the dead" (D&C 138:30). In a relatively short time, many significant things of eternal consequence had taken place.

Three Days in the Tomb

Each of the four New Testament Gospels clarifies our understanding of Jesus' life that the other three gospels may not. The testimony of Third Nephi is no exception. For example, it clarifies the following discrepancy among the other four Gospels. Jesus answered the scribes and Pharisees who sought a sign from him: "An evil and adulterous generation seeketh after a sign; and there shall no sign be given to it, but the sign of the prophet Jonas: For as Jonas was three days and three nights in the whale's belly; so shall the Son of man be three days and three nights in the heart of the earth" (Matthew 12:39–40). It is generally concluded that Jesus' body did not lie for a full three days in the sepulchre, but only from Friday afternoon until Sunday morning, parts of three days and two nights. The prophecy of his being in the grave for three days is justified by the explanation that from

Friday afternoon, with Sunday morning included, was a part or whole of three different days. There are other considerations.

A chronological sequence of the last week of Jesus' life upon earth shows no record of the day Wednesday. The last supper is considered to have been on Thursday evening, followed by his vigil of arrests, trials, and crucifixion that followed into Friday. Was there a discrepancy between the Galilean and Judean calendars? Had an error crept into the Jewish calendar, and Jesus ate the Passover meal on Wednesday, the true date, while the Jews were a day behind as some authorities suggest? Was the day of no record possibly out of chronological order, and was Christ really a day longer in the tomb? Was this a year of a dual Sabbath under the Jewish calendar, and thus his crucifixion was on Thursday, the first of the two Sabbaths—one being on a feast day— extending the time his body lay in the tomb? While the Book of Mormon does not clear up the chronology of days, it does give support to his being in the tomb for the fuller three days.

On the third hour in Jerusalem (9 A.M.), on the day of the crucifixion, Jesus was nailed to the cross (Mark 15:25). On the sixth hour there was darkness over all the land. This was noon according to Jewish time and would have been earlier in America, between 3:00 and 6:00 A.M., varying according to the time zone on the continent. The destructive storm recorded in Book of Mormon lasted for three hours (between 6 and 9 A.M.), and was followed by three days of "thick darkness upon all the face of the land" (3 Nephi 8:19–23). His resurrection in the morning in Jerusalem ("it was yet dark" John 20:1—before daylight) would have occurred six to nine hours earlier than Nephite time. Taking into account the natural darkness that would follow this hour among the Nephites, there would have been three full days of darkness on this continent from around 6:00 A.M. on Thursday to 6:00 A.M. on Sunday. In Jerusalem his body would have been without his spirit for about two and one-half days (3 P.M. Thursday to early Sunday morning), but the darkness among the Nephites would have been a full three days. Although the exact times are not known, the three days of darkness and Jesus' being in the tomb an extra day is verified in Third Nephi. Using Thursday as the day of his crucifixion instead of Friday, the accompanying chart illustrates these possible time parallels:

	Jerusalem	Reference	America	Reference
Thursday (or double Sabbath)	• 3rd Hour (9 A.M.) On the Cross • 6th Hour (Noon) Darkness • 9th Hour (3 P.M.) Gave up Ghost	Matt. 27:45 Mark 15:25,33 Luke 23:44	• Midnight to 3 A.M. 3 A.M. to 6 A.M. Storm 3 Hours • 6–9 A.M. Darkness 3 days Jesus Speaks Twice	3 Nephi 8:5–18 3 Nephi 8:19–10:7
Friday	No Record		Friday	3 Nephi 10:8–10
Saturday	No Record		Saturday	3 Nephi 10:8–10
Sunday	• First Day of Week • Early Yet Dark • Jesus Resurrected	John 21:1	• Saturday Evening • Light about 6 A.M. Sunday Morning	3 Nephi 10:9

The Gospel of Matthew, JST Mark, The Book of Mormon, and The Doctrine and Covenants (section 138) all testify that Jesus was in the spirit world for three full days between being crucified and resurrected. While the actual resurrection is more important than the time frame in between, the correlation of Jonah, Jesus' own teaching, the Book of Mormon, and Joseph Smith should be given serious consideration.

Mormon's Commentary

The remainder of 3 Nephi 10 is a commentary by Mormon as he abridged the record.

> 11 And thus far were the scriptures fulfilled which had been spoken by the prophets.

> 12 And it was the more righteous part of the people who were saved, and it was they who received the prophets and stoned them not; and it was they who had not shed the blood of the saints, who were spared—

13 And they were spared and were not sunk and buried up in the earth; and they were not drowned in the depths of the sea; and they were not burned by fire, neither were they fallen upon and crushed to death; and they were not carried away in the whirlwind; neither were they overpowered by the vapor of smoke and of darkness. [3 Nephi 10:11–13]

Before citing which of the prophets had foretold these calamitous events, he remarks about the people who had been spared. There are two distinct groups specified by Mormon. "They who received the testimony of Jesus, and believed on his name and were baptized" were the celestial-type people (D&C 76:51). "They who had not shed the blood of the Saints" were the terrestrial-type people; although they were not responsive to the prophets, "they who are honorable men of the earth" and would not participate in the devilish acts against the Saints or Church members (D&C 76:75). Both groups had escaped the burials, the drownings, and the burnings of their fellow Nephites (v. 13). The less righteous telestial-type people had been destroyed, and were candidates to be instructed in the spirit world.

14 And now, whoso readeth, let him understand; he that hath the scriptures, let him search them, and see and behold if all these deaths and destructions by fire, and by smoke, and by tempests, and by whirlwinds, and by the opening of the earth to receive them, and all these things are not unto the fulfilling of the prophecies of many of the holy prophets.

15 Behold, I say unto you, Yea, many have testified of these things at the coming of Christ, and were slain because they testified of these things.

16 Yea, the prophet Zenos did testify of these things, and also Zenock spake concerning these things, because they testified particularly concerning us, who are the remnant of their seed.

17 Behold, our father Jacob also testified concerning a remnant of the seed of Joseph. And behold, are not we a remnant of the seed of Joseph? And these things which testify of us, are they not written upon the plates of brass which our father Lehi brought out of Jerusalem? [3 Nephi 10:14–17]

Mormon specified some of the prophets who had foretold of the coming of Christ. The first two mentioned are Zenos and Zenock

(v. 16). Nephi, son of Lehi, had earlier written of these same two prophets by name, and of their particular prophecies. Zenock had foretold of Jesus being "lifted up [upon the cross]." Zenos had prophesied of his being "buried in a sepulcher," and "concerning the three days of darkness, which should be a sign given of his death unto those who should inhabit the isles of the sea." Nephi mentioned another prophet named Neum who had testified of Jesus being "crucified" (1 Nephi 19:10). Alma had also quoted the words of Zenos and Zenock, and because Zenock "testified of the Son of God" the people "stoned him to death." (Alma 33:3–17). Nephi, the son of Helaman, had referred to many that did "bear record that the Son of God should come" including Zenock, and that Zenos "did testify boldly; for the which he was slain" (Helaman 8:13–20).

Why had Mormon only included the names of Zenos and Zenock among the many prophets who had testified of Christ? Mormon answered this question. They had testified particularly concerning the Nephites (v. 16). He also gave a little more insight into these two men of God whose records were on the plates of brass, but were lost when the great and abominable church took away "many parts which are plain and most precious; and also many covenants of the Lord." (1 Nephi 13:26). These two prophets were in Mormon's ancestral line. Mormon was "a pure descendant of Lehi" and thus of "the seed of Joseph" (3 Nephi 5:20–21). Lehi "was a descendant of Manasseh, who was the son of Joseph who was sold into Egypt" (Alma 10:3). Thus, Zenos and Zenock are descendants of Joseph and possibly of Manasseh as well. They had "testified particularly concerning [the Nephites], who are the remnant of their seed" (v. 16).

As a further verification of these events having been foretold by the prophets, Mormon extends his ancestral line of prophecy to father Jacob, the progenitor of the twelve tribes of Israel. He too had spoken of "a remnant of the seed of Joseph."[2] Mormon, writing hundreds of years later, proclaims that he and his people are "a remnant of the seed of Joseph" and that the many prophecies of the Nephites are "written upon the plates of brass" (v. 17).

The vast majority of the members of the Church of Jesus Christ of Latter-day Saints are also remnants of the seed of Joseph. The Lord identified the elders of the Church in a revelation to Joseph Smith.

> 44 And now, verily, I say concerning the residue of the elders of my church, the time has not yet come, for many years, for them to receive their inheritance in this land, except they desire it through the prayer of faith, only as it shall be appointed unto them of the Lord.
>
> 45 For, behold, they shall push the people together from the ends of the earth. [D&C 58:44–45]

Verse forty-five is a quotation from Moses' blessing to the tribe of Joseph (Deuteronomy 33:17 see also vv. 15–16). Thus the restoration of the gospel in these latter days is fulfilling a blessing given by Moses to the tribe of Joseph.

The prophecies of these many prophets undoubtedly included much concerning the Nephites. Lehi prophesied that the "plates of brass should go forth unto all nations, kindreds, tongues, and people who were of his seed" (1 Nephi 5:18). When this happens, Mormon's words in Third Nephi will be verified.

---

[2] Part of the blessing of Jacob to his son Joseph was: "Joseph *is* a fruitful bough, *even* a fruitful bough by a well; *whose* branches run over the wall: . . . The blessings of thy father have prevailed above the blessings of my progenitors unto the utmost bound of the everlasting hills: they shall be on the head of Joseph, and on the crown of the head of him that was separate from his brethren" (Genesis 49:22,26). Latter-day Saints interpret this blessing as a prophecy of the people of Lehi. Another of Jacob's prophecies is 3 Nephi 20:22, to be discussed later.

PART 3

The Three-day Ministry—Shortly After His Ascension

DAY ONE • 3 Nephi 10:18–18:39

Jesus Christ appeared in person to the Nephites somewhat unexpectedly. It wasn't until he appeared to twenty-five hundred of them "round about the temple . . . in the land Bountiful" (3 Nephi 11:1; 17:25) that those who were there for another purpose "remembered that it had been prophesied among them that Christ should show himself unto them after his ascension into heaven (3 Nephi 11:12). The things that transpired on this occasion were of eternal consequence.

Christ visited them on this day to establish the foundation of The Church of Jesus Christ. He had fulfilled the law of Moses and had come to usher in his higher law. The recorded events are included in about seventeen pages of the 1981 edition of the Book of Mormon. Those seventeen pages are essential for an understanding of the doctrine of Christ. The following six chapters (4–9) will examine the content of the first day's recorded teachings.

Chapter 4

This Is My Doctrine

3 Nephi 11

The divine ministry of Jesus, his advent among the Nephites, came about with a spectacular introduction. It was undoubtedly one of the great theophanies of the history of the world. It would compare with Jesus being introduced by the Father at his baptism, on the Mount of Transfiguration (Matthew 17), or the First Vision in A.D. 1820. An outline of the Book of Mormon chapters follows as a preparation for further study.

Outline • 3 Nephi 10:18; 11:41

➤ 10:18–19　The ending of the thirty-fourth year, the Nephites and the Lamanites who were spared, had great blessings shown unto them.

    a.　Soon after Christ's ascension into heaven, he showed himself unto them. v. 18

    b.　He showed his body to them, and ministered to them. v. 19

Superscription: Jesus Christ showed himself to the Nephite multitude in Bountiful, and did minister to them.

➤ 11:1–2　A great multitude gathered around the temple in Bountiful.

      a. They were showing one another the marvelous change that had taken place. v. 1

      b. They were conversing about Jesus Christ, and the sign given of his death. v. 2

➤ 11:3–8   They heard a voice as if out of heaven, but did not understand the voice.

      a. It was not a harsh, nor a loud voice, but a small voice that pierced them to the center. v. 3

           1. It was a small voice that pierced them to the center, and caused their whole frames to shake.

           2. It pierced them to the very soul, and caused their hearts to burn.

      b. They heard the voice the second time and understood not. v. 4

      c. The third time they opened their ears to hear, their eyes to heaven, and understood the voice. vv. 5–7

           1. The voice said: Behold my Beloved Son—hear ye him.

           2. They beheld a man descending out of heaven, clothed in a white robe.

      d. He came and stood in their midst. v. 8

           1. Their eyes were upon him, but they dared not to speak to one another.

           2. They thought it was an angel.

➤ 11: 9–17   He stretched forth his hand and spoke.

      a. I am Jesus Christ whom the prophets testified should come into the world. vv. 10–11

           1. I am the life and light of the world.

           2. I have drunk the bitter cup, and have glorified his name by taking upon me the sins of the world.

      b. The whole multitude fell to the earth remembering the prophecy of his showing himself to the world shortly after his ascension. vv. 12–14

           1. He invited them to feel his side, and the nail prints in his hands and feet.

    2. They would then know he was the God of Israel and the whole world, and had been slain for the sins of the world.

  c. They came and thrust their hands into his side, and felt the nail prints in his hands and feet. v. 15

    1. They went one by one until all had felt and seen.

    2. They knew of a surety, and bare record that it was he of whom the prophets had written.

  d. They all cried with one accord, Hosanna! Blessed be the name of the Most High! And they fell down and worshipped him. vv. 16–17

➤ 11:18–41 The Lord called Nephi and he came and bowed before him, and kissed his feet. v. 19

  a. He commanded Nephi to arise, and he gave him power to baptize this people after he (Christ) had ascended into heaven. vv. 20–21

  b. The Lord called others also, and gave them power and the manner to baptize. vv. 22–27

    1. Whoso repents and desires to be baptized, shall go down into the water with you.

    2. Call them by name and baptize them in the name of the Father, the Son, and the Holy Ghost.

    3. Immerse them in the water, and bring them out of the water again.

    4. The Father, Son, and Holy Ghost are one.

  d. There shall be no disputations among you over baptism, or doctrine, as before. vv. 28–30

    1. The spirit of contention is not of me, but of the devil, the father of contention.

    2. He stirs up the hearts of men to contend with anger. This should be taken away.

  e. Jesus declared his doctrine, which is the doctrine the Father had given him. vv. 31–34

1. He bears record of the Father, the Father bears record of him, and the Holy Ghost bears record of the Father and Christ.

2. The Father commands all men everywhere to repent and believe in Christ.

3. Those who believe and are baptized shall be saved, and inherit the kingdom of God.

4. Those who do not believe and are not baptized shall be damned.

f. This is Christ's doctrine, and he bears record of it from the Father. vv. 35–36

1. Those who believe in me believe in the Father also.

2. The Father bears record of Christ by baptizing with fire and the Holy Ghost.

3. The Father, and Christ, and the Holy Ghost, are one.

g. Again he says you must repent, be baptized, and become as a little child to receive these things. v. 37

h. He repeats again the above with a different ending: "to inherit the kingdom of God." v. 38

i. Whoso builds upon Christ's doctrine, builds upon his rock, and the gates of hell shall not prevail against them. v. 39

j. Whoso declares more or less, and establishes it for doctrine, is not built upon Christ's rock. v. 40

1. He builds on a sandy foundation.

2. The gates of hell stand open to receive such when the floods and the winds come.

k. Go to this people and to the ends of the earth to declare the words Christ has spoken. v. 41

NOTES AND COMMENTARY

A contrast of Christ's appearance with the previous wickedness and destruction helps one to appreciate what was about to happen. A few weeks earlier, "all the inhabitants of the earth, upon the face of this land" who had survived the destruction at the time of his death had briefly heard his voice speak to them, but had not seen him (3 Nephi 9:1; 10:3). His appearance was to a multitude "in number about two thousand and five hundred souls, and they did consist of men, women, and children" (3 Nephi 17:25). That it was only a few weeks after the sign of his death is evidenced by several factors. First, as Mormon prepared his abridgment of the account of Jesus' visit to the Nephites, he gave us his objective.

> 18 And it came to pass that in the ending of the thirty and fourth year, behold, I will show unto you that the people of Nephi who were spared, and also those who had been called Lamanites, who had been spared, did have great favors shown unto them, and great blessings poured out upon their heads, insomuch that soon after the ascension of Christ into heaven he did truly manifest himself unto them—
>
> 19 Showing his body unto them, and ministering unto them; and an account of his ministry shall be given hereafter. Therefore for this time I make an end of my sayings. [3 Nephi 10:18–19]

Jesus Christ did show himself unto the people of Nephi, as the multitude were gathered together in the land Bountiful, and did minister unto them; and on this wise did he show himself unto them. (Superscription)

"After his ascension," when Jesus did appear, the multitude remembered it (3 Nephi 11:12). If it had been months later, it does not appear that it would have come into their minds. Secondly, the italicized Superscription, recorded above chapter 11, which, as mentioned before, was translated from the plates, appears to be a confirmation of what Mormon had just listed as his objective.

Thirdly, and probably the most convincing, is their having assembled before his appearance.

> 1 And now it came to pass that there were a great multitude gathered together, of the people of Nephi, round about the temple which was in the land Bountiful; and they were marveling and wondering one with another, and were showing one to another the great and marvelous change which had taken place.

> 2 And they were also conversing about this Jesus Christ, of whom the
> sign had been given concerning his death. [3 Nephi 11:1–2]

That they were still "marveling and wondering one with another, and were showing one to another the great and marvelous change which had taken place" (v. 1), does not suggest a very long time.[1] President Joseph Fielding Smith has commented:

> The fact that the multitude had gathered at the temple and were point-ing out to each other the great changes that had occurred is evidence that this was an event immediately following the resurrection of our Lord. If this event had occurred one year later, the multitude would have been perfectly familiar with these great changes, and they would not have been so awed by them. It was in great astonishment and wonder that they had gathered and were pointing out to each other what had occurred.
>
> Moreover it is contrary to reason that Jesus would make the Nephites and Lamanites, who had been faithful, wait for one whole year before he would make his appearance and give them instructions in relation to the closing of the period in which the law of Moses was in force, and the period when the fullness of the gospel was ushered in.[2]

This sudden appearance to begin the Nephite ministry is compara-ble to Jesus' post-resurrection ministry in Palestine. We have only a brief scriptural account of his "being seen of them forty days, and speaking of the things pertaining to the kingdom of God" (Acts 1:3; see vv. 4–9), but Paul later referred to his having been "seen of above five hundred brethren at once" following his resurrection (1 Corinthi-

---

[1] As Mormon abridged the record of 3 Nephi, he recorded "that in the ending of the thirty and fourth year," the people who were spared had great blessings poured out "insomuch that soon after the ascension of Christ into heaven, he did truly manifest himself unto them" (3 Nephi 10:18). The word "ending" is sometimes interpreted to mean the end of the year, but since Mormon had been abridging what had happened in the beginning of the year, "ending" could also be interpreted to mean that which followed the beginning or in the rest or remainder of the year. This interpretation of "ending" would be consistent with Mormon's statement of Christ's visit to the Nephites being "soon after the ascension."

[2] Joseph Fielding Smith, *Answers to Gospel Questions,* 5 vols. (Salt Lake City: Deseret Book, 1957–1966), 4:28–29.

ans 15:4–6). The New Testament account does not say if there were any women or children present, although it implies that there weren't. If there were women and children present, the total numbers who saw the resurrected Lord in both continents would be somewhat similar.

The Nephite group was "conversing about this Jesus Christ, of whom the sign had been given concerning his death" (v. 2). This also suggests that it was only a short time since the destruction had taken place.

> 3 And it came to pass that while they were thus conversing one with another, they heard a voice as if it came out of heaven; and they cast their eyes round about, for they understood not the voice which they heard; and it was not a harsh voice, neither was it a loud voice; nevertheless, and notwithstanding it being a small voice it did pierce them that did hear to the center, insomuch that there was no part of their frame that it did not cause to quake; yea, it did pierce them to the very soul, and did cause their hearts to burn.
>
> 4 And it came to pass that again they heard the voice, and they understood it not.
>
> 5 And again the third time they did hear the voice, and did open their ears to hear it; and their eyes were towards the sound thereof; and they did look steadfastly towards heaven, from whence the sound came.
>
> 6 And behold, the third time they did understand the voice which they heard; and it said unto them: [3 Nephi 11:3–6]

They heard the voice three times before they were able to understand it (vv. 5–6), probably due to their not being in tune with the Spirit. A group of Lamanites had also heard a voice from heaven three times some sixty years earlier, but they understood it all three times. Both accounts give a similar description of the voice:

> 30 And it came to pass when they heard this voice, and beheld that it was not a voice of thunder, neither was it a voice of a great tumultuous noise, but behold, it was a still voice of perfect mildness, as if it had been a whisper, and it did pierce even to the very soul— [Helaman 5:30; see also vv. 29–33]

The phrase in Third Nephi "did pierce them that did hear" (11:3) implies that some did not hear, also probably because they had not atuned themselves to the Spirit. Certain Greeks attending the last Passover of Christ's mortal ministry in Jerusalem had a similar experience. In response to Jesus' request, the Father spoke from heaven and glorified his name: "The people therefore, that stood by, and heard it, said that it thundered: others said, An angel spake to him. Jesus answered and said, This voice came not because of me, but for your sakes" (John 12:29–30). Once more, some apparently understood the voice and some did not. In Nauvoo, after the martyrdom of the Prophet Joseph, "Brigham Young was transfigured into the likeness of Joseph Smith—voice, person, and manner" as a witness that Brigham and other members of the Quorum of the Twelve were to lead the Church. However, some in the congregation did not receive the manifestation, and did not sustain the Twelve as their leaders (CHC 2:418). The Lord gives manifestations to those who are prepared. In a later revelation to the Saints through Brigham Young, the Lord said: "Let him that is ignorant learn wisdom by humbling himself and calling upon the Lord his God, that his eyes may be opened that he may see, and his ears opened that he may hear; for my Spirit is sent forth into the world to enlighten the humble and contrite" (D&C 136:32–33).[3]

The voice that was heard by the Nephites was the voice of the Father introducing his "Beloved Son" (v. 7). The Father had given an almost identical introduction and endorsement to the people who witnessed the baptism of Jesus: "This is my beloved Son, in whom I am well pleased" (Matthew 3:17), and to Peter, James, and John on the Mount of Transfiguration (see Matthew 17:5). The Prophet Joseph Smith also received this same proclamation in what is termed in the Church, the First Vision (see JS–H 1:17). The Father was not only

---

[3] King Benjamin gave similar instructions to his people. " My brethren, all ye that have assembled yourselves together, you that can hear my words which I shall speak unto you this day; for I have not commanded you to come up hither to trifle with the words which I shall speak, but that you should hearken unto me, and open your ears that ye may hear, and your hearts that ye may understand, and your minds that the mysteries of God may be unfolded to your view." (Mosiah 2:9)

placing his stamp of approval upon Jesus, but was also placing his divine investiture of authority upon him. The Father had previously delegated to his Son the responsibility to create and govern the earth, and was recognizing this fact to the Nephites as well as on those other occasions.[4] The principle is taught in the Testimony of John, "And no man hath seen God at any time, except he hath borne record of the Son" (JST John 1:19). The Nephites had received a witness of sound: the Father had verified the divine ministry of his Only Begotten Son as he had done in his mortal ministry, and has done again in these latter days.

> 8 And it came to pass, as they understood they cast their eyes up again towards heaven; and behold, they saw a Man descending out of heaven; and he was clothed in a white robe; and he came down and stood in the midst of them; and the eyes of the whole multitude were turned upon him, and they durst not open their mouths, even one to another, and wist not what it meant, for they thought it was an angel that had appeared unto them.
>
> 9 And it came to pass that he stretched forth his hand and spake unto the people, saying:
>
> 10 Behold, I am Jesus Christ, whom the prophets testified shall come into the world.
>
> 11 And behold, I am the light and the life of the world; and I have drunk out of that bitter cup which the Father hath given me, and have glorified the Father in taking upon me the sins of the world, in the which I have suffered the will of the Father in all things from the beginning. [3 Nephi 11:8–11]

Once the Nephite people understood the voice, they did not dare open their mouths "for they thought it was an angel that had appeared unto them" (v. 8). Their reluctance to speak was certainly not because of fear, but rather because of awe or amazement. Their thinking it was an angel, even though the Father had just invited them to behold his Son, could have been for various reasons. The appearances of angels

---

[4] See "The Father and the Son, A Doctrinal Exposition by the First Presidency and the Twelve." James R. Clark, *Messages of the First Presidency*, (Salt Lake City: Bookcraft, 1971) 5: 26–34.

were not common, let alone the appearance of the Son of God. While "angels did minister unto [Nephi] daily" prior to Jesus' appearance (3 Nephi 7:18), almost all of those assembled had not seen angels or the Son of God. They didn't know what to expect from the Father's invitation. Furthermore, they may have assumed an angel would precede or accompany Christ. Nonetheless, their thinking was immediately corrected.

Jesus, at this point, introduced himself. His introduction contained several of the same items he had spoken to the inhabitants of all the land during the three days of darkness. There were slight variations, however. The prophets he referred to who had testified of his coming "into the world" were probably the Nephite prophets rather than the broader "scriptures concerning my coming" referred to during the period of darkness (3 Nephi 9:16). Alma had foretold of Jesus being born to Mary at Jerusalem, a chosen [foreordained] vessel who would be a virgin and would "conceive by the power of the Holy Ghost" (Alma 7:10). Alma, Amulek, and many others had gone throughout the land, testifying of the coming of the Son of God (at Jerusalem) and of his appearance to the Nephites alter his resurrection (see Alma chapters 5–16).

Jesus then testified, as his voice had declared during the three days of darkness, that he was "the light and the life of the world," but added that he had "drunk out of that bitter cup which the Father hath given me," (v. 11). At the feast of tabernacles (the third year of his ministry), where great lights were illuminated, Jesus told the festive crowd, "I am the light of the world: he that followeth me shall not walk in darkness, but shall have the light of life" (John 8:12). The Jews rejected his testimony, unlike the Nephites, showing again the difference between the two ministries.

The bitter cup has reference to his suffering in the garden of Gethsemane where he paid the demands of justice for the sins of the world. As a part of the celebration of the Passover meal, the Israelites drank of a cup brewed "with bitter herbs" that was in commemoration of the atonement that Christ would make (Exodus 12:8). The bitterness of his suffering was further shown by Jesus' prayer as he approached the assignment. En route to the garden, he "fell on his face, and prayed, saying, O my Father, if it be possible, let this cup pass from me: nevertheless not as I will, but as thou wilt" (Matthew 26:39). His announcement of the completion of the Gethsemane assignment was a second witness to the Nephites of his divinity as Jesus Christ, the Son of God. They had seen him descend out of heaven, and he had verified that he was not an angel, but rather the Son of God, as his Father had testified.

The people's response changed from one of awe to being totally overcome, and they fell to the ground.

> 12 And it came to pass that when Jesus had spoken these words the whole multitude fell to the earth; for they remembered that it had been prophesied among them that Christ should show himself unto them after his ascension into heaven.
>
> 13 And it came to pass that the Lord spake unto them saying:
>
> 14 Arise and come forth unto me, that ye may thrust your hands into my side, and also that ye may feel the prints of the nails in my hands and in my feet, that ye may know that I am the God of Israel, and the God of the whole earth, and have been slain for the sins of the world.
>
> 15 And it came to pass that the multitude went forth, and thrust their hands into his side, and did feel the prints of the nails in his hands and in his feet; and this they did do, going forth one by one until they had all gone forth, and did see with their eyes and did feel with their hands, and did know of a surety and did bear record, that it was he, of whom it was written by the prophets, that should come. [3 Nephi 11:12–15]

There was another witness to follow. Jesus invited the Nephites to physically feel the marks of his crucified body. The multitude accepted his invitation to feel the wounds, and one by one went forth (vv. 14–15). The logistics of twenty-five hundred people personally meeting and feeling his wounds is astounding. If each person averaged fifteen seconds, it would take more than ten hours for the group to proceed past him. This may illustrate the patience that Jesus exemplified in establishing his identity. But establish it he did, and they now knew by touch as well as by sight and sound. The Lord had proven that he was "the God of Israel and the God of the whole earth" (v. 14) through three physical witnesses, as the law of Moses had taught, and as he had taught in his mortal ministry, "in the mouth of two or three witnesses every word may be established" (Matthew 18:16; quoting from the law, Deuteronomy 19:15).

There is another witness that was undoubtedly present. The text says that they "did know of a surety and did bear record" (v. 15). Their bearing record suggests that they testified of his divinity. A testimony comes by the Spirit. "No man can know that Jesus is the Lord, but by the Holy Ghost" (TPJS, 223).[5] Therefore, the Holy Ghost had confirmed their temporal witness. The law of witnesses was again exemplified. Just as the two sets of witnesses to the Book of Mormon were a combination of the spiritual (3 witnesses) and temporal (8 witnesses), the Nephite multitude had two types of witnesses, a temporal and a spiritual.

The same types of witnesses had been provided in Jerusalem. As Jesus ascended into heaven following his post-resurrection, forty-day ministry, the faithful apostles and probably others beheld him taken up and received into a cloud out of their sight. As they beheld his ascension, "two men stood by them in white apparel" and testified, "this same Jesus, which is taken up from you into heaven, shall so come in like manner as ye have seen him go into heaven" (Acts 1:9–11). They had a witness by sight and by sound. Earlier these apostles had been invited to "handle me, and see; for a spirit hath not flesh and bones, as ye see me have . . . he shewed them his hands and his feet" (Luke 24:39–40). The doubting Thomas was invited to "Reach hither thy finger, and behold my hands; and reach hither thy hand, and thrust it into my side: and be not faithless, but believing" (John 20:27). On the day of Pentecost, the promised "power, after that the Holy Ghost is come upon you" came and "they were all filled with the Holy Ghost." The Jerusalem multitude received a spiritual witness

---

[5] Joseph Smith's comment is a correction of 1 Corinthians 12:3 that did not find its way into the JST.

(Acts 1:8; 2:2–4). Today we have the two witnesses of the Jerusalem account and the Nephite account. We are also promised a personal witness "by the power of the Holy Ghost" (Moroni 10:4). The Lord consistently establishes his truths through various aspects of the law of witnesses.

> 16 And when they had all gone forth and had witnessed for themselves, they did cry out with one accord, saying:
>
> 17 Hosanna! Blessed be the name of the Most High God! And they did fall down at the feet of Jesus, and did worship him. [3 Nephi 11:16–17]

The chief cornerstone, Jesus Christ, was laid in place. The testimony of Jesus Christ is the cornerstone or anchor of our individual lives as well. The time to lay the sure foundation of the apostles was now at hand. Jesus called Nephi to come forth, who came and bowed down, kissing Jesus' feet, undoubtedly in a gesture of respect and total submission.

> 18 And it came to pass that he spake unto Nephi (for Nephi was among the multitude) and he commanded him that he should come forth.
>
> 19 And Nephi arose and went forth, and bowed himself before the Lord and did kiss his feet.
>
> 20 And the Lord commanded him that he should arise. And he arose and stood before him.
>
> 21 And the Lord said unto him: I give unto you power that ye shall baptize this people when I am again ascended into heaven.
>
> 22 And again the Lord called others, and said unto them likewise; and he gave unto them power to baptize. And he said unto them: On this wise shall ye baptize; and there shall be no disputations among you. [3 Nephi 11:18–22]

How the power was conferred upon Nephi is not stated at this time in the record, but Moroni later taught that Jesus laid his hands upon the Twelve and gave them "power that to him upon whom ye shall lay your hands, ye shall give the Holy Ghost" (Moroni 2:1–2). "The elders of the church ordained priests and teachers by laying "their hands upon them" (Moroni 3:1–2). It is assumed that when Christ "laid his hands upon [the twelve]," the power he conferred was the priesthood (Moroni 2:1–2). The Lord called others and also gave them the power to baptize (v. 22 above). The others are not specified, but Mormon inserts an editorial comment later that twelve were "called, and received power and authority to baptize" (3 Nephi 12:1). Before Christ's appearance, "there were ordained of Nephi, men unto this ministry" (3 Nephi 7:25). Although they already had the priesthood, Jesus apparently gave them power pertaining to this dispensation. More will be said on this subject later. "The Lord called [eleven] others" (3 Nephi 12:1) who must have been those who later became the Quorum of the Twelve Disciples that Jesus organized as the foundation of the Church. Joseph Smith taught that the Nephites had Apostles and other officers of the Church.[6] "The foundation of the apostles and prophets, Jesus Christ himself being the chief corner-stone," as taught by the Apostle Paul (Ephesians 2:20), was being set in place.

Having called the twelve Nephites and given them power to baptize, Jesus gave them instructions on how to baptize.

> 23 Verily I say unto you, that whoso repenteth of his sins through your words, and desireth to be baptized in my name, on this wise shall ye baptize them—Behold, ye shall go down and stand in the water, and in my name shall ye baptize them.
>
> 24 And now behold, these are the words which ye shall say, calling them by name, saying:
>
> 25 Having authority given me of Jesus Christ, I baptize you in the name of the Father, and of the Son, and of the Holy Ghost. Amen.
>
> 26 And then shall ye immerse them in the water, and come forth again out of the water.
>
> 27 And after this manner shall ye baptize in my name; for behold, verily I say unto you, that the Father, and the Son, and the Holy Ghost

---

[6] [The Book of Mormon] also tells us that our Savior made His appearance upon this continent after His resurrection; that He planted the Gospel here in all its fullness, and richness, and power, and blessing; that they had Apostles, Prophets, Pastors, Teachers, and Evangelists; the same order, the same priesthood, the same ordinances, gifts, powers, and blessings, as were enjoyed on the eastern continent (HC 4:538).

are one; and I am in the Father, and the Father in me, and the Father and I are one.

28 And according as I have commanded you thus shall ye baptize. And there shall be no disputations among you, as there have hitherto been; neither shall there be disputations among you concerning the points of my doctrine, as there have hitherto been. [3 Nephi 11:23–28]

These instructions on baptism were necessary to make sure that the ordinance was performed correctly because there had been some disputations in the past regarding the manner of baptism (vv. 22, 28). There are presently, and have always been, disputations over the mode of baptism. Changing this ordinance shows that an apostasy is in progress or has taken place. God told Abraham:

4 My people have gone astray from my precepts, and have not kept mine ordinances, which I gave unto their fathers;

5 And they have not observed mine anointing, and the burial, or baptism wherewith I commanded them;

6 But have turned from the commandment, and taken unto themselves the washing of children, and the blood of sprinkling; [JST Genesis 17:4–6]

Thus, the importance of the instructions given here by the Savior are significant. They were also revealed to the Prophet Joseph Smith in this dispensation.

71 No one can be received into the church of Christ unless he has arrived unto the years of accountability before God, and is capable of repentance.

72 Baptism is to be administered in the following manner unto all those who repent—

73 The person who is called of God and has authority from Jesus Christ to baptize, shall go down into the water with the person who has presented himself or herself for baptism, and shall say, calling him or her by name: Having been commissioned of Jesus Christ, I baptize you in the name of the Father, and of the Son, and of the Holy Ghost. Amen.

74 Then shall he immerse him or her in the water, and come forth again out of the water. [D&C 20:71-74]

There are some prerequisites for entering into the waters of baptism. John the Baptist "did preach the baptism of repentance for the remission of sin" (Mark 1:4). The Savior's instructions to the Nephites enlarged somewhat upon the general New Testament admonition. The ordinance was for "whoso repenteth of his sins through [the disciples'] words, and desireth to be baptized in my name" (v. 23). To repent is to change. This change was to be based upon the words they had received from the disciples. This strongly implies faith in those words. "Faith comes by hearing the word of God, through the testimony of the servants of God; that testimony is always attended by the Spirit of prophecy and revelation" (TPJS 148).[7] A desire to be baptized also implies faith. To be baptized in Christ's name exemplifies a faith in him and his teachings. Therefore, the prerequisites for baptism "are: first, Faith in the Lord Jesus Christ; second, Repentance" (Articles of Faith 1:4; see also D&C 20:37).

Those Nephites who desired to meet these prerequisites were instructed by the Savior to "go down and stand in the water," where the disciples, having the power and the authority, were to baptize them (v. 24). Jesus gave the Nephites the exact words of the baptismal prayer (v. 25). This is one of the few set prayers in the Church.[8] The same prayer for baptism was also revealed to Joseph Smith. However, there is one word difference between the Nephite prayer and the one revealed in the latter days. The word "authority" in the Nephite prayer is substituted with "been commissioned" in the revelation to Joseph Smith (D&C 20:73). While this is a difference without significance, the prayer revealed in this dispensation is the one that is followed in the Church today.

After the baptismal prayer was recited, and following the calling of the baptismal candidate by name, the person being baptized was

---

[7] Joseph Smith's comment begins with Romans 10:17; "So then faith cometh by hearing, and hearing by the word of God . . ."

[8] The sacrament prayers and temple ordinances are also to be given precisely.

immersed (vv. 24–26). The gospel of John strongly implies that John baptized by immersion.

> 23 And John also was baptizing in Aenon near to Salim, because there was much water there: and they came, and were baptized. [John 3:23]

The Matthew account implies even stronger that Jesus himself was immersed.

> 16 And Jesus, when he was baptized, went up straightway out of the water: and, lo, the heavens were opened unto him, and he saw the Spirit of God descending like a dove, and lighting upon him: [Matthew 3:16]

As revealed to us by Paul, complete immersion is symbolic of the death, burial, and resurrection. "Know ye not, that so many of us as were baptized into Jesus Christ were baptized into his death? Therefore we are buried with him by baptism into death: that like as Christ was raised up from the dead by the glory of the Father, even so we also should walk in newness of life" (Romans 6:4). The record does not say that Jesus explained this symbolism to the Nephites, but he may have and was probably the source for Paul's analysis. He did, however, comment on the baptism being performed in the name of the three members of the Godhead. The reason he gave was that the three of them are one (v. 27). It is significant that the plural verb "are" was used in the prayer. The three are thus plural in their being, but are unified in the plan of salvation, of which baptism is an ordinance. Through this ordinance, entrance to the Church of Jesus Christ was thereby established among the Nephites.

> 29 For verily, verily I say unto you, he that hath the spirit of contention is not of me, but is of the devil, who is the father of contention, and he stirreth up the hearts of men to contend with anger, one with another.
>
> 30 Behold, this is not my doctrine, to stir up the hearts of men with anger, one against another; but this is my doctrine, that such things should be done away. [3 Nephi 11:29–30]

Jesus again cautioned the Nephites against contentions. He added the warning that "he that hath the spirit of contention is not of me, but is of the devil, who is the father of contention, (v. 29). Just as Nephi had warned that those who spoke harshly against the Book of Mormon would "be of the spirit of the devil" (2 Nephi 33:5), those who have, through the history of the world, contended over and changed the ordinance of baptism, or any of the points of Christ's gospel, have been influenced by the devil. The doctrine of Christ is not "to stir up the hearts of men with anger one against another; but this is my doctrine, that such things should be done away" (v. 30). The Lord then expounded upon his doctrine.

> 31 Behold, verily, verily, I say unto you, I will declare unto you my doctrine.
>
> 32 And this is my doctrine, and it is the doctrine which the Father hath given unto me; and I bear record of the Father, and the Father beareth record of me, and the Holy Ghost beareth record of the Father and me; and I bear record that the Father commandeth all men, everywhere, to repent and believe in me.
>
> 33 And whoso believeth in me, and is baptized, the same shall be saved; and they are they who shall inherit the kingdom of God.
>
> 34 And whoso believeth not in me, and is not baptized, shall be damned. [3 Nephi 11:31–34]

The doctrine of Christ is also the doctrine of the Father, because it is the doctrine that "the Father hath given unto me" (32). In the temple at Jerusalem, Jesus answered the Jews who marveled at his teachings, "My doctrine is not mine, but his that sent me. If any man will do his will, he shall know of the doctrine, whether it be of God, or whether I speak of myself" (John 7:16–17). As Nephi, son of Lehi, taught, it "is the only and true doctrine of the Father, and of the Son, and of the Holy Ghost, which is one God, without end. Amen" (2 Nephi 31:21). All three members of the Godhead bear record of each other. Christ told the Nephites on this occasion, "I bear record of the Father, and the Father beareth record of me, and the Holy Ghost beareth record of the Father and me" (v. 32).

The three members of the Godhead work together for the salvation of all mankind. Joseph Smith taught: "Everlasting covenant was made between three personages before the organization of this earth, and relates to their dispensation of things to men on the earth; these personages, according to Abraham's record, are called God the first, the Creator; God the second, the Redeemer; and God the third, the witness or Testator" (TPJS, 190). Although they have separate roles, they supplement and compliment each other through testimony.

The doctrine of the Father that Jesus was declaring to the Nephite Twelve is the same as was given to the Twelve in Jerusalem when he concluded his mortal ministry, but he added the promise that "these signs shall follow them that believe."

> 15 And he said unto them, Go ye into all the world, and preach the gospel to every creature.
>
> 16 He that believeth and is baptized shall be saved; but he that believeth not shall be damned.
>
> 17 And these signs shall follow them that believe; In my name shall they cast out devils; they shall speak with new tongues; [Mark 16:15–17]

Many scholars feel that the "longer ending" of Mark has been added to the text, which ending includes the 3 Nephi 11:33–34 quotation of Jesus to the Nephites cited above. Moroni later quotes Jesus as teaching the almost identical "longer ending" of Mark (Mormon 9:22–25). Moroni also gives it as an admonition to the reader in the Book of Ether (4:18). Again the Book of Mormon is "Proving to the world that the holy scriptures are true" (D&C 20:11), and "shall establish the truth of the first" (1 Nephi 13:39).

Having taught the correct doctrine of baptism and the Godhead, Jesus amplified his explanation of the roles of the three personages of Deity.

> 35 Verily, verily, I say unto you, that this is my doctrine, and I bear record of it from the Father; and whoso believeth in me believeth in the Father also; and unto him will the Father bear record of me, for he will visit him with fire and with the Holy Ghost.
>
> 36 And thus will the Father bear record of me, and the Holy Ghost will bear record unto him of the Father and me; for the Father, and I, and the Holy Ghost are one.

37 And again I say unto you, ye must repent, and become as a little child, and be baptized in my name, or ye can in nowise receive these things.

38 And again I say unto you, ye must repent, and be baptized in my name, and become as a little child, or ye can in nowise inherit the kingdom of God. [3 Nephi 11:35–38]

Jesus bore record that the doctrine was from the Father; therefore, those who believed in Christ believed also in the Father. Those who so believed would have the Father bear record of Christ through a visit of fire and the Holy Ghost (v. 35). The fire is the cleansing power that remits a person's sins. "And after they had been received unto baptism, and were wrought upon and cleansed by the power of the Holy Ghost, they were numbered among the people of the church of Christ" (Moroni 6:4).

In an epistle written to Moroni by his father Mormon, we learn the purpose of the baptism of the Holy Ghost.

25 And the first fruits of repentance is baptism; and baptism cometh by faith unto the fulfilling the commandments; and the fulfilling the commandments bringeth remission of sins;

26 And the remission of sins bringeth meekness, and lowliness of heart; and because of meekness and lowliness of heart cometh the visitation of the Holy Ghost, which Comforter filleth with hope and perfect love, which love endureth by diligence unto prayer, until the end shall come, when all the saints shall dwell with God. [Moroni 8:25–26]

The Father thus bears record of his Son through the Holy Ghost, while the Holy Ghost bears record to those baptized of the Father and of Christ. The three deities are one in testifying of the doctrine of salvation for mankind (v. 36).

As a matter of summary or emphasis, the Savior taught, "And again I say unto you, ye must repent, and become as a little child, and be baptized in my name, or ye can in nowise receive these things" (v. 37). Jesus then repeated the same instructions with a different order, becoming as a little child following repentance and baptism instead of before baptism. He also gave a different conclusion: "And again I say unto you, ye must repent, and be baptized in my name, and become as a little child, or ye can in nowise inherit the kingdom of God" (v. 38).

The different order is probably to distinguish the procedure before baptism and after. Those who repent and become as a little child are fit candidates for baptism. The instructions to the newly restored in April 1830 was:

> 37 *And again, by way of commandment to the church concerning the manner of baptism*—All those who humble themselves before God, and desire to be baptized, and come forth with broken hearts and contrite spirits, and witness before the church that they have truly repented of all their sins, and are willing to take upon them the name of Jesus Christ, having a determination to serve him to the end, and truly manifest by their works that they have received of the Spirit of Christ unto the remission of their sins, shall be received by baptism into his church. [D&C 20:37]

If the Nephites or modern-day candidates would not meet these prerequisites, they would not "receive these things"—the testimony of the various members of the Godhead (v. 37). Furthermore, those who are baptized and do receive the testimonies promised must again become as a little child so they can be taught and prepared for an inheritance in "the kingdom of God" (v. 38). In responding to the question by his disciples in Jerusalem, "Who is the greatest in the kingdom of heaven?" Jesus said, "Except ye be converted, and become as little children, ye shall not enter into the kingdom of heaven. Whosoever therefore shall humble himself as this little child is greatest in the kingdom of heaven" (Matthew 8:3–4). These baptized symbolic children are the Saints, spoken of by an angel to King Benjamin, who become "submissive, meek, humble, patient, full of love, willing to submit to all things which the Lord seeth fit to inflict upon him, even as a child doth submit to his father" (Mosiah 3:19). The doctrine of Christ, the Father, and the Holy Ghost is the plan to bring eternal life to the inhabitants of the earth. Their work is "to bring to pass the immortality and eternal life of man" (Moses 1:39).

> 39 Verily, verily, I say unto you, that this is my doctrine, and whoso buildeth upon this buildeth upon my rock, and the gates of hell shall not prevail against them.

> 40 And whoso shall declare more or less than this, and establish it for my doctrine, the same cometh of evil, and is not built upon my rock; but he buildeth upon a sandy foundation, and the gates of hell stand open to receive such when the floods come and the winds beat upon them.
>
> 41 Therefore, go forth unto this people, and declare the words which I have spoken, unto the ends of the earth. [3 Nephi 11:39–41]

For the third time the Savior declared to the Nephite Twelve that "this is my doctrine" (v. 39). Was he establishing his doctrine by three witnesses? Perhaps, but it may have been as an introductory explanation, followed by a more specific explanation, and a concluding reemphasis and warning against contending over his doctrine. It was such contention that had brought his initial explanation. Those who build upon the doctrine of Christ build upon his rock, "and the gates of hell shall not prevail against them" (v. 39). Jesus gave the same promise to Peter; "thou art Peter, and upon this rock I will build my church; and the gates of hell shall not prevail against it." (Matthew 16:18). The same promise was given in this dispensation.

> 67 Behold, this is my doctrine—whosoever repenteth and cometh unto me, the same is my church.
>
> 68 Whosoever declareth more or less than this, the same is not of me, but is against me; therefore he is not of my church.
>
> 69 And now, behold, whosoever is of my church, and endureth of my church to the end, him will I establish upon my rock, and the gates of hell shall not prevail against them.
>
> 70 And now, remember the words of him who is the life and light of the world, your Redeemer, your Lord and your God. Amen. [D&C 10:67–70]

Those who declare more or less than his teachings and establish it as doctrine, are not built on the rock of Christ, but rather on a sandy foundation. The gates of hell will receive those who pervert the gospel when the winds of contention and the floods of deception sweep people away (v. 40 above). These cautions are significant.

Those familiar with the Palestine Sermon on the Mount will recognize the ending of this sermon to the Nephite Twelve as the same as that ending. The Nephite Twelve were instructed to teach the people these sayings (v. 41). Following these instructions, Jesus taught the multitude basically as he had in the Sermon on the Mount, and ended in a similar manner (3 Nephi 14:24–27). Certainly the conclusions are the same for all people. As the Godhead is united in the doctrine of Christ, so are they united in its effect upon the people. However, the building upon the rock of Christ was not a new concept. Helaman had taught his two sons Lehi and Nephi to build their foundation upon the rock of our Redeemer, who is Christ, the Son of God, and warned of the devil sending his mighty winds, hail, and storm. He called the rock of Christ a sure "foundation whereon if men build they cannot fail" (Helaman 5:12). This concept, taught by Helaman about sixty years before Christ taught it, seems to be a well-known one. Apparently it was a part of "the many plain and precious things taken out of the [Old Testament] (1 Nephi 13:29). Perhaps Jesus was reminding the people of a well-known principle. Regardless, to come back to the doctrine of Christ taught to the Nephites, the correct doctrine was the foundation upon which one was to build, and the building was to be raised from the testimony of Christ, the chief cornerstone.

The well-built foundation would keep people out of hell, but the sandy foundation would cause these gates to open wide and receive the storm-tossed inhabitants of the earth. A sure foundation is well worth building upon. In our dispensation, the cornerstone of Christ was set through the First Vision when "two Personages," one being the others "Beloved Son" appeared to Joseph Smith (JS–H 1:17), and subsequent appearances of Christ to chosen servants of the Lord. Joseph Smith and Sidney Rigdon testified:

> 22 And now, after the many testimonies which have been given of him, this is the testimony, last of all, which we give of him: That he lives!
>
> 23 For we saw him, even on the right hand of God; and we heard the voice bearing record that he is the Only Begotten of the Father— [D&C 76:22–23].

Joseph Smith and Oliver Cowdery also saw Christ in the temple at Kirtland, Ohio on April 3, 1836.

1 The veil was taken from our minds, and the eyes of our understanding were opened.

2 We saw the Lord standing upon the breastwork of the pulpit, before us; and under his feet was a paved work of pure gold, in color like amber.

3 His eyes were as a flame of fire; the hair of his head was white like the pure snow; his countenance shone above the brightness of the sun; and his voice was as the sound of the rushing of great waters, even the voice of Jehovah, saying:

4 I am the first and the last; I am he who liveth, I am he who was slain; I am your advocate with the Father. [D&C 110:1–4]

The foundation of the Church was also laid upon the apostolic calling to men upon the earth.

9 And now, Oliver Cowdery, I speak unto you, and also unto David Whitmer, by the way of commandment; for, behold, I command all men everywhere to repent, and I speak unto you, even as unto Paul mine apostle, for you are called even with that same calling with which he was called.

26 And now, behold, there are others who are called to declare my gospel, both unto Gentile and unto Jew;

27 Yea, even twelve; and the Twelve shall be my disciples, and they shall take upon them my name; and the Twelve are they who shall desire to take upon them my name with full purpose of heart.

33 And I, Jesus Christ, your Lord and your God, have spoken it.

34 These words are not of men nor of man, but of me; wherefore, you shall testify they are of me and not of man;

35 For it is my voice which speaketh them unto you; for they are given by my Spirit unto you, and by my power you can read them one to another; and save it were by my power you could not have them;

36 Wherefore, you can testify that you have heard my voice, and know my words. [D&C 18:9; 26–27; 33–37]

We must build upon that sure foundation and the testimony of Christ as the chief cornerstone today just as the Nephites were commanded to build upon Jesus Christ, the Son of God.

Chapter 5

The Higher Law of Christ

3 Nephi 12:1–16

T he Christian world looks upon the sermon that Jesus delivered on the mount by the Sea of Galilee as one of the greatest sermons on morals and ethics ever given. While the teachings of this sermon can be applied to our lives and the lives of others in many moral and ethical ways, the purpose and content of the sermon was much more specific. The Sermon on the Mount was the higher law promised to replace the law of Moses. It was "the law and the commandments of [the] Father . . . and the law [was] fulfilled" (3 Nephi 12:19). It was "the gospel of the kingdom" that "Jesus went about all Galilee, teaching in their synagogues, and preaching" (Matthew 4:23).[1] In the words of Paul, "the law was our schoolmaster to bring us to Christit. . . . But . . . we are no longer under a schoolmaster." (Galatians 3:24). The sermon, in Jerusalem and in Bountiful, was a deep theological treatise of how to build upon the doctrinal foundation of the apostles and prophets, with Jesus Christ being the chief cornerstone as discussed

---

[1] As he went about Galilee, "there followed him great multitudes of people from Galilee, and from Decapolis, and from Jerusalem, and from Judea, and from beyond Jordan" (Matthew 4:25). He probably taught these same doctrines elsewhere, but on the mount by Galilee is where his teachings were recorded, again probably at his request, and was more complete because it would be recorded. The fact that the sermons in Jerusalem and in Bountiful were identical lends support to this theory.

in the previous chapter. Among the Nephites, the testimony of Jesus to establish the cornerstone had just been given to the multitude, and the doctrine taught to Nephi and other chosen disciples had been given as a solid foundation upon which to build (3 Nephi 11). Jesus next turned to the multitude to show them how to build upon his doctrinal rock (3 Nephi 12:1).

The first part of the sermon that Jesus delivered to the multitude, here and in Galilee, is generally referred to as "the beatitudes," a series of short, descriptive characteristics, each followed by a promised reward or blessing. Each is introduced with the phrase "blessed are." There are eight or nine of these "blessed" conditions outlined in the Galilean sermon, depending on whether the last two beatitudes are counted as one or two. They will be treated here as two separate ones. The Book of Mormon account begins with two additional "blessed" statements. Therefore, some are prone to say that the Book of Mormon has two more beatitudes. However, these two initial "blessed" statements are a summation to the multitude of the doctrine that Jesus had just taught to Nephi and others. They constitute the doctrinal foundation that they had to accept if they wanted to build upon the rock of Christ. An outline of the first part of the sermon follows as an overview in preparation for a deeper analysis of the text of his sermon.

Outline • 3 Nephi 12:1–16

➤ 12:1–16   After Jesus had spoken to Nephi and the other twelve, and given them power and authority to baptize, he spoke to the multitude.

     a. Blessed are you if you give heed to these twelve, chosen to minister and be your servants. v. 1

        1. They have power to you with water, and I will baptize you with fire and the Holy Ghost.

        2. Blessed are you if you will be baptized after seeing me and knowing I am.

     b. Blessed are those who will believe in your testimony and are baptized, for I will baptize them with fire and the Holy Ghost, and they shall receive a remission of sins. vv. 2–12

1. The poor in spirit who come to Christ shall inherit the kingdom of heaven.
2. Those who mourn shall be comforted.
3. The meek shall inherit the earth.
4. Those who hunger and thirst after righteousness shall be filled with the Holy Ghost.
5. The merciful shall obtain mercy.
6. The pure in heart shall see God.
7. The peacemakers shall be called the children of God.
8. Those persecuted for my name's sake shall inherit the kingdom of heaven.
9. Those reviled and persecuted for my sake will have great joy in heaven for so persecuted they the prophets before you.

c. Those baptized are given the opportunity to be the salt of the earth. v. 13

1. If the salt loses its savor, how shall the earth be salted?
2. The salt is no good and shall be trodden under foot of men.

d. Those baptized are given the opportunity to be the light of this people. vv. 14–16

1. A city set on a hill cannot be hid.
2. A candle is not lighted and put under a bushel, but on a candlestick to light the whole house.
3. Let your good works glorify your Father in Heaven to all his people.

NOTES AND COMMENTARY

1 And it came to pass that when Jesus had spoken these words unto Nephi, and to those who had been called, (now the number of them who had been called, and received power and authority to baptize, was twelve) and behold, he stretched forth his hand unto the multitude, and cried unto them, saying: Blessed are ye if ye shall give heed unto the words of these twelve whom I have chosen from among you to minister unto you, and to be your servants; and unto them I have given power that they may baptize you with water; and after that ye are baptized with water, behold, I will baptize you with fire and with the Holy Ghost; therefore blessed are ye if ye shall believe in me and be baptized, after that ye have seen me and know that I am.

2 And again, more blessed are they who shall believe in your words because that ye shall testify that ye have seen me, and that ye know that I am. Yea, blessed are they who shall believe in your words, and come down into the depths of humility and be baptized, for they shall be visited with fire and with the Holy Ghost, and shall receive a remission of their sins. [3 Nephi 12:1–2]

Although there were "about two thousand and five hundred souls; and they did consist of men, women, and children" present at the Bountiful temple site (3 Nephi 17:25), there were many, many more people throughout the Nephite lands. Those among the twenty-five hundred, who were baptized with water and fire and the Holy Ghost, were to go out and testify to others not present of what they had seen and been taught. Those who heard their message, and humbled themselves and believed, and would be baptized with water would also "be visited with fire and with the Holy Ghost, and shall receive a remission of their sins" (v. 2). As stated before, this is the doctrine of Christ that Jesus had just taught the twelve disciples (see 3 Nephi 11:32–37). The Joseph Smith Translation text is the same as the Third Nephi text quoted above, showing that these same prerequisites for building upon the doctrinal foundation, or the rock of Christ, were given to the Galilean multitude. As instructed through the Spirit, Joseph added these same truths to that text (JST Matthew 5:1–2).

Why the two "blessed" prerequisites had been removed from the original text cannot be definitely ascertained. It was probably the work of the "great and abominable church" taking "away from the gospel of the Lamb many parts which are plain and most precious . . . that they might pervert the right ways of the Lord, that they might blind the eyes and harden the hearts of the children of men" (1 Nephi 13:26–27). Other deletions from the original text support this notion. A comparison of the Bible and Book of Mormon texts illustrate these deletions.

Blessed are the poor in spirit: for theirs is the kingdom of heaven. (Matthew 5:3)	Yea, blessed are the poor in spirit who come unto me, for theirs is the kingdom of heaven. (3 Nephi 12:3)

Many people emphasize the retention of "who come unto me" in the Book of Mormon text. However, just as important is the retention of the word "yea" that introduces the verse. "Yea" connects or reemphasizes what has just been said with what is now being said. Jesus had just explained the necessity of baptism as the doctrinal foundation. He now reemphasizes this requirement to be in "the kingdom of heaven."[2] Only those baptized with water, and with fire and the Holy Ghost will receive the blessed condition promised. To "come unto me [Christ]" is to come to the waters of baptism. In defining his gospel, Jesus said: "Repent, all ye ends of the earth, and come unto me and be baptized in my name" (3 Nephi 27:20; see also 21:6). Those who are not baptized "are under the bondage of sin, because they come not unto me" (D&C 84:49–51). Baptism brings a remission of sin through repentance followed by the baptism of fire

---

[2] Jesus taught the Nephite disciples: "And whoso believeth in me, and is baptized, the same shall be saved; and they are they who shall inherit the kingdom of God.

And whoso believeth not in me, and is not baptized, shall be damned." (3 Nephi 11:33–34)

Jesus taught the Jerusalem apostles: "And he said unto them, Go ye into all the world, and preach the gospel to every creature. He that believeth and is baptized shall be saved; but he that believeth not shall be damned." (Mark 16:15–16)

and the Holy Ghost. Those who are poor in spirit, or who lack the Spirit, will attain it if they "come down into the depths of humility and be baptized, for they shall be visited with fire and the Holy Ghost, and shall receive a remission of their sins" (3 Nephi 12:2).

The Christian world gives many interpretations of being "poor in spirit." Most of them center around humility. While humility is required for baptism (3 Nephi 12:2 quoted just above), the context of Jesus' teaching implies a further condition. To be poor may be associated with having a lack of something, such as riches or other material things. Therefore, to be "poor in spirit," as suggested above, is to be lacking the Spirit. Those who come unto Christ will receive that Spirit through a baptism of the Holy Ghost. To be baptized means to be immersed. An immersion in the Spirit will be the blessing given to those who recognize, in humility, that they are without the Spirit, and after repentance and a baptism of water, they are promised they will receive an immersion in the Holy Ghost. Through this baptism of the Spirit, they are on the "strait and narrow path which leads eternal life" (2 Nephi 31:17). Having entered the path, they are ready to build upon the doctrinal foundation of Christ, as outlined in the other beatitudes.

The second beatitude is introduced in the Book of Mormon with the words "And again." The Bible does not contain this introduction. These introductory words tie the beatitude back to those who have been baptized with water, and with fire and the Holy Ghost. It is another way of confirming that the promised blessing is based upon accepting the ordinances connected with the doctrine of Christ, and with membership in Christ's church through baptism.

And again blessed are all they that mourn, for they shall be comforted. (3 Nephi 12:4)	Blessed are they that mourn; for they shall be comforted. (Matthew 5:4)

The Nephite sermon contains the word "*all* they that mourn" (italics added). This is significant since the promise is to all who are baptized with water, and with fire and the Holy Ghost. The ethical application recognizes the tendency of those who profess to follow Christ to show compassion to those who experience tragedy or sorrow. While this is commendable and desirable, there is a deeper doctrinal teaching. Just as a person who is taught of Christ and his doctrine recognizes that they are lacking in the Spirit, they will acknowledge that they have been living a life that does not conform to Christ's gospel. As taught by the Apostle Paul: "For all have sinned, and come short of the glory of God" (Romans 3:23). However, only the people who recognize and mourn over their past sins, and come unto Christ, will "be comforted." They will feel Christ's healing influence upon the mourning soul. Part of Christ's self-proclaimed mission, in the synagogue in Nazareth, was "to heal the brokenhearted" (Luke 4:18). He was quoting the prophecy of Isaiah; "he hath sent me to bind up the broken hearted," regarding his mission (Isaiah 61:2).

People become brokenhearted when they recognize they have contributed to the agony of Christ suffered in Gethsemane, as well as to the suffering they may have caused others. The gate to enter the path to eternal life "is repentance and baptism by water, and then comes a remission of your sins by fire and the Holy Ghost" (2 Nephi 31:17). The healing comes through being "cleansed by the power [fire] of the Holy Ghost" (Moroni 6:4), and the renewal of their spirits with "the visitation of the Holy Ghost, which Comforter filleth with hope and perfect love, which love endureth by diligence unto prayer, until the end shall come, when all the saints shall dwell with God" (Moroni 8:25–26). Therefore, the real comforter is the Holy Ghost as taught by Christ in the New Testament: "But the Comforter, *which is* the Holy Ghost, whom the Father will send in my name, he shall teach you all things, and bring all things to your remembrance, whatsoever I have said unto you." (John 14:26).

Only those who are baptized with water are eligible to receive the baptism of fire and the Holy Ghost. Although, "by the power of the Holy Ghost [anyone] may know the truth of all things" (Moroni 10:5), only the legally baptized members of Christ's church are given it as a gift. The Nephite Twelve were given "power that to him upon whom ye shall lay your hands, ye shall give the Holy Ghost" (Moroni 2:2). The apostles, Peter and John, "laid they their hands on [those baptized in Samaria], and they received the Holy Ghost" (Acts 8:14–17). When Simon offered the apostles money for this power, ". . . Peter said unto him, Thy money perish with thee, because thou hast thought that the gift of God may be purchased with money" (Acts 8:20). Therefore, those who mourn over their sins and come unto Christ will be comforted by a baptism of the Holy Ghost, and they will know that their sins have been forgiven.

The Prophet Joseph also taught that those who lost a beloved marriage partner would be comforted by the knowledge that they would "soon have the company of [that] companion in a world of glory" as well as the association of friends and loved ones there (TPJS, 296; see also 347). Of course this knowledge is based upon the principle of marriage and the family unit being for time and eternity,[3] and would come from a witness of the Holy Ghost.

Each of the next seven beatitudes are prefaced with an "and" that is not in the biblical text. These prefaces seem to also tie back to the prerequisite of being baptized. This assumption is strengthened, if not confirmed, by the rewards that are promised under each "blessed" condition. As will be shown for each, the rewards are only attained by those who are baptized into the Church. Mention of the "and"

---

[3] ". . . verily I say unto you, if a man marry a wife by my word, which is my law, and by the new and everlasting covenant, and it is sealed unto them by the Holy Spirit of promise, by him who is anointed, unto whom I have appointed this power and the keys of this priesthood; and it shall be said unto them—Ye shall come forth in the first resurrection; and if it be after the first resurrection, in the next resurrection; and shall inherit thrones, kingdoms, principalities, and powers, dominions, all heights and depths—then shall it be written in the Lamb's Book of Life, that he shall commit no murder whereby to shed innocent blood, and if ye abide in my covenant, and commit no murder whereby to shed innocent blood, it shall be done unto them in all things whatsoever my servant hath put upon them, in time, and through all eternity; and shall be of full force when they are out of the world; . . . as hath been sealed upon their heads, which glory shall be a fulness and a continuation of the seeds forever and ever." (D&C 132:19)

preface will be made here, but not necessarily with each succeeding beatitude.

> 5 And blessed are the meek, for they shall inherit the earth. [3 Nephi 12:5 cp Matthew 5:5]

The third beatitude, "blessed are the meek," is worded the same in Matthew and Third Nephi, except for the "And." The promise that those who attain this characteristic will inherit the earth will be fulfilled when the earth is celestialized. Only those who are baptized with water and with fire and the Holy Ghost, and endure in faith to the end will live upon the celestial earth. In a revelation to Joseph Smith, the Lord said:

> 17 And the redemption of the soul is through him that quickeneth all things, in whose bosom it is decreed that the poor and the meek of the earth shall inherit it.
>
> 18 Therefore, it must needs be sanctified from all unrighteousness, that it may be prepared for the celestial glory;
>
> 19 For after it hath filled the measure of its creation, it shall be crowned with glory, even with the presence of God the Father;
>
> 20 That bodies who are of the celestial kingdom may possess it forever and ever; for, for this intent was it made and created, and for this intent are they sanctified. [D&C 88:17–20]

But, who are the meek? The meek are often interpreted to be the shy, the introverts, or those who are not aggressive. This interpretation is not scripturally sound. Jesus described himself as being "meek and lowly in heart" (Matthew 11:29). The Prophet Joseph commented on this passage:

> Some of the company thought I was not a very meek Prophet; so I told them: 'I am meek and lowly in heart,' and will personify Jesus for a moment, to illustrate the principle, and cried out with a loud voice, 'Woe unto you, ye doctors; woe unto you, ye lawyers; woe unto you, ye scribes, Pharisees, and hypocrites!' But you cannot find the place where I ever went that I found fault with their food, their drink, their house, their lodgings; no, never; and this is what is meant by the meekness and lowliness of Jesus. [TPJS, 270]

Therefore, the meek are not the shy introverts, but those who follow the example of the Lord. The Lord called Moses "very meek, above all the men which were upon the face of the earth" (Numbers 12:3). The Bible does not sustain Moses as shy, an introvert, or non-aggressive. The context of the Lord's statement about Moses being meek reveals him as the faithful mouthpiece of the Lord.

> 6 Hear now my words: If there be a prophet among you, *I* the LORD will make myself known unto him in a vision, *and* will speak unto him in a dream.
>
> 7 My servant Moses *is* not so, who *is* faithful in all mine house.
>
> 8 With him will I speak mouth to mouth, even apparently, and not in dark speeches; and the similitude of the LORD shall he behold: wherefore then were ye not afraid to speak against my servant Moses? [Numbers 12:6–8]

In other words, he was teachable, the most teachable man upon the earth. The most meek and, therefore, teachable man upon the face of the earth today is the President of the Church.

> 91 And again, the duty of the President of the office of the High Priesthood is to preside over the whole church, and to be like unto Moses—
>
> 92 Behold, here is wisdom; yea, to be a seer, a revelator, a translator, and a prophet, having all the gifts of God which he bestows upon the head of the church. [D&C 107:91–92; see also 28:2; 103:16]

He is the Lord's mouthpiece. Those who inherit the earth as a celestial home will be those who are teachable through the Spirit. The Spirit is given as a gift to those who are baptized and through meekness grow "in the knowledge of . . . that . . . which is just and true" (Mosiah 4:12).

The fourth "blessed" condition enumerated by the Savior was:

Blessed are they which do hunger and thirst after righteousness; for they shall be filled. (Matthew 5:6)	And blessed are all they who do hunger and thirst after righteousness, for they shall be filled with the Holy Ghost. (3 Nephi 12:6)

The Bible promises that those who so hunger and thirst will be filled. The Book of Mormon text retains the important principle that "all" those who meet this "blessed" condition will be filled "with the Holy Ghost." To be filled with the Holy Ghost is to be immersed, or baptized, in the Spirit. This was the original promise extended to the multitude if they would be baptized with water. This beatitude is the formula to sustain a fullness of the Spirit in their lives. However, "A man may receive the Holy Ghost, and it may descend upon him and not tarry with him" (D&C 130:23). Those who maintain the Spirit in their lives are sanctified "because of their yielding their hearts unto God" (Helaman 3:35); because they "love and serve God with all their mights, minds, and strength" (D&C 20:31); or "by the reception of the Holy Ghost, that ye may stand spotless before me at the last day" as Jesus later taught the Nephites (3 Nephi 27:20). To be "sanctified by the Holy Spirit" is the prerequisite for being in the celestial kingdom.

> 10 Now, as I said concerning the holy order, or this high priesthood, there were many who were ordained and became high priests of God; and it was on account of their exceeding faith and repentance, and their righteousness before God, they choosing to repent and work righteousness rather than to perish;
>
> 11 Therefore they were called after this holy order, and were sanctified, and their garments were washed white through the blood of the Lamb.
>
> 12 Now they, after being sanctified by the Holy Ghost, having their garments made white, being pure and spotless before God, could not look upon sin save it were with abhorrence; and there were many, exceedingly great many, who were made pure and entered into the rest of the Lord their God. [Alma 13:10–12]

The rest of the Lord "is the fullness of his glory" (D&C 84:24).

Although the concept of being filled with the Holy Ghost and then maintaining the Spirit unto sanctification is not clearly taught in the New Testament Gospels, Paul taught it to the saints in Thessalonica.

> 13 But we are bound to give thanks alway to God for you, brethren beloved of the Lord, because God hath from the beginning chosen you

to salvation through sanctification of the Spirit and belief of the truth.
[2 Thessalonians 2:13]

Paul's teachings strongly imply that Jesus also taught this concept in his mortal ministry since Paul was taught the gospel not by man, "but by the revelation of Jesus Christ" (Galatians 1:12). Modern revelation confirms that Jesus taught sanctification by the Spirit.

Jesus' admonition to hunger and thirst after righteousness is a comparison of a spiritual need with a physical need. When a man has physical hunger or thirst, his body drives him to satisfy those appetites. Those who are attuned to the Spirit can receive a similar drive to satisfy their spiritual needs. However, without the Spirit, the desire for spiritual needs is diminished and people suffer spiritual malnutrition without recognition of their condition. Their suffering from the lack of the Spirit must be drawn to their attention through others' teachings, or they remain spiritually deficient. They will be filled spiritually to the degree that they seek after righteousness.

> 7 And blessed are the merciful, for they shall obtain mercy. [3 Nephi
> 12:7 cp Matthew 5:5]

Those who bless the merciful are promised mercy in return. The ethical interpretation of this beatitude may be referred to as the law of the boomerang: if I am merciful to others, they will be merciful to me. However, the mercy that is needed in everyone's life is the mercy of Jesus Christ. To those who extend mercy to their fellow beings, the Lord says, "Inasmuch as ye have done it unto one of the least of these my brethren, ye have done it unto me," and thus he counts them as inheritors of the kingdom of heaven (Matthew 25:34–40). The law of mercy takes effect and satisfies the demands of justice to those who are baptized, through the Atonement. Alma teaches that:

> . . . God did call on men, in the name of his Son, (this being the plan
> of redemption which was laid) saying: If ye will repent, and harden not
> your hearts, then will I have mercy upon you, through mine Only
> Begotten Son;

Therefore, whosoever repenteth, and hardeneth not his heart, he shall have claim on mercy through mine Only Begotten Son, unto a remission of sins; and these shall enter into my rest. [Alma 12:33–34]

And blessed are all the pure in heart, for they shall see God. (3 Nephi 12:8)	Blessed *are* the pure in heart for they shall see God. (Matthew 5:8)

In the sixth "blessed" condition, the Book of Mormon text retains the word "all the pure in heart," and the Prophet Joseph added it to the JST. The promised reward for attaining this state is to "see God." To become pure in heart one must overcome all sin, both literally and mentally, thus having no more disposition to do evil, but rather to do good continually. This comes through "the Spirit of the Lord Omnipotent" (Mosiah 5:2). It happens initially to those who are "born of God, and . . . filled with the Holy Ghost" (Alma 36:24). This initial condition of righteousness must be maintained or developed in order to become "partakers of the divine nature" (2 Peter 1:4). The obtaining of this nature is also a part of the sanctification process. We must consecrate our minds to "become single to [the glory of] God, and the days will come that [we] shall see him; for he will unveil his face unto [us], and it shall be in his own time, and in his own way, and according to his own will" (D&C 88:68). The Lord revealed the formula for seeing his face to the Latter-day Saints. "Verily, thus saith the Lord: It shall come to pass that every soul who forsaketh his sins and cometh unto me, and calleth on my name, and obeyeth my voice, and keepeth my commandments, shall see my face and know that I am" (D&C 93:1).

An interpretation of this verse is suggested: Those who forsake their sins (repent), come unto him (baptism), call on his name (pray continually for guidance), obey his voice (receive personal revelation from the Holy Ghost), and keep his commandments (live by the scriptures) shall see his face and know that he is (D&C 93:1). Thus, those who diligently follow this formula will become pure in heart, and shall see God.

9 And blessed are *all* the peacemakers, for they shall be called the children of God. [3 Nephi 12:9; italics added]

In the sixth beatitude, the Book of Mormon again retains "all" the peacemakers, which the KJV Matthew 5:9 has lost. From an ethical viewpoint, a person should be a moderator among his peers to help settle arguments or disagreements. However, from a doctrinal point, the gospel is the only solution for lasting peace. Therefore, Christ is the epitome of a peacemaker, or the "founder of peace" as taught by Isaiah and interpreted by Abinadi (Isaiah 52:8; Mosiah 15:18). Furthermore, the prophets, "they who have published peace, who have brought good tidings of good, who have published salvation," and all others who have and will teach the gospel are peacemakers (Mosiah 15:13–17; cp. Isaiah 52:7). Paul also understood Isaiah, and testified that a person cannot teach the gospel without knowing well the teachings of Christ. Furthermore, he must, in the fullest sense, be called and have authority to preach it, as Paul taught.

13 For whosoever shall call upon the name of the Lord shall be saved.

14 How then shall they call on him in whom they have not believed? and how shall they believe in him of whom they have not heard? and how shall they hear without a preacher?

15 And how shall they preach, except they be sent? as it is written, How beautiful are the feet of them that preach the gospel of peace, and bring glad tidings of good things! [Romans 10:13–15]

Thus, Latter-day Saints are commissioned to "testify and warn the people, and it becometh every man who hath been warned to warn his neighbor" (D&C 88:80–81). Those who are peacemakers will be called the children of God because they will have been born of God through the baptism of fire and the Holy Ghost. They shall be and have "become his sons and daughters," or have been spiritually begotten or adopted as Christ's children (Mosiah 5:7). Having taken upon themselves his name, they will testify of him as the only "name given whereby salvation cometh" (Mosiah 5:8). Peter bore the same testimony. "Neither is there salvation in any other: for there is none other name under heaven given among men, whereby we must be saved" (Acts 4:12). Those who so live and testify are the blessed peacemakers.

The eighth and ninth beatitudes both concern persecution and are often linked together, as mentioned above. Although the persecution and the promised blessings overlap, there are two kinds of persecution. The first is being "persecuted for my name's sake" or for "righteousness' sake" as stated in the Matthew account.

Blessed are they which are persecuted for righteousness' sake: for theirs is the kingdom of heaven. (Matthew 5:10)	And blessed are all they who are persecuted for my name's sake, for theirs is the kingdom of heaven. (3 Nephi 12:10)

When people enter the waters of baptism, they should be "willing to take upon them the name of Jesus Christ" (D&C 20:37), and thus "come into the fold of God," or family, and are "called his people" (Mosiah 18:8). Many who are thus baptized are persecuted because of their membership in Christ's true Church. They may be disowned by family, fired from their employment, ostracized by their friends, or ridiculed for being willing to take Christ's name. This is external persecution brought upon Christ's followers from the world. The persecuted must remember, however, that they are potential members of the kingdom of heaven, and if they endure these worldly persecutions, they will be blessed both here and in eternity for so doing.

The Prophet Joseph Smith gave this timely admonition to the persecuted Saints:

> The enemies of this people will never get weary of their persecution against the Church, until they are overcome. I expect they will array every thing against me that is in their power to control, and that we shall have a long and tremendous warfare. He that will war the true Christian warfare against the corruptions of these last days will have wicked men and angels of devils, and all the infernal powers of darkness continually arrayed against him. When wicked and corrupt men oppose, it is a criterion to judge if a man is warring the Christian warfare. When all men speak evil of you falsely, blessed are ye. Shall a man be considered bad, when men speak evil of him? No. If a man stands and opposes the world of sin, he may expect to have all wicked and corrupt spirits arrayed

against him. But it will be but a little season, and all these afflictions will be turned away from us, inasmuch as we are faithful, and are not overcome by these evils. By seeing the blessings of the endowment rolling on, and the kingdom increasing and spreading from sea to sea, we shall rejoice that we were not overcome by these foolish things. [TPJS, 259]

The second kind of persecution is basically internal in regards to the Church. This persecution comes from professed members of the earthly kingdom of God.

> 11 And blessed are ye when men shall revile you and persecute, and shall say all manner of evil against you falsely, for my sake; [3 Nephi 12:11]

The Matthew account has "you" following "persecute," a difference not affecting the meaning. "For my sake" implies criticism for doing the work of the Church, or the kingdom. The first persecution was for taking Christ's name; the second persecution is for carrying out his assignments. It is "the persecution of your brethren, who humble themselves and do walk after the holy order of God, wherewith they have been brought into this church, having been sanctified by the Holy Spirit, and they do bring forth works which are meet for repentance" (Alma 5:54). These revilings are often spawned by jealousies, rationalizations, or self-justifications for one's own failures. The internal ridicule is more difficult to withstand than the external. As the Prophet Joseph Smith said:

> My life is more in danger from some little dough-head of a fool in this city than from all my numerous and inveterate enemies abroad. I am exposed to far greater danger from traitors among ourselves than from enemies without, although my life has been sought for many years by the civil and military authorities, priests, and people of Missouri; and if I can escape from the ungrateful treachery of assassins, I can live as Caesar might have lived, were it not for a right-hand Brutus. I have had pretended friends betray me. [HC 6:152]

The Savior said, probably referring to both types, that such persecution would result in great joy and bring exceeding gladness and great reward in heaven.

Rejoice, and be exceeding glad: for great is your reward in heaven: for so persecuted they the prophets which were before you. (Matthew 5:12)	For ye shall have great joy and be exceeding glad, for great shall be your reward in heaven; for so persecuted they the prophets who were before you. (3 Nephi 12:12)

This joy and gladness is an inner peace or self-satisfaction, "or an actual knowledge that the course of life which one is pursuing is according to [Christ's] will" (Lectures on Faith, 3:5). It is the reward of "even peace in this world, and eternal life in the world to come" (D&C 59:23). As some consolation, the Savior added, "For so persecuted they the prophets who were before you." The scriptures are full of accounts of the prophets being persecuted (e.g., Jeremiah 20). If the prophets were persecuted for their work, it is comforting to know that, when persecuted, we are experiencing what such good men had endured. Said the Prophet Joseph:

> Now, dear brethren, if any men ever had reason to claim this promise, we are the men; for we know that the world not only hate us, but they speak all manner of evil of us falsely, for no other reason than that we have been endeavoring to teach the fullness of the Gospel of Jesus Christ. [TPJS, 124]

There will always be opposition to the work of God. "The devil always sets up his kingdom at the very same time in opposition to God" (TPJS, 365). When that opposition ceases, we are probably not doing his will. It is easier to endure persecution when we know we are right.

The nine beatitudes were given as the higher law of Christ to build upon the rock of the doctrine of Christ. They were given in their fullest sense to the baptized members of the Church of Jesus Christ in any dispensation. They represent the commandments to be lived to gain eternal life. They can be summarized into two commandments.

The Two Great Commandments

When Jesus was asked, "Master, which is the great commandment in the law? Jesus said unto him, Thou shalt love the Lord thy God with all thy heart, and with all thy soul, and with all thy mind. This is the first and great commandment. And the second is like unto it, Thou shalt love thy neighbour as thyself. On these two commandments hang all the law and the prophets" (Matthew 22:36–40). The nine beatitudes can be categorized into these two commandments. The first four beatitudes are ways we should show our love for the Lord our God. When we turn to the Lord with all our heart, we turn our spirit to his Spirit. For the Hebrews, the heart was synonymous with the Spirit. All things "are revealed to our spirits precisely as though we had no bodies at all; and those revelations that will save our spirits will save our bodies" (TPJS, 355). Therefore, "blessed are the poor in spirit who come unto me" (3 Nephi 12:3).

When we mourn over our sins, we are involved physically. We turn to the Lord with our might. The meek are the teachable. They are taught through their mind, and the Spirit "will tell you in your mind and in your heart" (D&C 8:2–3). Those who hunger and thirst seek to obtain strength from food and drink. Those who hunger and thirst after righteousness seek spiritual strength; therefore, they turn to the Lord for strength. The first four beatitudes instruct us to love God by turning to him with all of our heart, might, mind, and strength.

Love God	Beatitudes	Promised Blessings
Heart—spirit	Poor in Spirit—come unto me	Kingdom of Heaven—Celestial
Might—physical	Mourn—over our sins	Comforted—sins forgiven
Mind—wisdom	Meek—teachable	Inherit the Earth
Strength—spiritual	Hunger and thirst after righteousness	Filled with the Holy Ghost

The second great commandment was like unto the first, to love thy neighbor as thyself. It is the second commandment because a person cannot know how to love his neighbor unless he or she first knows how to love God. Through loving God, he will be shown how to love his neighbor. Loving a neighbor includes acting towards them in compliance with God's laws. Our love towards our neighbors will be measured by our interactions with them. Alma told Zeezrom that "our words will condemn us, yea, all our works will condemn us . . . and our thoughts will also condemn us" (Alma 12:14). King Benjamin admonished his subjects to "watch yourselves, and your thoughts, and your words, and your deeds" (Mosiah 4:30). All three of these areas are covered in the beatitudes that follow.

The fifth beatitude, "blessed are the merciful," relates to our deeds; our actions towards our fellowmen, and our works in the Church in serving our fellowmen. "When ye are in the service of your fellow beings ye are only in the service of your God" (Mosiah 2:17). The sixth beatitude, "blessed are the pure in heart," is concerning our thoughts and our attitudes, or how we judge others from within our hearts. "With what judgment ye judge, ye shall be judged" (3 Nephi 14:2; Matthew 7:2). While we all must make judgments, we must "Judge not according to the appearance, but judge righteous judgment. (John 7:24). "The way to judge . . . is [by] the light of Christ" (Moroni 7:16–19). The seventh beatitude, "blessed are the peacemakers," addresses our words, those words we share with our neighbors in endeavoring to teach them the gospel. "It becometh every man who hath been warned to warn his neighbor" (D&C 84:81). Jesus chastised the Pharisees with these words:

> 34 O generation of vipers, how can ye, being evil, speak good things? for out of the abundance of the heart the mouth speaketh.
>
> 35 A good man out of the good treasure of the heart bringeth forth good things: and an evil man out of the evil treasure bringeth forth evil things.
>
> 36 But I say unto you, That every idle word that men shall speak, they shall give account thereof in the day of judgment.
>
> 37 For by thy words thou shalt be justified, and by thy words thou shalt be condemned. [Matthew 12:34–37]

Love Neighbor	Beatitudes	Promised Bless-ings
Deeds or Works	Merciful	Mercy of Christ
Thoughts and Atti-tudes	Pure in Heart	See God
Words	Peacemakers	Children of God

Thus, these three beatitudes help us to love our neighbors as we should.

But who is my neighbor? This question prompted the Savior to give the Parable of the Good Samaritan.

30 And Jesus answering said, A certain man went down from Jerusalem to Jericho, and fell among thieves, which stripped him of his raiment, and wounded him, and departed, leaving him half dead.

31 And by chance there came down a certain priest that way: and when he saw him, he passed by on the other side.

32 And likewise a Levite, when he was at the place, came and looked on him, and passed by on the other side.

33 But a certain Samaritan, as he journeyed, came where he was: and when he saw him, he had compassion on him,

34 And went to him, and bound up his wounds, pouring in oil and wine, and set him on his own beast, and brought him to an inn, and took care of him.

35 And on the morrow when he departed, he took out two pence, and gave them to the host, and said unto him, Take care of him; and whatsoever thou spendest more, when I come again, I will repay thee.

36 Which now of these three, thinkest thou, was neighbour unto him that fell among the thieves?

37 And he said, He that shewed mercy on him. Then said Jesus unto him, Go, and do thou likewise. [Luke 10:30–37]

"The Jews [had] no dealings with the Samaritans" (John 4:9). The priest and the Levite were the priesthood holders, and responsible to care for those in need. The message of the parable was essentially that every one of God's children is our neighbor, and we must love them as we would ourselves. Therefore, those who would persecute us, whether externally from outside the Church, or internally from within the Church membership, are our neighbors, and we should love them as God would love them. We must act for their good as God directs us, and not react to their actions. This is the law and the prophets, "all things whatsoever ye would that men should do to you, do ye even so to them" (3 Nephi 14:12).

Love Enemies	Beatitudes	Promised Blessings
External Persecution	For my name's sake (for Church Membership)	Kingdom of Heaven
Internal Persecution	For Christ's sake (for works within the Church)	Reward in Heaven

As we love our neighbors, we will gain a greater appreciation for God and will love him more. As we love him more, we will have a greater depth of love for our neighbors. We will be the benefactors from both loving God and loving our neighbor.

The Role of Church Members

Having given instructions to the multitude, Jesus drew some comparisons for them to consider. The first likened the members of the Church unto salt and said:

Ye are the salt of the earth: but if the salt have lost his savour, wherewith shall it be salted? it is thenceforth good for nothing, but to be cast out, and to be trodden under foot of men. (Matthew 5:13)

Verily, verily, I say unto you, I give unto you to be the salt of the earth; but if the salt shall lose its savor wherewith shall the earth be salted? The salt shall be thenceforth good for nothing, but to be cast out and to be trodden under foot of men. (3 Nephi 12:13)

The Nephite account shows that the baptized member has the potential to become the salt of the earth; it is not automatic as the Matthew account implies. Those who were baptized would have a similar function to the world as their use of salt had among them.

Salt has two basic uses, as a seasoning and as a preservative. Both uses are for food. In comparing salt to people, Jesus was saying that they were to season the world with his teachings. They were to take the gospel throughout the land as salt is sprinkled in food for flavor. The Lord used the same comparison with the Latter-day Saints: "When men are called unto mine everlasting gospel, and covenant with an everlasting covenant, they are accounted as the salt of the earth and *the savor of men*" (D&C 101:39; italics added). To savor is to add to, to improve the taste. Those who are members of the Church enter into "a new and an everlasting covenant" (D&C 22:1), and are thereby commissioned to spread the gospel to the world. Since most of the world to whom the gospel was taken first in this dispensation were already Christian, they were not to give them a totally new diet, but were to savor their belief in Christ and make it palatable for celestial living.

As a preservative, salt was used as a brine to enable food to be kept without spoiling (before refrigeration). In the gospel sense, he that believeth and was baptized would be saved from the spoils of the world. The Lord also used this analogy with the Latter-day Saints: "For they were set to be a light unto the world, and to be *the saviors of men*" (D&C 103:9; italics added). Through the performing of ordinances for those who accept the teachings of Jesus, the doors of salvation and even exaltation in the celestial kingdom are opened. Through the saving ordinances of the gospel, the world will be preserved and "not wasted at [Christ's] coming" (D&C 2:3). Through the ordinances for both the living and the dead, all the inhabitants of the earth will have the opportunity to be preserved from the spoiling effects of Satan and his followers.

Jesus attached a warning to his analogy: "If the salt shall lose its savor . . . the salt shall be thenceforth good for nothing, but to be cast out and to be trodden under foot of men" (v. 13). Salt does not decompose. However, it loses its usability when it is mixed with impurities such as dirt or other foreign elements. Therefore, the Savior is warning the people against their mixing foreign cultures, the philosophies of men, or the revelations of the devil with the doctrine of Christ. To do so loses the savor of the gospel. The Lord attached this same warning to both of the revelations to the Latter-day Saints concerning their being salt (D&C 101:40; 103:10 quoted above). If the gospel is perverted, or the ordinances are changed or performed without authority, the savoring influence of the gospel and saving ordinances of the gospel are no more efficacious. As salt was cast out and used in Jesus' day for rooftops or walkways when it had lost its savor, those members of the Church who perverted the gospel were to be cast out into the worldly element with which they had mixed.

The second comparison that Jesus likened the people unto was a light.

Ye are the light of the world. A city that is set on a hill cannot be hid. Neither do men light a candle and put in under a bushel, but on a candlestick; and it giveth light unto all that are in the house. Let your light so shine before men, that they may see your good works, and glorify your Father which is in heaven. (Matthew 5:14–16)	Verily, verily, I say unto you, *I give unto you to be the light of this people.* A city that is set on a hill cannot be hid. Behold, do men light a candle and put it under a bushel? Nay, but on a candlestick, and it giveth light to all that are in the house; Therefore let your light so shine before this people, that they may see your good works and glorify your Father who is in heaven. (3 Nephi 12:14–16; italics added)

To glorify the Father we must do his work. The work and glory of the Father and of Christ is "to bring to pass the immortality and the eternal life of man" (Moses 1:39). We must do "the works which ye have seen me do," or be the "manner of [man]" that Christ was while he was upon the earth (3 Nephi 27:21, 27). Example is the best teacher. Jesus had set the example for the disciples to follow in Jerusalem. He was "the way, the truth, and the life: no man cometh unto the Father, but by me" (John 14:6). He also gave that same example to the Nephites. He was "the light which ye shall hold up—that which ye have seen me do" (3 Nephi 18:24). He had set the example, "the way"; he had taught them his gospel, "the truth"; and he had given them the authority to perform the saving ordinances, "the life."

The higher law of Christ was now revealed. He had previously established the foundation of his Church by teaching the twelve disciples his doctrine, and made them special witnesses of his divinity as the chief cornerstone (3 Nephi 11). The multitude of about twenty-five hundred people had been given the opportunity to build upon the foundation, and upon the testimony the twelve had been given. They had also been instructed to share it with others throughout the land (3 Nephi 12:1–16). They were now ready to be instructed concerning the law and the prophets.

Chapter 6

The Law and the Prophets Fulfilled

3 Nephi 12:17–13:24

The higher law of the gospel of Jesus Christ was revealed to Adam.[1] It was taught and lived through various dispensations from Adam's day until a lesser law was given through Moses. Paul verifies that God "preached before the gospel unto Abraham" (Galatians 3:8), that "the law was our schoolmaster to bring us [back] unto Christ" (Galatians 3:24), and that "as many of you as have been baptized into Christ have put on Christ . . . then are ye Abraham's seed, and heirs according to the promise" (Galatians 3:27,29). The Nephites had previously come to Christ through baptism:

> 24 And, notwithstanding we believe in Christ, we keep the law of Moses, and look forward with steadfastness unto Christ, until the law shall be fulfilled.
>
> 25 For, for this end was the law given; wherefore the law hath become dead unto us, and we are made alive in Christ because of our faith; yet we keep the law because of the commandments. [2 Nephi 25:24–25]

---

[1] 58 And thus the Gospel began to be preached, from the beginning, being declared by holy angels sent forth from the presence of God, and by his own voice, and by the gift of the Holy Ghost.

59 And thus all things were confirmed unto Adam, by an holy ordinance, and the Gospel preached, and a decree sent forth, that it should be in the world, until the end thereof; and thus it was. Amen. (Moses 5:58–59)

However, they kept only "those outward performances [of the law] until the time that he should be revealed unto them" (Alma 25:15). Nephi, son of Helaman, testified "that even since the days of Abraham there have been many prophets, that have testified [of] these things" (Helaman 8:19). After his resurrection, Jesus walked with two disciples, "And beginning at Moses and all the prophets, he expounded unto them in all the scriptures the things concerning himself" (Luke 24:27).

When Jesus came to the Nephites, he clarified for them the role of both the law of Moses and the prophets. An outline of the part of the sermon discussed in this chapter follows as an overview to prepare for a deeper analysis of the text.

Outline • 3 Nephi 12:17–13:24

➤ 12:17–48   Christ does not come to destroy the law or the prophets, but to fulfill.

     a. Every jot or tittle of the law has been fulfilled in Christ. v. 18

     b. Christ has given them the higher law of the Father, to come unto him. vv. 19–20

         1. The commandments are before you, come unto me and be saved.

         2. Except you keep the commandments you cannot inherit the kingdom of heaven.

     c. Six comparisons of the law of Moses and the higher law are given. vv. 21–45

         1. Not kill and anger.

         2. Adultery and no lust.

         3. Bill of divorce, and fornication only cause.

         4. Oaths and communication.

         5. An eye for an eye, and not resist evil.

         6. Love your neighbor and hate your enemies, and love your enemies.

    d. Things under the old law (of Moses) are fulfilled, and the higher law is new. vv. 46–47

    e. Be perfected by the higher law as your Father in Heaven and Christ are perfected. v. 48

➤ 13:1–18   Guidelines for giving alms to the poor, praying, and fasting.

    a. Alms are not to be done to be seen of men, or you have your reward. vv. 1–2

        1. Those who sound a trumpet to get the glory of men have their reward.

        2. Let thine alms be done in secret.

        3. Thy Father who sees in secret will reward thee openly.

    b. Do not pray as the hypocrites in the synagogue and on the street corners to be seen of men. vv. 5–15

        1. They have their reward.

        2. Enter thy closet, close the door, and pray to thy Father in secret.

        3. Thy Father shall reward thee openly.

        4. Use not vain repetitions as the heathen, thinking of being heard for much speaking.

        5. The Father knows what you need before you ask.

        6. After this manner pray, (the so-called Lord's Prayer).

        7. If you forgive men their trespasses, your Father will forgive you your trespasses.

    c. Do not fast as the hypocrites, with sad countenances, to appear unto men to fast. vv. 16–18

        1. They have their reward.

        2. Anoint your head, and wash your face, that you not appear to be fasting.

        3. Thy father, who seeth in secret, shall reward thee openly.

➤ 13:19–21   Lay not up treasures on earth, but lay up treasures in heaven.

    a. Moth and rust corrupt earthly treasures, and thieves break through and steal. v. 19

    b. Moth and rust do not corrupt heavenly treasures, and thieves cannot steal. v. 20

    c. Where your treasure is, your heart is also. v. 21

➢ 13:22–23 The light of the body is the eye.

    a. If the eye is single (to the glory of God), the whole body shall be full of light. v. 22

    b. If the eye is evil, the whole body shall be full of darkness. v. 23

    c. How great is that darkness. v. 23

➢ 13:24 You cannot serve two masters, God and mammon.

    a. You will hate one and love the other.

    b. You will hold to one and despise the other.

NOTES AND COMMENTARY

17 Think not that I am come to destroy the law or the prophets. I am not come to destroy but to fulfil; [3 Nephi 12:17]

The Matthew account (5:17) is identical to Third Nephi. The law of Moses was a good law, "it was added because of transgression" (Galatians 3:19). Joseph Smith declared; "It must be plain that it was added to the gospel, since we learn that they had the gospel preached to them" (TPJS, 60). However, when Jesus visited the Nephites, it had been fulfilled, every jot and tittle. The meaning of the phrase "every jot and tittle" is significant. The jot is what is presently referred to as the yod, the smallest letter of the Hebrew alphabet. The tittle was a part of various Hebrew letters of the alphabet. It was an extension of a line that differentiated between two letters such as the Hebrew bet and the koph, or the dalet and the rosh. Thus, Jesus was saying that every letter of the law, including the smallest and even the smallest part of every letter, had now been fulfilled. The Nephite people were now prepared to be taught the higher law of Christ.

Jesus gave the Nephites some instructions that are not presently included in the biblical account, although perhaps they were originally. He was giving a new law by commandment of the Father. This was to replace the law of Moses:

And behold, I have given you the law and the commandments of my Father, that ye shall believe in me, and that ye shall repent of your sins, and come unto me with a broken heart and a contrite spirit. Behold, ye have the commandments before you, and the law is fulfilled.	Whosoever therefore shall break one of these least commandments, and shall teach men so, he shall be called the least in the kingdom of heaven: but whosoever shall do and teach *them*, the same shall be called great in the kingdom of heaven.
Therefore, come unto me and be saved; for verily I say unto you, that except ye shall keep my commandments, which I have commanded you at this time, ye shall in no case enter into the kingdom of heaven. (3 Nephi 12:19–20)	For I say unto you, That except your righteousness shall exceed *the righteousness* of the scribes and Pharisees, ye shall in no case enter into the kingdom of heaven. (Matthew 5:19–20)

The commandments they were given were to prepare them to accept the ordinance of baptism. This was necessary to bring them salvation. From this point on they were to keep the commandments that he had and would give them, or they would not enter the kingdom of heaven.

Although the prophets had foretold of Christ's coming, and these prophecies had been fulfilled, they knew of his bringing a higher law. To make sure that the people understood the higher law, he contrasted his teachings with those of the law of Moses, and of other teachings and traditions. This comparison illustrated the superiority of the higher law. While the law of Moses was a good law, "salvation doth not come by the law alone" (Mosiah 13:27–28). It was a terrestrial law. The higher law of Christ was a celestial law, one that would bring salvation. The law of Moses was designed to produce honorable people of the earth in preparation for a higher law, but until that higher law was given they would "receive of his [terrestrial] glory, but not of his fullness" (D&C 76:76). When Christ visited the Nephites, the telestial-type people had been destroyed, leaving those "who received the prophets" (celestial), and those honorable people (terrestrial) "who had not shed the blood of the saints" (3 Nephi 10:12), even though they had not accepted the prophet's message. This was not the case in Palestine. The Sermon on the Mount was given early in his mortal ministry. There were all classes of people who listened to him as he went about all Galilee "preaching the gospel of the (celestial) kingdom" (Matthew 4:23). Although the Nephites did not at this time have telestial people among them, nor did Jesus make mention of them in Galilee, this analysis will include the contrast of telestial and terrestrial-type living with the higher law of Christ in order that the higher law may be even more appreciated.

The first law that Jesus compared was the sixth of the Ten Commandments, "Thou shalt not kill" (Exodus 20:13; Mosiah 13:21).

Ye have heard that it hath been said by them of old time, and it is also written before you, that thou shalt not kill, and whosoever shall kill shall be in danger of the judgment of God; But I say unto you that whosoever is angry with his brother shall be in danger of his judgment. And whosoever shall say to his brother, Raca, shall be in danger of the council; and whosoever shall say, Thou fool, shall be in danger of hell fire (3 Nephi 12:21–22).	Ye have heard that it was said by those of old time, Thou shalt not kill; and whosoever shall kill shall be in danger of judgment. By I say unto you, that whosoever is angry with his brother without a cause shall be in danger of the judgment: and whosoever shall say to his brother, Raca, shall be in danger of the council: but whosoever shall say, Thou fool, shall be in danger of hell fire (Matthew 5:21–22).

Although to "not kill" was to be lived under the law of Moses, and was "written" before them, it was also a part of the higher law that was lived before the law was given; thus "it hath been said by them of old time." It is always a part of the law of God. Noah was told: "whosoever sheddeth man's blood, by man shall his blood be shed" (Genesis 9:6). It was revealed to the Church in this dispensation: "Thou shalt not kill; and he that kills shall not have forgiveness in this world, nor in the world to come" (D&C 42:18). The telestial law was the survival of the fittest, to kill or be killed. Nevertheless, if a person only restrains himself from killing, he is only living on a terrestrial level. The higher law of Christ was to not be angry with a brother (v. 22). Under the lesser laws, violators would be "in danger of the judgments of God" (v. 21). Under the higher law, the violator was subjected to several types of judgment.

Regarding being angry with a brother, the New Testament account contains the phrase, "without a cause," but it is not in the Book of Mormon. The phrase was apparently added by someone through the years in an attempt to make it more reasonable. However, everyone who is angered has a cause. It may not be justified, or a good cause, but they have a cause. Regardless, we should deal with our fellow beings in a rational manner, and if we don't, that person will judge our actions in his or her life, and will also stand as a witness of our actions in the life to come.

But there was a second judgment. For calling a brother Raca, one could be called before the council (v. 22). The term Raca has no direct translation, but is probably the equivalent of labeling someone as an imbecile, a thief, or other slandering title. The council has reference to a Disciplinary Council of the Church. The charge would be for unchristian-like conduct. As brothers and sisters in the gospel, we should be able and willing to settle our differences in a calm and rational manner.

There was also a third judgment pronounced by the Savior. Those who called someone "Thou fool," would be in danger of hell fire (v. 22). The capitalization of the word Thou may suggest that Deity is being profaned. Regardless, the judgment is from God, since the punishment may be hell fire. We are all God's children, and he will judge us. We must leave judgment up to him, and not take it upon ourselves to curse or give derogatory designations to others.

Based upon these three possible judgments, the Lord counseled:

Therefore, if ye shall come unto me, or shall desire to come unto me, and rememberest that thy brother hath aught against thee—	Therefore if thou bring thy gift to the alter, and there rememberest that they brother hath ought against thee;
Go thy way unto thy brother, and first be reconciled to thy brother, and then come unto me with full purpose of heart, and I will receive you.	Leave there thy gift before the alter, and go thy way; first be reconciled to thy brother, and then come and offer thy gift.
Agree with thine adversary quickly while thou art in the way with him, lest at any time he shall get thee, and thou shalt be cast into prison. (3 Nephi 12:23–25)	Agree with thine adversary quickly, whiles thou art in the way with him; lest at any time the adversary deliver thee to the judge, and the judge deliver thee to the officer, and thou be cast into prison. (Matthew 5:23–25)

This strict and seemingly one-sided counsel requires some explanation. To come unto Christ would be to come to the sacrament service to renew our baptismal covenants. In the New Testament, the instructions were concerning the bringing of a gift to the altar, a sacrifice of a type and shadow of Christ and, thus, were for a similar purpose. To remember that our brother has aught against us presupposes that we do not have aught against him. We should already have solved that difference, but if we know he has ill feelings toward us, we should endeavor to resolve those differences before our coming unto Christ. If we don't, our coming unto Christ is not acceptable.

To "agree with thine adversary quickly" does not suggest that we must immediately submit to whatever the brother desires. The word reconcile in the previous verse suggests otherwise. It gives us an opportunity to explain our position, and if we have unknowingly offended, to apologize and make things right. If we have been falsely accused or misunderstood, we can clear up those errors. Perhaps the other party is not willing to make reconciliation. Are we not to partake of the sacrament? Of course we may. The responsibility is then shifted to the other party, and our desires will be acceptable to the Lord. However, if we fail to take the initiative, we will be accountable to him and to the Lord. Failure to do so may result in our spiritual impairment in this life, or in our serving time in the spirit prison. Having rejected the counsel of Jesus Christ, we will have to suffer for our own sins rather than have them paid for through the Atonement. "I, God, have suffered these things for all, that they might not suffer if they would repent; But if they would not repent they must suffer even as I" (D&C 19:16–18):

Verily, verily I say unto thee, thou shalt by no means come out thence until thou hast paid the uttermost senine. And while ye are in prison can ye pay even one senine? Verily, verily, I say unto you, Nay. (3 Nephi 12:26)	Verily I say unto thee, Thou shalt by no means come out thence, till thou hast paid the uttermost farthing. (Matthew 5:26)

The celestial way of handling anger-producing situations may sound difficult and against our human nature, but it is the way to eternal happiness.

The seventh of the ten commandments, "thou shalt not commit adultery," was the second comparison made by Jesus.

Behold, it is written by them of old time, that thou shalt not commit adultery; But I say unto you, that whosoever looketh on a woman, to lust after her, hath committed adultery already in his heart. (3 Nephi 12:27–28)	Ye have heard that it was said by them of old time, Thou shalt not commit adultery: But I say unto you, That whosoever looketh on a woman and lust after her hath committed adultery with her already in his heart. (Matthew 5:27–28)

Again, the law was "written by them of old time," showing it preceded the law of Moses. "Thou shalt not commit adultery; and he that committeth adultery and repenteth not, shall be cast out" is the law to the Church in this dispensation, showing that it is an eternal law (D&C 42:24). But there is a higher law. Mere abstinence is honorable, but is only a terrestrial law. By comparison, the telestial law is really to have no law, or the law of animals in which sexual gratification is sought. Christ said "that whosoever looketh on a

woman, to lust after her, hath committed adultery already in his heart"
(v. 28). The Book of Mormon does not contain the biblical
"committeth adultery *with her*" (Matthew 5:27–28; italics added). As
worded there, it may imply guilt on the part of the woman, who is
looked upon with lust, which of course is not correct.

> 29 Behold, I give unto you a commandment, that ye suffer none of
> these things to enter into your heart;
>
> 30 For it is better that ye should deny yourselves of these things,
> wherein ye will take up your cross, than that ye should be cast into hell.
> [3 Nephi 12:29–30]

Committing adultery in one's heart takes the sin from the physical
act to the thinking or mental area. This is typical of the higher law.
We must control our thoughts as well as our actions. Of course there
is a difference between lust and admiration. While it is only natural
to observe and recognize beauty, to lust is to physically crave, and is
of the carnal mind, inspired of the devil. While such thoughts may
come unbidden, they must not be entertained. Thus Christ commanded that we "suffer [allow] none of these things to enter into your
heart" (v. 29), even though they may come into our mind. The
celestial person seeks the Spirit of the Lord to keep his thoughts
wholesome. Those who do not deny the lustful desires permit
themselves to be led into hell. If we "take up [the] cross" of Christ
(v. 30), we will occupy our minds with good things.

The above instructions to the Nephites, on avoiding immoral
thoughts and actions, differs with the admonition to the Galilean
multitude.

> 29 And if thy right eye offend thee, pluck it out, and cast it from thee:
> for it is profitable for thee that one of thy members should perish, and not
> that thy whole body should be cast into hell.
>
> 30 And if thy right hand offend thee, cut it off, and cast it from thee:
> for it is profitable for thee that one of thy members should perish, and not
> that thy whole body should be cast into hell. [Matthew 5:29–30]

The right eye or the right hand plucked out, or cut off, may have had reference to an eastern custom that still exists in isolated areas, to sever one's hand if caught stealing or guilty of similar offenses. However, JST Matthew labels the teachings as a parable. "And now this I speak, a parable concerning your sins; wherefore, cast them from you, that ye may not be hewn down and cast into the fire" (5:34). The Savior's higher law, in this case was not to be taken literally, but was emphasizing that our work should be done "with an eye must be single to the glory of God;" (D&C 4:5; see also 27:2; 55:1; 59:1), the same context as Jesus' instructions to "take up your cross" (v. 30). Such commitment will lead to our own glorification. Disregard of the warning leads to being cast into hell.

The law of Moses allowed a man who "found some uncleanness in [his wife]: then let him write her a bill of divorcement" (Deuteronomy 24:1). Jesus taught:

It hath been written, that whosoever shall put away his wife, let him give her a writing of divorcement. Verily, verily, I say unto you, that whosoever shall put away his wife, saving for the cause of fornication, causeth her to commit adultery; and whose shall marry her who is divorced committeth adultery. (3 Nephi 12:31-32)	It hat been said, Whosoever shall put away his wife, let him give her a writing of divorcement: But I say unto you, That whosoever shall put away his wife, saving for the cause of fornication, causeth her to commit adultery: and whosoever shall marry her that is divorced committeth adultery. (Matthew 5:31–32)

Jesus, in the higher law, removed the law of divorce except for "the cause of fornication" (v. 32). His instructions regarding divorce are difficult to understand and often misinterpreted. The usual interpretation is that adultery is the only grounds for divorce. This is not what the text states. The text says fornication is the only allowable cause for divorce. Adultery and fornication are related sins, but there is a difference. Adultery is usually defined as extramarital sexual relations, and fornication as premarital. Some, therefore, interpret Jesus' teachings regarding fornication as premarital sexual relations by one of the parties as the grounds for divorce. This does not have scriptural support. An analysis of the scriptures reveals that the law of divorce also relates to the heart rather than just the physical sexual act. This requires some explanation.

Jeremiah chastised the Jewish people for not learning from the poor example of her sister nation, Northern Israel. The Lord had followed the Mosaic law "whereby backsliding Israel committed adultery I had put her away, and given her a bill of divorce;" because she had "gone up upon every high mountain and under every green tree, and there hath played the harlot" or worshipped Baal, the pagan god. Later, Judah "went and played the harlot also" (Jeremiah 3:6–9). Both of the nations of Israel had sinned because the house of Israel (all twelve tribes) was symbolically married to Christ by covenant. "For thy Maker is thine husband; the Lord of hosts is his name; and thy Redeemer the Holy One of Israel" (Isaiah 54:5). Through Israel's worship of Baal they had an affair, or committed adultery with another god, rather than worship or keep their covenant with Israel's symbolic husband, Christ. This sin was adultery, not fornication.

Scripturally, fornication was the prophesied sin of Babylon at the time John "saw another angel fly in the midst of heaven, having the everlasting gospel to preach unto them that dwell on the earth, and to every nation, and kindred, and tongue, and people." Another angel followed "saying, Babylon is fallen . . . because she made all nations drink of the wine of the wrath of her fornication" (Revelation 14:6,8). Who is Babylon and what is her fornication? Babylon represents the wickedness of the world or spiritual Babylon. Modern day revelation commands Israel to "Go ye out from among the nations, even from Babylon, from the midst of wickedness, which is spiritual Babylon" (D&C 133:14). Her fornication with all nations seems to be the deception of introducing pagan practices and beliefs into the true religion. It is the corruption of the Church through its incorporation into the political systems, or in the ultimate extreme, the making of state religions. As apostate Christianity spread throughout the Gentile nations of the world, it was infiltrated with pagan ritual and philosophies. These nations, thereby, commit fornication by pretending to worship the true God while having ulterior motives for power and control. They "draw near unto me [Christ] with their mouth, and with their lips do honor me, but have removed their hearts far from me, and their fear towards me is taught by the precepts of men" (2 Nephi 27:25; quoting Isaiah 29:13). Therefore, their love for Christ is a pretended or false love.

Examples of this definition of fornication from the past include the introduction of pagan practices under Jehoran, king of Judah, into the true religion, which "caused the inhabitants of Jerusalem to commit fornication, and compelled Judah thereto" (2 Chronicles 21:11). Paul accuses Esau of committing fornication by selling his birthright "for one morsel of meat" (Hebrews 12:16). He was giving up spiritual things for the satisfaction of the physical desires. Such is the description of fornication in the scriptures.

Under the higher law of Christ, then, the allowable divorce is for the apostasy of one's marriage partner. It is, in the words of Elder Bruce R. McConkie, "in a spiritual sense, infidelity to and a forsaking of the true God for false gods."[2] The Savior said, "whosoever shall put away his wife, saving for the cause of fornication, causeth her to commit adultery; and whoso shall marry her who is divorced committeth adultery (v. 32). This is hard doctrine, but if the higher law were fully lived, this would be followed. However, the Lord has allowed lesser laws to be followed: to the Jews he declared, "Moses because of the hardness of your hearts suffered you to put away your wives: but from the beginning it was not so" (Matthew 19:7–9). A similar situation seems to be in effect in our time.

Today we live in a corrupt society where divorce is prevalent. In Jesus' day, the law of Moses had been watered down to where divorce was granted for almost any reason. Our society has become even

---

[2] Bruce R. McConkie, *Mormon Doctrine,* 2nd ed. (Salt Lake City: Bookcraft, 1966), 298.

worse. The telestial law of "free love" is advocated and lived. The Lord has again allowed a more lenient policy to the membership of his Church because of the effect of this environment, the Gentile culture, upon innocent or repentant individuals. The Church does not consider one to be living in adultery when the laws of the land have been conformed with, especially when one partner has become the victim of the other partner's apostasy. However, the higher law has not changed. Individually, we are expected to live according to the knowledge that has been revealed to us.

The fourth comparison made by Jesus was in regards to the making of oaths:

> 33 And again it is written, thou shalt not forswear thyself, but shalt perform unto the Lord thine oaths;
>
> 34 But verily, verily, I say unto you, swear not at all; neither by heaven, for it is God's throne;
>
> 35 Nor by the earth, for it is his footstool;
>
> 36 Neither shalt thou swear by thy head, because thou canst not make one hair black or white;
>
> 37 But let your communication be Yea, yea; Nay, nay; for whatsoever cometh of more than these is evil. [3 Nephi 12:33–37]

The Matthew account is not written above because the variation between the two accounts seems insignificant. The principle here is the people's involvement of the Lord in their communication. This is not dealing with profanity, but with one's verbal or written agreements. To forswear means to perjure or falsify. The taking of an oath was a binding commitment among the house of Israel, and thus also among the Nephites. An oath unto the Lord was a solid commitment. Nephi "spake unto [Zoram], even with an oath, that he need not fear; that he should be a free man." Zoram "also made an oath with us that he should tarry with us from that time forth" (1 Nephi 4:31–35). Both complied with the law of Moses. An Israelite was instructed that it was better "that thou shouldest not vow, than that thou shouldest vow and not pay" (Ecclesiastes 5:5). The keeping of an oath was the mark of an honorable man, but a terrestrial man. Again, in Jesus' day, the oath had become desecrated. To swear by the temple meant nothing. To swear by the gold on the temple made compliance with the oath obligatory. To swear by the altar was nothing, but to swear by the gift on the altar, and not keep the oath brought condemnation. Jesus gave some of his severest criticism to such practices.

16 Woe unto you, ye blind guides, which say, Whosoever shall swear by the temple, it is nothing; but whosoever shall swear by the gold of the temple, he is a debtor!

17 Ye fools and blind: for whether is greater, the gold, or the temple that sanctifieth the gold?

18 And, Whosoever shall swear by the altar, it is nothing; but whosoever sweareth by the gift that is upon it, he is guilty.

19 Ye fools and blind: for whether is greater, the gift, or the altar that sanctifieth the gift?

20 Whoso therefore shall swear by the altar, sweareth by it, and by all things thereon.

21 And whoso shall swear by the temple, sweareth by it, and by him that dwelleth therein.

22 And he that shall swear by heaven, sweareth by the throne of God, and by him that sitteth thereon. [Matthew 23:16–22]

These were indeed telestial observances. Today our society has become similar. We sign contracts and then look for loopholes in the contract or the law. We commit ourselves in writing, and say that it means nothing for one reason or another. We indeed live in a telestial world.

Jesus instructed his people to swear not at all, or that oaths were not required, but to let their communication be" Yea, yea or Nay, nay." To make more than this commitment was considered evil or at least of a lesser or temporal law (vv. 12:34–37 above). These teachings were not directed to our use of adjectives or adverbs as descriptive language. He was teaching that "our word is our bond." We do not need to bind ourselves with an oath, but should do all in our power short of death, or impairment through sickness or accident, to fulfill that which we have verbally agreed or not agreed to do. Such is the nature of a celestial man.

Because of a correct understanding of some, there is in the laws of the land the constitutional right to affirm. This means that we do not have to swear upon a Bible or make other kinds of oaths that we will tell the truth, but that our lives affirm that we are men or women of integrity and our word is our bond. We must live to be impeccable, beyond reproach, so that our word will be so honored. However, because we live in a telestial world, we are not violating the gospel principles by swearing upon a Bible, signing contracts, and other forms of terrestrial laws. We have no control over our death or impairments, so we must enter into some agreements in writing or similar means to protect our families and associates in long-range commitments. The ideal, however, is to live as a celestial being and keep our verbal agreements as well as our written ones, and above all else, to not stoop to the telestial level of excusing ourselves through legalities or rationalizations.

The next comparison of the higher law and the law of Moses was concerning retaliation for injury or harm. The two accounts, Third Nephi and Matthew, are the same except for the introductions, which are the same as the previous comparisons, and so again only the Third Nephi account is quoted.

> 38 And behold, it is written, an eye for an eye, and a tooth for a tooth;
>
> 39 But I say unto you, that ye shall not resist evil, but whosoever shall smite thee on thy right cheek, turn to him the other also; [3 Nephi 12:38–39]

The law of Moses thus required an equal remuneration or penalty: "Breach for breach, eye for eye, tooth for tooth" (Leviticus 24:20). However, the more detailed instructions given by Moses allowed for compensations for the injury or harm under certain conditions. There were values placed on the losses of various body parts similar to our liability laws of today.[3] This represented justice, the honorable responsibility for one's conduct. Again, this is the terrestrial law.

The telestial law is one of revenge. The telestial-type reasoning is: if you accidentally or purposely put out my eye, I will put out both of your eyes. It is the supremacy of the macho man. It is the natural-man tendency to show that I am more powerful, or more intelligent, or more clever than you are.

The celestial law taught by Christ is one of mercy rather than justice or revenge. It is to not resist evil or to resist the ways of the world. All that is evil cometh from the devil and is the way of the world. All that is good is from God and less than this is evil. Therefore, if a man "smite thee on the right cheek, turn to him the other also (v. 39). This is often misunderstood. To properly understand, one must read Doctrine and Covenants 98:23–32 and some Book of Mormon passages. We are not obligated to suffer bodily harm and not defend ourselves. "The Lord has said that: Ye shall "defend your families [and ourselves] even unto bloodshed" in defense of "their homes and their liberties, their wives and their children, and their all, yea, for their rites of worship and their church" (Alma 43:45–47).

The smiting on the "right cheek" is significant in the analysis of this scripture. Since most people are right-handed, the scriptures often

---

[3] 18 And if men strive together, and one smite another with a stone, or with *his* fist, and he die not, but keepeth *his* bed:

19 If he rise again, and walk abroad upon his staff, then shall he that smote *him* be quit: only he shall pay *for* the loss of his time, and shall cause *him* to be thoroughly healed.

20 And if a man smite his servant, or his maid, with a rod, and he die under his hand; he shall be surely punished.

21 Notwithstanding, if he continue a day or two, he shall not be punished: for he *is* his money.

22 If men strive, and hurt a woman with child, so that her fruit depart *from her*, and yet no mischief follow: he shall be surely punished, according as the woman's husband will lay upon him; and he shall pay as the judges *determine*. (Exodus 21:18–22; see the following verses for other examples.)

use the prominent hand in examples. Even though it was a parable, Jesus referred to the "right eye offend thee" and the "right hand offend thee" when tempted to commit adultery (JST Matthew 5:32–34 discussed above). Therefore, it is assumed that being smitten on the right cheek would be by a right-handed person as he faces his assailant. The only way a right-handed person could smite another on the right cheek is with a back-handed slap, not a forceful thrust of the fist causing injury. The backhand will sting, but it will be more of an insult than injury. Therefore, the Savior is saying to swallow your pride and resist the natural reaction to retaliate, although if you do, "it shall be accounted unto you as being meted out as a just measure unto you" but you will receive no mercy from him (D&C 98:24). "Blessed are the merciful for they shall obtain mercy" (3 Nephi 12:7). Therefore, the turning of the other cheek does not suggest that we invite our assailant to hit us again, but that we are willing to overlook his worldly reaction and settle our differences in a more rational manner. It shows that we are trying to live according to a higher law than is he.

The following two examples given by Jesus, to sustain his teachings on retaliation, are identical in the Bible and the Book of Mormon. However, they were modified by the Prophet Joseph Smith in the JST.

And if any man will sue thee at the law and take away thy coat, let him have thy cloak also; And whosoever shall compel thee to go a mile, go with him twain. (3 Nephi 12:40–41)	And if any man will sue thee at the law, and take away thy coat, let him have it; and if he sue thee again, let him have thy cloak also. And whosoever shall compel thee to go a mile, go with him a mile; and whosoever shall compel thee to go with him twain, thou shalt go with him twain. (JST Matthew 5:42–43)

These changes indicate that we must do all in our power to meet the justice of the law of the land. If the law finds us guilty; "we believe in obeying, honoring, and sustaining the law" (Articles of Faith 1:12). We must always meet the full measure of justice.

Jesus concluded this section of his comparisons of the laws of retaliation by admonishing us again to be merciful. "Give to him that asketh thee, and from him that borrow of thee turn thou not away" (3 Nephi 12:42; Matthew 5:42 has no significant differences). Again, we must read more to get the full answers. We must help the poor "both spiritually, and temporally, according to their wants," and if we indiscriminately give, we may be harming him spiritually. We must make agreements on borrowing, or we may "commit sin and perhaps thou shalt cause thy neighbor to commit sin also." (Mosiah 4:26–28). In general, the higher law of Christ is to extend mercy, but there is to be a proper balance of justice and mercy.

The last of the series of comparisons of the laws, according to the Nephite record, was also based upon what was written. The Matthew account again says, "ye have heard that it hath been said" (Matthew 5:43).

> 43 And behold it is written also, that thou shalt love thy neighbor and hate thine enemy;
>
> 44 But behold I say unto you, love your enemies, bless them that curse you, do good to them that hate you, and pray for them who despitefully use you and persecute you;
>
> 45 That ye may be the children of your Father who is in heaven; for he maketh his sun to rise on the evil and on the good. [3 Nephi 12:43–45]

This quotation is not written in the present Old Testament. Perhaps he was quoting from the traditions or writings of the elders or priests, or perhaps this teaching was lost from the original text. If it was once in the Bible, it was probably to keep the Israelites from associating with the surrounding nations and their pagan worship. It was probably in the context of "abstain from all appearance of evil" (1 Thessalonians 5:22). It is normal and even honorable to show respect and love towards those with whom you associate, and to avoid or refrain from association with those who make your life miserable by wrongful acts or words. However, it is still a terrestrial law, not the celestial.

The telestial-type people trust no one and take advantage of everyone they can. They are deceitful and hypocritical. They are not honorable as are the terrestrial.

In teaching the higher law, Jesus commanded his followers to love their enemies (v. 44). The easiest way to eliminate your enemies is to make them your friends. The easiest way to make friends is to do "whatsoever ye would that men should do to you, do ye even so to them" (3 Nephi 14:12). To return good for evil, as suggested by Jesus, and to enlist the power of the Spirit to soften hearts through prayer, shows character, and attracts people as well as changes their hearts and attitudes toward you. President Joseph F. Smith gave some wise counsel regarding those who despitefully use us:

> Do you love these slanderers, these liars, these defamers, these persecutors of the innocent and of the unoffending—do you love them? [several voices, No, no.] I can scarcely blame you. But that is not according to the law of God. I want to tell you how I feel towards them. I love them so much that if I had it in my power to annihilate them from the earth I would not harm a hair of their heads—not one hair of their heads. I love them so well that if I could possibly make them better men, convert them from the error of their ways I would do it, God being my helper. I love them so much that I would not throw a straw in their way to prosperity and happiness, but so far as possible I would hedge up their headlong and downward course to destruction, and yet I detest and abominate their infamous actions and their wicked course. That is how I feel towards them, and that is how much I love them, and if this is not the love that Jesus desired us to have for our enemies, tell me what kind of love we should have for them? I do not love them so that I would take them into my bosom, or invite them to associate with my family, or that I would give my daughters to their embraces, nor my sons to their counsels. I do not love them so well that I would invite them to the councils of the Priesthood, and the ordinances of the House of God, to scoff and jeer at sacred things which they do not understand, nor would I share with them the inheritance that God, my Father, has given me in Zion; I do not love them well enough for this, and I do not believe that God ever designed that I should; but I love them so much that I would not hurt them, I would do them good, I would tell the truth about them, I would benefit them if it was in my power, and I would keep them to the utmost of my ability from doing harm to themselves and to their neighbors. I love them that much; but I do not love them with that affection

with which I love my wife, my brother, my sister or my friend. There is
a difference between the love we should bear towards our enemies and
that we should bear towards our friends. [JD 23:284:85]

This is the higher law of Christ. Those who live this commandment
become like God, and will thus be his children eternally in the
celestial kingdom. The Father "maketh his sun to rise on the evil and
on the good." The Matthew account adds "and sendeth rain on the just
and the unjust" (Matthew 5:45). It also adds a comparison to the
publicans that apparently was not applicable to the Nephites.

> 46 For if ye love them which love you, what reward have ye? do not
> even the publicans the same?
>
> 47 And if ye salute your brethren only, what do ye more than others?
> do not even the publicans so? [Matthew 5:46–47; see also Luke 6:32–36]

Jesus concluded the above comparisons by again confirming that
the law of Moses was fulfilled in him.

> 46 Therefore those things which were of old time, which were under
> the law, in me are all fulfilled.
>
> 47 Old things are done away, and all things have become new.
>
> 48 Therefore I would that ye should be perfect even as I, or your
> Father who is in heaven is perfect. [3 Nephi 12:46–48][4]

A new dispensation and a higher law were now in effect. This higher
law was to make us perfect as were he and his Father (v. 48). In the
Matthew account, Jesus only included his Father as being perfect.
This was apparently because he was not yet perfect in body since he
had not yet been resurrected. He came to the Nephites as a perfect,
resurrected being. He was now perfect and we were to become like
him as well as like his Father.

---

[4] JST Matthew reading is, "ye are commanded to be perfect," suggesting a long
term goal.

Perfection comes by living the celestial law. Is it possible for us to reach perfection in this life? Elder James E. Talmage made the following qualifications of the commandment:

> Our Lord's admonition to men to become perfect, even as the Father is perfect (Matthew 5:48) cannot rationally be construed otherwise than as implying the possibility of such achievement. Plainly, however, man cannot become perfect in mortality in the sense in which God is perfect as a supremely glorified Being. It is possible, though, for man to be perfect in his sphere in a sense analogous to that in which superior intelligences are perfect in their several spheres; yet the relative perfection of the lower is infinitely inferior to that of the higher. A college student in his freshman or sophomore year may be perfect as freshman or sophomore; his record may possibly be a hundred per cent on the scale of efficiency and achievement; yet the honors of the upper classman are beyond him, and the attainment of graduation is to him remote, but of assured possibility, if he do but continue faithful and devoted to the end.[5]

The Bible describes the relative perfection of some Old Testament characters. "Noah was a just man and perfect in his generations, and Noah walked with God (Genesis 9:6; Moses 8:27). There were others.

> 29 Abraham received all things, whatsoever he received, by revelation and commandment, by my word, saith the Lord, and hath entered into his exaltation and sitteth upon his throne. [D&C 132:29; see also v. 37, and Helaman 10:4–5]

President Spencer W. Kimball also taught the Brigham Young University students that perfection was a relative process. He said:

> To be perfect, then, one must begin early in his life. He or she must become the perfect husband, the perfect wife, the perfect father, the perfect mother, the perfect leader, and the perfect follower. One's marriage must be perfectly performed and perfectly kept on a hallowed plane. One must keep his life circumspect. Each person must keep himself clean and free from lusts. He must shun ugly, polluted thoughts and

---

[5] Talmage, James E., *Jesus the Christ*, 19th ed. (Salt Lake City, Utah: Deseret Book Co., 1951), p. 248.

acts as he would an enemy. Pornographic and erotic stories and pictures are worse than polluted food. Shun them. The body has power to rid itself of sickening food. That person who entertains filthy stories or porno-graphic pictures and literature records them in his marvelous human computer, the brain, which can't forget this filth. Once recorded, it will always remain there, subject to recall-filthy images.

As we have stated before, the way to perfection seems to be a changing of one's life—to substitute the good for the evil in every case. Changes can come best if we take one item at a time. For instance, it's not difficult to be perfect in tithe paying, for if one pays one-tenth of his income annually, he is perfect in that respect. It is not difficult to become perfect in avoiding a swearing habit, for if one locks his mouth against all words of cursing, he is en route to perfection in that matter. If one studies the scriptures with all reasonable devotion, he has approached perfection in that matter also.[6]

While perfection, or "a fullness of joy" is not complete until the "spirit and element [body]" are "inseparably connected [resurrected]" (D&C 93:33), we can and must work towards perfection of our spirits to inhabit a perfect tabernacle. The celestial law of Christ challenges all of us to seek the goals outlined by Christ in this glorious section of his sermon. "Be ye therefore perfect" (v. 48).

Upon completion of the comparisons of the laws by Jesus, he continued to instruct the multitude on matters of worship. He instruc-ted them concerning the giving of alms, praying, and fasting. These teachings also illustrate the three classes of people: celestial, terres-trial, and telestial.

1 Verily, verily, I say that I would that ye should do alms unto the poor; but take heed that ye do not your alms before men to be seen of them; otherwise ye have no reward of your Father who is in heaven.

2 Therefore, when ye shall do your alms do not sound a trumpet before you, as will hypocrites do in the synagogues and in the streets, that they may have glory of men. Verily I say unto you, they have their reward.

---

[6] Spencer W. Kimball, "Be Ye Therefore Perfect," *Speeches of the Year: BYU Devotional and Ten-Stake Fireside Addresses, 1974* (Provo, UT: Brigham Young University Press, 1975), 241–42.

3 But when thou doest alms let not thy left hand know what thy right hand doeth;

4 That thine alms may be in secret; and thy Father who seeth in secret, himself shall reward thee openly. [3 Nephi 13:1–4]

The Matthew account is the same as Third Nephi except it does not have the introductory phrase telling us we should do alms; therefore Matthew is not quoted above. The care of the poor is high on the Lord's priority list, but "it must needs be done in [the Lord's] own way" (D&C 104:15–18). Those who give alms to be seen of men, or for the glory of men, will be rewarded by the plaudits of men in this life, not from their Father in Heaven (vv. 1–2). These may be good and honorable efforts, but it is only a terrestrial-type giving. Those who are hypocritical, or give alms to get men subjected to them, are operating on a telestial level. They are serving the devil. The celestial way is to "let not thy left hand know what thy right hand doeth" (v. 3). This means to anonymously help those in need. Those acts done secretly so as not to obtain the recognition of men, but to help those in need, will be rewarded openly by our Father in Heaven (v. 4). The Lord knows the thoughts and the intents of the heart, and knows our reasons for helping. The main reason should be out of love and concern for our fellowmen, not to obtain our Father in Heaven's blessing.

5 And when thou prayest thou shalt not do as the hypocrites, for they love to pray, standing in the synagogues and in the corners of the streets, that they may be seen of men. Verily I say unto you, they have their reward.

6 But thou, when thou prayest, enter into thy closet, and when thou hast shut thy door, pray to thy Father who is in secret; and thy Father, who seeth in secret, shall reward thee openly.

7 But when ye pray, use not vain repetitions, as the heathen, for they think that they shall be heard for their much speaking.

8 Be not ye therefore like unto them, for your Father knoweth what things ye have need of before ye ask him.

9 After this manner therefore pray ye: Our Father who art in heaven, hallowed be thy name.

10 Thy will be done on earth as it is in heaven.

11 And forgive us our debts, as we forgive our debtors.

12 And lead us not into temptation, but deliver us from evil.

13 For thine is the kingdom, and the power, and the glory, forever. Amen.

14 For, if ye forgive men their trespasses your heavenly Father will also forgive you;

15 But if ye forgive not men their trespasses neither will your Father forgive your trespasses. [3 Nephi 13:5–15]

The instructions Jesus gave on prayer were similar to those on alms. Some people pray to be seen of men or to become Lord over other men. Such are also terrestrial or telestial-type individuals. Those who pray in closets (private conference rooms), or in secret, will be rewarded or receive answers to their prayers by their Father in Heaven (v. 6). This is the celestial way. But the Lord added a caution against the use of vain repetition, as the heathen who think their reward comes through the quantity or length of time praying (v. 7). The meaning of vain is "useless" or "meaningless." Vain repetitions are, therefore, thoughtless or insincere recitations of trite phrases with no meaning. However, it is not only appropriate, but necessary to repeatedly pray for meaningful things. Although our Father in Heaven knows what we need before we ask (v. 8), there is a law that governs our prayer: "Ask, and it shall be given unto you" (3 Nephi 14:7). If we don't ask we will not receive. Therefore, we must sincerely analyze our needs, and seek guidance in our prayers lest we "ask anything that is not expedient for [us], and it turn unto [our] condemnation" (D&C 88:63–65). In the New Testament, James warns to not "ask amiss" (James 5:3). Nephi says: "God will give me, if I ask not amiss" (2 Nephi 4:35).

How we pray is also important. The Savior revealed what is commonly called "The Lord's Prayer" (vv. 9–13). However, it is not a set prayer, as many suppose, but it is a "manner" or a pattern for prayer. The prayer includes a recognition of the greatness of God (v. 9); a commitment to obey his will (v. 10); a seeking for forgiveness based upon our willingness to forgive (v. 11); a request to deliver us from evil influences (v. 12); and an acknowledgment of his kingdom, power, and glory (v. 13). Our prayers should include like requests and acknowledgments.

There are some noted differences between the Nephite pattern of prayer and the pattern revealed on the mount in Galilee. Perhaps these were deliberate differences to show that the prayer was not a set prayer. Perhaps the needs in Galilee were different. The Galilean prayer contained a request for "Thy kingdom [of God] come" (Matthew 6:10). The kingdom had not yet been established in Palestine when Jesus gave the instructions, but it was now being established among the Nephites and so was not requested to come. In Galilee, there was a request to "Give us this day our daily bread." Perhaps the Nephites knew and had demonstrated their dependence on God for their sustenance and needed not to be reminded, or perhaps the people in Galilee were prone to "seek [Christ], not because ye saw the miracles, but because ye did eat of the loaves, and were filled," or seeking a handout rather than work for their living (John 6:26–27). These are conjectures at best.

After the pattern of prayer was given, the Savior added emphasis on the importance of obtaining forgiveness. While we all need forgiveness, its being obtained is not based as much upon our prayers as it is upon our actions. We will be forgiven as we are willing to forgive (vv. 14–15).

The last item of instruction was about fasting. It was essentially the same as those on alms and prayer.

> 16 Moreover, when ye fast be not as the hypocrites, of a sad countenance, for they disfigure their faces that they may appear unto men to fast. Verily I say unto you, they have their reward.
>
> 17 But thou, when thou fastest, anoint thy head, and wash thy face;
>
> 18 That thou appear not unto men to fast, but unto thy Father, who is in secret; and thy Father, who seeth in secret, shall reward thee openly. [3 Nephi 13:16–18]

The telestial people seek to subject men to themselves, the terrestrial people receive the rewards of those other men whom they serve, and celestial people receive rewards of their Heavenly Father because they turn to him in secret in their fasting (vv. 17–18). The higher law does not give details concerning fasting. The prophet Isaiah is the most complete source for those desiring to find further information on the subject (see Isaiah 58:1–12). The higher law of Christ shows that we can worship him through the giving of alms, prayer, and fasting.

> 19 Lay not up for yourselves treasures upon earth, where moth and rust doth corrupt, and thieves break through and steal;
>
> 20 But lay up for yourselves treasures in heaven, where neither moth nor rust doth corrupt, and where thieves do not break through nor steal.
>
> 21 For where your treasure is, there will your heart be also. [3 Nephi 13:19–21]

Jacob, brother of Nephi, earlier warned against seeking earthly treasures. "But wo unto the rich, who are rich as to the things of the world. For because they are rich they despise the poor, and they persecute the meek, and their hearts are upon their treasures; wherefore, their treasure is their god. And behold, their treasure shall perish with them also" (2 Nephi 9:30). The heart is the equivalent of the spirit. Our eyes influence our spirit. Therefore, if our "eye be single to the glory of God" (JST Matthew 6:22), our whole bodies will be full of light (vv. 22–23). This is the state of being "sanctified, even them of the celestial world," and is also the prerequisite to "see [Christ]; for he will unveil his face unto you" (D&C 88:2, 67–68). It is the attaining of "eternal life, that they might know thee the only true God, and Jesus Christ" (John 17:3), the end result of proper worship.

The final conclusion drawn by Jesus to the multitude in Galilee was: "No man can serve two masters; for either he will hate the one and love the other, or else he will hold to the one and despise the other. Ye cannot serve God and Mammon" (3 Nephi 13:24). To serve

Mammon[7] is to follow the desires of the world. It is to serve ourselves and other men. These may be honorable attempts, but are terrestrial nonetheless. These worldly desires "giveth the spirit of the devil power to captivate, to bring you down to hell" (2 Nephi 2:29). To follow Satan is to be "the servant of sin" (John 8:34). To serve Christ properly is to do so with an eye single to his glory without the reward of men. If we do serve him through keeping the higher law, we will receive the highest reward possible from our Heavenly Father, the celestial kingdom.

---

[7] Mammon is capitalized in Third Nephi but not in Matthew. The capitalization suggests a worship of worldly things (see D&C 124:84) .

The Fulfillment of the Law and the New Commandments

THE LAW OF CHRIST	THE LAW OF MOSES	THE LAW OF THE JUNGLE
Celestial Law	**Terrestrial Law**	**Telestial Law**
1. Murder—3 Nephi 12:12–26 Do not be angry Reconcile your brother	Thou shalt not kill	Survival of the fittest Revenge
2. Adultery—3 Nephi 12:27–30 No lust in your heart	Thou shalt not commit adultery	Sexual gratification
3. Divorce—3 Nephi 12:31–32 No cause except fornication	Letter of divorcement	Free love
4. Communication—3 Nephi 12:33–37 Nay and Yea (Your word is good)	Oaths unto the Lord	Trust no one
5. Retaliation—3 Nephi 12:38–43 Do not resist evil (Mercy)	Eye for an eye (Justice)	Revenge plus (Supremacy)
6. Love—3 Nephi 12:43–45 Love your enemies and neighbors as self	Love neighbors as self Hate enemy	Love self

Summation: Be ye therefore perfect—Through Celestial Law—3 Nephi 2:46–48

7. Alms—3 Nephi 14:1–4 In secret	Rewards of men	Subject men to you
8. Prayer—3 Nephi 14:5–15 In secret	Seen of men	Power over men
9. Fasting—3 Nephi 14:16–18 In secret	Seen of men	Power over men
10. Treasures—3 Nephi 14:19–21 In Heaven	On Earth	Corrupted

Summation: No man can serve two masters—Love or hate (3 Nephi 13:22–24).

Chapter 7

Instructions to the Twelve
and Missionaries

3 Nephi 13:25–14:27

Bertrand Russell, the British philosopher, categorized the Christian religion as the greatest religion in the world, but he chose not to follow it because he couldn't live it. He claimed it was too idealistic and impractical. He based at least part of his judgment on the verses treated in this chapter. It was, he reasoned, not realistic to take no thought for the morrow concerning what to eat or wear.[1] Had Mr. Russell had access to the Book of Mormon, his criticisms would have been alleviated.

The Book of Mormon text shows that the instructions in question were addressed only to "the twelve whom [Jesus] had chosen . . . to minister to this [the Nephite] people," and not to the general Church populace (3 Nephi 13:25). In the New Testament account, it is not clear whether the Twelve had yet been chosen; nevertheless, the JST shows that the Matthew text was also not to the people in general, but was addressed to either the Twelve or to select disciples who were

---

[1] *Why I Am Not A Christian,* pp. 15–16 (New York: Freethought Press Association, 1940).

going out to preach the gospel.[2] An outline of the remainder of the sermon gives us an overview to prepare for a deeper study.

Outline • 3 Nephi 13:25–14:27

➤ 13:25–34 Jesus speaks to the Twelve he had chosen to minister to his people.

    a.   Take no thought for the morrow, what to eat, drink, or wear. vv. 25–32

        1.   Life is more than meat and the body raiment.

        2.   The Father takes care of the fouls, and ye are better than they.

        3.   You cannot add to your stature one cubit.

        4.   The Father takes care of the lilies, and even Solomon was not arrayed as these.

        5.   He will clothe you if you are not of little faith.

        6.   He knows you have need of all these things.

    b.   Seek ye first the kingdom of God, and all these things shall be added to you. vv. 33–34

        1.   Take no thought for the morrow, and the morrow shall take thought for itself.

        2.   Sufficient is the day unto the evil thereof.

➤ 14:1–27 After Jesus had spoken to the Twelve, he again taught the multitude.

    a.   Judge not that ye be not judged. vv. 1–5

        1.   You are judged as you judge others.

---

[2] According to Elders James E. Talmage and Bruce R. McConkie, the calling of the Twelve was in the beginning of the second year of Jesus' ministry just prior to his delivering the Sermon on the Mount *(Jesus The Christ,* pp. 217–31; *Doctrinal New Testament Commentary,* pp. 14; 209–11). However, President J. Reuben Clark places the sermon prior to the Twelve being called *(Our Lord of the Gospels,* pp. 209, 227). The same chronological differences exist among Bible scholars of other faiths.

    2. You behold a mote in your brother's eye, but not the beam in your own.

    3. First cast out the beam in your eye, and then you shall see to cast out the mote in your brother's eye.

  b. Do not give holy things to the dogs, or cast pearls before swine. v. 6

  c. Ask and it shall be given, seek and you shall find, knock and it shall be opened. vv. 7:11

    1. If a son asks for bread, you do not give him a stone.

    2. If a son asks for a fish, you do not give him a serpent.

    3. If you, being evil, know how to give good gifts, how much more will your Father in heaven know how to give good gifts to those who ask.

  d. The Golden Rule, as you would have done unto you, so do unto others. v. 12

  e. Enter the strait gate that leads to life and few find, not the gate that leads to destruction. vv. 13–14

  f. Beware of false prophets who come in sheep's clothing, but are wolves inwardly. vv. 15–20

    1. You shall know them by their fruits, men do not gather thorns or thistles.

    2. A good tree brings good fruit, and a corrupt tree brings corrupt fruit.

    3. A tree not bringing good fruit is hewn down and cast into the fire.

  g. He who does the will of the Father shall enter the kingdom of heaven. vv. 21–23

    1. Many will say we have done works in thy name.

    2. I will profess to them that I never knew them, depart from me.

  h. He who hears these words, and does them, is like the man who builds his house on a rock. vv. 24–25

    1. The rains, floods, and winds beat upon the house.

     2. It falls not because it is built upon the rock.

   i. Not hearing these words, and not following, is like a man building on a sand foundation. vv. 26–27

     1. The rains, floods, and winds beat upon the house.

     2. The house falls and great is the fall.

NOTES AND COMMENTARY

JST Matthew 5:1 says, "And *Jesus,* seeing the multitudes, went up into a mountain; and when he was set *down*, his disciples came unto him" (italics added). "His disciples" may refer to the Twelve. If the Twelve had not yet been chosen, they would still have been among the disciples that went up to him. JST Matthew 6:1 also adds that Jesus is still addressing his disciples, "And it came to pass that, as Jesus taught his disciples, he said unto them, . . ." The beginning of the text being considered in this chapter is likewise slightly changed in the JST. A comparison of the three accounts below illustrates that the Book of Mormon and the JST confirm that the verses that follow were given to either the Apostles or a select group of disciples that followed Jesus into the mountain in Galilee.

And now it came to pass that when Jesus had spoken these words he looked upon the twelve whom he had chosen, and said unto them: Remember the words which I have spoken. For behold, ye are they whom I have chosen to minister unto this people		And, again, I say unto you, go ye into the world, and care not for the world; for the world will hate you, and will persecute you, and will turn you out of their synagogues. Nevertheless, ye shall go forth from house to house, teaching the people; and I will go before you. And your Heavenly Father will provide for you, whatsoever things ye need for food, what ye shall eat; and for raiment, what ye shall wear or put on.

Therefore I say unto you, take no thought for your life, . . . (3 Nephi 13:25).	Therefore I say unto you, Take no thought for your life, . . . (Matthew 6:25).	Therefore I say unto you, take no thought for your life (JST Matthew 6:25–28).

Therefore, the concept of taking no thought for the morrow is limited to Apostles or missionaries who are in the full-time service of the Lord. A further comparison of the text shows that the remainder of these two great sermons is regarding appropriate missionary work. The first part was addressing what the Twelve, or the missionaries, were to do, and the last part "are the words which Jesus taught his disciples that they should say unto the people" (JST Matthew 7:1). In the Book of Mormon, Jesus "turned again to the multitude" and addressed them. This was probably because the multitude was with him, while in Galilee only the select disciples were present. Nonetheless, it set the pattern for the teaching of the gospel. We will consider the words to the twelve or chosen disciples first.

> 26 Behold the fowls of the air, for they sow not, neither do they reap nor gather into barns; yet your heavenly Father feedeth them. Are ye not much better than they?
>
> 27 Which of you by taking thought can add one cubit unto his stature?
>
> 28 And why take ye thought for raiment? Consider the lilies of the field how they grow; they toil not, neither do they spin;
>
> 29 And yet I say unto you, that even Solomon, in all his glory, was not arrayed like one of these.
>
> 30 Wherefore, if God so clothe the grass of the field, which today is, and tomorrow is cast into the oven, even so will he clothe you, if ye are not of little faith.
>
> 31 Therefore take no thought, saying, What shall we eat? or, What shall we drink? or, Wherewithal shall we be clothed?
>
> 32 For your heavenly Father knoweth that ye have need of all these things. [3 Nephi 13:26–32]

JST Matthew adds, "How much more will he not feed you? Wherefore take no thought for these things, but keep my commandments wherewith I have commanded you" (6:29–30). This addition shows that these promises are conditional, based upon the obedience of the recipients.

As further evidence of God's ability to care for his full-time servants, Jesus reminded his listeners that they were unable to add one cubit to their stature by themselves, yet God had produced and glorified the lilies of the field (vv. 27–29). Again, a condition of their having faith is placed upon God's caring for them even more than the lilies (vv. 30–31).

Matthew includes (v. 32) a declaration: (For after all of these things do the Gentiles seek). The JST precedes this remark with, *"Why is it that ye murmur among yourselves, saying, We cannot obey thy word because ye have not all these things*, and *seek to excuse yourselves*, saying that after all these things do the Gentiles seek" (6:36; emphasis added). Jesus was reading their thoughts that questioned the ability of the Father to provide, and rationalized that the Gentiles were no different than they. The deletion of this from the Nephite account was undoubtedly because there were no Gentiles in America. Regardless, Jesus taught both groups the same principle, "your heavenly Father knoweth that ye have need of all things" (v. 32).

In the Nephite and the Matthew record, having sustained that their Father in Heaven would care for his Twelve, Jesus announced their mission: "But seek ye first the kingdom of God and his righteousness and all these things shall be added unto you" (v. 33). The Gospels of Matthew and Luke, and the JST of Luke and Matthew, have a slightly different rendering of these instructions:

But seek ye first the kingdom of God and his righteousness, and all these things shall be added unto you (2 Nephi 13:33; Matthew 6:33).	Wherefore, seek not the things of this world but seek ye first to build up the kingdom of God, and to establish his right-eousness, and all these things shall be added unto you (JST Matthew 6:38).	But rather seek ye the kingdom of God; and all these things shall be added unto you (Luke 12:31).	And ye are sent unto them to be their ministers, and the laborer is worthy of his hire; for the law saith, That a man shall not muzzle the ox that treadeth out the corn. Therefore seek ye to bring forth the kingdom of God, and all these things shall be added unto you (JST Luke 12:33-34).

Remembering that these instructions in the New Testament are addressed to the select disciples as guidelines to missionaries gives a different understanding. Although a missionary commits him or herself to full-time service of the Lord, it is a temporary commitment, not a lifetime commitment as with the apostles. Therefore, Jesus' instruction to those called on missions was: "Wherefore, *seek not the things of this world but seek ye first to build up the kingdom of God, and to establish his righteousness*, and all these things shall be added unto you" (JST Matthew 6:38; emphasis added). The admonition in Luke to seek to bring forth the kingdom was also addressed to the select disciples and emphasizes their role as ministers or servants of the people. While the JST changes may be to clarify Jesus' original instructions to select disciples, as well as to the Twelve, the Book of Mormon being addressed specifically to the Twelve suggests that the Apostles are unique in their calling to "seek ye first the kingdom of God." An apostle dedicates himself to the Lord and his kingdom and is, therefore, responsible to seek first the kingdom of God for the rest of his mortal life.

Following the admonitions concerning the kingdom of God, both the Nephite and Matthew accounts repeat the charge to take no thought for the morrow (v. 34; JST Matthew 6:39). Luke's later charge is slightly different and conforms to the above context. He advises the listeners to "fear not, little flock; for it is your Father's good pleasure to give you the kingdom" (Luke 12:32). The kingdom had not yet come when the New Testament sermon was given, but was soon to be established.

There was one more item of instruction that Jesus gave the Twelve and the full-time missionaries. This provocative statement was attached to the previous admonition to take no thought for the morrow: "for the morrow shall take thought for the things of itself. Sufficient is the day unto the evil thereof" (v. 34). The JST Matthew account renders it in the future: "Sufficient unto the days *shall be* the evil thereof" (6:39; emphasis added). What Jesus seems to be saying is that each day will bring its own challenges, problems, and opportunities for teaching the gospel. These will not all be pleasant; in fact, much will be from the opposition of Satan, and will be quite adequate to keep one humble and in need of the Lord's help. This concept is illustrated in today's missionary work, but is more pronounced in the work of the Twelve. As they travel throughout the Church and the world, the local authorities are anxious to receive the Twelve's counsel in the more serious problems of each area. Thus, the Twelve are constantly faced with serious situations to which they must respond. They do not need to anticipate future problems; each day will have it's own challenges, and these should be taken as they come. (Of course long-range planning, and the taking of preventive measures, is not only desirable, but also necessary.)

The special instructions were completed for now. That Jesus later followed the pattern of giving his chosen disciples special instructions that were not shared with the multitude is further verified in the Gospel of Luke where Peter seeks clarification of some of Jesus' deeper teachings with the question, "Lord, speakest thou this parable unto us, or even to all?" (Luke 12:41). They are his special witnesses and are to build up his kingdom.

The Instructions to the Multitude

1 And now it came to pass that when Jesus had spoken these words he turned again to the multitude, and did open his mouth unto them again, saying: Verily, verily, I say unto you, Judge not, that ye be not judged.

2 For with what judgment ye judge, ye shall be judged; and with what measure ye mete, it shall be measured to you again. [3 Nephi 14:1–2]

The Nephite record discloses that, after Jesus instructed the Twelve, he turned back to the multitude to continue his teachings. The Matthew account begins with "Judge not . . .," but the JST Matthew testimony states: "Now these are the words which Jesus taught his disciples that they should say unto the people" (JST Matthew 7:1). The JST has extensive additions in its text. Some may wonder why Joseph Smith made these additions since after the Book of Mormon was translated it was revealed to him, "and as your Lord and your God liveth it is true" (D&C 17:6), and was essentially the same as the KJV Bible text. The answer to this question seems to be that, since the meanings and understandings of words and concepts change through time, Joseph is making sure that we understand what Jesus' instructions mean. They were translated correctly, but our ability to grasp the meanings of that far-removed day is inadequate; thus, he renders "a plainer translation."[3]

Jesus told the multitude to "judge not, that ye be not judged." Although what he meant was probably clearly understood by both the Jewish people and the Nephite peoples, it needs a plainer rendition today. It is impossible to live in today's world, or at any other time,

---

[3] When the angel Moroni appeared to Joseph Smith in September of 1823, he quoted Malachi 4:5–6 quite differently (see D&C 2). The Book of Mormon quotes Malachi precisely as it is recorded in the Bible. In an epistle to the Church in September 1842, Joseph quoted the passage precisely as it is in Malachi and the Book of Mormon. He then added; "I might have rendered a plainer translation to this, but it is sufficiently plain to suit my purpose as it stands" (D&C 128:17–18). The conclusion drawn above is based on this experience.

without making judgments each day. Life is a series of judgments. Therefore, Joseph rendered this passage, "Judge not unrighteously, that ye be not judged; but *judge righteous judgment*" (JST Matthew 7:1; emphasis added). That this was the original intent of his instruction is shown by a later instruction that Jesus gave in Palestine, "Judge not according to the appearance, but judge righteous judgment" (John 7:24). The latter part of the original statement, "that ye be not judged" and the words that follow, was a warning against unrighteous judgment. Luke's account reads:

> 37 Judge not, and ye shall not be judged: condemn not, and ye shall not be condemned: forgive, and ye shall be forgiven:
>
> 38 Give, and it shall be given unto you; good measure, pressed down, and shaken together, and running over, shall men give into your bosom. For with the same measure that ye mete withal it shall be measured to you again. [Luke 6:37–38]

Joseph Smith's additions in his translation of the Bible are certainly consistent with Jesus' other teachings in the New Testament, and in the Book of Mormon.

The Book of Mormon later gives a much more complete explanation of how to make righteous judgments and their consequences:

> 14 Wherefore, take heed, my beloved brethren, that ye do not judge that which is evil to be of God, or that which is good and of God to be of the devil.
>
> 15 For behold, my brethren, it is given unto you to judge, that ye may know good from evil; and the way to judge is as plain, that ye may know with a perfect knowledge, as the daylight is from the dark night.
>
> 16 For behold, the Spirit of Christ is given to every man, that he may know good from evil; wherefore, I show unto you the way to judge; for every thing which inviteth to do good, and to persuade to believe in Christ, is sent forth by the power and gift of Christ; wherefore ye may know with a perfect knowledge it is of God.
>
> 17 But whatsoever thing persuadeth men to do evil, and believe not in Christ, and deny him, and serve not God, then ye may know with a perfect knowledge it is of the devil; for after this manner doth the devil

work, for he persuadeth no man to do good, no, not one; neither do his angels; neither do they who subject themselves unto him.

18 And now, my brethren, seeing that ye know the light by which ye may judge, which light is the light of Christ, see that ye do not judge wrongfully; for with that same judgment which ye judge ye shall also be judged. [Moroni 7:14–18]

Righteous judgments are made through the Spirit of Christ that is given to all men for that very purpose.

Jesus continued his instructions regarding judgments with a question about introspection. As the JST shows, this question was to be asked of others:

And why beholdest thou the mote that is in thy brother's eye, but considerest not the beam that is in thine own eye?	And again, ye shall say unto them, Why is it that thou beholdest the mote that is in they brother's eye, but considerest not the beam that is in thine own eye?
Or how wilt thou say to thy brother: Let me put the mote out of thine eye and behold, a beam is in thine own eye?	Or how wilt thou say to thy brother, Let me pull out the mote out of thine eye; and canst not behold a beam in thine own eye? (JST Matthew 7:4–5)
Thou hypocrite, first cast the beam out of thine own eye; and then shalt thou see clearly to cast the mote out of they brother's eye. (3 Nephi 14:3–5)	

The KJV Matthew account is identical to the Book of Mormon, and Luke 6:41–42 is basically the same.

A mote is a small speck or particle, and a beam is a large construction timber. The comparison was, of course, an exaggeration to illustrate who was guilty of the most serious sin. The following addition to the JST Matthew testimony identifies those who were thus guilty. This may have been in the original text of Matthew, and a part of the "plain and precious things which have been taken out of the book" (1 Nephi 13:29), but was not given in the Nephite sermon because it was not applicable to them.

> And Jesus said unto his disciples, Beholdest thou the Scribes, and the Pharisees, and the Priests, and the Levites? They teach in their synagogues, but do not observe the law, nor the commandments; and all have gone out of the way, and are under sin.
>
> Go thou and say unto them, Why teach ye men the law and the commandments, when ye yourselves are the children of corruption? [JST Matthew 7:6–7]

In Jerusalem, having identified the serious sinners, Jesus instructed the multitude to "*Say unto them* [the scribes, the Pharisees, the priests, and the Levites], Ye hypocrites, first cast out the beam out of thine own eye; and then shalt thou see clearly to cast out the mote out of thy brother's eye" (JST Matthew 7:8; Matthew 7:5 is identical except for the italicized introduction). This is one of the most scathing denouncements that Jesus gave. He also called the same group of Jews "hypocrites" later in his Jerusalem ministry (see Matthew 23:13–33 partially quoted in the previous chapter). Unless they repented, these Jewish leaders were destined to be judged harshly. Jesus continued his instructions to the faithful disciples: "Go ye into the world, saying unto all, Repent, for the kingdom of heaven has come nigh unto you" (JST Matthew 7:9).

The same basic message was given to the world in this generation: "The thing which will be of the most worth unto you will be to declare repentance unto this people, that you may bring souls unto me, that you may rest with them in the kingdom of my Father" (D&C 15:6). Also in latter-day revelation, the Lord told Hyrum Smith to "say nothing but repentance to this generation" (D&C 11:9). This is consistent with the next instruction that Jesus gave to the multitude in America and Palestine. The identical Matthew and Third Nephi accounts warn against teaching holy or sacred things to those who were unprepared for them, but the JST makes it plainer that only the basic truths are to be used in preaching the gospel to the world:

Give not that which is holy unto the dogs, neither cast ye your pearls before swine, let they trample them under their feet, and turn again and rend you. (3 Nephi 14:6)	And the mysteries of the kingdom ye shall keep within yourselves; for it is not meet to give that which is holy unto the dogs; neither cast ye your pearls unto swine, let they trample them under their feet. (JST Matthew 7:10)

The "mysteries of the kingdom" are those things that the Lord has not seen fit to reveal to the world. "Unto him that keepeth my [the Lord's] commandments I will reveal the mysteries of my kingdom" (D&C 63:23), or the truths of the gospel that are reserved for those Saints who are willing to receive them. To reveal the sacred mysteries to "the dogs" is to reveal them to the unbelievers, as used in the Book of Mormon. In the New Testament, it would be "to take the children's bread, and cast it to the dogs [those not of the house of Israel]" (Matthew 15:21–26). To cast pearls before swine, in both accounts, would be symbolic of revealing those precious truths of the gospel before those who served the devil. Jesus illustrated this in the New Testament when Herod "questioned with him in many words; but [Jesus] answered him nothing" (Luke 23:9). Earlier Jesus had told the Pharisees: "Go ye and tell that fox, Behold, I cast out devils," implying his association with devils (Luke 13:31–32). While the unbelievers, or the Gentiles, would not understand the mysteries of the kingdom, the devil's servants would attempt to ridicule or twist them to defeat missionaries' purposes. The Prophet Joseph cautioned: "Strive not about the mysteries of the kingdom; cast not your pearls before swine, give not the bread of the children to dogs, lest you and the children should suffer, and you thereby offend your righteous Judge" (TPJS 77).

Once more the JST adds another dimension of reasoning to the caution of not teaching the mysteries of God: "For the world cannot receive that which ye, yourselves, are not able to bear; wherefore ye shall not give your pearls unto them, lest they turn again and rend you" (JST Matthew 7:11). Before a person should teach the deeper things of the kingdom, he must first understand them himself. Hyrum

Smith was similarly admonished: Seek not to declare my word, but first seek to obtain my word, and then shall your tongue be loosed; then, if you desire, you shall have my Spirit and my word, yea, the power of God unto the convincing of men" (D&C 11:21). You cannot teach what you do not understand.

Jesus gave one more item of instruction regarding the multitude teaching the gospel: "Ask, and it shall be given unto you; seek, and ye shall find; knock, and it shall be opened unto you. For every one that asketh, receiveth; and he that seeketh, findeth; and to him that knocketh, it shall be opened" (3 Nephi 14:7–8; the Matthew 7:7–8 is identical). The JST prefaces this with, "Say unto them, Ask of God" (JST Matthew 7:12). Undoubtedly, this addition was to ensure that we understand to whom we are to ask. This triad for understanding the mysteries of God may be paraphrased in this way: pray, study, and live according to what you know and are trying to understand. The Book of Mormon shows that this formula for understanding was not unique to the Sermon on the Mount or the Nephite sermon. Nephi, son of Lehi, had taught the same principles six hundred years earlier:

> 3 Angels speak by the power of the Holy Ghost; wherefore, they speak the words of Christ. Wherefore, I said unto you, feast [*seek*] upon the words of Christ; for behold, the words of Christ will tell you all things what ye should do.
>
> 4 Wherefore, now after I have spoken these words, if ye cannot understand them it will be because ye *ask* not, neither do ye *knock*; wherefore, ye are not brought into the light, but must perish in the dark. [2 Nephi 32:3–4; emphasis added]

These principles were probably also taught and recorded in the Old Testament before the "many plain and precious things" were removed (1 Nephi 13:29).

JST Matthew adds several verses at this point. These additions represent the disciples' anticipation of the responses they will get from people as they endeavor to teach them the gospel. The first anticipated response was: "And then said his disciples unto him, they will say unto us, We ourselves are righteous, and need not that any man should teach us. God, we know, heard Moses and some of the prophets; but us he will not hear" (JST Matthew 7:14). Paraphrased, this verse claims that revelation has ceased. People are willing to accept that former prophets received revelation, but are not ready to accept modern-day prophets and revelation. Things are no different today.

The second anticipated response was, "And they will say, We have the law for our salvation, and that is sufficient for us" (JST Matthew 7:15). To paraphrase this response, they will say that our religion is good enough for us; we are already Christians. God will save us if we believe. Again, this is a common response in these latter days.

Jesus' response appealed to the normal reactions of mankind:

> Then Jesus answered, and said unto his disciples, thus shall ye say unto them, What man among you, having a son, and he shall be standing out, and shall say, Father, open thy house that I may come in and sup with thee, will not say, Come in, my son; for mine is thine, and thine is mine? [JST Matthew 7:16–17]

The following verses that are common in KJV Matthew and Third Nephi are the other examples of a rational man's reaction to a son's request.

> 9 Or what man is there of you, who, if his son ask bread, will give him a stone?
>
> 10 Or if he ask a fish, will he give him a serpent?
>
> 11 If ye then, being evil, know how to give good gifts unto your children, how much more shall your Father who is in heaven give good things to them that ask him? [3 Nephi 14:9–11; see also Luke 11:11–12]

The lost parts from the Matthew account quoted above, when restored, make the text much more readable. Why Jesus did not use them among the Nephites can only be a matter of conjecture, but perhaps the Nephites did not anticipate the responses, as did the Jewish people. Nevertheless, Jesus wanted the principles taught regarding the Father answering their prayers, so he tied these principles to his admonition to ask in order to receive revelation. Our Father in Heaven obviously responds in like manner as do earthly fathers. Although the text does not read as well without the JST restoration, the messages are the same.

Having established how normal, rational, earthly fathers will react, Jesus teaches that our Heavenly Father is much more understanding and willing to bless his children with good gifts if they will just ask (v. 11). Luke states: "how much more shall your heavenly Father give the Holy Spirit to them that ask him" (Luke 11:13). The JST Luke account adds that the Father will "give *good gifts* through the Holy Spirit to them who ask him" (JST Luke 11:14; emphasis added). Revelation has not ceased; it is available for the asking. Thus, Jesus answered the first anticipated response.

The Savior answered the second anticipated response concerning the law as being sufficient. He also included the people's tendency to accept former prophets in his corrective answer: "Therefore, all things whatsoever ye would that men should do to you, do ye even so to them, for this is the law and the prophets" (3 Nephi 14:12). This principle has become known throughout the Christian world as the "golden rule," but what Jesus is also teaching here is that, if people really believed in the Law and the Prophets of the Old Testament, they would understand that both of these ancient Hebrew texts taught what he had been teaching.[4] They taught of a loving Father who was desirous to pour out gifts through his Spirit upon his children, but since he was a God of law, these blessings were conditioned upon the principle of "ask and ye shall receive."

With the concept of God as a loving Father being implanted in their minds, Jesus turned to other conditions that man must meet in order to obtain the Father's blessings.

---

[4] The Hebrew Bible was divided into three parts. The Law referred to the first five books of Moses. The Prophets consisted of eight books: Joshua, Judges, 1&2 Samuel (as one book), 1&2 Kings (as one book), Isaiah, Jeremiah, Ezekiel, and the Twelve prophets (Hosea through Malachi). The other books of the Old Testament were collected into a third book that was called the Hagiographa, mostly poetic books.

13 Enter ye in at the strait gate; for wide is the gate, and broad is the way, which leadeth to destruction, and many there be who go in thereat;

14 Because strait is the gate, and narrow is the way, which leadeth unto life, and few there be that find it. [3 Nephi 14:13–14; Matthew 7:13–14 is identical]

Jesus repeated this instruction with some variant wording when he defined the gospel to his disciples in an appearance following his ministry.

. . . He said unto his disciples: Enter ye in at the strait gate; for strait is the gate, and narrow is the way that leads to life, and few there be that find it; but wide is the gate, and broad the way which leads to death, and many there be that travel therein, until the night cometh, wherein no man can work. [3 Nephi 27:33]

The gate that they were to enter was baptism. Nephi, son of Lehi, made this point very clear as he concluded his record and testified of the doctrine of Christ: "And again, it showeth unto the children of men the straitness of the path, and the narrowness of the gate, by which they should enter, he having set the example before them" (2 Nephi 31:9). The JST adds, "Repent, therefore and enter," making it consistent with a further statement of Nephi, " the gate by which you enter is repentance and baptism by water" (2 Nephi 31:17). The word *strait*[5] means restricted or limited access. Thus, there is only one acceptable method and one prayer for that baptism to be administered which is recorded in 3 Nephi 11:23–28. The wide gate through which many others enter may well be the various modifications and perversions of the ordinance of baptism. These lead to destruction.

"This strait and narrow path . . . leads to eternal life" as Nephi had previously stated (2 Nephi 31:18). It is the path that one trods after baptism. Following entrance into the Church, the parameters are set

---

[5] The spelling in the 1981 edition was changed from "straight" in previous editions to "strait." The original spelling was probably due to Oliver Cowdery's spelling and was not corrected until 1981.

by scripture, living prophets, and priesthood leaders. Once we are on that path, we:

> 20 . . . must press forward with a steadfastness in Christ, having a perfect brightness of hope, and a love of God and of all men. Wherefore, if ye shall press forward, feasting upon the word of Christ, and endure to the end, behold, thus saith the Father: Ye shall have eternal life.
>
> 21 And now, behold, my beloved brethren, this is the way; and there is none other way nor name given under heaven whereby man can be saved in the kingdom of God. And now, behold, this is the doctrine of Christ, and the only and true doctrine of the Father, and of the Son, and of the Holy Ghost, which is one God, without end. Amen. [2 Nephi 31:20–21, see also Jacob 6:11–12]

As Jesus said, "few there be that find [the path to eternal life]" (3 Nephi 14:14; Matthew 7:14). The number who accept baptism is small by percentages. The number of those who accept baptism and press forward is also small, hopefully not as small a percentage as those who accept baptism but, nevertheless, small.

The next condition outlined by Jesus to obtain the blessings of the Father was in the form of a warning: "Beware of false prophets, who come to you in sheep's clothing, but inwardly they are ravening wolves" (3 Nephi 14:15; Matthew 7:15).

The fact that Jesus said that the false prophets "would come to you" implies that these prophets would not be from within the Church, but from without. They come to the people dressed "in sheep's clothing but inwardly they are ravening wolves" (v. 15). They pretend to be saving the people from the wolves, but they themselves are the wolves. This applies to religious leaders who claim to be saving their people from the ravages of the world, but are themselves the wolves ravaging the message and the effect of the gospel of Jesus Christ.

> 16 Ye shall know them by their fruits. Do men gather grapes of thorns, or figs of thistles?
>
> 17 Even so every good tree bringeth forth good fruit; but a corrupt tree bringeth forth evil fruit.

18 A good tree cannot bring forth evil fruit, neither a corrupt tree bring forth good fruit.

19 Every tree that bringeth not forth good fruit is hewn down, and cast into the fire.

20 Wherefore, by their fruits ye shall know them. [3 Nephi 14:15–20]

Because Jesus warned of false prophets, it must be acknowledged that there would be true prophets. If not so, he would merely have warned about so-called prophets coming among them, and declared that there were to be no more prophets. Furthermore, he would not have given a criterion to discern a true prophet from a false prophet. The symbolism used as the criterion was a tree that produced fruit. A good tree brings forth good fruit; a corrupt tree brings forth corrupt fruit. Trees that do not bring forth good fruit are to be cut down and burned for firewood. "By their fruits ye shall know them" (vv. 16–20). Does the Book of Mormon teach good things and bring forth good people? Nephi testified that it did:

4 And the words which I have written in weakness will be made strong unto them; for it persuadeth them to do good; it maketh known unto them of their fathers; and it speaketh of Jesus, and persuadeth them to believe in him, and to endure to the end, which is life eternal.

5 And it speaketh harshly against sin, according to the plainness of the truth; wherefore, no man will be angry at the words which I have written save he shall be of the spirit of the devil.

10 And now, my beloved brethren, and also Jew, and all ye ends of the earth, hearken unto these words and believe in Christ; and if ye believe not in these words believe in Christ. And if ye shall believe in Christ ye will believe in these words, for they are the words of Christ, and he hath given them unto me; and they teach all men that they should do good. [2 Nephi 33:4–5, 10]

Does the Church of Jesus Christ of Latter-day Saints collectively bring forth good people? This question must be answered by the observers, but are the members of the Church honest, God-fearing, hard-working, and devout people? If they are, the tree is producing good fruit.

After warning the people of the external forces that would lead them astray, the Savior cautioned those within the Church. The Luke account renders an interesting phrasing of the principle:

Not every one that saith unto me, Lord, Lord, shall enter into the kingdom of heaven; but he that doeth the will of my Father who is in heaven. (3 Nephi 14:21; Matthew 7:21)	And why call ye me, Lord, Lord, and do not the things which I say? Whosoever cometh to me, and heareth my sayings, and doeth them, I will shew you to whom he is like. (Luke 6:46–47)

Again, the Lord gives a discerning factor. Those who do the Father's will are those to whom one should look, not necessarily to those who profess to be Christ's followers, but only give lip service. It is their works that count, not their verbal pronouncements. The JST makes this more pronounced as well as showing that a qualifying discernment will be made at the judgment bar if they are not discerned in this life: "For the day soon cometh, that men shall come before me to judgment, to be judged according to their works" (JST Matthew 7:31).

Jesus gave another warning regarding Church members. He warned those who relied upon their past efforts as justification for salvation: "Many will say to me in that day: Lord, Lord, have we not prophesied in thy name, and in thy name have cast out devils, and in thy name done many wonderful works?" (3 Nephi 14:22; Matthew 7:22).

These are people who rationalize that serving a full-time mission, or giving some other period of Church service is sufficient. They will, at the day of judgment, recount their having been instruments in the Lord's hands as missionaries, priesthood bearers, or leaders. To these the Lord will respond negatively. The JST has an interesting rendition.

And then will I profess unto them: I never knew you; depart from me, ye that work iniquity. (3 Nephi 14:23; Matthew 7:23)	And then will I say, Ye never knew me; depart from me ye that work iniquity. (JST Matthew 7:33)

These people seem to be those who were socially members of Christ's church, and even fulfilled positions and assignments, but did so without conviction and testimony of the Lord and his work.

The Savior concluded his great sermon as it had begun, likening his audience to him who builds a house:

> 24 Therefore, whoso heareth these sayings of mine and doeth them I will liken him unto a wise man, who built his house upon a rock
>
> 25 And the rain descended, and the floods came, and the winds blew, and beat upon that house; and it fell not, for it was founded upon a rock.
>
> 26 And every one that heareth these sayings of mine and doeth them not shall be likened unto a foolish man, who built his house upon the sand—
>
> 27 And the rain descended, and the floods came, and the winds blew, and beat upon that house; and it fell, and great was the fall of it. [3 Nephi 14:24–27; Matthew 7: 24–27]

The Luke account likens the building upon the rock or the sand to those who come unto Christ (baptism), and do or not do the things that the Lord says.

> 47 Whosoever cometh to me, and heareth my sayings, and doeth them, I will shew you to whom he is like:
>
> 48 He is like a man which built an house, and digged deep, and laid the foundation on a rock: and when the flood arose, the stream beat vehemently upon that house, and could not shake it: for it was founded upon a rock.
>
> 49 But he that heareth, and doeth not, is like a man that without a foundation built an house upon the earth; against which the stream did beat vehemently, and immediately it fell; and the ruin of that house was great. [Luke 6:47–49]

Our eternal salvation is dependent upon our building upon the rock of Christ by following his teachings. As noted in chapter 4, the rock that we are to build upon is the Rock of Christ. It is a testimony of his divinity as the Son of God. The rain, the floods, and the winds that come are the temptations of the devil and the philosophies of men that attempt to erode away the gospel of Jesus Christ. Those who have a testimony and continue to nourish it will endure in spite of those temptations. On the other hand, those who base their salvation upon the reasoning power of man, instead of upon the revelation of the Holy Spirit, will see their reasoning taken away by others more wise in the ways of the world, or more cunning in the deceptions of the devil. The foundation of Christ will stand. If we build upon it, we will endure.

Chapter 8

The Gentiles and the House of Israel

3 Nephi 15:1–17:4

The Lord covenanted with Abraham that, through him and his seed "shall all the families of the earth be blessed, even with the blessings of the Gospel, which are the blessings of salvation, even of life eternal" (Abraham 2:11; see also Genesis 12:3; 1 Nephi 22:9; 3 Nephi 20:25). After Jesus had explained the higher laws of the gospel to the Nephites, he defined the various families of the earth, and showed the order in which his teachings were to be offered to them. Before he proceeded, Jesus perceived that a few questions needed to be answered. There are also things that we must understand before we proceed to Jesus' explanation of the gospel going to the nations of the earth.

It is important, as previously shown, to note the audience to whom Jesus is speaking. To the multitude he gave general or basic information, but to the Twelve he gave specific and intimate or personalized items of instruction. In this section of the Nephite record, the first ten verses are addressed to the multitude, but the following thirty-four verses (3 Nephi 15:11–16:20) are the deeper doctrines shared only with his chosen disciples, (the Twelve). The first four verses of chapter seventeen are again addressed to the multitude. An outline of all forty-eight of the verses, as an overview to prepare us for a deeper study, follows.

Outline • 3 Nephi 15:1–17:4

➤ 15:1–10   Jesus again addresses the Multitude.

   a   You have heard what I taught before I ascended to my Father, and if you do these things you will be lifted up at the last day. v. 1

   b.   He perceived that some wondered concerning the law of Moses. vv. 2–8

   1.   They understood not that old things had passed away, and all things had become new.

   2.   The law given to Moses was fulfilled in me, and is ended.

   3.   I gave the law, and I covenanted with my people Israel .

   4.   I do not destroy the prophets, and all that is not fulfilled shall be.

   5.   I do not destroy things that are to come.

   6.   The covenant with my people is not all fulfilled.

   c.   I am the law and the light, look unto me, and endure to the end, and ye shall gain eternal life. vv. 9–10

   1.   I have given the commandments; therefore, keep them.

   2.   The law and the prophets truly testify of me.

➤ 15:11–24   Jesus again instructs the Twelve whom he had chosen.

   a.   Ye are my disciples, and a light to this people. vv. 12–13

   1.   You are a remnant of the house of Joseph.

   2.   The Father hath given you this land as your inheritance.

   b.   The Father did not command me to tell your brethren at Jerusalem of you, or of the other tribes he had led away. vv. 14–15

c. The Father did command me to tell them that other sheep he had that were not of their fold. vv. 16–20

    1. They were to hear my voice, and there would be one fold and one shepherd.

    2. Because of stiffneckedness and unbelief, they did not understand my words.

    3. You were separated from them because of their iniquity, and they did not know of you.

    4. The other tribes were also separated, and they did not know of them because of their iniquity.

d. You are those that I said were the other sheep not of their fold. vv. 21–24

    1. They thought I spoke of the Gentiles, and understood not that the Gentiles were to be converted through their preaching.

    2. They understood not that the Gentiles would not hear my voice at any time, and I would not manifest myself to them except by the Holy Ghost.

    3. You have heard my voice and seen me, and are among the sheep my Father hath given me.

➢ 16:1–5   I have other sheep that are not of this land, nor of Jerusalem, nor of any lands where I have ministered.

a. They have not as yet heard my voice, nor have I ministered to them. vv. 2–3

    1. The Father hath commanded me to go to them, and they shall hear my voice and be numbered among my sheep to become one fold with one shepherd.

    2. I go to show myself to them.

b. I command you to write these things after I am gone. vv. 4–5

    1. If those in Jerusalem do not ask and receive a knowledge of you and the other tribes by the Holy Ghost, these sayings shall be kept and manifested to you through the fullness of the Gentiles.

     2.   The remnant of their seed (the Jews), who are scattered upon all the earth because of unbelief, shall come to a knowledge of their Redeemer.

     3.   Then will I gather them, and fulfill the covenant to all the house of Israel.

➤ 16:6–20   Blessed are the Gentiles because of their belief in me through the Holy Ghost.

    a.   Because of the Gentiles' belief, and the unbelief of the house of Israel, in the latter days the truth will come unto the Gentiles. vv. 6–8

     1.   Wo to the unbelieving Gentiles who scattered my people on this land, and cast them out and have trodden them under foot.

     2.   Because of the Father's mercies to the Gentiles, and his judgments on the house of Israel, Israel has been smitten and hated by the Gentiles.

    b.   The father commanded, that when the Gentiles sin against my gospel, and reject the fullness of my gospel, and are full of all manner of wickedness, I will bring the fulness of my gospel from them. v. 10

    c.   Then I will remember my covenant with Israel, and bring my gospel to them. vv. 11–15

     1.   The Gentiles shall have no power over you, and you shall come to a knowledge of the gospel.

     2.   If the Gentiles repent, they shall be numbered among the house of Israel, and not be trodden down.

     3.   If they do not repent, Israel will tread them down.

     4.   They shall be as salt that has lost its savor.

    d.   The Father commanded me to give you this land for your inheritance, which will fulfill the words of Isaiah (52:8–10). vv. 16–20

     1.   Thy watchman shall sing together when the Lord brings again Zion.

     2.   They shall sing that the Lord has redeemed Jerusalem.

       3.   The Lord has made bare his arm in the eyes of all nations, and all shall see the salvation of God.

➤ 17:1–4   Jesus again turns to the multitude, and says his time is at hand.

       a.   He perceives they are weak, and cannot understand the words he was commanded to speak. v. 2

       b.   Go to your homes and ponder, pray, and prepare for the morrow when I will come again. v. 3

       c.   I go to the Father, and to show myself to the lost tribes of Israel. v. 4

       d.   They are not lost to the Father; he knows where he has taken them.

Although today both parts of his sermon have been made general to the reader, the deeper doctrines should be savored as sacred preaching for "Christ's sake, and for the sake of [his] people" (Jacob 1:4).

NOTES AND COMMENTARY

To the Nephite multitude, Jesus declared that they had now been taught the things he had taught the people in Palestine during his mortal ministry. He also promised redemption at the last day to those who followed what he had taught.

> 1 And now it came to pass that when Jesus had ended these sayings he cast his eyes round about on the multitude, and said unto them: Behold, ye have heard the things which I taught before I ascended to my Father; therefore, whoso remembereth these sayings of mine and doeth them, him will I raise up at the last day. [3 Nephi 15:1]

This seemingly insignificant summary is of vital importance to the Saints of the latter days when their faith is tested by the theories of men proclaiming that the Sermon on the Mount is not an actual discourse of the Savior, but is the work of an editor who compiled the variant teachings of the Master into its present form.[1] Such foolish concepts water down one of the greatest sermons ever recorded, taking away its doctrinal significance as well as throwing a shadow on its validity, calling it the work of a man, rather than the higher law of Jesus Christ.

Following his brief but poignant statement confirming the importance of the sermon on the higher law, the Savior perceived the multitudes' apprehension over the law of Moses and its fulfillment.

> 2 And it came to pass that when Jesus had said these words he perceived that there were some among them who marveled, and wondered what he would concerning the law of Moses; for they understood not the saying that old things had passed away, and that all things had become new.
>
> 3 And he said unto them: Marvel not that I said unto you that old things had passed away, and that all things had become new.
>
> 4 Behold, I say unto you that the law is fulfilled that was given unto Moses.
>
> 5 Behold, I am he that gave the law, and I am he who covenanted with my people Israel; therefore, the law in me is fulfilled, for I have come to fulfil the law; therefore it hath an end. [3 Nephi 15:2–5]

To ease their concern, he verified that "the law is fulfilled that was given unto Moses." To substantiate his pronouncement, he declared: "I am he that gave the law, and I am he who covenanted with my people Israel," (vv. 4–5). At Capernaum in Galilee, Jesus had indirectly taught the same thing. The people asked for a sign and justified their asking by saying: "Our fathers did eat manna in the desert; as it is written, He gave them bread from heaven to eat. Then Jesus said unto them, Verily, verily, I say unto you, Moses gave you not that bread from heaven; but my Father giveth you the true bread from heaven. For the bread of God is he which cometh down from heaven,

---

[1] See Johnson, Sherman E., "The Gospel According to Matthew" The *Interpreter's Bible,* Vol. 7, p. 279, and Wilder, Amos N. "The Teachings of Jesus—The Sermon on the Mount." Vol. 7, pp. 155–162.

and giveth you true bread from heaven" (John 6:31–33). In essence, he stated: "Moses did not give you that manna, I did." Also, there was a "spiritual Rock that followed them [in the wilderness]: and that Rock was Christ" (1 Corinthians 10:1–4). He also gave them the law (v. 5). Since he was the author of the law, he certainly had the authority and, as the Son of God, the power to bring it to closure. He was, therefore, the beginning and the end of the law of Moses as well as "the author and finisher of our faith" (Moroni 6:4, Hebrews 12:2).

However, lest he be misunderstood, Jesus had not fulfilled all that was foretold in the Old Testament.

> 6 Behold, I do not destroy the prophets, for as many as have not been fulfilled in me, verily I say unto you, shall all be fulfilled.
>
> 7 And because I said unto you that old things have passed away, I do not destroy that which hath been spoken concerning things which are to come.
>
> 8 For behold, the covenant which I have made with my people is not all fulfilled; but the law which was given unto Moses hath an end in me.
>
> 9 Behold, I am the law, and the light. Look unto me, and endure to the end, and ye shall live; for unto him that endureth to the end will I give eternal life.
>
> 10 Behold, I have given unto you the commandments; therefore keep my commandments. And this is the law and the prophets, for they truly testified of me. [3 Nephi 15:6–10]

There were many prophecies of the prophets yet to be fulfilled. The fulfillment of the covenant that he had made with Abraham, and had extended to Israel, was yet to come in the future. Both the fulfillment of the prophecies and the covenant to Israel were vital to his gospel, and were tied to him, as was the law of Moses. He was the total law of this world, and the light that governed its destiny. Those who kept his commandments would therefore attain eternal life. The multitude's questions were satisfied, but do we realize that we are living in the day this covenant and these prophecies are being fulfilled? Hopefully, this work will help bring about such a realization.

As Jesus had spoken to the multitude, the Twelve had heard his broad declarations concerning the prophets and the covenants with Israel. To these trusted disciples, he now turned to reveal the finer details of how these promises would be fulfilled, particularly their role in these future happenings.

The Twelve—The Land of Joseph

The Twelve had been chosen to direct the Nephites in the fulfillment of their part in the covenant made to Israel. The Nephites were descendants of Joseph, son of Jacob, who had been instrumental in preserving the house of Israel in the land of Egypt. These people, as a remnant of Joseph, were inheritors of the Americas as their promised land.

> 11 And now it came to pass that when Jesus had spoken these words, he said unto those twelve whom he had chosen:
>
> 12 Ye are my disciples; and ye are a light unto this people, who are a remnant of the house of Joseph.
>
> 13 And behold, this is the land of your inheritance; and the Father hath given it unto you.
>
> 14 And not at any time hath the Father given me commandment that I should tell it unto your brethren at Jerusalem.
>
> 15 Neither at any time hath the Father given me commandment that I should tell unto them concerning the other tribes of the house of Israel, whom the Father hath led away out of the land. [3 Nephi 15:11–15]

This privileged information had not been revealed to "the brethren at Jerusalem" (vv. 14–15). It is not clear if the "brethren at Jerusalem" had reference to the Saints in general at Jerusalem, or to the twelve Apostles there. Regardless, to either group, this knowledge was available through the power of the Holy Ghost, and if it were not manifest through that means, it would eventually "be manifested unto the Gentiles" through the writings of these Nephite disciples (3 Nephi 16:4). Had the Jerusalem brethren searched the scriptures, the Holy Ghost would probably have manifested it unto them. Furthermore, there were several Old Testament prophecies that alluded to the

Nephites in America through which the people in Jerusalem could have known of them.

Father Jacob had promised his son Joseph that the branches of his seed "would run over the wall [of the ocean] . . . to the utmost bound of the everlasting hills" (Genesis 49:22–26). Lehi, "who was a descendant of Manasseh, who was the son of Joseph who was sold into Egypt" (Alma 10:3), and Ishmael, being a descendant of Ephraim,[2] the sons of Joseph, had laid the foundation for this promise. Moses had made a similar prophecy regarding "the ancient mountains" and "the lasting hills" whereunto "the ten thousands of Ephraim, and . . . the thousands of Manasseh" would be pushed [gathered] together (Deuteronomy 33:13–17). The Lord revealed that the elders of the latter-day Restoration would fulfill Moses' prophecy. They would eventually "receive their inheritance in this land . . . For, behold, they shall push the people together from the ends of the earth" (D&C 58:44–45).

Furthermore, in what is obviously a part of "the many plain and precious things which have been taken out of the book [Bible]" (1 Nephi 13:29), the Lord had made a covenant with Jacob, father of Joseph: "And behold, this people will I establish in this land [Americas], unto the fulfilling of the covenant which I made with your father Jacob; and it shall be a New Jerusalem. And the powers of heaven shall be in the midst of this people; yea, even I will be in the midst of you" (3 Nephi 20:22). Perhaps this precious truth had been lost by the time Jesus had ministered in Jerusalem. Jesus warned the scheming lawyers: "ye have taken away the key of knowledge, *the fulness of the scriptures*, ye entered not in yourselves into the kingdom; and those who were entering in, ye hindered" (JST Luke 11:53; italics added). Nonetheless, the covenant made to Jacob had been recorded, and even if then lost, the same information could have been revealed by the

---

[2] Elder Erastus Snow, a former member of the Quorum of the Twelve Apostles said: "The Prophet Joseph informed us that the record of Lehi, was contained on the 116 pages that were first translated and subsequently stolen . . . that Ishmael was of the lineage of Ephraim." JD 23:184

Holy Ghost. Apparently, the Jewish people never learned of the Nephites through either of these means. Therefore, it is today being "manifested unto the Gentiles, that through the fulness of the Gentiles, the remnant of [the Jewish seed], who [have been] scattered forth upon the face of the earth because of their unbelief, may be brought in, or may be brought to a knowledge of [Christ], their Redeemer" (3 Nephi 16:4).

As birthright holders, the tribe of Ephraim, son of Joseph, who were also scattered among the Gentiles, are now being gathered to bring about this promised blessing to his father's land. This is verified by the following scriptures. The Lord promised the Gentiles who would repent when the gospel and the Church came among them, that they would be able to assist "the remnant of Jacob unto whom I have given this land for their inheritance" in building the New Jerusalem (3 Nephi 21:22–23). In June 1831, the Lord identified the elders of his recently restored church as "my people, which are a remnant of Jacob, and those who are heirs according to the covenant," and Missouri as the land "which I will consecrate unto" them (D&C 52:1–2). After Ephraim is firmly established, the rest of Joseph's seed and others of the house of Israel will be gathered to them (3 Nephi 21:23–27). This gathering will be discussed in chapter twelve of this work.

The Other Sheep

16 This much did the Father command me, that I should tell unto them:

17 That other sheep I have which are not of this fold; them also I must bring, and they shall hear my voice; and there shall be one fold, and one shepherd.

18 And now, because of stiffneckedness and unbelief they understood not my word; therefore I was commanded to say no more of the Father concerning this thing unto them.

19 But, verily, I say unto you that the Father hath commanded me, and I tell it unto you, that ye were separated from among them because of

their iniquity; therefore it is because of their iniquity that they know not of you.

20 And verily, I say unto you again that the other tribes hath the Father separated from them; and it is because of their iniquity that they know not of them. [3 Nephi 15:16–20]

Jesus had spoken as much to the Jews about the Nephites as his Father had commanded. He had identified himself as the Good Shepherd who "giveth his life for the sheep" and declared that "other sheep I have, which are not of this fold; them also I must bring, and they shall hear my voice" (John 10:11–16). Those in Jerusalem had not comprehended this message because of stiffneckedness and unbelief (v. 18). This unbelief probably has reference to the populace of Jerusalem, and possibly (but probably not) to the Saints of Galilee, but certainly not to the Twelve. It is possible, that if the Twelve knew, they had been commanded to not make it public. This probability is drawn from Jesus' statement concerning the iniquity of the people in Jerusalem (vv. 19–20). Jesus' statement about the other sheep was made at "the feast of the dedication" in Jerusalem, in the winter, a few months before his crucifixion. "There was a division therefore again among the Jews for these sayings" (John 10:19). The wicked element prevailed and "Then the Jews took up stones again to stone him" (John 10:31). The Twelve Apostles were not a part of this iniquitous attempt to take Jesus' life, nor were the disciples in Galilee.

After informing the Nephites that it was they to whom he had referred as "the other sheep," Jesus told them of the misunderstanding of the Jews:

21 And verily I say unto you, that ye are they of whom I said: Other sheep I have which are not of this fold; them also I must bring, and they shall hear my voice; and there shall be one fold, and one shepherd.

22 And they understood me not, for they supposed it had been the Gentiles; for they understood not that the Gentiles should be converted through their preaching.

23 And they understood me not that I said they shall hear my voice; and they understood not that the Gentiles should not at any time hear my

> voice—that I should not manifest myself unto them save it were by the Holy Ghost.
>
> 24 But behold, ye have both heard my voice, and seen me; and ye are my sheep, and ye are numbered among those whom the Father hath given me. [3 Nephi 15:21–24]

The Gentiles did not hear his voice during his mortal ministry. The Gentile woman of Canaan cried unto him for mercy over her grievously ill daughter, but "he answered her not a word." His disciples urged him to send her away, but he responded, "I am not sent but unto the lost sheep of the house of Israel" (Matthew 15:21–24). Although he did then speak to her, "O woman, great is thy faith: be it unto thee even as thou wilt. And her daughter was made whole that very hour" (15:28), his doctrine was established; his mission was to speak to the house of Israel, and the Gentiles would not hear his voice.

Earlier Jesus had commanded his Twelve Apostles: "Go not into the way of the Gentiles, and into any city of the Samaritans enter ye not: But go rather to the lost sheep of the house of Israel" (Matthew 10:5–6). At the conclusion of his ministry, he commanded them to "Go ye therefore and teach all nations" (Matthew 28:19). However, the full implication of these instructions was not perceived until Peter, as the President of the Church, received his vision of the unclean meats. "Of a truth I perceive that God is no respecter of persons: But in every nation he that feareth him, and worketh righteousness, is accepted of him" (Acts 10:34–35). The Lord had opened the door for the preaching to the Gentiles. As Lehi had prophesied in 600 B.C., Christ "should make himself manifest, by the Holy Ghost, unto the Gentiles" (1 Nephi 10:11). This manifestation would come through the message of the Apostles being confirmed by that Spirit.

> 1 And verily, verily, I say unto you that I have other sheep, which are not of this land, neither of the land of Jerusalem, neither in any parts of that land round about whither I have been to minister.
>
> 2 For they of whom I speak are they who have not as yet heard my voice; neither have I at any time manifested myself unto them.

3 But I have received a commandment of the Father that I shall go unto them, and that they shall hear my voice, and shall be numbered among my sheep, that there may be one fold and one shepherd; therefore I go to show myself unto them.

4 And I command you that ye shall write these sayings after I am gone, that if it so be that my people at Jerusalem, they who have seen me and been with me in my ministry, do not ask the Father in my name, that they may receive a knowledge of you by the Holy Ghost, and also of the other tribes whom they know not of, that these sayings which ye shall write shall be kept and shall be manifested unto the Gentiles, that through the fulness of the Gentiles, the remnant of their seed, who shall be scattered forth upon the face of the earth because of their unbelief, may be brought in, or may be brought to a knowledge of me, their Redeemer.

5 And then will I gather them in from the four quarters of the earth; and then will I fulfil the covenant which the Father hath made unto all the people of the house of Israel. [3 Nephi 16:1–5]

Through the writings of the Nephites that were to come forth to the Gentiles in the latter days, the Jews who would be scattered among those Gentile nations would be brought to a knowledge of Christ their Redeemer (v. 4). As the Book of Mormon was taken to the Gentile nations, the scattered remnants of Judah among them would have the opportunity to accept the gospel, and be gathered together in fulfillment of the covenant made to Israel's descendants (v. 5).

Following Jesus' visit among the Nephites, his Father had commanded him to visit another group of the house of Israel, the lost tribes. These he designated as still other sheep that he must visit (vv. 1–3). The sheep of the lost tribes also came to a knowledge of Jesus Christ through his visit, "and the Nephites and the Jews shall have the words of the lost tribes of Israel; and the lost tribes of Israel shall have the words of the Nephites and the Jews" (2 Nephi 29:13). Thus, the Book of Mormon contains the fullness of the gospel, and is "Another Testament of Jesus Christ" to others of the house of Israel. However, this blessing will follow the times of the Gentiles.

The Times of the Gentiles

The gospel being "manifested unto the Gentiles" (3 Nephi 16:4) often raises the question, "Who are the Gentiles?" While there are many different definitions of Gentiles used in the world today, it is important to understand the Book of Mormon interpretation. Otherwise, the sequence of latter-day events will not be understood. Since the Book of Mormon definition was given by the Savior, it is certainly an accurate description.

> 6 And blessed are the Gentiles, because of their belief in me, in and of the Holy Ghost, which witnesses unto them of me and of the Father.
>
> 7 Behold, because of their belief in me, saith the Father, and because of the unbelief of you, O house of Israel, in the latter day shall the truth come unto the Gentiles, that the fulness of these things shall be made known unto them.
>
> 8 But wo, saith the Father, unto the unbelieving of the Gentiles—for notwithstanding they have come forth upon the face of this land, and have scattered my people who are of the house of Israel; and my people who are of the house of Israel have been cast out from among them, and have been trodden under feet by them;
>
> 9 And because of the mercies of the Father unto the Gentiles, and also the judgments of the Father upon my people who are of the house of Israel, verily, verily, I say unto you, that after all this, and I have caused my people who are of the house of Israel to be smitten, and to be afflicted, and to be slain, and to be cast out from among them, and to become hated by them, and to become a hiss and a byword among them— [3 Nephi 16:6–9]

Jesus defined the Gentiles as those who have a "belief in [Christ], in and of the Holy Ghost, which witnesses unto them of me, and of the Father" (v. 6). This definition correlates with Jesus' statement to the Nephites discussed above, "that the Gentiles should not at any time hear my voice—that I should not manifest myself unto them save it were by the Holy Ghost" (3 Nephi 15:24). Following the revelation to Peter, and through the efforts of the Twelve, spearheaded by Paul, "the apostle of the Gentiles" (Romans 11:13), the gospel spread through Asia and Europe. As the work of the Twelve went forth to the

Gentiles, the Holy Ghost bore witness of the divinity of Jesus. Although the new converts had not at anytime heard the voice of the Lord, they had had Christ manifest unto them by the Holy Ghost. Thus, the Gentiles believed in Christ "in and of the Holy Ghost" (v. 6).

The acceptance of the gospel accelerated until Christianity became the dominant, or even the state religion of many nations. These nations are primarily in Europe and the Americas. Thus, the Book of Mormon definition labels the Christian nations as the Gentiles. It was to these nations that the truth was to come in the latter days (v. 7). This was according to Jesus' prophecy that the "first shall be last; and the last shall be first" (Matthew 20:1–16; Luke 13:22–30). In Paul's missionary work, "It was necessary that the word of God should first have been spoken to [the Jews]," and after they rejected the gospel, "lo, we turn to the Gentiles" (Acts 13:46). In this dispensation, it was to "go forth unto the ends of the earth, unto the Gentiles first, and then, behold, and lo, they shall turn to the Jews" (D&C 90:9). Thus, we are living in the times of the Gentiles, as defined in a revelation to Joseph Smith:[3] "And when the times of the Gentiles is come in, a light shall break forth among them that sit in darkness, and it shall be the fulness of my gospel" (D&C 45:28). It is the time for the Gentiles to have their opportunity to accept the gospel and be numbered with Israel.

After the Savior announced the glorious promise of taking the gospel to the Gentiles in the latter days, he added a warning to "the unbelieving of the Gentiles (v. 8). Many will reject the message of truth. This he repeated a little later in his three-day ministry to the Nephites; "there shall be among them those who will not believe it" (3 Nephi 21:9), and in his Jerusalem ministry; "But [the Gentiles]

---

[3] The revelation to Joseph Smith cited here is actually the words that Jesus spoke to his disciples in Jerusalem just prior to his crucifixion and recited in this dispensation (see D&C 45:16–59).

receive it not; for they perceive not the light, and they turn their hearts from me because of the precepts of men" (D&C 45:29). Isaiah had earlier foretold that Israel, as the Lord's servant, would "seek [the Gentiles], and shalt not find them, even them that contended with thee" (41:12). Those who contended are, of course, the Gentiles who inhabited the land of America at the time the Book of Mormon came forth, and fought against those servants of Israel who brought it forth. While the percentages or numbers of unbelievers are not given anywhere in scripture, Joseph Smith declared that "few of [the Gentiles] will be gathered with the chosen family" (TPJS, 15). Jesus' teachings during his mortal ministry are applicable here: "for many be called, but few chosen" (Matthew 20:16).

Before pronouncing the fate upon the unbelieving Gentiles, the Savior diverted his speech to the seriousness of the Gentiles' rejection. Because of the unbelief and idolatry of the Nephite nation, the Lord had "reserved their blessings which they might have received in the land, for the Gentiles who shall possess the land" (Mormon 5:19). The Father had thus been merciful unto the Gentiles in allowing them to come to this land and scatter his people who are of the house of Israel, the Lamanites, and trod them down, hate them, and make them a hiss and a by-word among the Gentiles (16:8–9). The Father's mercy was further extended to the Gentiles through his bringing forth the Book of Mormon that would "make known the plain and precious things which have been taken away from them" (1 Nephi 13:40), and would be "unto the taking away of their stumbling blocks" (1 Nephi 14:1), caused by "the most plain and precious parts of the gospel of the Lamb which have been kept back by that abominable church" (1 Nephi 13:34). Having been given the rich blessing of living in a choice land above all other lands, and an opportunity for even richer blessings, serious consequences would follow the rejection of the Book of Mormon and the truth it contains.

Returning to the warning, the Savior announced the causes of the future Gentile judgment by the Father and what that judgment would be.

> 10 And thus commandeth the Father that I should say unto you: At that day when the Gentiles shall sin against my gospel, and shall reject the fulness of my gospel, and shall be lifted up in the pride of their hearts above all nations, and above all the people of the whole earth, and shall be filled with all manner of lyings, and of deceits, and of mischiefs, and all manner of hypocrisy, and murders, and priestcrafts, and whoredoms, and of secret abominations; and if they shall do all those things, and shall reject the fulness of my gospel, behold, saith the Father, I will bring the fulness of my gospel from among them. [3 Nephi 16:10]

The first cause was that "the Gentiles shall sin against [his] gospel." To sin against the gospel is to live contrary to what it teaches. King Benjamin defined sin as "having transgressed the law of God contrary to his own knowledge" (Mosiah 2:33). Therefore, the Savior seems to be saying that the Gentiles will knowingly go against the truths of the gospel.

The second cause was that the Gentiles "shall reject the fulness of my gospel." Since "the fulness of the everlasting gospel was contained in the [Book of Mormon]" (JS–H 1:34), he is foretelling the rejection of that great book. "A knowledge of [The Book of Mormon] must come unto the remnant of these people, and also unto the Gentiles" (Mormon 5:9). To reject it, implies the rejection of its messengers, the servants of God who are to take it "to every nation, and kindred, and tongue, and people" (Revelation 14:6–7). Therefore, the blessings of the Book of Mormon, and the subsequent rejection of it will be extended to all the Gentile nations or Christian nations. While it will also eventually go to all non-Christian nations as well, we are concerned in this time period with the Gentile nations.

The Gentiles' rejection of this book will come, according to the Savior, because the Gentiles are "lifted up in the pride of their hearts above all nations, and above all the people of the whole earth, and shall be filled with all manner of lyings, and of deceits, and of mischiefs, and all manner of hypocrisy, and murders, and priestcrafts, and whoredoms, and of secret abominations" (v. 10). "Because of the pride of [Nephi's] seed, and the temptations of the devil," the Nephite nation was overpowered (1 Nephi 12:19). The Lord has warned us:

"beware of pride lest ye become as the Nephites of old" (D&C 38:39). President Ezra Taft Benson has warned us of pride in our society. He gave various definitions and consequences of pride, and declared that: "We must cleanse the inner vessel of pride."[4]

All of the various sins enumerated by the Savior are prevalent in our society today. While the society is guilty of these sins, they have not as yet rejected the messengers who are offering its message of salvation to them; therefore, the Lord has not as yet brought about his judgment of bringing "the fullness of the gospel from among them" (v. 10). When he does, "in that generation shall the times of the Gentiles be fulfilled" (D&C 45:29; see also Luke 21:25–32; JST Luke 21:24–25, 32 as footnoted in the LDS edition of the Bible, and in its appendix). An overflowing scourge and "a desolating sickness shall cover the land. But the Lord's disciples shall stand in holy places and not be moved" (D&C 45:30–32). These days will probably come piecemeal. Just as nations are opened to the preaching of the gospel one by one, it seems plausible that the rejection of the gospel will come in a similar manner. The piecemeal theory is also evidenced by the fact that some of the Gentile (Christian) nations have recently been given their opportunity to accept the gospel, while others have had the opportunity for many years. While every nation does not have to have an equal time period of having the gospel among them, it is within the justice of God that each nation will have an opportunity to accept or reject the gospel. As the rejection comes, the servants, and thus the gospel, will be withdrawn. The gospel will then be taken to the house of Israel.

The Times of Israel

> 11 And then will I remember my covenant which I have made unto
> my people, O house of Israel, and I will bring my gospel unto them.

---

[4] CR April 1989 pp. 3–7 This inspired sermon is too long to be included here , but should be read by every member of the Church. All those who are not members of the Church are also invited to read it. It was published in the Church's *Ensign* magazine, May 1989.

12 And I will show unto thee, O house of Israel, that the Gentiles shall not have power over you; but I will remember my covenant unto you, O house of Israel, and ye shall come unto the knowledge of the fulness of my gospel.

13 But if the Gentiles will repent and return unto me, saith the Father, behold they shall be numbered among my people, O house of Israel. [3 Nephi 16:11–13]

There is a chronological sequence in the fulfillment of this prophecy. There are three separate groups of the house of Israel: the lost tribes, the Jews, and the Lamanites, naming them in the order of their having been taken away from Palestine and scattered in the Lord's vineyard or the world. According to Zenos' allegory of the house of Israel, these are to be gathered in the reverse order of their dispersion; "begin at the last that they may be first, and that the first may be last" (Jacob 5:63). Thus, the Lamanites are the first to receive the gospel. The gospel has already begun to go to the Lamanites, although much of the thrust of missionary work is still towards the Gentiles. This is indicative of a piecemeal transition from the teaching of the gospel to the Gentiles to the teaching of Israel. Although the gathering of Israel has commenced, we learn from the Book of Mormon that the main thrust of their return will not happen until the New Jerusalem has been built in Missouri. "And then shall the work of the Father commence at that day, even when this gospel shall be preached among the remnant of this people [the Lamanites]," followed by other groups of Israel (3 Nephi 21:23–27). The gathering of these groups will be discussed in future chapters. The Lord briefly mentioned it here to show the house of Israel "that the Gentiles shall not have power over [them]; but [he] will remember [his] covenant unto" them, and they "shall come unto the knowledge of the fullness of the gospel" (v. 12).

The Lord continued to speak of the Gentiles, promising that, if they "will repent and return unto me, saith the Father, behold they shall be numbered among my people, O house of Israel" (v. 13). A careful analysis of this verse and the verses that follow indicates some dual meanings. For example, although the times of Israel are yet to come, there are those of the house of Israel who have already been established. This requires some explanation.

Israel Among The Gentiles

As prophesied by Amos, the Old Testament prophet, the Lord said: "I will sift [scatter] the house of Israel among all nations" (Amos 9:8–9). The purpose of this scattering was to fulfill a part of the covenant made to Abraham that: 'In thy seed shall all the kindreds of the earth be blessed"; (1 Nephi 22:9; see also Genesis 12:3)). As the gospel was taken to the Gentiles, all of them would eventually be given an opportunity to accept or reject the gospel. However, those among them who had the blood of Israel would respond to the teachings of the gospel, and gather together. As the Savior taught, "My sheep hear my voice, and I know them, and they follow me" (John 10:27).[5] The gathering of these scattered remnants of Israel from among the Gentiles would thus establish "the natural tree," spoken of in Zenos' allegory of the house of Israel, into which the three branches of Israel, the Lamanites, the Jews, and the ten tribes, would be "grafted into their mother tree" (Jacob 5:54–56). The mother trunk would logically and scripturally be the birthright holders; "and Ephraim is my firstborn" (Jeremiah 31:9). As determined by revelation through patriarchal blessings, it is no accident, therefore, that the blood of Ephraim is being primarily gathered today. In the words of President Joseph F. Smith, "A striking peculiarity of the Saints gathered from all parts of the earth is that they are almost universally of the blood of Ephraim.[6]

> 14 And I will not suffer my people, who are of the house of Israel, to go through among them, and tread them down, saith the Father.

---

[5] For a fuller analysis of the gathered Latter-day Saints being of the literal blood of Israel see Nyman, Monte S., *Doctrines of Exaltation,* Chap. 14 "The Second Gathering of the Literal Seed" Deseret Book, Salt Lake City, Utah 1989.

[6] Smith, Joseph F., *Gospel Doctrine* , November 1, 1902, 11th ed. (Salt Lake City, Utah: Deseret Book Co., 1959), p. 115.

15 But if they will not turn unto me, and hearken unto my voice, I will suffer them, yea, I will suffer my people, O house of Israel, that they shall go through among them, and shall tread them down, and they shall be as salt that hath lost its savor, which is thenceforth good for nothing but to be cast out, and to be trodden under foot of my people, O house of Israel. [3 Nephi 16:14–15]

Those who are gathered together, Ephraim and adopted Gentiles who accept the gospel, are promised by the Savior that they will not be trodden down by the house of Israel (v. 14). The manner of this fulfillment will be discussed more fully later, but for now let us note that the treading down is not a conditional prophesy; "the remnants who are left of the land will marshal themselves, and shall become exceedingly angry, and shall vex the Gentiles with a sore vexation" (D&C 87:5). It suggests that the treading down is to be by those who are not yet members of the restored Church, since the members of the Church are to be safe. However, the Savior gives a warning to those who are gathered as well.

The Savior said that those who would "not turn unto me, and hearken unto my voice," shall be trodden down, and shall be as salt that hath lost its savor (v. 15; see also Matthew 5:13). The people who reject the gospel will, of course, be subjected to the uprising of the house of Israel, but who are the salt of the earth? The salt of the earth is identified in latter-day revelation as the members of the Church:

When men are called unto mine everlasting gospel, and covenant with an everlasting covenant, they are accounted as the salt of the earth and the savor of men;

They are called to be the savor of men; therefore, if that salt of the earth lose its savor, behold, it is thenceforth good for nothing only to be cast out and trodden under the feet of men. [D&C 101:39–40; see also D&C 103:8–10]

Therefore, this prophecy includes the gathered members of the Church who do not keep the commandments or follow the admonitions of the living prophets. Those who do keep the commandments and follow the prophets will not only escape being trodden, but will also inherit the land of America as the descendants of Joseph. The Father had commanded Jesus to promise this to the Nephites.

> 16 Verily, verily, I say unto you, thus hath the Father commanded me—that I should give unto this people this land for their inheritance.

> 17 And then the words of the prophet Isaiah shall be fulfilled, which say:

> 18 Thy watchmen shall lift up the voice; with the voice together shall they sing, for they shall see eye to eye when the Lord shall bring again Zion.

> 19 Break forth into joy, sing together, ye waste places of Jerusalem; for the Lord hath comforted his people, he hath redeemed Jerusalem.

> 20 The Lord hath made bare his holy arm in the eyes of all the nations; and all the ends of the earth shall see the salvation of God. [3 Nephi 16:16–20]

Having detailed the work in the Americas among the Lamanites and the Gentiles, the Lord proclaimed that the prophet Isaiah had prophesied of these very things. He then quoted Isaiah 52:8–10. In this prophecy the prophet Isaiah said; "thy watchmen [priesthood servants] shall lift up the voice." From the context of Jesus' explanation, this would be the missionaries declaring the gospel among the Gentiles to gather out Israel. Isaiah said further, "With the voice together shall they sing, for they shall see eye to eye when the Lord shall bring again Zion" (v. 18; Isaiah 52:8). The servants of the Lord will be purified through the still small voice of the Spirit to bring forth and establish the cause of Zion. Those who have been gathered will be purified and prepared to become a Zion people. Those who are not prepared will be trodden down with the unrepentant Gentiles, as Jesus explained earlier.

The next verse of Isaiah was not explained by Jesus at this time, but is again quoted and then explained a few chapters later in Third Nephi. At this point he is merely quoting Isaiah to show that there will be a similar restoration to Jerusalem among the Jews (v. 19; Isaiah 52:9).

Jesus then quoted a final verse from Isaiah (52:10), "The Lord hath made bare his holy arm in the eyes of all nations" (v. 20). From Jesus' previous explanation, the nations mentioned here must be viewed as the Gentile nations. The Lord's holy arm that has been made bare is symbolically his power shown forth among the Gentiles in two ways: first, the power of his spirit in bringing about the restoration of his Church and kingdom among the Gentiles; and second, the treading down of the Gentiles and the unrepentant gathered Israel who reject the gospel or lose their savor (testimonies and commitment to live the principles). The last phrase, "and all the ends of the earth shall see the salvation of God," may be an example of Hebrew parallelism in which the same thought is repeated, or it may be a declaration that the other nations of the earth (Israel and all others) will then be given their opportunity to hear and accept the gospel. From the context of Jesus' prior words, the latter seems to be more appropriate. Truly Isaiah had foretold the destiny of the nations of the earth, and verified that Abraham's covenant to bless all of these nations will be fulfilled. The deeper doctrines had been explained.

The Lost Tribes of Israel

1 Behold, now it came to pass that when Jesus had spoken these words he looked round about again on the multitude, and he said unto them: Behold, my time is at hand.

2 I perceive that ye are weak, that ye cannot understand all my words which I am commanded of the Father to speak unto you at this time.

3 Therefore, go ye unto your homes, and ponder upon the things which I have said, and ask of the Father, in my name, that ye may understand, and prepare your minds for the morrow, and I come unto you again.

4 But now I go unto the Father, and also to show myself unto the lost tribes of Israel, for they are not lost unto the Father, for he knoweth whither he hath taken them. [3 Nephi 17:1–4]

Jesus turned to the multitude, having taught his disciples some of the mysteries of God and having perceived their spiritual (and possibly physical) weakness, and instructed them to go to their homes and prepare their minds for the morrow when he would come again

(vv. 1–3). Understanding of the things of God is based upon one's willingness to ponder and pray about them. To ponder is to weigh back and forth both intellectually and spiritually. It must be "in your mind and in your heart" that the Holy Ghost bears witness (D&C 8:2). These are appropriate instructions for our reading the Book of Mormon today.

While they were pondering, Jesus intended to visit the lost tribes of Israel (v. 4). These were the still "other sheep" to whom he had earlier referred to his disciples (3 Nephi 16:1). Although he detained his departure for a little while because he had compassion for the faithful Nephite multitude, he did indeed visit the lost tribes. Someday we will have an account of that visit. He had taught the Nephites as he had the people in Palestine, and being no respecter of persons, he was going to do the same for the rest of the house of Israel. They were also a part of Abraham's covenant and the last group of Israel that he would visit. His ministry of the meridian of time would then be completed.

Today we are living in the dispensation of the fullness of times, when the things of which he prophesied are being fulfilled. It is a day that will eventually bless all the nations of the earth; those of the Gentiles, those of Israel, and those of all other nations. The covenant made to Abraham will then be fulfilled. Mormon said it would be fulfilled "after [the Lamanites] had been driven and scattered by the Gentiles" (Mormon 5:20). Mormon's prophecy has been fulfilled, and the nations are being offered the blessings of the gospel. The blessings offered to those nations are the same as those he gave to the Nephites after he returned from his visit to the ten tribes, as discussed in the following chapters.

Chapter 9

The New Dispensation

3 Nephi 17:5–18:39; 20:1–9; Moroni 4–5

The blessings of the gospel to be ministered by Abraham's seed through the priesthood of God were "the blessings of salvation, even of life eternal" (Abraham 2:9–11). The Church's third Article of Faith states, "through the Atonement of Christ, all mankind may be saved, by obedience to the laws and ordinances of the Gospel." Some ordinances are necessary for salvation (saving ordinances), while others bless the members of the Church, but are not essential for salvation. Ordinances are a vital part of the gospel today and were a part of the gospel that Jesus introduced to the Nephites.

Prior to the advent of Jesus Christ among the Nephites, Nephi had ordained "men unto this ministry, that all such as should come unto them should be baptized with water" [a saving ordinance] (3 Nephi 7:25). Therefore, priesthood ordinations and baptism were already a Nephite practice. Yet Jesus had just given twelve Nephite disciples (including Nephi) "power and authority to baptize" (3 Nephi 11:22; 12:1). On the second day of Jesus' ministry, "Nephi went down into the water and was baptized." Nephi then "baptized all those whom Jesus had chosen" (3 Nephi 19:11–12). Later, as Moroni recorded some of Jesus' teachings and actions during his Nephite ministry, he stated: "elders, priests, and teachers were baptized" (Moroni 6:1). Why were these priesthood holders baptized when they had already been baptized?[1] The answer to this question may be drawn from the instructions given to the Church in these latter days through the Prophet Joseph:

> 1 Behold, I say unto you that all old covenants have I caused to be done away in this thing; and this is a new and an everlasting covenant, even that which was from the beginning.
>
> 2 Wherefore, although a man should be baptized an hundred times it availeth him nothing, for you cannot enter in at the strait gate by the law of Moses, neither by your dead works. [D&C 22:1–2]

A new dispensation was being ushered in. "The law [was] fulfilled that was given unto Moses" (3 Nephi 15:14), and his dispensation was ended. Although many of the same ordinances and principles of the gospel were still to be followed, Jesus gave specific instructions regarding his dispensation that was now beginning. The order in which the ordinances were introduced was at least partially determined by the reaction of the multitude, and is not significant. What he said and did was the pattern that the Nephites were to follow. An outline of the chapters introducing the ordinances follows, as an overview to prepare for a deeper study.

Outline • 3 Nephi 17:5–18:39; 20:1–9; Moroni 4–5

➤ 17:5–25   Jesus perceives the multitude's desire for him to remain a little longer, is filled with compassion and remains with them.

        a.   He invites them to bring their sick and afflicted, and he will heal them. vv. 7–10

---

[1] They were apparently also reordained to priesthood offices. Moroni, in speaking of Jesus' ministry states that men were ordained to various offices as "they laid their hands upon them." He also outlined the ordination prayer that was followed and the bestowal of "the gifts and callings of God unto men; and they ordained them by the power of the Holy Ghost, which was in them" (Moroni 3:1–4). This procedure suggests that individual and specific blessings were bestowed upon each individual.

1. He perceives their desire to be shown what he had done in Jerusalem.

2. He sees they have faith to be healed.

3. They bring forth their sick and afflicted, and they are healed.

4. Those healed and those whole bowed and worshipped him, kissing and bathing his feet with tears.

b. He commands them, and they bring their little children and set them round about him. vv. 11–17

1. He commands the multitude to kneel down.

2. He tells the Father he is troubled because of the wickedness of the people of Israel.

3. He kneels and prays words that could not be written, nor had been heard.

4. No one can conceive the joy that filled their souls as he prayed.

c. Jesus arose, but the multitude was overcome with joy. He commanded them to arise, and he blessed their little children one by one. vv. 18–25

1. He said they were blessed because of their faith, and his joy was full.

2. He invited them to behold their little ones.

3. They looked up and saw angels descend in the midst of fire, encircle and minister to their children.

4. About two thousand five hundred men, woman, and children saw and heard these things.

➢ 18:1–16 Jesus commanded the disciples to bring forth bread and wine, and for the multitude to sit down.

a. He broke the bread and blessed it, and had them drink of the wine and were filled. v. 3

b. They were to give it to the multitude. v. 4

c. One was given power to break and bless the bread, and give it to those baptized. vv. 5–7

    1.   They should always break and bless the bread as he had done.

    2.   It was to be done in remembrance of his body.

    3.   It was to be a testimony to the Father of always remembering Christ.

    4.   If they always remember, they will have his Spirit to be with them.

  d.   The baptized were to drink the wine to fulfill Christ's commandment. vv. 8–11

    1.   It was a witness to the Father that they would do as Christ commanded.

    2.   It was in remembrance of Christ's blood which was shed for them.

    3.   If they always remember him, they will have his Spirit to be with them.

  e.   The disciples are commanded to partake of the bread and wine. vv. 12–14

    1.   Those who do are built upon his rock.

    2.   Those who do more or less than this are not built on his rock, and will fall.

  f.   The disciples are to watch and pray always lest they be led away by the devil. vv. 15–16

    1.   Pray among the church as he prayed among them.

    2.   He is the light and has set an example to them.

➤ 18:17–25   Jesus instructed the multitude to watch and pray always lest they be led into temptation.

  a.   Satan desires to sift you as wheat. v. 18

  b.   Always pray unto the Father in Christ's name. vv. 19–21

    1.   Whatsoever they ask, that is right, shall be received if they believe.

    2.   Pray in your families that your wives and children be blessed.

  c.   Meet together oft, and do not forbid any to come unto you. vv. 22–23

        1.   Pray for them, and do not cast them out.

        2.   If they come unto you oft, pray unto the Father for them.

    d.   Hold up your light that it may shine unto the world. vv. 24–25

        1.   Christ is the light they should hold up.

        2.   Do the things he has done and commanded.

        3.   Those who break this commandment allow themselves to be led into temptation.

➢ 18:26–35   Jesus commands the disciples to not allow anyone to knowingly partake of his flesh and blood unworthily.

    a.   Those who eat and drink unworthily eateth and drinketh damnation to his soul. vv. 29–32

        1.   Do not cast him out, but minister to him and pray for him.

        2.   If he repents and is baptized, ye shall give him Christ's flesh and blood.

        3.   If not, he shall not be numbered among my people that he may destroy them.

        4.   Ye shall still not cast him out, but continue to minister to him, and be the means of his salvation.

    b.   Keep these commandments that you come not unto condemnation. vv. 33–34

        1.   Wo unto those whom the Father condemns.

        2.   These commandments were given because of disputations among you.

        3.   Blessed are you if you have no disputations.

    c.   It is expedient for Christ to go to the Father for your sakes. v. 35

➢ 18:36–39   Jesus touched and spoke to the disciples one by one, and a cloud overshadowed the multitude.

    a.   They bore record that he gave them power to give the Holy Ghost as Mormon will show later. v. 37

    b.   The multitude could not see Jesus. v. 38

         c.   The disciples saw and bore record that he ascended into heaven. v. 39

➤ 20:1–9   On the second day, the Savior commanded the multitude and the disciples to cease to pray, but to continue to pray in their hearts.

         a.   He brake bread again gave it to the disciples and the multitude, and gave them wine to drink. vv. 3–4

         b.   There had been no bread or wine brought, but he truly gave it to them. vv. 6–7

         c.   Those who ate of his body and drank of his blood shall never hunger or thirst, but be filled. vv. 8–9

            1.   They were all filled with his Spirit.

            2.   They cried with one voice, and gave glory to Jesus.

➤ Moroni 4–5   The manner of administering the flesh and blood of Christ unto the church.

         a.   The elders or priests administered according to the commandment of Christ, which is true. 4:2

         b.   They knelt down with the church, and prayed to the Father in the name of Christ. 4:2; 5:2

         c.   The words of the prayer on the bread. 4:3

         d.   The words of the prayer on the wine. 5:2

NOTES AND COMMENTARY

5 And it came to pass that when Jesus had thus spoken, he cast his eyes round about again on the multitude, and beheld they were in tears, and did look steadfastly upon him as if they would ask him to tarry a little longer with them. [3 Nephi 17:5]

After Jesus announced that he was going to visit the ten tribes, he noted the response of the multitude. Being filled with compassion towards them, he did tarry and performed several ordinances before he departed. However, as noted above, some of these ordinances had been performed in the previous dispensation since the Nephites had the Melchizedek priesthood among them then also

Healing the Sick

> 6 And he said unto them: Behold, my bowels are filled with compassion towards you.
>
> 7 Have ye any that are sick among you? Bring them hither. Have ye any that are lame, or blind, or halt, or maimed, or leprous, or that are withered, or that are deaf, or that are afflicted in any manner? Bring them hither and I will heal them, for I have compassion upon you; my bowels are filled with mercy.
>
> 8 For I perceive that ye desire that I should show unto you what I have done unto your brethren at Jerusalem, for I see that your faith is sufficient that I should heal you.
>
> 9 And it came to pass that when he had thus spoken, all the multitude, with one accord, did go forth with their sick and their afflicted, and their lame, and with their blind, and with their dumb, and with all them that were afflicted in any manner; and he did heal them every one as they were brought forth unto him.
>
> 10 And they did all, both they who had been healed and they who were whole, bow down at his feet, and did worship him; and as many as could come for the multitude did kiss his feet, insomuch that they did bathe his feet with their tears. [3 Nephi 17:6–10]

Jesus invited those who were afflicted in any way to come forth, perceiving that their faith was sufficient to be healed (vv. 7–8). The multitude responded to Jesus' invitation, and all who came forth were healed. The result of these many miracles was that those healed, and also those who were whole, fell down and worshipped Jesus, kissing his feet and bathing them with their tears (vv. 9–10). Through these healings, the Nephites had a similar experience as the people during part of the Galilean ministry when Jesus went about healing.

> 23 And Jesus went about all Galilee, teaching in their synagogues, and preaching the gospel of the kingdom, and healing all manner of sickness and all manner of disease among the people.
>
> 24 And his fame went throughout all Syria: and they brought unto him all sick people that were taken with divers diseases and torments, and those which were possessed with devils, and those which were lunatick, and those that had the palsy; and he healed them. [Matthew 4:23–24; see also Luke 6:17–19]

Neither the abbreviated Nephite text, nor the Galilean account, gives any detail of how Jesus performed his healings. We can safely assume that he laid his hands upon them and anointed them with oil. He at least taught them this procedure, even if he did not use it himself. The New Testament instructs the Saints to heal in this manner.

> 14 Is any sick among you? let him call for the elders of the church; and let them pray over him, anointing him with oil in the name of the Lord:
>
> 15 And the prayer of faith shall save the sick, and the Lord shall raise him up; and if he have committed sins, they shall be forgiven him. [James 5:14–15]

Modern-day revelation gives similar instructions.

> 43 And whosoever among you are sick, and have not faith to be healed, but believe, shall be nourished with all tenderness, with herbs and mild food, and that not by the hand of an enemy.
>
> 44 And the elders of the church, two or more, shall be called, and shall pray for and lay their hands upon them in my name; and if they die they shall die unto me, and if they live they shall live unto me. [D&C 42:43–44]

The gospel is eternal and would function the same way in all dispensations.[2] Also, it should be noted that healing is not a saving ordinance, but rather an ordinance for blessing the membership of the Church. However, it is an important part of Christ's higher law.

---

[2] The eternal nature of the gospel is verified in a revelation to Joseph Smith.

25 That as many as would believe and be baptized in his holy name, and endure in faith to the end, should be saved—

26 Not only those who believed after he came in the meridian of time, in the flesh, but all those from the beginning, even as many as were before he came, who believed in the words of the holy prophets, who spake as they were inspired by the gift of the Holy Ghost, who truly testified of him in all things, should have eternal life,

27 As well as those who should come after, who should believe in the gifts and callings of God by the Holy Ghost, which beareth record of the Father and of the Son; [D&C 20:25–27]

The Blessing of Little Children

> 11 And it came to pass that he commanded that their little children should be brought.
>
> 12 So they brought their little children and set them down upon the ground round about him, and Jesus stood in the midst; and the multitude gave way till they had all been brought unto him.
>
> 13 And it came to pass that when they had all been brought, and Jesus stood in the midst, he commanded the multitude that they should kneel down upon the ground.
>
> 14 And it came to pass that when they had knelt upon the ground, Jesus groaned within himself, and said: Father, I am troubled because of the wickedness of the people of the house of Israel. [3 Nephi 17:11–14]

The ages of these children are not given, nor is the number of children given, but the total persons present "were in number about two thousand and five hundred souls; and they did consist of men, women, and children" (3 Nephi 17:25). A conservative estimate would suggest that several hundred little children were gathered around Jesus. The number was so great that the multitude enlarged the exterior of the circle to make room for the children to be close to him (v. 12).

When all the multitude had come to the kneeling position, Jesus groaned within himself because of the wickedness of the house of Israel (v. 14). To which tribes of the house of Israel Jesus was referring is not stated. From the context of the rest of this chapter, it would seem that he was not speaking of the Nephites,[3] but was speaking of those in Jerusalem, and perhaps of the ten tribes to whom he had shortly before announced that he was going to visit. It may also

---

[3] Further evidence that Jesus was not speaking of the Nephites is this later statement: "And it came to pass that when Jesus had made an end of praying he came again to the disciples, and said unto them: So great faith have I never seen among all the Jews; wherefore I could not show unto them so great miracles, because of their unbelief" (3 Nephi 19:35).

have included some of the Nephites in other areas of the land besides Bountiful where he was ministering. The setting of his message being in the midst of the children would further suggest that the wickedness of the house of Israel may have been in relationship to their children. They were probably not bringing them up "in light and truth" as Jesus has commanded (D&C 93:40).

After he groaned over the wickedness of Israel, Jesus knelt and prayed unto the Father. The prayer was beyond the ability of man to record. The Nephite multitude only recorded this:

> 15 And when he had said these words, he himself also knelt upon the earth; and behold he prayed unto the Father, and the things which he prayed cannot be written, and the multitude did bear record who heard him.
>
> 16 And after this manner do they bear record: The eye hath never seen, neither hath the ear heard, before, so great and marvelous things as we saw and heard Jesus speak unto the Father;
>
> 17 And no tongue can speak, neither can there be written by any man, neither can the hearts of men conceive so great and marvelous things as we both saw and heard Jesus speak; and no one can conceive of the joy which filled our souls at the time we heard him pray for us unto the Father. [3 Nephi 17:15–17]

Finishing his prayer, Jesus arose, but the multitude was overcome with joy and apparently sat somewhat spellbound. His joy was likely full because he had been able to "bring many souls" to experience great joy (cp. D&C 18:10–16).

> 18 And it came to pass that when Jesus had made an end of praying unto the Father, he arose; but so great was the joy of the multitude that they were overcome.
>
> 19 And it came to pass that Jesus spake unto them, and bade them arise.
>
> 20 And they arose from the earth, and he said unto them: Blessed are ye because of your faith. And now behold, my joy is full.
>
> 21 And when he had said these words, he wept, and the multitude bare record of it, and he took their little children, one by one, and blessed them, and prayed unto the Father for them.

> 22 And when he had done this he wept again; [3 Nephi 17:18–22]

Undoubtedly Jesus wept because of his joy. He blessed the children and prayed unto the Father for them, one by one (vv. 21–22). Once more the time element of this must have been staggering. To spend a few minutes with each one of several hundreds of children would require several hours. Coupled with the multitude's touching of the nail prints in his body and the healing of their sick, it was a long day for Jesus and the Nephite Saints. That the blessings took place after he had announced his intended visit to the lost tribes indicates that the day was drawing to a close as he began to take the children into his arms. This also repeated the ordinance he had introduced among the Judean people.

> 13 And they brought young children to him, that he should touch them: and his disciples rebuked those that brought them.
>
> 14 But when Jesus saw it, he was much displeased, and said unto them, Suffer the little children to come unto me, and forbid them not: for of such is the kingdom of God.
>
> 15 Verily I say unto you, Whosoever shall not receive the kingdom of God as a little child, he shall not enter therein.
>
> 16 And he took them up in his arms, put his hands upon them, and blessed them. [Mark 10:13–16; see also Matthew 19:13–15]

The Lord has directed the members of the Church in this dispensation to likewise bless their children.

> 70 Every member of the church of Christ having children is to bring them unto the elders before the church, who are to lay their hands upon them in the name of Jesus Christ, and bless them in his name. [D&C 20:70]

The blessing of children is not a saving ordinance, but nonetheless a sacred one to parents as well as to the Savior.

> 23 And he spake unto the multitude, and said unto them: Behold your little ones.
>
> 24 And as they looked to behold they cast their eyes towards heaven, and they saw the heavens open, and they saw angels descending out of

heaven as it were in the midst of fire; and they came down and encircled those little ones about, and they were encircled about with fire; and the angels did minister unto them.

25 And the multitude did see and hear and bear record; and they know that their record is true for they all of them did see and hear, every man for himself; and they were in number about two thousand and five hundred souls; and they did consist of men, women, and children. [3 Nephi 17:23–25]

To see angels ministering unto their children was a glorious manifestation shared by all. It was no doubt a stabilizing influence to them for the rest of their lives. Such an event is not recorded as happening in Jerusalem. If it didn't happen, it was because of their lack of faith. Jesus later told the Nephites: "So great faith have I never seen among all the Jews; wherefore I could not show unto them so great miracles, because of their unbelief" (3 Nephi 19:35). The divine ministry of Jesus as a God among the Nephites was off to a magnificent start, and there was still more to come.

The Sacrament

1 And it came to pass that Jesus commanded his disciples that they should bring forth some bread and wine unto him.

2 And while they were gone for bread and wine, he commanded the multitude that they should sit themselves down upon the earth.

3 And when the disciples had come with bread and wine, he took of the bread and brake and blessed it; and he gave unto the disciples and commanded that they should eat.

4 And when they had eaten and were filled, he commanded that they should give unto the multitude. [3 Nephi 18:1–4]

The Nephite disciples partaking of the sacrament would be comparable to the last supper with his apostles in Jerusalem.[4] Following the multitude's eating and being filled, the Savior instructed them about the ordinance in which they had just participated. Before reviewing those instructions, it should be noted that the filling of the disciples and multitude, through partaking of the bread, was not a physical filling with food, but a filling of the soul by the Spirit being poured out upon them. This will be discussed later in this chapter.

> 5 And when the multitude had eaten and were filled, he said unto the disciples: Behold there shall one be ordained among you, and to him will I give power that he shall break bread and bless it and give it unto the people of my church, unto all those who shall believe and be baptized in my name.
>
> 6 And this shall ye always observe to do, even as I have done, even as I have broken bread and blessed it and given it unto you.
>
> 7 And this shall ye do in remembrance of my body, which I have shown unto you. And it shall be a testimony unto the Father that ye do always remember me. And if ye do always remember me ye shall have my Spirit to be with you. [3 Nephi 18:5–7]

The one ordained among them to whom the Savior would give power to administer this ordinance was not identified. However, this does not mean that there was only one person who was authorized to break and bless the bread. From modern revelation, it can be learned that the one to whom this power was given was the presiding authority of the Church. To the Nephites it was probably Nephi. Nephi was the first one that Jesus gave the power to baptize, and then he gave it to the other eleven chosen disciples (3 Nephi 11:18–21; discussed in

---

[4] 26 And as they were eating, Jesus took bread, and blessed *it*, and brake *it*, and gave *it* to the disciples, and said, Take, eat; this is my body.

27 And he took the cup, and gave thanks, and gave *it* to them, saying, Drink ye all of it;

28 For this is my blood of the new testament, which is shed for many for the remission of sins. (Matthew 26:26–28)

chapter 4). Nephi was apparently the President of the Nephite Quorum of the Twelve. Today that power is vested in the President of the Church. He has "all the gifts which [the Lord] bestows upon the head of the church" (D&C 107:91–92). On the local level, "From the [president] comes the administering of ordinances and blessings upon the church, by the laying on of hands" (D&C 107:67). The bishop in every ward of the Church, or the presiding authority of each branch, has been delegated the authority to supervise the administering of the sacrament. The blessing of the sacrament may be delegated to other priesthood holders. In Moroni's later addition of Jesus' teachings, he recorded "the manner of their elders and priests administering the flesh and blood of Christ unto the church; and they administered it according to the commandments of Christ; wherefore we know the manner to be true; and the elder or priest did administer it" (Moroni 4:1). Modern revelation directs: "The priest's duty [in the Aaronic priesthood] is to . . . administer the sacrament," and "the elder [Melchizedek priesthood] or priest shall administer it" (D&C 20:46, 76). The authority to administer the sacrament was given to the Nephites by the resurrected Lord. The same authority was certainly given to the Jerusalem Church, although there is no record of it in the New Testament. That authority has been restored to the earth today.

According to the Savior's instructions, the sacrament is to be administered "unto all those who shall believe and be baptized in my name" (v. 5). The sacrament is a covenant ordinance, and in a sense, a saving ordinance. It is partaken of as a continuance of our baptismal covenant. Blessings are promised conditionally upon one's keeping the commandments agreed upon. It is a weekly reminder of our initial commitment to be a member of Christ's Church. The prayer, or blessing upon the sacrament emblems, specifies these commitments and the promised blessings. Since the two parts of the sacred ordinance symbolize different aspects of the covenant, each part must be analyzed separately.

The breaking of the bread was in remembrance of Christ's "body, which I have shown unto you" (vv. 6–7). His body was a resurrected body. Thus, it was to be remembered that Christ had laid it down "in remembrance of my body which I give as a ransom for you" (JST Matthew 26:22). Through the mortality that he had obtained from his mother Mary, he had the ability to die, and because of his divine nature obtained from his Father, he had the power to break "the bands of death that the grave should have no victory, and that death should have no sting" (Mosiah 16:7). Paul says: "then shall be brought to pass the saying that is written, Death is swallowed up in victory. O death, where is thy sting? O grave, where is thy victory?" (1 Corinthians 15:54–55).[5] Through this victory over death, Christ ransomed us from the grave, or paid the demands of justice that had all mankind within its grasp because of the fall of Adam. Again quoting Paul: "For as in Adam all die, even so in Christ shall all be made alive" (1 Corinthians 15:22). As we partake of the bread, we do so as "a testimony unto the Father that [we] do always remember [Christ]. And if [we] do always remember [Christ we] shall have [his] Spirit to be with [us]" (v. 7).

After the bread is broken, it is to be blessed. The exact prayer to be used on the blessing of the bread was revealed by Christ, probably on this occasion, since he was introducing the ordinance. Mormon did not record the prayer in his abridgment, however. Moroni later recorded it sometime between A.D. 400–421 as he hid himself from the Lamanites who were seeking to kill him.

> 1 The manner of their elders and priests administering the flesh and blood of Christ unto the church; and they administered it according to the commandments of Christ; wherefore we know the manner to be true; and the elder or priest did minister it—
>
> 2 And they did kneel down with the church, and pray to the Father in the name of Christ, saying:
>
> 3 O God, the Eternal Father, we ask thee in the name of thy Son, Jesus Christ, to bless and sanctify this bread to the souls of all those who

---

[5] Note that, in Paul's letter to Corinth, he is quoting from a written text. Abinadi, in Mosiah, is probably quoting from the same source, undoubtedly written on the plates of brass, but now lost from the Old Testament.

partake of it; that they may eat in remembrance of the body of thy Son, and witness unto thee, O God, the Eternal Father, that they are willing to take upon them the name of thy Son, and always remember him, and keep his commandments which he hath given them, that they may always have his Spirit to be with them. Amen. [Moroni 4:1–3]

The same prayer was revealed to this generation (see D&C 20:77). The elders, or priest, having been delegated that privileged authority from the one "ordained among [them]" (3 Nephi 18:5), was to "kneel down with the church, and pray to the Father in the name of Christ" (Moroni 4:1–2). Based upon the practice of the Church today, which is a valid interpretation, to "kneel with the church" is to kneel in behalf of the Church. As one having authority addresses the Father, he represents the entire congregation. The congregation mentally follows the prayer and sanctions it by saying "amen" at the conclusion of the prayer.

The prayer confirms that it represents all who partake of it, and that it is in remembrance of Christ's body (that was laid down and then resurrected). It then specifies man's part of the covenant and God's promised blessings to follow. There are three parts of man's commitment: (1) To be willing to take upon them the name of Christ; (2) To always remember him; and (3) To keep his commandments. If these three commitments are kept, God promises that they will always have his Spirit to be with them (v. 3).

A comparison with the baptismal covenant recorded in Mosiah 18 shows the commitment made at the sacrament ordinance to be the same as that made in the waters of baptism when one enters into the Church. To take upon us the name of Christ is to become a part of his family. It is to "come unto the fold of God, and to be called his people." It is to accept other members of the Church as brothers and sisters, and to be "willing to bear one another's burdens, that they may be light; Yea, and [be] willing to mourn with those that mourn; yea, and comfort those that stand in need of comfort" (Mosiah 18:8–9).

A commitment to always remember Christ is to agree "to stand as witnesses of God at all times and in all things, and in all places that ye may be in, even until death" (Mosiah 18:9). This means that we are mindful of his example and will follow it seven days a week, not just on Sunday; that we will exemplify in our lives the principles that he taught in our everyday activities of business or occupation, and in all other associations with our fellow human beings. It also means that we conform our lives to the pattern of Christ's life in our social activities, and in our traveling to any other area of the world. We are his children and should be proud of his family name.

The third commitment of man is to "serve him and keep his commandments" (Mosiah 18:10). As our Father of eternal life, we accept Christ as the head of the family who will delegate our stewardship to us through revelation to his servants, and he will give us the rules to govern us as members of his household. In exchange for following these family rules, Christ agrees to "pour out his Spirit more abundantly upon us" (Mosiah 18:10). Since all men are born with the light of Christ, the members of his family are promised an additional source of light and truth, the guidance of the Holy Spirit. Through the sacrament, the covenant of baptism is reaffirmed by both man and God, but more should be remembered. Through the breaking of the bread, symbolic of his body, we are to remember that, through his resurrection, we too may be resurrected. We should acknowledge this and give thanks to our Father in Heaven for this blessing of his Son.

The Lord has given us certain commandments that make our bodies fit tabernacles for the Spirit.[6] As we live in this mortal state of probation, we are preparing ourselves "for that endless state ... which is after the resurrection of the dead" (Alma 12:24). There are degrees of resurrection commensurate with the degree of glory that we have prepared ourselves to receive. "For he who is not able to abide the law of a celestial kingdom cannot abide a celestial glory" (D&C 88:22).

---

[6] Know ye not that ye are the temple of God, and *that* the Spirit of God dwelleth in you?

If any man defile the temple of God, him shall God destroy; for the temple of God is holy, which *temple* ye are. (1 Corinthians 3:16–17)

A reflection of our past week's activities in relationship to our bodies as temples of God, and being worthy of his spirit, would be fitting as we partake of the bread. We should also make personal commitments to do better the following week in our areas of weakness, as well as to thank our Father for the blessings of the past week. Through the partaking of the bread, we have an opportunity to periodically evaluate our progress toward immortality. Other opportunities and blessings follow.

> 8 And it came to pass that when he said these words, he commanded his disciples that they should take of the wine of the cup and drink of it, and that they should also give unto the multitude that they might drink of it.
>
> 9 And it came to pass that they did so, and did drink of it and were filled; and they gave unto the multitude, and they did drink, and they were filled.
>
> 10 And when the disciples had done this, Jesus said unto them: Blessed are ye for this thing which ye have done, for this is fulfilling my commandments, and this doth witness unto the Father that ye are willing to do that which I have commanded you.
>
> 11 And this shall ye always do to those who repent and are baptized in my name; and ye shall do it in remembrance of my blood, which I have shed for you, that ye may witness unto the Father that ye do always remember me. And if ye do always remember me ye shall have my Spirit to be with you. [3 Nephi 18:8–11]

Again they witnessed to the Father that they would keep the commandments. However, the wine was to be partaken of "in remembrance of [Christ's] blood, which [was] shed for [them]." Again, the Spirit was promised to those who would "always remember [Christ]" (3 Nephi 18:8–11). Moroni also recorded the exact prayer for the wine as he concluded the record of the Nephites.

> 1 The manner of administering the wine—Behold, they took the cup, and said:
>
> 2 O God, the Eternal Father, we ask thee, in the name of thy Son, Jesus Christ, to bless and sanctify this wine to the souls of all those who drink of it, that they may do it in remembrance of the blood of thy Son, which was shed for them; that they may witness unto thee, O God, the

Eternal Father, that they do always remember him, that they may have
his Spirit to be with them. Amen. [Moroni 5:1–2]

The blessing upon the wine was also revealed in this dispensation
(D&C 20:79).[7] It is identical to the Nephite blessing, and so will not
be included here. The blessing on the wine is essentially the same
prayer as the blessing on the bread, with appropriate changes for the
emblems being wine rather than bread, and the wine being in remembrance of Christ's blood which was shed for them. There is no
mention of the participant's covenant to take Jesus' name or to keep
the commandments in the blessing on the wine. This may be because
they have already committed themselves to take his name and keep
his commandments, and are to now remember a different aspect of the
Atonement, the blood of Christ that was shed in Gethsemane, a vicar-
ious payment for their sins. Thus, they reflect upon the great sacrifice
that he made, how their past sins contributed to his suffering, and how
those sins have been forgiven. Their thoughts should, therefore, be of
worship for the willingness of their Savior to make the Atonement and
pay for their sins. Perhaps they might extend those thoughts to what
they are doing to share the knowledge of Christ and his atonement to
others, both in word and in deed.

12 And I give unto you a commandment that ye shall do these things.
And if ye shall always do these things blessed are ye, for ye are built
upon my rock.

13 But whoso among you shall do more or less than these are not built
upon my rock, but are built upon a sandy foundation; and when the rain
descends, and the floods come, and the winds blow, and beat upon them,
they shall fall, and the gates of hell are ready open to receive them.

14 Therefore blessed are ye if ye shall keep my commandments, which
the Father hath commanded me that I should give unto you. [3 Nephi
18:12–14]

---

[7] The common use of water as the sacrament emblem today came about because of
an angel warning Joseph against purchasing wine from the enemies of the Church (see
D&C 27 heading and vv. 1–4).

Jesus concluded his instructions on the bread and the wine by making his afore-given instructions a commandment (v. 12). According to Moroni's later-recorded testimony of Christ's ministry, the Church "did meet together oft to partake of bread and wine, in remembrance of the Lord Jesus" (Moroni 6:6). Neither account clarifies the meaning of "oft." In this dispensation, we are given this sacred opportunity weekly. Jesus further attested that the proper partaking of the sacrament would result in one's building upon his rock (v. 12). Just as proper baptism was the beginning of the building upon the rock, so was the covenant of the sacrament. While the ordinance of baptism is a one-time, long-term commitment, the sacrament serves as a weekly opportunity to keep a proper foundation under our quest for eternal life, and to build upon it. For those who fail to observe their sacrament covenants, their foundation becomes one of sand, and leads to entrance in the gates of hell, just as it does for those who dishonor their baptismal covenant (v. 13).

The Savior instructed the Nephites regarding prayer after he spoke of the bread and wine, but then he returned to the subject of the sacrament.

> 26 And now it came to pass that when Jesus had spoken these words, he turned his eyes again upon the disciples whom he had chosen, and said unto them:
>
> 27 Behold verily, verily, I say unto you, I give unto you another commandment, and then I must go unto my Father that I may fulfil other commandments which he hath given me.
>
> 28 And now behold, this is the commandment which I give unto you, that ye shall not suffer any one knowingly to partake of my flesh and blood unworthily, when ye shall minister it;
>
> 29 For whoso eateth and drinketh my flesh and blood unworthily eateth and drinketh damnation to his soul; therefore if ye know that a man is unworthy to eat and drink of my flesh and blood ye shall forbid him. [3 Nephi 18:26–29]

Those who are unworthy to partake of the sacrament are still God's children, and are to be given special attention in order for them to become worthy to partake.

> 30 Nevertheless, ye shall not cast him out from among you, but ye shall minister unto him and shall pray for him unto the Father, in my name; and if it so be that he repenteth and is baptized in my name, then shall ye receive him, and shall minister unto him of my flesh and blood.
>
> 31 But if he repent not he shall not be numbered among my people, that he may not destroy my people, for behold I know my sheep, and they are numbered.
>
> 32 Nevertheless, ye shall not cast him out of your synagogues, or your places of worship, for unto such shall ye continue to minister; for ye know not but what they will return and repent, and come unto me with full purpose of heart, and I shall heal them; and ye shall be the means of bringing salvation unto them.
>
> 33 Therefore, keep these sayings which I have commanded you that ye come not under condemnation; for wo unto him whom the Father condemneth.
>
> 34 And I give you these commandments because of the disputations which have been among you. And blessed are ye if ye have no disputations among you. [3 Nephi 18:30–34]

Those who do not repent are exercising their agency, a God-given right. However, the Lord will also protect his Church. This concept was stated clearly to Alma the younger by an angel who called him to repentance. The angel cried again, saying:

> 13 Alma, arise and stand forth, for why persecutest thou the church of God? For the Lord hath said: This is my church, and I will establish it; and nothing shall overthrow it, save it is the transgression of my people.
>
> 16 And now I say unto thee, Alma, go thy way, and seek to destroy the church no more, that their prayers may be answered, and this even if thou wilt of thyself be cast off [Mosiah 27:13, 16].

Those who neglect to help the unworthy, or those who contend against the Church for allowing the unworthy to attend, are endangering themselves to be condemned. "The devil, who is the father of contention, and . . . stirreth up the hearts of men to contend with anger, one with another" delights in the member's contentions (3 Nephi 11:29). Jesus also gave these same instructions to the people in Palestine. Paul instructed the Corinthian Saints similarly and based his teachings upon what Jesus had taught at the last supper.

> 23 For I have received of the Lord that which also I delivered unto you, That the Lord Jesus the same night in which he was betrayed took bread:
>
> 24 And when he had given thanks, he brake it, and said, Take, eat: this is my body, which is broken for you: this do in remembrance of me.
>
> 25 After the same manner also he took the cup, when he had supped, saying, This cup is the new testament in my blood: this do ye, as oft as ye drink it, in remembrance of me.
>
> 26 For as often as ye eat this bread, and drink this cup, ye do shew the Lord's death till he come.
>
> 27 Wherefore whosoever shall eat this bread, and drink this cup of the Lord, unworthily, shall be guilty of the body and blood of the Lord.
>
> 28 But let a man examine himself, and so let him eat of that bread, and drink of that cup.
>
> 29 For he that eateth and drinketh unworthily, eateth and drinketh damnation to himself, not discerning the Lord's body.
>
> 30 For this cause many are weak and sickly among you, and many sleep [1 Corinthians 11:23–30].

Paul added that many among the Corinthians were weak, sick, or even slept [had died] because of their partaking unworthily (v. 30). Elder John Taylor said: "People wonder sometimes why we have sickness amongst us," and then he quoted 1 Corinthians 11:30 as an answer to the question (JD 20:360). Moroni also later warned: "see that ye partake not of the sacrament of Christ unworthily" (Mormon 9:29).

On the second day of his divine Nephite ministry, Jesus again gave the sacrament to his disciples and commanded them to administer it to the multitude.

1 And it came to pass that he commanded the multitude that they should cease to pray, and also his disciples. And he commanded them that they should not cease to pray in their hearts.

2 And he commanded them that they should arise and stand up upon their feet. And they arose up and stood upon their feet.

3 And it came to pass that he brake bread again and blessed it, and gave to the disciples to eat.

4 And when they had eaten he commanded them that they should break bread, and give unto the multitude.

5 And when they had given unto the multitude he also gave them wine to drink, and commanded them that they should give unto the multitude.

6 Now, there had been no bread, neither wine, brought by the disciples, neither by the multitude;

7 But he truly gave unto them bread to eat, and also wine to drink.

8 And he said unto them: He that eateth this bread eateth of my body to his soul; and he that drinketh of this wine drinketh of my blood to his soul; and his soul shall never hunger nor thirst, but shall be filled.

9 Now, when the multitude had all eaten and drunk, behold, they were filled with the Spirit; and they did cry out with one voice, and gave glory to Jesus, whom they both saw and heard. [3 Nephi 20:1–9]

Jesus performed a miracle parallel to those of his Palestine ministry. He had miraculously provided bread and wine for the multitude similar to his feeding of the "five thousand men, beside women and children" in the desert of Palestine (Matthew 14:13–21), or his later feeding of "four thousand men, beside women and children" (Matthew 15:32–38), or his filling "the waterpots with water" . . . and the water "was made wine" at the marriage in Cana (John 2:7–9). The Nephite record does not describe how he did it, nor does the New Testament, but he did miraculously provide (v. 7).

The multitude experienced the promised fulfillment of the sacrament covenant; they were filled with the Spirit, as mentioned previously. The result was a united voice of praise and "glory to Jesus, whom they both saw and heard" (v. 9). We too, as we partake of the sacrament, should give praise and glory to our Lord for the resurrection and the atonement that he provided.

Prayer

15 Verily, verily, I say unto you, ye must watch and pray always, lest ye be tempted by the devil, and ye be led away captive by him.

16 And as I have prayed among you even so shall ye pray in my church, among my people who do repent and are baptized in my name. Behold I am the light; I have set an example for you.

17 And it came to pass that when Jesus had spoken these words unto his disciples, he turned again unto the multitude and said unto them:

18 Behold, verily, verily, I say unto you, ye must watch and pray always lest ye enter into temptation; for Satan desireth to have you, that he may sift you as wheat.

19 Therefore ye must always pray unto the Father in my name;

20 And whatsoever ye shall ask the Father in my name, which is right, believing that ye shall receive, behold it shall be given unto you.

21 Pray in your families unto the Father, always in my name, that your wives and your children may be blessed. [3 Nephi 18:15–21]

Jesus' next teaching to the Nephites was a combination of a principle and a warning regarding the necessity of prayer. Although both the twelve disciples and the multitude were given the basic admonition to "watch and pray always" lest they be tempted by the devil (vv. 15, 18), each group had separate instructions. The disciples' warning of temptation by the devil was that they would become captive by him. This may suggest the power that Satan has to deceive those of the Twelve if they are not prayerful. While the vast majority of those called to the Twelve are already prayerful men, perhaps this is why Judas and some of this dispensation fell.

The only additional teaching given to the disciples at this time was to follow the example that Jesus had set as he prayed among them. He was the light to which they were to look (v. 16). The example referred to is known as the Lord's Prayer and is discussed in Chapter 6 of this work (3 Nephi 13:6–15). Later Jesus promised the disciples [Twelve]:

"whatsoever things ye shall ask the Father in my name shall be given unto you" (3 Nephi 27:28). This promise was also given to the Apostles (Twelve) in Palestine: "whatsoever ye shall ask of the Father in my name, he may give it you" (John 15:16). Such an unconditional promise is based upon Jesus' knowledge that these servants were so in tune with the Spirit that they, like Nephi, son of Helaman, would "not ask that which is contrary to [his] will" (Helaman 10:5).

Jesus warned the multitude that "Satan desireth to have you, that he may sift you as wheat" (v. 18). This same warning was given in the New Testament to Simon (Peter), but the Prophet Joseph rendered it slightly different: "Satan hath desired you, that he may *sift the children of the kingdom* as wheat (JST Luke 22:31; emphasis added). This rendering is consistent with the Book of Mormon text addressing the multitude. To sift "the children of the kingdom" as wheat is to separate the chaff and smaller or broken kernels out from the wholesome and fuller ones. Satan makes "war with the Saints of God, and encompasseth them round about" (D&C 76:29). When a Church member (child of the kingdom) yields to Satan and breaks the commandments, it is the equivalent of fragmenting the soul, and they may be sifted out of the kingdom or excluded from the company of the Church and the Saints. The fall of a child of the kingdom through the sieve is pleasing unto Satan. Once more, prayer is the deterrent to this happening.

The Nephite Saints were instructed to "always pray unto the Father in [Christ's] name" (v. 19). This instruction gives the appropriate pattern concerning to whom we pray, and is consistent with Old Testament period instructions. Jacob, son of Lehi, said "they believed in Christ and worshipped the Father in his name" (Jacob 4:5). In modern revelation, we learn the same pattern for today: "we ask thee, Holy Father, in the name of Jesus Christ" (D&C 109:4).

If their desires were to be granted, there were two conditions that had to be met when the multitude (lay people) prayed: first, the request must be right, and second, the person must believe or have faith that the request would be granted (v. 20). The first condition was dependent upon the giver, the Father, and the second one upon the person praying. A further caution is given in modern revelation: "If ye ask anything that is not expedient for you, it shall turn to your condemnation" (D&C 88:65). Therefore, we should seek the Spirit as a guide to our prayers, and should conclude with a submission to our Father in Heaven's wisdom, "Thy will be done" (3 Nephi 13:10).

Jesus also instructed the Nephites to "Pray in your families unto the Father, always in my name, that your wives and your children may be blessed" (v. 21). There seem to be two significant principles involved in this instruction: first, the reminder of to whom and through whom they were to pray; and second, the power of prayer as a blessing upon family members. It is implied in the latter that the father, as patriarch in the home, is responsible to conduct the family prayer as well as to analyze and give guidance to the family members.

> 22 And behold, ye shall meet together oft; and ye shall not forbid any man from coming unto you when ye shall meet together, but suffer them that they may come unto you and forbid them not;
>
> 23 But ye shall pray for them, and shall not cast them out; and if it so be that they come unto you oft ye shall pray for them unto the Father, in my name. [3 Nephi 18:22–23]

The Lord had instructed them individually and by families; he now extends his instructions to public gatherings. The public meetings were to be held often and were to be open to those who were not of the Church. None were to be forbidden from attending (v. 22). This repetitious admonition to pray for those who attended and were not baptized members of the Church seems to be a general concern and prayer for anyone who attended, but more importantly is a specific appeal for a blessing upon those who attend often. The Father would, undoubtedly, then bear witness to them if they were prepared and ready to receive that witness.

> 24 Therefore, hold up your light that it may shine unto the world. Behold I am the light which ye shall hold up—that which ye have seen me do. Behold ye see that I have prayed unto the Father, and ye all have witnessed.

25 And ye see that I have commanded that none of you should go away, but rather have commanded that ye should come unto me, that ye might feel and see; even so shall ye do unto the world; and whosoever breaketh this commandment suffereth himself to be led into temptation. [3 Nephi 18:24–25]

In addition to praying for those who were not as yet members, Jesus reminded the members that they were to be "the light of this people," as he had previously taught them (3 Nephi 12:14). The light they were to hold up was Jesus Christ, and his examples and teachings he had set while visiting among them (v. 24). Since this was the first day of his ministry among the Nephites, he must have had reference to the events of that day. His following comments sustain this observation. They had witnessed his prayer unto the Father (3 Nephi 17:14–15). He had invited the people to come unto him and they "did see with their eyes and did feel with their hands and did know of a surety" (3 Nephi 11:15). The multitude was to extend a similar invitation by declaring to the world their testimony of what they had seen and heard, and by living as he had commanded them.

There was a caution attached to the commandment to be a light to the world. He who breaks this commandment [is not a light] and "suffereth himself to be led into temptation" (v. 25). There is a natural consequence attached to this warning. The word suffer means "to allow." People who are willing to openly proclaim their allegiance to Christ, both by word and by deed, will be more cognizant of their responsibility to live his example. Similarly, those who know of a person's values and commitment will respect him or her for it, and often will endeavor to protect or assist in maintaining their standards. Of course, there is also an outpouring of the Spirit upon the person who is holding up the light. This is observable, in a spiritual sense, by those who are in tune with the Spirit. There is another scriptural caution given by Alma to his son Shiblon that is applicable to our holding up the light of Christ. Alma admonished him to "use boldness, but not overbearance" (Alma 38:12). Sometimes, in our eagerness to proclaim our allegiance to the gospel, we may appear arrogant or self-righteous.

Christ's Ascension

35 And now I go unto the Father, because it is expedient that I should go unto the Father for your sakes.

36 And it came to pass that when Jesus had made an end of these sayings, he touched with his hand the disciples whom he had chosen, one by one, even until he had touched them all, and spake unto them as he touched them.

37 And the multitude heard not the words which he spake, therefore they did not bear record; but the disciples bare record that he gave them power to give the Holy Ghost. And I will show unto you hereafter that this record is true.

38 And it came to pass that when Jesus had touched them all, there came a cloud and overshadowed the multitude that they could not see Jesus.

39 And while they were overshadowed he departed from them, and ascended into heaven. And the disciples saw and did bear record that he ascended again into heaven. [3 Nephi 18:35–39]

Jesus announced that he was now going to "the Father for [the disciples'] sake" (v. 35). He was probably reporting his ministry to the Father, and making known his intercession for the Nephite Twelve. As their advocate, he was possibly vowing for their righteousness and their stewardship. Having completed his teaching, he touched each of the disciples and gave them power to give the Holy Ghost to others. This will be the subject of the following chapter Mormon promised to hereafter show the reader that Jesus "gave them power to give the Holy Ghost" v. 37). Although the Nephite multitude did not witness Jesus' ascension, the disciples did (vv. 37–39). They were given the same privilege that the Twelve of Galilee had had.

9 And when he had spoken these things, while they beheld, he was taken up; and a cloud received him out of their sight.

10 And while they looked stedfastly toward heaven as he went up, behold, two men stood by them in white apparel;

11 Which also said, Ye men of Galilee, why stand ye gazing up into heaven? this same Jesus, which is taken up from you into heaven, shall

so come in like manner as ye have seen him go into heaven. [Acts 1:9–11]

The witness of his ascension by the Nephite Twelve is once more "Another Testament of Jesus Christ."

The first day of Jesus' divine ministry had drawn to a close—and what a day it had been! The righteous Nephites in the land Bountiful had been given a glorious manifestation of the position and divinity of Jesus Christ. They had also been instructed in the higher law of the gospel, some parts of which were limited to the Nephite Twelve. Jesus had clarified the various groups of the house of Israel and identified the Gentiles, and the sequence of each receiving the gospel. Last of all, he had introduced various ordinances and principles of the gospel to them. But the morrow would be just as stimulating.

DAY TWO

3 Nephi 19:1–26:13

1 And now it came to pass that when Jesus had ascended into heaven, the multitude did disperse, and every man did take his wife and his children and did return to his own home.

2 And it was noised abroad among the people immediately, before it was yet dark, that the multitude had seen Jesus, and that he had ministered unto them, and that he would also show himself on the morrow unto the multitude.

3 Yea, and even all the night it was noised abroad concerning Jesus; and insomuch did they send forth unto the people that there were many, yea, an exceedingly great number, did labor exceedingly all that night, that they might be on the morrow in the place where Jesus should show himself unto the multitude. [3 Nephi 19:1–3]

Preparation for the second day of Jesus' ministry began the night before. That evening, following Jesus' ascension into heaven, the families returned to their homes and immediately spread the word of the first day's visit, and announced his coming visit on the morrow. The news of his second day's visit caused "an exceeding great number" to labor all night in order for them to gather to the place where Jesus would visit (vv. 1–3). Thus, the number who were gathered must have far exceeded the twenty-five hundred souls (3 Nephi 17:25) of the first day.

The first day had been a day of instruction, partaking of the sacrament, and conferring of the priesthood and the power to give the Holy Ghost. The second day was a day of the baptism of the twelve disciples, their baptism of fire and the Holy Ghost, and further instruction to the multitude. The day's events that were recorded constitute about twelve and a half pages in the 1981 edition of the Book of Mormon. However, this represents not "even a hundredth part of the things which Jesus did truly teach" (3 Nephi 26:6). What was recorded is vital to our understanding of the last days before the Second Coming of Christ. Chapters 10 through 13 will analyze this day's events.

Chapter 10

The Reception of the Holy Ghost

3 Nephi 19:4–36; Moroni 2

When the Savior appeared to the Nephites after his resurrection, he promised that "unto [the believer] will the Father bear record of [Christ], for he will visit them with fire and with the Holy Ghost" (3 Nephi 11:35). Later the same day, "he gave them power to give the Holy Ghost" (3 Nephi 18:37). The Father's promise was fulfilled on the second day of Jesus' divine ministry among the Nephites. This chapter enumerates some of the great blessings that came through the baptism of the Holy Ghost, and the receiving of the gift of the Holy Ghost. An outline of the Book of Mormon text in this chapter, as an outline to prepare for a deeper study, follows.

Outline • 3 Nephi 19:4–36; Moroni 2

➢ 19:1–3   The multitude returns to their homes, and many labor all night to tell others of his visit on the morrow.

➢ 19:4–14   On the morrow, the people assemble with Nephi and the other disciples standing in their midst.

    a. The multitude was so big that they separated into twelve bodies, and the Twelve teach them. vv. 5–9

        1.   They taught them to pray unto the Father in the name of Jesus.

        2.   They ministered the same words spoken by Jesus, nothing varying.

        3.   They prayed for what they desired most, that the Holy Ghost be given them.

    b.   The disciples went to the water's edge, and the multitude followed. vv. 10–14

        1.   Nephi went into the water and was baptized, and then he baptized the other disciples.

        2.   When they came out of the water, they were filled with the Holy Ghost and with fire.

        3.   They were encircled as if by fire from heaven, of which the multitude bore record.

        4.   Angels came down from heaven and ministered unto them.

➤ 19:15–36   As the angels ministered, Jesus came and commanded the disciples and the multitude to pray.

    a.   They prayed unto Jesus calling him their Lord and their God. v. 18

    b.   Jesus departed a little way and prayed to the Father. vv. 19–23

        1.   He thanked him for giving the Holy Ghost to the chosen disciples.

        2.   He asked that the Holy Ghost be given to all who believed in their words.

        3.   The disciples were given the Holy Ghost because they believed in Christ.

        4.   They believed and prayed to him because he was with them.

        5.   Jesus prayed for the disciples and all who believed in their words, and that they may be one as he and the Father were one.

    c.   Jesus came to the disciples, and they continued to pray to him. vv. 24–26

    1. They did not multiply words for it was given them what to pray.

    2. He blessed them, his countenance was upon them, and they were white.

    3. Their whiteness exceeded all the whiteness of the earth.

    4. Jesus told them to pray on, and they did not cease.

  d. He went a little way off, and prayed again to the Father. vv. 27–29

    1. He thanked him that he had purified the disciples.

    2. He asked that those who believed the disciples words would also be purified.

    3. He prayed not for the world, but for those given him out of the world.

    4. He prayed that they might be one as the Father and he were one, and that he might be glorified in them.

  e. He came to his disciples, who continued to pray to him, and they were white even as Jesus. v. 30

  f. He went a little way off, and prayed to the Father again. vv. 31–34

    1. Tongue cannot speak and the words cannot be written which he prayed.

    2. The multitude heard and bore record that they understood in their hearts.

  g. Jesus came to the disciples and said he had not seen so great faith among the Jews. vv. 35–36

    1. He could not show the Jews so great miracles because of their unbelief.

    2. The Jews had not seen nor heard what the Nephites had.

➢ Moroni 2:1–3   The words Christ spoke as he laid his hands on his twelve disciples and gave them power to give the Holy Ghost.

a. In my name shall you give it, for thus do my apostles. v. 2

b. Christ spoke these words when he first appeared, but only the disciples heard them. v. 3

c. On as many as the disciples laid their hands, fell the Holy Ghost. v. 3

NOTES AND COMMENTARY

The importance of the baptism of the Holy Ghost, and the reception of the gift of the Holy Ghost for the Nephite Saints, may be exemplified by some statements made by the Prophet Joseph Smith in this dispensation of the gospel. In December 1839, Joseph Smith and Elias Higbee wrote to Hyrum Smith and the High Council of The Church of Jesus Christ of Latter-day Saints regarding their visit to Washington, D.C. to seek redress for the suffering of the Saints in Missouri. In a postscript to that letter, obviously written by Elias Higbee, we read: "In our interview with the President, he interrogated us wherein we differed in our religion from the other religions of the day. Brother Joseph said we differed in mode of baptism and the gift of the Holy Ghost by the laying on of hands. We considered that all other considerations were contained in the gift of the Holy Ghost" (HC 4:42). On a later occasion, the Prophet stated, "You might as well baptize a bag of sand as a man, if not done in view of the remission of sins and getting of the Holy Ghost. Baptism by water is but half a baptism, and is good for nothing without the other half that is, the baptism of the Holy Ghost" (TPJS, 314). Jesus' instructions to the Nephites sustain the Prophet's views.

As previously mentioned, at the end of the first day of his visit, Jesus "touched with his hand the disciples whom he had chosen, one by one, . . . the disciples bare record that he gave them power to give the Holy Ghost." Mormon then recorded, "And I will show unto you hereafter that this record is true" (3 Nephi 18:36–37). Although Mormon never fulfilled his pledge, undoubtedly because of the extreme pressures of his military tasks and social environment, his son Moroni did record more details of the Savior conferring the power upon the disciples to give the Holy Ghost to the Church members. As he concluded his father's record, Moroni gave:

> The words of Christ, which he spake unto his disciples, the twelve whom he had chosen, as he laid his hands upon them—(Thus showing that his touching them, as recorded in 3 Nephi 18:36, was the laying on of hands) And (Jesus) called them by name, saying: Ye shall call on the Father in my name, in mighty prayer; and after ye have done this ye shall have power that to him upon whom ye shall lay your hands, ye shall give the Holy Ghost; and in my name shall ye give it, for thus do mine apostles. [Moroni 2:1–2]

Modern scripture confirms that an Apostle has power "to confirm the church by the laying on of the hands, and the giving of the Holy Ghost" (D&C 20:43).

Since these newly called Nephite Twelve had previously been "ordained of Nephi [held the Melchizedek Priesthood]" (3 Nephi 7:25), the laying on of hands upon their heads by Jesus was not an ordination to the priesthood, but an additional power given them as Apostles. It may have even been part of their ordination to the apostleship. However it came, it was fulfilled. After recording the words of Jesus to the Twelve, Moroni bore witness that this power was indeed received. "Now Christ spake these words unto them at the time of his first appearing; and the multitude heard it not, but the disciples heard it; and on as many as they laid their hands, fell the Holy Ghost" (Moroni 2:3). Mormon's brief account confirms the Holy Ghost coming upon the Twelve.

Jesus promised the Jerusalem Twelve that, if they loved him and kept his commandments, "I will pray the Father, and he shall give you another Comforter, that he may abide with you for ever; Even the Spirit of truth; whom the world cannot receive, because it seeth him not, neither knoweth him: but ye know him; for he dwelleth with you, and shall be in you" (John 14:15–17). Following the resurrection of Christ in Jerusalem, it is recorded: "And when he had said this he breathed on them, and saith unto them, Receive ye the Holy Ghost"

(John 20:22). Based upon the Third Nephi and Moroni accounts, we can rest assured that "breathed" on them is an incorrect translation. As promised they were later "endued [endowed] with power from on high" (Luke 24:49), or collectively baptized with fire and the Holy Ghost on the day of Pentecost.[1] That they individually received the gift of the Holy Ghost by the laying on of hands is evidenced by the account of Peter and John being sent to Samaria and conferring the Holy Ghost by the laying on of hands upon those who had been baptized.

> 14 Now when the apostles which were at Jerusalem heard that Samaria had received the word of God, they sent unto them Peter and John:
>
> 15 Who, when they were come down, prayed for them, that they might receive the Holy Ghost:
>
> 16 (For as yet he was fallen upon none of them: only they were baptized in the name of the Lord Jesus.)
>
> 17 Then laid they *their* hands on them, and they received the Holy Ghost. [Acts 8:14–17]

Certainly the Nephite Apostles had received the Holy Ghost in the same manner.

> 4 And it came to pass that on the morrow, when the multitude was gathered together, behold, Nephi and his brother whom he had raised from the dead, whose name was Timothy, and also his son, whose name was Jonas, and also Mathoni, and Mathonihah, his brother, and Kumen, and Kumenonhi, and Jeremiah, and Shemnon, and Jonas, and Zedekiah, and Isaiah—now these were the names of the disciples whom Jesus had

---

[1]　1 And when the day of Pentecost was fully come, they were all with one accord in one place.

2 And suddenly there came a sound from heaven as of a rushing mighty wind, and it filled all the house where they were sitting.

3 And there appeared unto them cloven tongues like as of fire, and it sat upon each of them.

4 And they were all filled with the Holy Ghost, and began to speak with other tongues, as the Spirit gave them utterance. (Acts 2:1–4)

chosen—and it came to pass that they went forth and stood in the midst of the multitude.

5 And behold, the multitude was so great that they did cause that they should be separated into twelve bodies.

6 And the twelve did teach the multitude; and behold, they did cause that the multitude should kneel down upon the face of the earth, and should pray unto the Father in the name of Jesus.

7 And the disciples did pray unto the Father also in the name of Jesus. And it came to pass that they arose and ministered unto the people.

8 And when they had ministered those same words which Jesus had spoken—nothing varying from the words which Jesus had spoken—behold, they knelt again and prayed to the Father in the name of Jesus.

9 And they did pray for that which they most desired; and they desired that the Holy Ghost should be given unto them. [3 Nephi 19:4–9]

The first event of the second day of Jesus' divine ministry was the going of the Twelve into the midst of the increased multitude that had gathered because of the spreading news of his promise to "also show himself on the morrow unto the multitude" (3 Nephi 19:1–3). The Twelve are named individually, but will not be enumerated or commented on. The multitude was so large that the Twelve divided the group into twelve bodies of people, and each of those Twelve taught an individual group. They instructed the multitude to pray unto the Father in the name of Jesus, and they also prayed for that which they desired most, that the Holy Ghost should be given to them (vv. 6–9). They, too, recognized the importance of its baptism and receiving it as a gift.

10 And when they had thus prayed they went down unto the water's edge, and the multitude followed them.

11 And it came to pass that Nephi went down into the water and was baptized.

12 And he came up out of the water and began to baptize. And he baptized all those whom Jesus had chosen. [3 Nephi 19:10–12]

Nephi was baptized, and then the remainder of the Twelve were baptized by Nephi (vv. 11–12). Who baptized Nephi is not recorded, but any one of the Twelve had that authority. It would have been similar to when "[Joseph Smith] baptized [Oliver Cowdery] first, and afterwards [Oliver] baptized [Joseph]." They had both been given "the Priesthood of Aaron, which holds the keys of the ministering of angels, and of the gospel of repentance, and of baptism by immersion for the remission of sins" by the angelic John the Baptist, "who commanded us to go and be baptized, and gave us directions" to baptize each other (JS–H 1:69–71). The ordinance was to be performed by mortal beings since it was obviously an earthly ordinance. The desire of the Nephite Twelve to receive the Holy Ghost was then granted.

> 13 And it came to pass when they were all baptized and had come up out of the water, the Holy Ghost did fall upon them, and they were filled with the Holy Ghost and with fire.
>
> 14 And behold, they were encircled about as if it were by fire; and it came down from heaven, and the multitude did witness it, and did bear record; and angels did come down out of heaven and did minister unto them. [3 Nephi 19:13–14]

Baptism is a prerequisite to receiving the Holy Ghost as a gift. "The voice of the Son came unto [Nephi], saying: He that is baptized in my name, to him will the Father give the Holy Ghost, like unto me" (2 Nephi 31:12). As the twelve disciples individually came up out of the waters of baptism, "the Holy Ghost did fall upon them, and they were filled with the Holy Ghost and with fire." The multitude was humble and spiritually attuned enough to witness the outpouring of the Holy Ghost upon the Twelve. They saw and bore record that the Twelve were "encircled about as if by fire" (vv. 13–14). The phrase "as if by fire" is probably the best way that the glory of the Holy Ghost could be described. The spirit "can only be discerned by purer eyes" (D&C 131:7), but they lacked the earthly words to describe this glorious manifestation.

While the Holy Ghost was being poured out upon the twelve disciples, angels also ministered to them. How the angels ministered is not recorded, but they were probably strengthening them and preparing them for their ministry. "There appeared an angel unto [Christ] from heaven, strengthening him" as he suffered in Gethsemane (Luke 22:43). As the angels were ministering unto the Nephites, Jesus made his second-day appearance.

> 15 And it came to pass that while the angels were ministering unto the disciples, behold, Jesus came and stood in the midst and ministered unto them.
>
> 16 And it came to pass that he spake unto the multitude, and commanded them that they should kneel down again upon the earth, and also that his disciples should kneel down upon the earth.
>
> 17 And it came to pass that when they had all knelt down upon the earth, he commanded his disciples that they should pray.
>
> 18 And behold, they began to pray; and they did pray unto Jesus, calling him their Lord and their God.
>
> 19 And it came to pass that Jesus departed out of the midst of them, and went a little way off from them and bowed himself to the earth, and he said: [3 Nephi 19:15–19]

The disciples praying to Jesus was contradictory to his instructions given the day before to "always pray unto the Father in my name" (3 Nephi 18:19). The reason that they prayed to him, rather than following the previous day's instructions, was later given in the prayer that Jesus uttered to the Father.

Jesus explained: "they pray unto me because I am with them" (3 Nephi 19:22). When a glorified being has attained godhood, and appears to someone, it is most likely that they would communicate directly with each other. Support of this concept is shown in Joseph Smith's dedicatory prayer of the Kirtland Temple. In this prayer, which "was given to [Joseph] by revelation" (preface to Section 109), Joseph Smith spoke directly to the "Lord God of Israel [Christ]" as he began his prayer (D&C 109:1), and repeatedly thereafter (109:34, 42, 56). These addresses were interspersed with other appeals to the Holy Father, including the formal salutation of the prayer, "we ask thee Holy Father, in the name of Jesus Christ" (v. 4), which is consistent with Jesus' previous instruction to "always pray unto the Father in my name" (3 Nephi 18:19; see also D&C 109:10, 14, 22, 24, 29, 47, 77). Was Jesus present? His house was being dedicated, and it seems probable that he was there, which was why Joseph addressed him personally.

The prayer of Jesus to the Father after he departed from the Nephites' midst is only four verses long, but contains some great lessons for us. Perhaps the four verses were not the entire prayer, but were only the significant things that were pertinent to what Mormon was recording. Since Jesus was away from the disciples when he prayed, it may be that only some of the words of his prayer were revealed to the disciples. When the "greater things [are] made manifest," as the large plates come forth, we may have further information about this prayer (3 Nephi 26:9).

The first recorded part of the prayer was a thanks to the Father for giving the disciples, whom Jesus had chosen, that which they desired most, the Holy Ghost. Jesus also acknowledged that he had chosen those disciples "because of their belief in [him]" (3 Nephi 19:20). Their belief in Christ could be equated with a "desire to take upon them [Christ's] name with full purpose of heart," a prerequisite revealed in this dispensation for becoming one of the chosen disciples of the Lord (D&C 18:26–28). Jesus then asked the Father to "give the Holy Ghost unto all them that shall believe in [the disciples'] words," who had power to confer it (3 Nephi 19:21). The Holy Ghost does not come automatically, or unconditionally, upon the person to whom it is given. "A man may receive the Holy Ghost, and it may descend upon him and not tarry with him" (D&C 130:23). Jesus reminded the Father, and us through our reading, that the disciples were given the Holy Ghost because of their belief in Christ. Their belief was exemplified through the prayers that the Father heard (3 Nephi 19:22).

Jesus concluded by praying for unity between the disciples and those who would believe in their words. He desired the same oneness for them that existed between him and the Father (3 Nephi 19:23). The prayer is shorter but quite similar to part of the intercessory prayer offered by Jesus in Gethsemane. The part that is similar is paralleled here with Jesus' prayer to show the similarities:

Father, I thank thee that thou has given the Holy Ghost unto these whom I have chosen; and it is because of their belief in me that I have chosen them out of the world. Father, I pray thee that thou wilt give the Holy Ghost unto all them that shall believe in their words. Father, thou has given them the Holy Ghost because they believe in me; and thou seest that they believe in me because thou hearest them, and they pray unto me; and they pray unto me because I am with them. And now Father, I pray unto thee for them, and also for all those who shall believe on their words, that they may believe in me, that I may be in them as thou, Father, art in me, that we may be one. (3 Nephi 19:20–23)	Neither pray I for these alone, but for them also which shall believe on me through their word; That they all may be one; as thou, Father, art in me, and I in thee, that they also may be one in us: that the world may believe that thou has sent me. And the glory which thou gavest me I have given them; that they may be one, even as we are one: I in them, and thou in me, that they may be made perfect in one; and that the world may know that thou hast sent me, and hast loved them, as thou hast loved me. (John 17:20–23)

Unity is a requirement for being the Lord's people. The Lord called Enoch's "people Zion, because they were of one heart and one mind" (Moses 7:18). As Jesus revealed in this dispensation, "Be one; and if ye are not one ye are not mine" (D&C 38:1, 27). The Book of Mormon teaches that those who seek to bring forth the Lord's Zion "shall have the gift and the power of the Holy Ghost" (1 Nephi 13:37). Jesus' Nephite prayer illustrates the importance of the Holy Ghost in attaining the oneness of the Father and the Son, and becoming a Zion people.

> 24 And it came to pass that when Jesus had thus prayed unto the Father, he came unto his disciples, and behold, they did still continue, without ceasing, to pray unto him; and they did not multiply many words, for it was given unto them what they should pray, and they were filled with desire. [3 Nephi 19:24]

The description of these disciples praying shows one of the great principles of communication through prayer. Although the amount of time that the disciples had been praying is not given, it implies that it was a rather lengthy prayer. However, their prayers were not vain repetitions that they had been previously warned against (3 Nephi 13:7); they were sincere and meaningful words. They were guided by the Spirit as to what they were to say. This is the key to meaningful prayer. This key is also taught in the New Testament. Paul taught the Romans, "Likewise the Spirit also helpeth our infirmities: for we know not what we should pray for as we ought: but the Spirit itself maketh intercession for us with groanings [striving] which cannot be uttered [expressed]" (Romans 8:26).[2] Paul gave similar instructions to the Ephesians: "Praying always with all prayer and supplication in the Spirit" (Ephesians 6:18). Jude admonished his readers to pray "in the Holy Ghost" (Jude 1:20). Thus, it is appropriate to ask for the Holy Ghost to guide us in our prayers that we may pray for that "which is right" (3 Nephi 18:20). As we pray, the Holy Ghost will also fill us "with desire," as were the Nephite disciples (v. 24).

> 25 And it came to pass that Jesus blessed them as they did pray unto him; and his countenance did smile upon them, and the light of his countenance did shine upon them, and behold they were as white as the countenance and also the garments of Jesus; and behold the whiteness thereof did exceed all the whiteness, yea, even there could be nothing upon earth so white as the whiteness thereof.
>
> 26 And Jesus said unto them: Pray on; nevertheless they did not cease to pray. [3 Nephi 19:25–26]

Were the Twelve temporarily transfigured? The answer to this question can only come from the Savior himself. Whatever happened, their souls were purified as shown by the next prayer that Jesus offered to the Father as he again left the disciples to pray.

---

[2] TPJS, 278. The Prophet Joseph gave the bracketed words as a better wording, but they were never added to the JST.

27 And he turned from them again, and went a little way off and bowed himself to the earth; and he prayed again unto the Father, saying:

28 Father, I thank thee that thou hast purified those whom I have chosen, because of their faith, and I pray for them, and also for them who shall believe on their words, that they may be purified in me, through faith on their words, even as they are purified in me." [3 Nephi 19:27–28]

The desire for others to be purified gives us insight into what had already happened to the twelve disciples. To be purified is to be sanctified. The disciples had become sanctified through the Spirit. This is the ultimate role of the Holy Ghost, "the purifying and the sanctification of their hearts, which sanctification cometh because of their yielding their hearts unto God" (Helaman 3:35). To the Twelve it happened in a brief period, but to most, sanctification is usually a life-long process. The extent of the Twelve's experience was undoubtedly beyond the normal. How long their whiteness remained is not stated, but when Jesus returned, "they were white even as Jesus" (v. 30). This represents the ultimate of being "purified even as he is pure" (Moroni 7:48), or being "partakers of the divine nature" (2 Peter 1:4).

The last part of Jesus' second prayer to the Father also has a parallel with the intercessory prayer in Gethsemane:

Father, I pray not for the world, but for those whom thou hast given me out of the world, because of their faith, that they may be purified in me, that I may be in them as thou, Father, art in me, that we may be one, that I may be glorified in them. (3 Nephi 19:29)	I pray for them: I pray not for the world, but for them which thou hast given me; for they are thine. And all mine are thine, and thine are mine; and I am glorified in them. And now I am no more in the world, but these are in the world, and I come to thee. Holy Father, keep through thine own name those whom thou hast given me, that they may be one, as we are. (John 17:9–11)

Another glorious manifestation of the divinity of Jesus had occurred on the second day of his divine ministry.

> 30 And when Jesus had spoken these words he came again unto his disciples; and behold they did pray steadfastly, without ceasing, unto him; and he did smile upon them again; and behold they were white, even as Jesus.
>
> 31 And it came to pass that he went again a little way off and prayed unto the Father;
>
> 32 And tongue cannot speak the words which he prayed, neither can be written by man the words which he prayed.
>
> 33 And the multitude did hear and do bear record; and their hearts were open and they did understand in their hearts the words which he prayed.
>
> 34 Nevertheless, so great and marvelous were the words which he prayed that they cannot be written, neither can they be uttered by man. [3 Nephi 19:30–34]

The third successive prayer that Jesus offered was so glorious that "tongue cannot speak the words which he prayed, neither can be written by man." However the multitude "did understand in their hearts" (vv. 31–34). Perhaps as the Millennium is ushered in we will receive the words of this last prayer, and we too will be able to understand it.

> 35 And it came to pass that when Jesus had made an end of praying he came again to the disciples, and said unto them: So great faith have I never seen among all the Jews; wherefore I could not show unto them so great miracles, because of their unbelief.
>
> 36 Verily I say unto you, there are none of them that have seen so great things as ye have seen; neither have they heard so great things as ye have heard. [3 Nephi 19:35–36]

Jesus' commendation for their great faith demonstrated that his ministry among them was really the ultimate in importance and spirituality. The Jews had not been shown "so great miracles, because of their unbelief" nor "seen so great things" nor heard so great things as had the Nephites (vv. 35–36). The miracles and the teachings among the Nephites were greater than among the Jews. Although there were multiple miracles performed in Jerusalem, as cited earlier (see Matthew 4:23–24; Luke 7:17–19), these miracles were probably not as many, nor of such quality, as those done among the Nephites. Possibly that is why there are no accounts of individual miracles in 3 Nephi. There were so many and they were so great that there was not space to record them.

Following Jesus' mortal ministry in Jerusalem, the apostles did perform great miracles by the power of the Holy Ghost. Peter, shortly after the day of Pentecost when the Holy Ghost was given, healed the "man lame from his mother's womb" (Acts 3:1–11). He later healed a man confined to "his bed for eight years." Tabitha, a woman of Joppa, who "was sick and died," he told to "arise. And she opened her eyes; and when she saw Peter, she sat up . . . and when he had called the saints and widows, presented her alive" (Acts 9:36–41). Many more miracles could be cited, and all came by the power of the Holy Ghost.

The ministry of Jesus among the Nephites was indeed a divine ministry. The divine ministry can be attributed to the Holy Ghost that was so graciously poured out upon them because of their unwavering acceptance of Jesus as the Christ. The example of the Nephites on this occasion should be one to emulate. We should desire most that we attain the Spirit in our lives, should pray verbally for it, and always have that Spirit in our hearts. The Savior "commanded the multitude that they should cease to pray, and also his disciples. And he commanded them that they should not cease to pray in their hearts" (3 Nephi 20:1). Great blessings had been poured out upon the Nephites, and as they continued to pray verbally, and in their hearts, these blessings would continue.

The Prophet Joseph Smith also taught the supreme importance of the Holy Ghost. President Brigham Young related a dream that he had in February 1847 when he saw and spoke with the Prophet Joseph following the martyrdom of the Prophet. President Young asked Joseph if he had any counsel for him.

Joseph stepped toward me, and looking very earnestly, yet pleasantly said, 'Tell the people to be humble and faithful, and be sure to keep the spirit of the Lord and it will lead them right. Be careful and not turn away the small still voice; it will teach you what to do and where to go; it will yield the fruits of the kingdom. Tell the brethren to keep their hearts open to conviction, so that when the Holy Ghost comes to them, their hearts will be ready to receive it. They can tell the Spirit of the Lord from all other spirits; it will whisper peace and joy to their souls; it will take malice, hatred, strife and all evil from their hearts; and their whole desire will be to do good, bring forth righteousness and build up the kingdom of God. Tell the brethren if they will follow the spirit of the Lord they will go right. Be sure to tell the people to keep the Spirit of the Lord; and if they will, they will find themselves just as they were organized by our Father in Heaven before they came into the world. Our Father in Heaven organized the human family, but they are all disorganized and in great confusion.'

Joseph then showed me the pattern, how they were in the beginning. This I cannot describe, but I saw it, and saw where the Priesthood had been taken from the earth and how it must be joined together, so that there would be a perfect chain from Father Adam to his latest posterity. Joseph again said, "Tell the people to be sure to keep the Spirit of the Lord and follow it, and it will lead them just right.[3]

Thus, the Prophet Joseph Smith is a second witness to the Book of Mormon of the importance of our receiving the Holy Ghost. To obtain the Spirit in our lives we must accept Jesus Christ without reservation, and show our desire to have that Spirit through the way that we live and by sincere prayer, as did the Nephites.

---

[3] Watson, Elden J. (Ed.), *Manuscript History of Brigham Young 1846–1847*, pp. 528–530.

Chapter 11

The Covenant of Abraham and the Gathering of Israel

3 Nephi 20:10–42, 46

The second day of Jesus' divine ministry began with a great spiritual experience for all who had assembled. The Nephite Twelve were baptized with water and with the Holy Ghost, and angels ministered to them, all of which was witnessed by the multitude. Jesus appeared and commanded the twelve to pray, and he prayed for them. He miraculously produced bread and wine, and gave the sacrament again to all the multitude. All were filled with the Spirit. They were prepared to be taught, which Jesus did. His topic, given him by the Father, was the covenant made to the Nephite people, a remnant of the house of Israel. His text was words that he had revealed some seven hundred years earlier to the prophet Isaiah. An outline of part of that text, an overview to prepare for a deeper study, follows. The remainder of the abridged text of his second day's teachings will be discussed in the following two chapters.

Outline • 3 Nephi 20:10–42, 46

➤ 20:10–42, 46   The commandment given by the Father concerning this people, a remnant of the house of Israel.

a.   When the words of Isaiah are fulfilled, then will the covenant of the Father be fulfilled. vv. 11–13

   1.   They are written and are before you, search them.

   2.   The remnants scattered on the face of the earth shall be gathered.

   3.   They shall be brought to the knowledge of the Lord their God.

b.   The Father commanded me to give you this land for your inheritance. vv. 14–20 (Micah 4:8–9,12)

   1.   If the Gentiles do not repent, after receiving so many blessings, then this remnant of Jacob shall tread them down.

   2.   All thine enemies shall be cut off.

   3.   I will gather my covenant people, and beat in pieces many people.

   4.   The sword of justice shall hang upon all the nations of the Gentiles.

c.   I will establish my people, the house of Israel. vv. 21–23

   1.   The covenant made to father Jacob shall be fulfilled.

   2.   The New Jerusalem shall be built in this land, and the power of heaven will be in their midst.

   3.   I am the prophet spoken of by Moses (Deuteronomy 18:15).

d.   All the prophets from Samuel and after have testified of me. vv. 24–28

   1.   Ye are the children of the prophets, of Israel, and · of the covenant of Abraham.

   2.   The Father has sent me to you first to turn you from your iniquities.

   3.   After you are blessed, the Holy Ghost shall be poured out through me upon the Gentiles.

   4.   The Gentiles shall scatter my people, and be a scourge upon the people of this land.

    5.   When the Gentiles receive the fulness of the gospel, their iniquities will return on their own heads.

  e. I will remember the covenant to my own people (Jews) to gather them to Jerusalem. vv. 29–35

    1.   The fulness of my gospel shall be preached unto them.

    2.   They shall believe in me and pray to the Father in my name.

    3.   Their watchman shall sing together, and shall see eye to eye.

    4.   Then the Father will gather them to Jerusalem.

    5.   They will sing that the Father hath redeemed Jerusalem.

    6.   The Father shall bare his arm to all nations, and all shall see the salvation of the Father and me.

  f.   The words written (by Isaiah) shall be fulfilled. vv. 36–42

    1.   Zion is to put on her strength, and Jerusalem shall put on her beautiful garments.

    2.   Jerusalem shall shake off her dust, and Zion the bands of her neck.

    3.   They shall be redeemed without money.

    4.   My people shall know my name, and know that I speak.

    5.   They will recognize those that publish peace.

    6.   A cry shall go forth; be ye clean that bear the vessels of the Lord.

    7.   They will not go out with haste or by flight, but the Lord will go before and in their rearward.

  g. All these things shall surely come as the Father hath commanded. v. 46

    1.   The covenant of the Father will be fulfilled with his people (the house of Israel).

2. Jerusalem will be inhabited again with [Christ's] people.

Notes and Commentary

10 And it came to pass that when they had all given glory unto Jesus, he said unto them: Behold now I finish the commandment which the Father hath commanded me concerning this people, who are a remnant of the house of Israel.

11 Ye remember that I spake unto you, and said that when the words of Isaiah should be fulfilled—behold they are written, ye have them before you, therefore search them—

12 And verily, verily, I say unto you, that when they shall be fulfilled then is the fulfilling of the covenant which the Father hath made unto his people, O house of Israel. [3 Nephi 20:10–12]

This is the first of three admonitions to search the words, or prophecies, of Isaiah. Two of these came from the Savior, the second one being a commandment, and one from Moroni (v. 11; 3 Nephi 23:1, and Mormon 8:23).[1] They were to search Isaiah's prophecies because "when they shall be fulfilled then is the fulfilling of the covenant which the Father hath made unto his people, O house of Israel" (v. 12).

The historical setting and the text that follows illustrates that the fulfilling of the covenant to Israel would be in the latter days. Jesus was instructing the Nephite Saints in A.D. 34, following the completion of his mortal ministry upon the earth. He was speaking of the time after a further scattering of Israel, the taking of the gospel to the Gentiles, and the future gathering of Israel (see 3 Nephi 20:13–14

---

[1] These prophecies were originally upon the plates of brass that Nephi and his brothers had obtained from Laban (1 Nephi 4:20–24; 5:10–13). The Book of Mormon also shows that copies of these texts had been made and were used by the people as also indicated here. For example, all of the sons of Mosiah read from the scriptures as they were individually in different parts of the land of Lehi-Nephi doing missionary work among the Lamanites (see Mosiah 13:11; Alma 14:1; 21:9; 22:12; 33:2).

quoted below). As stated before, Mormon prophesied that the covenant of Abraham would be fulfilled after his people had been scattered by the Gentiles. "But behold, it shall come to pass that they shall be driven and scattered by the Gentiles; and after they have been driven and scattered by the Gentiles, behold, then will the Lord remember the covenant which he made unto Abraham and unto all the house of Israel" (Mormon 5:20). Following A.D. 34, the branch of Judah, the branches of Joseph [Nephites and Lamanites], and possibly other branches of Israel were scattered. The gospel has again been going to the Gentiles since A.D. 1830, and a few of the branches of Israel are today having the gospel taken to them. Since these events are now in the process of being fulfilled, it seems evident that the prophecies of Isaiah, and the covenants to Israel are being fulfilled in our day. Furthermore, there have been no other claims of their fulfillment since A.D. 34. As they are fulfilled, it should be kept in mind that the prophecies will be fulfilled at different times to different branches of Israel.

Jacob, the brother of Nephi, testified that "Isaiah spake concerning *all the house of Israel*" (2 Nephi 6:5; italics added). A careful study of Isaiah's prophesies shows that he did this through a form of dual prophesy; the same prophecy being applicable to each of the individual branches of Israel. Jesus illustrated this through the slight modification of Isaiah's words as he spoke of different branches of Israel. To the Nephites he quoted Isaiah saying *"thy* watchmen" (3 Nephi 16:18), and he quoted the same passage in reference to the Jews as *"their* watchmen [shall] lift up their voice" (3 Nephi 20:32; Isaiah 52:8; italics added). The third branch of Israel, the lost tribes, shall undoubtedly also have their own watchmen lift up their voices among their own people.

As Jesus ministered on the American continent, he spoke of the Nephite people, of the Jewish people, and of all the house of Israel. He spoke of one group for a time, then of another, and then of the collective house of Israel. Because of this pattern, our analysis will follow the sequence that he established. There seems to be a purpose in this sequence.

The Scattered Remnant

> 13 And then shall the remnants, which shall be scattered abroad upon the face of the earth, be gathered in from the east and from the west, and from the south and from the north; and they shall be brought to the knowledge of the Lord their God, who hath redeemed them. [3 Nephi 20:13]

The scattering and gathering of Israel is consistent with the prophets of the Bible and the Book of Mormon. Amos had foretold that Israel would be sifted "among *all nations*" (Amos 9:9; italics added). Lehi prophesied that the branches of Israel "should be broken off and should be scattered *upon all the face of the earth*" (1 Nephi 10:12–13; italics added). Nephi, in explaining Isaiah to Laman and Lemuel, said that the house of Israel "sooner or later, will be scattered *upon all the face of the earth, and also among all nations*" (1 Nephi 22:3; italics added). The extent of Israel's scattering is shown by Jesus' prophecy that Israel will "be gathered in from the east and from the west, and from the south and from the north" (v. 13). Jesus had taught this same concept during his mortal ministry in Palestine. To these whom he called "workers of iniquity," he prophesied:

> 28 There shall be weeping and gnashing of teeth, when ye shall see Abraham, and Isaac, and Jacob, and all the prophets, in the kingdom of God, and you yourselves thrust out.
>
> 29 And they shall come from the east, and from the west, and from the north, and from the south, and shall sit down in the kingdom of God.
>
> 30 And, behold, there are last which shall be first, and there are first which shall be last [Luke 13:28–30, see also Matthew 8:11].

The house of Israel was first to hear the gospel in the meridian of time, and the Gentiles were last. In the latter days, the gospel would be restored first among the Gentiles, and after they had an opportunity to accept or reject it, the house of Israel would be the last ones to hear.

His above prophecies are, therefore, not only the gathering of the branches of Israel, but also a gathering of those who were dispersed among the Gentile nations.[2] Therefore, the Gentiles would also be given opportunity to receive the gospel as the scattered remnants were gathered. As he continued to prophesy, Jesus spoke of the Nephites, a specific branch of the house of Israel, and how their gathering related to the gathering of all of Israel.

The Nephite Remnant

> 14 And the Father hath commanded me that I should give unto you this land, for your inheritance.
>
> 15 And I say unto you, that if the Gentiles do not repent after the blessing which they shall receive, after they have scattered my people— [3 Nephi 20:14–15]

The Father had commanded Jesus to give the lands of America to the Nephites, descendants of Joseph who was sold into Egypt (v. 14). He had filled this commandment on the first day of his visit (3 Nephi 15:12–13, discussed in chapter 8 of this work).[3] However, because the Nephites later lost "the Spirit of the Lord" and were "led about by Satan, even as chaff is driven before the wind," the Lord "reserved their blessings, which they might have received in the land, for the

---

[2] Jacob, brother of Nephi, in commenting on Zenos' allegory of the house of Israel, states that God is merciful "for he remembereth the house of Israel, both roots and branches" (Jacob 6:4). This shows that the roots are a segment of the house of Israel and not Jesus Christ or gospel covenants as some have supposed. The branches are shown in the allegory to be three distinct segments of Israel that were taken away (Jacob 5:38–39). The roots, therefore, must be those scattered among all nations and primarily Ephraim, the birthright holder, who would be established as the mother tree into which the branches would be grafted back (Jacob 5:52–56).

[3] The Nephites, as used here, is a general term for the righteous descendants of Lehi, a descendant of Manasseh, son of Joseph (Alma 10:3), and of Ishmael, a descendant of Ephraim, son of Joseph *(see JD* 23:184). Collectively, they represent the branches of Joseph that were to "run over the wall [ocean], unto the utmost bound of the everlasting hills [Americas]" (Genesis 49:22–26).

Gentiles who shall possess the land" (Mormon 5:16–19). The day before, Jesus had taught the Nephites that the blessing of the gospel would come to the Gentiles upon the land of the Americas. Therefore, the gathering spoken of in verse 13 above would be centered in the Americas. He also warned the Gentiles of their sinning against the opportunity for accepting the gospel, and being trodden down by the house of Israel when this happened (3 Nephi 16:10–15; see chapter 8). Therefore, he is reviewing the previous day's teaching concerning the Gentiles (3 Nephi 20:15), and enlarging upon the role of the various branches of the house of Israel.

The key to understanding the segments of Israel to whom Jesus refers in his explanations is given in the end of 3 Nephi 20. In verse 46 Jesus said, "Verily, verily, I say unto you, all these things shall surely come, even as the Father hath commanded me. Then shall this covenant which the Father hath covenanted with his people be fulfilled; and then shall Jerusalem be inhabited again with my people, and it shall be the land of their inheritance." From this passage we learn that the Father's people are the whole house of Israel with whom he made a covenant, while Jesus' people are the tribe of Judah through whom his mortal birth came. Therefore, when spoken of individually, the Father's people would include any of the tribes of Israel except Judah. It could also include Judah when spoken of in the context of the Father's covenant to the whole house of Israel. A clear designation of the group of whom Jesus speaks, as he addresses the Nephites, is vital to a correct understanding of the text.

The first group that Jesus refers to is clearly the Nephite remnant. He begins by saying that the Father had commanded him to give the land of America to the Nephites as the land of their inheritance, and then says, "and I say *unto you*" (vv. 14–15; italics added). Continuing, he then quotes, with slight modification, the prophet Micah.[4] A comparison of the KJV text and the Book of Mormon illustrates these slight differences, and the retention of a more complete text in the Third Nephi account. However, the KJV text more correctly identifies the Gentiles as the people among whom the Nephites will be.

Then shall ye, who are a remnant of the house of Jacob, go forth among them; and ye shall be in the midst of them who shall be many; and ye shall be among them as a lion among the beasts of the forest, and as a young lion among the flocks of sheep, who, if he goeth through both treadeth down and teareth in pieces, and none can deliver. Thy hand shall be lifted up upon thine adversaries, and all thine enemies shall be cut off. (3 Nephi 20:16–17; italics added)	And the remnant of Jacob shall be among the Gentiles in the midst of many people as a lion among the beasts of the forest, as a young lion among the flocks of sheep: who, if he go through, both treadeth down, and teareth in pieces, and none can deliver. Thine hand shall be lifted up upon thine adversaries, and all thine enemies shall be cut off. (Micah 5:8–9; italics added)

The Gentiles are to be trodden down by the Lamanites, who will cut them off from the blessings of the gospel. The full interpretation of these verses will be discussed later when they are again quoted by Jesus.

Jesus continued quoting Micah (or Isaiah), but from a different chapter. He also changes subjects as determined by the key, the father's people, and my people, cited above. He speaks of "my people" or of the Jews. Again there are slight differences in the Book of Mormon and the biblical text.

---

[4] The words were probably from Isaiah because Isaiah was the source that he had admonished them to search. Isaiah and Micah were contemporaries and both of them quote other similar prophecies (Isaiah 2:2–3; Micah 4:1–2). If this thesis is correct, the verses quoted by Jesus here would be a part of the plain and precious parts lost from Isaiah.

And I will gather my people together as a man gathereth his sheaves into the floor.

For I will make my people with whom the Father hath covenanted, yea, I will make thy horn iron, and I will make thy hoofs brass. And thou shalt eat in pieces many people; and I will consecrate their gain unto the Lord, and their substance unto the Lord of the whole earth. And behold, I am he who doeth it. (3 Nephi 20:18–19)

But they know not the thoughts of the Lord, neither understand they his counsel: for he shall gather them as the sheaves into the floor.

Arise and thresh, O daughter of Zion: for I will make thine horn iron, and I will make thy hoofs brass: and thou shalt beat in pieces many people: and I will consecrate their gain unto the Lord, and their substance unto the Lord of the whole earth. (Micah 4:12–13)

Jesus is using the symbolism in Micah (or Isaiah) of the threshing floor where the grain is separated from the chaff by the animals walking upon the grain stalks that have been gathered upon the threshing floor. It represents the gleaning of Judah (wheat) out of the gentile nations (chaff). The Jews are to be gathered and be victorious over many people (Gentiles) because the Lord is behind them, but as shown by the KJV text, the Jews are not aware of his help, or of his intended program for them. The sequential order of the prophecies of the two groups, the Nephites and the Jews, seems to occur simultaneously, as indicated by the text. The word "then" (v. 16) introduces a new time frame, and the word "and" (v. 18) seems to designate the same period as verses 16 and 17. Therefore, while the Nephites are treading down the unrepentant Gentiles, the Jews will be gathering, but will have opposition from the Gentiles. The Father's justice will then come upon all the gentile nations. "And it shall come to pass, saith the Father, that the sword of my justice shall hang over them at that day; and except they repent it shall fall upon them, saith the Father, yea, even upon all the nations of the Gentiles" (3 Nephi 20:20). The introductory phrase, "And it shall come to pass," also indicates a lapse of time following the gathering out of "my people," the Jews.

Another "And it shall come to pass" introduces the next step of the fulfilling of the covenant made to Israel. "And it shall come to pass that I will establish my people, O house of Israel" (3 Nephi 20:21). From other scriptures that follow, it is apparent that this step is simultaneous with the time period of the sword of justice falling upon all the nations of the Gentiles, but after Israel and the Jews have been gathered from among the Gentiles. Following their gathering, and during the Gentile oppression, the Father will establish his people (v. 21), the tribes of Israel. Jesus speaks to the Nephites of their part in that step.

The Nephite people were to be established in this land (the Americas). Being established apparently means the building of the New Jerusalem, or "the center place" for "the city of Zion" (D&C 57:2–3). This will fulfill a covenant made to Jacob, the father of the twelve tribes of Israel. "And behold, this people will I establish in this land, unto the fulfilling of the covenant which I made with your father Jacob; and it shall be a New Jerusalem. And the powers of heaven shall be in the midst of this people; yea, even I will be in the midst of you" (3 Nephi 20:22). The covenant to Jacob sheds some additional light upon the blessing he gave to his son Joseph. The phrase "branches [of Joseph] run over the wall [ocean] . . . unto the utmost bound of the everlasting hills" (Genesis 49:22–26) was not some unknown terminology that Jacob did not comprehend. He knew of his sons' posterity coming to the Americas and of the eventual building of the New Jerusalem. (The Nephites' role in this project will be discussed in the next chapter.) Nor was Jacob the sole possessor of this knowledge. Earlier, Ether, the Jaredite prophet, had foreseen "that a New Jerusalem should be built up upon this land, unto the remnant of the seed of Joseph, for which things there has been a type " (Ether 13:6). As Moroni abridged the Jaredite records, he acknowledged Ether's prophecy and compared "Joseph [bringing] his father down into the land of Egypt," with "the Lord [bringing] a remnant of the seed of Joseph out of the land of Jerusalem[5] (Ether 13:7–8).

After the building of the New Jerusalem, Jesus promises that "the powers of heaven shall be in the midst of this people [who reside in the New Jerusalem]; yea, even I will be in the midst of you" (v. 22). Some would interpret this wording as a declaration that the New Jerusalem would be built in the Millennium. While such may be the case, there may be another valid interpretation. The New Jerusalem will have "a spot for the temple" to be built in this marvelous city (D&C 57:3). The temple is the Lord's house, and, thus, he could come to his house periodically in fulfillment of his promise to be in their midst. Elder Harold B. Lee taught:

> I know that this is the Lord's work, I know that Jesus Christ lives and that he is closer to this Church and appears more often in Holy places than any of us realize, excepting sometimes those to whom he makes personal appearance. I know it and the time is hastening when he shall come again to reign as Lord of Lords and King of Kings.[6]

Furthermore, even without the appearances of the Lord, the powers of heaven being in the midst of the people is the power of the priesthood. Again, as interpreted by President Harold B. Lee:

> How does he reign in our midst? How shall he have power over his saints? If you had been in the meeting of the priesthood last night, you would have seen the great power that was in evidence there, where there were two thousand holders of the priesthood, the power of God by which

---

[5] Moroni seems to be the person speaking in Ether 13:7–8 since he speaks in the past tense regarding Joseph having brought his father Jacob down into the land of Egypt. Had this been a continuation of Ether's prophecy, it would have continued in the future tense.

[6] Harold B. Lee, MIA June Conference, June 29, 1969 as quoted in *Teachings of the Living Prophets,* Brigham Young University Press, p. 24.

he works through men to the accomplishment of his purposes. He is reigning in our midst through them.[7]

Thus the Lord may be in the people's midst in the New Jerusalem before the Millennium. The Prophet Joseph Smith said: "Judah must return, Jerusalem must be rebuilt, and the temple, . . . before the Son of Man will make his appearance" (TPJS, 286). This statement, correlated with the teachings of Jesus in 3 Nephi 21, and the following verses of 3 Nephi 20, indicate it will be before the millennial reign.

When the New Jerusalem has been established and the powers of heaven, even Jesus Christ, are in the midst of the Nephite people, there will be a fulfillment of the prophecy made by Moses concerning Jesus Christ.

> Behold, I am he of whom Moses spake, saying: A prophet shall the Lord your God raise up unto you of your brethren, like unto me; him shall ye hear in all things whatsoever he shall say unto you. And it shall come to pass that every soul who will not hear that prophet shall be cut off from among the people. [3 Nephi 20:23, see also 1 Nephi 22:20–21]

Moses' prophecy is recorded in Deuteronomy 18:15. To be cut off from the Lord's people seems to be the pre-millennial separation of the righteous and the wicked, although it could possibly refer to the terrestrial people being separated from the celestial during the millennium. What Nephi, son of Lehi, said of Isaiah's prophecies, is applicable here; "in the days that the prophecies . . . shall be fulfilled men shall know of a surety, at the times when they shall come to pass" (2 Nephi 25:7). Peter bore the same testimony in Jerusalem of these events associated with the Second Coming.

> 20 And he shall send Jesus Christ, which before was preached unto you:
>
> 21 Whom the heaven must receive until the times of restitution of all things, which God hath spoken by the mouth of all his holy prophets since the world began.

---

[7] Harold B. Lee, *Ensign,* November 1971, 12.

22 For Moses truly said unto the fathers, A prophet shall the Lord your God raise up unto you of your brethren, like unto me; him shall ye hear in all things whatsoever he shall say unto you.

23 And it shall come to pass, that every soul, which will not hear that prophet, shall be destroyed from among the people.

24 Yea, and all the prophets from Samuel and those that follow after, as many as have spoken, have likewise foretold of these days.

25 Ye are the children of the prophets, and of the covenant which God made with our fathers, saying unto Abraham, And in thy seed shall all the kindreds of the earth be blessed. [Acts 3:20–25]

Further details of the fulfillment of this prophecy are given by the Savior, and will be discussed in the next chapter. Jesus is here, not only affirming his being the prophet spoken of by Moses, but also that all of the prophets from Samuel on have known and testified of him.[8]

He again relates the prophecy to the Nephites. Peter's prophecy, quoted above, is also a second witness to what Jesus next told the Nephites.

24 Verily I say unto you, yea, and all the prophets from Samuel and those that follow after, as many as have spoken, have testified of me.

25 And behold, ye are the children of the prophets; and ye are of the house of Israel; and ye are of the covenant which the Father made with your fathers, saying unto Abraham: And in thy seed shall all the kindreds of the earth be blessed.

26 The Father having raised me up unto you first, and sent me to bless you in turning away every one of you from his iniquities; and this because ye are the children of the covenant— [3 Nephi 20:24–26]

---

[8] The question as to why Jesus used Samuel as the focal point of the prophets testifying of him needs some explanation. Samuel was the first prophet following the period of the judges, a period of repeated corruption in Israel that left them without prophets. Moses was the author of the first five books of the Old Testament that contain many prophecies of Christ. Thus, having cited Moses' prophecy, Jesus is stating that those prophets who followed after Moses' time had also testified of Him, the first one being Samuel.

The Nephites, being descendants of Joseph, were the children, or the posterity, of the prophets of Israel, and therefore of the house of Israel and of Abraham to whom the covenant was made that "in thy seed shall all the kindreds of the earth be blessed" (v. 25; Acts 3:25; Genesis 12:3). Being of the covenant entitled them to the blessing of the Savior's visit. Because of that visit they could repent of their iniquities and receive the blessings promised to Abraham's seed (v. 26). The Father's covenant made to Abraham that he would bless the Gentiles was to follow the Savior's visit to the branches of Israel.

> 27 And after that ye were blessed then fulfilleth the Father the covenant which he made with Abraham, saying: In thy seed shall all the kindreds of the earth be blessed—unto the pouring out of the Holy Ghost through me upon the Gentiles, which blessing upon the Gentiles shall make them mighty above all, unto the scattering of my people, O house of Israel.
>
> 28 And they shall be a scourge unto the people of this land. Nevertheless, when they shall have received the fulness of my gospel, then if they shall harden their hearts against me I will return their iniquities upon their own heads, saith the Father. [3 Nephi 20:27–28]

Jesus was "not sent but unto the lost sheep of the house of Israel" (Matthew 15:24). "The Gentiles should not at any time hear [his] voice" (3 Nephi 15:23). They were blessed, however, as a part of the Abrahamic covenant, through "the pouring out of the Holy Ghost through [the Father]" that would "make them mighty above all, unto the scattering of [the Father's] people, O house of Israel" (v. 27). The Gentiles became a mighty people in many ways through the blessing of the Holy Ghost collectively being poured out upon them. They became the political leaders of the world. They became the discoverers of new lands. They prospered through education and inventions.[9] As Nephi was shown:

> 13 And it came to pass that I beheld the Spirit of God, that it wrought upon other Gentiles; and they went forth out of captivity, upon the many waters.
>
> 14 And it came to pass that I beheld many multitudes of the Gentiles upon the land of promise; and I beheld the wrath of God, that it was upon the seed of my brethren; and they were scattered before the Gentiles and were smitten.
>
> 15 And I beheld the Spirit of the Lord, that it was upon the Gentiles, and they did prosper and obtain the land for their inheritance; and I beheld that they were white, and exceedingly fair and beautiful, like unto my people before they were slain.
>
> 16 And it came to pass that I, Nephi, beheld that the Gentiles who had gone forth out of captivity did humble themselves before the Lord; and the power of the Lord was with them.
>
> 17 And I beheld that their mother Gentiles were gathered together upon the waters, and upon the land also, to battle against them.
>
> 18 And I beheld that the power of God was with them, and also that the wrath of God was upon all those that were gathered together against them to battle.
>
> 19 And I, Nephi, beheld that the Gentiles that had gone out of captivity were delivered by the power of God out of the hands of all other nations.
> [1 Nephi 13:13–19]

In their mighty condition, the Gentiles would scatter the house of Israel, which includes being a scourge to the Lamanites, but they were also to have the opportunity to accept the gospel. The Holy Ghost being poured out upon them would have also prepared them for this opportunity. Elder Wilford Woodruff, speaking in 1876, taught:

---

[9] For verification that blessings upon the Gentiles are attributable to the Holy Ghost, see Joseph Fielding Smith, *Doctrines of Salvation* 1:174–183. Compiled by Bruce R. McConkie, SLC, Bookcraft, 1954.

> The principle of gathering has been preached for the past thirty-seven years. Before this principle was preached by the Elders, a great many of the people had received the spirit of it; and the consequence was, that no sooner had it been taught by the Presidency of the Church, than the people everywhere were ready to receive it . . . revealed to them by the Holy Ghost, whose office it is to reveal that which is past, present, and that which is to come, and no surer, stronger testimony can be given to any one than it affords. [JD 18:221]

After the fullness of the gospel has been preached to the Gentiles, "if they shall harden their hearts against me I will return their iniquities upon their own heads, saith the Father" (v. 28). The Savior had enlarged upon this prophecy the previous day (3 Nephi 16; see chapter 8 of this work). The gospel opportunity was then to return to Israel. As Jesus taught in the parable of the vineyard: "So the last shall be first, and the first last" (Matthew 20:16).

My People, the Jews

> 29 And I will remember the covenant which I have made with my people; and I have covenanted with them that I would gather them together in mine own due time, that I would give unto them again the land of their fathers for their inheritance, which is the land of Jerusalem, which is the promised land unto them forever, saith the Father.
>
> 30 And it shall come to pass that the time cometh, when the fulness of my gospel shall be preached unto them;
>
> 31 And they shall believe in me, that I am Jesus Christ, the Son of God, and shall pray unto the Father in my name.
>
> 32 Then shall their watchmen lift up their voice, and with the voice together shall they sing; for they shall see eye to eye. [3 Nephi 20:29–32]

Having quoted the Father concerning the Gentiles, Jesus speaks of his own people, the Jews. He had covenanted to gather them to the land of Jerusalem in his own due time. This was the land of their fathers and the Father had said it was a promised land to the Jewish people forever (v. 29). Jesus then gave a chronological sequence of their gathering.

The first step of the Jewish gathering was the preaching to them of the fulness of [Christ's] gospel. The phrase, "the time cometh" (v. 29), implies a somewhat lengthy time in the future. It has certainly been a long time since Jesus said that "the time cometh," and the gospel has not yet been preached to them to any extent. When that time comes, however, through the preaching of the gospel, the Jews "shall believe in Jesus Christ, the Son of God, and shall pray unto the Father in [Jesus Christ's] name" (v. 31). Those Jews who are converted will initiate the second step of the Jewish gathering; their own watchmen, the converted Jews, will teach their fellow Jewish friends, neighbors and families. This will unite the Jewish people and cause them to see eye to eye (v. 32). The time period of the gospel being preached to the Jews is implied in the text of Jesus' prophecy. In verse 32, Jesus is quoting the first part of Isaiah 52:8, but he does not quote the last phrase of that verse "when the Lord shall bring again Zion." This may suggest that the preaching to the Jews will commence before the establishment of the New Jerusalem, or Zion, in Independence, Missouri.[10]

> 33 Then will the Father gather them together again, and give unto them Jerusalem for the land of their inheritance.
>
> 34 Then shall they break forth into joy—Sing together, ye waste places of Jerusalem; for the Father hath comforted his people, he hath redeemed Jerusalem.
>
> 35 The Father hath made bare his holy arm in the eyes of all the nations; and all the ends of the earth shall see the salvation of the Father; and the Father and I are one. [3 Nephi 20:33–35]

---

[10] That Jesus did not quote the last phrase of Isaiah 52:8 is another interesting variation of a dual prophecy. He did include the phrase "when the Lord shall bring again Zion" as he applied the same prophecy to the Nephites (3 Nephi 16:18). Perhaps it was deleted in reference to the Jews because the Jews would not be involved with the establishment of the New Jerusalem, but it seems more logical to be a time frame condition based upon 3 Nephi 21:26–27. This will be discussed further in chapter 12.

As the introductory phrase "then" (v. 33) implies, the third step of the gathering is that the Father will "gather them together again, and give unto them Jerusalem for the land of their inheritance." The general promise of a gathering had been cited previously (v. 29), but now it is specifically stated that the gathering home to Jerusalem would follow their acceptance of Jesus Christ and his gospel as they were living among the Gentiles. This is consistent with latter-day revelation. In the appendix to the Doctrine and Covenants, the Lord revealed: "Let them, therefore, who are among the Gentiles flee unto Zion. And let them who be of Judah flee unto Jerusalem, unto the mountains of the Lord's house" (D&C 133:12–13). However, in reply to Orson Hyde's letter, as he prepared to go to Palestine to dedicate the land for the return of the Jewish people, Joseph Smith informed him that "converted Jews must come here" and not to Jerusalem (TPJS, 180). The third step of the Jewish gathering will be fulfilled when those who are converted will be encouraged, and will want to gather to Jerusalem.

The fourth step of the gathering is the redemption of Jerusalem. The joy of the gospel will be taught in Jerusalem, and the unification will commence of the unconverted Jewish people, who previously had gathered to Jerusalem, with those who had been converted before gathering. The Lord will "gather all nations, and will bring them down into the valley of Jehoshaphat, and will plead with them there for my people . . . Multitudes, multitudes in the valley of decision: for the day of the Lord is near . . . but the Lord will be the hope of his people, . . . then shall Jerusalem be holy" (Joel 3:2–17). All nations will see the power of the Father as he bares his arm in defense of the Jewish nation. Thus "all the ends of the earth shall see the salvation of the Father; and the Father and I are one" (vv. 34–35; quoting Isaiah 52:9–10). The redemption of the promised land to Judah will have happened.

36 And then shall be brought to pass that which is written: Awake, awake again, and put on thy strength, O Zion; put on thy beautiful

garments, O Jerusalem, the holy city, for henceforth there shall no more come into thee the uncircumcised and the unclean.

37 Shake thyself from the dust; arise, sit down, O Jerusalem; loose thyself from the bands of thy neck, O captive daughter of Zion.

38 For thus saith the Lord: Ye have sold yourselves for naught, and ye shall be redeemed without money. [3 Nephi 20:36–38; quoting Isaiah 52:1–3]

The fifth step of the covenant to Judah is for Jerusalem to be "built up again, a holy city unto the Lord" (Ether 13:5). The sequence of verse 36 suggests that the building of the New Jerusalem will precede Jerusalem becoming a holy city. Zion putting on her strength is for "those whom God should call in the last days, who should hold the power of priesthood to bring again Zion, and the redemption of Israel; and to put on her strength is to put on the authority of the priesthood, which she, Zion, has a right to by lineage; also to return to that power which she had lost" (D&C 113:8). The New Jerusalem will thus be built, "the fulfilling of the covenant which I made with your father Jacob" (3 Nephi 20:22). This will include the building of the temple in Independence, Missouri, "the land which I [the Lord] have appointed and consecrated for the gathering of the saints" (D&C 57:1). As will be explained later, and in the same sequence as suggested above, the building of this temple will precede the building of the temple in Jerusalem, but Jerusalem is to "put on [her] beautiful garments," which may have reference to the temple. The Prophet Joseph taught, as partially quoted above:

> Judah must return, Jerusalem must be rebuilt, and the temple, and water come out from under the temple, and the waters of the Dead Sea be healed. It will take some time to rebuild the walls of the city and the temple, &c.; and all this must be done before the Son of Man will make His appearance. [TPJS, 286]

Elder Orson Pratt taught that "the Temple at Jerusalem will undoubtedly be built, by those who believe in the true Messiah."[11] Those who believe in the true Messiah are those who have become members of The Church of Jesus Christ of Latter-day Saints.

Continuing to quote Isaiah, the Savior said that Jerusalem was to "Shake thyself from the dust; arise, sit down" (v. 37; quoting Isaiah 52:2). To "shake thyself" suggests that it will be an internal rebuilding. The previous verse proclaimed that "the uncircumcised [Gentiles] and the unclean [those who were not converted]" would no longer come into Jerusalem. Jerusalem has been battled over for centuries, but at this point she will throw off the dust of the battlefield and "arise" as a beautiful city. It will "sit down" or be established as a permanent habitat for the children of Judah and others of the house of Israel. Moroni's prophecy would thus be fulfilled:

> And then also cometh the Jerusalem of old; and the inhabitants thereof, blessed are they, for they have been washed in the blood of the Lamb; and they are they who were scattered and gathered in from the four quarters of the earth, and from the north countries, and are partakers of the fulfilling of the covenant which God made with their father, Abraham.
>
> And when these things come, bringeth to pass the scripture which saith, there are they who were first, who shall be last; and there are they who were last, who shall be first. [Ether 13:11–12]

The time of Judah will have come in.

Meanwhile, in America, Zion will "loose thyself from the bands of thy neck, O captive daughter of Zion" (v. 37; quoting Isaiah 52:2). By revelation, the Prophet Joseph Smith explained: "the bands of her

---

[11] *JD* 19:20. See also Elder Bruce R. McConkie's The *Millennial Messiah,* SLC: Deseret Book , pp. 379–80. See also *Church News* Editorial, August 7, 1971, p. 16. The *Church News* editorial was written by Elder Mark E. Petersen. Thus, three modern-day apostles have testified that the Jerusalem temple will be built by members of the restored Church.

neck are the curses of God upon her, or the remnants of Israel in their scattered condition among the Gentiles" (D&C 113:9–10). As the scattered remnants are gathered, they must follow the ways of the Lord rather than the cultural ways of the Gentiles with whom they have been associated. They must live by the teachings of the Book of Mormon and other modern-day revelations. Another statement of the Prophet Joseph substantiates this concept.

> Take away the Book of Mormon and the revelations, and where is our religion? We have none; for without Zion, and a place of deliverance, we must fall; because the time is near when the sun will be darkened, and the moon turn to blood, and the stars fall from heaven, and the earth reel to and fro. Then, if this is the case, and if we are not sanctified and gathered to the places God has appointed, with all our former professions and our great love for the Bible, we must fall; we cannot stand; we cannot be saved; for God will gather out his Saints from the Gentiles, and then comes desolation and destruction, and none can escape except the pure in heart who are gathered. [TPJS, 71]

Those who gather and fail to follow the admonitions of latter-day revelation are subject to "a scourge and judgment to be poured out upon the children of Zion" (D&C 84:55–59).[12] Those who do gather, and sanctify themselves, "shall be redeemed without money," although their forefathers had sold themselves "for naught" (v. 38; quoting Isaiah 52:3). Their fathers had followed the ways of the world that had led them into captivity, but now their posterity was delivered through the power of Jesus Christ.

---

[12] See Benson, Ezra Taft President,/1 *Witness and a Warning* especially chapters 3–5, Deseret Book, 1988. President Benson was obviously raised up to get the Saints to take the Book of Mormon seriously. At the conclusion of the April 1986 General Conference of the Church, he testified "Now in our day, the Lord has revealed the need to reemphasize the Book of Mormon to get the Church and all the children of Zion out from under condemnation—the scourge and judgment. [See D&C 84:54–58.] This message must be carried to the members of the Church throughout the world. . . . I know that Christ is at the helm. This is His world. This is His Church. His purposes will be accomplished *(CR,* April 5 and 6, 1986, 100).

39 Verily, verily, I say unto you, that my people shall know my name; yea, in that day they shall know that I am he that doth speak.

40 And then shall they say: How beautiful upon the mountains are the feet of him that bringeth good tidings unto them, that publisheth peace; that bringeth good tidings unto them of good, that publisheth salvation; that saith unto Zion: Thy God reigneth!

41 And then shall a cry go forth: Depart ye, depart ye, go ye out from thence, touch not that which is unclean; go ye out of the midst of her; be ye clean that bear the vessels of the Lord.

42 For ye shall not go out with haste nor go by flight; for the Lord will go before you, and the God of Israel shall be your rearward. [3 Nephi 20:39–42]

The gathered Saints in both Zion and Jerusalem shall know the name of the Lord, and know that he directs them by revelation (v. 39; quoting Isaiah 52:6; see also Isaiah 26:4, 13; 2 Nephi 25:18–20). The recognition of his name by the Jews will be completed when he appears to them, and they recognize him as he who was crucified among them.

51 And then shall the Jews look upon me and say: What are these wounds in thine hands and in thy feet?

52 Then shall they know that I am the Lord; for I will say unto them: These wounds are the wounds with which I was wounded in the house of my friends. I am he who was lifted up. I am Jesus that was crucified. I am the Son of God.

53 And then shall they weep because of their iniquities; then shall they lament because they persecuted their king. [D&C 45:51–53]

The Jew's question and Jesus' answer was foretold by the Old Testament Prophet Zechariah.

6 And one shall say unto him, What are these wounds in thine hands? Then he shall answer, Those with which I was wounded in the house of my friends. [Zechariah 13:6; see also 12:10]

With this knowledge of Christ firmly established, the sixth phase of the gathering will commence. "And then shall they [the converted

Saints] say: How beautiful upon the mountains are the feet of him that bringeth good tidings unto them, that publisheth peace" (3 Nephi 20:40; quoting Isaiah 52:7). The Jewish people who have come to know Christ will teach the good tidings of Christ and his gospel. The children of Judah will acknowledge that Jesus Christ "is the founder of peace, yea, even the Lord, who has redeemed his people; yea, him who has granted salvation unto his people" (Mosiah 15:18; see also Romans 10:15).

The last phase of the work among the Jews will be the final gathering from other parts of the world. The knowledge of Jesus Christ shall give those who are still living in the world the incentive to depart from it, and to refrain from evil and "touch not that which is unclean." Those priesthood holders of the house of Israel shall be "clean that bear the vessels of the Lord" (v. 41; quoting Isaiah 52:11). The gathering to the promised lands of Israel, either Jerusalem or Zion, will not be in a mass exodus as when the Lord took them out of Egypt, but, nonetheless, it will be under his direction as it was then. They will not go out with haste, nor by flight; "for the Lord will go before you, and the God of Israel shall be your rearward" (v. 42; quoting Isaiah 52:12).

The Savior testified that "these things shall surely come, even as the Father hath commanded." The prophecies of Isaiah, that "the Father hath covenanted with his people [the whole house of Israel], and with Judah, "[Jesus Christ's] people," to be gathered to the promised lands of Zion and Jerusalem will thus be fulfilled (3 Nephi 20:46). Ephraim, the servant of the Lord, will be the instrument through which these gatherings will be initiated, as further discussed in the next chapter.

Chapter 12

The Lord's Servant and The
Sign of the Covenant

3 Nephi 20:43–22:17

There is no record of the people in Palestine being taught the concepts of the covenant of Abraham in the detail that it was taught by Jesus to the Nephites. We know it was not one of the "many covenants of the Lord have they taken away" told to Nephi by an angel of the Lord (1 Nephi 13:26). However, a comparison of Genesis 12:2–3 with Abraham 2:9–11 shows that much was taken away from the original text.

> 2 And I will make of thee a great nation, and I will bless thee, and make thy name great; and thou shalt be a blessing:
>
> 3 And I will bless them that bless thee, and curse him that curseth thee: and in thee shall all families of the earth be blessed. [Genesis 12:2–3]

> 9 And I will make of thee a great nation, and I will bless thee above measure, and make thy name great among all nations, and thou shalt be a blessing unto thy seed after thee, that in their hands they shall bear this ministry and Priesthood unto all nations;
>
> 10 And I will bless them through thy name; for as many as receive this Gospel shall be called after thy name, and shall be accounted thy seed, and shall rise up and bless thee, as their father;
>
> 11 And I will bless them that bless thee, and curse them that curse thee; and in thee (that is, in thy Priesthood) and in thy seed (that is, thy

Priesthood), for I give unto thee a promise that this right shall continue in thee, and in thy seed after thee (that is to say, the literal seed, or the seed of the body) shall all the families of the earth be blessed, even with the blessings of the Gospel, which are the blessings of salvation, even of life eternal. [Abraham 2:9–11]

Perhaps the covenant to Abraham was not taught because of the Jews' pious claim: "We be Abraham's seed, and were never in bondage to any man" for which Jesus severely chastised them (John 8:33–40). Or, perhaps, it was because of their lack of faith. Jesus said the great faith of the Nephites was "never seen among all the Jews" (3 Nephi 19:35). Since the Book of Mormon is to go to the Jews "that they may be persuaded that Jesus is the Christ, the Son of the living God; that the Father may bring about . . . his great and eternal purpose, in restoring the Jews . . . unto the fulfilling of his covenant" (Mormon 5:14), the blessings of the covenant will be made known to them through the account of Jesus' teaching the Nephites. An outline of Jesus' teachings discussed in this chapter, as an overview to prepare for a deeper study, follows. It continues from where the last chapter ended.

Outline • 3 Nephi 20:43–22:17

➤ 20:43–45   The Lord's servant shall be exalted and highly extolled.

   a.   His visage shall be marred more than any man. v. 44

   b.   Kings shall shut their mouths and see great things. v. 45

➤ 21:1–7   A sign is given for when the house of Israel will be gathered and Zion established.

   a.   The things declared to you [the Nephites] by me, and by the power of the Holy Ghost [The Book of Mormon], shall be made known to the Gentiles. vv. 2–3

      1.   They may know that this people is a remnant of Jacob whom they shall scatter.

      2.   These things shall come forth of the Father from the Gentiles unto you.

  b. The wisdom and power of the Father will establish the Gentiles in this land as a free people. vv. 4–6

   1. The covenant of the Father to the house of Israel will be fulfilled.

   2. These works will come forth of the Gentiles because of your unbelief and iniquity.

   3. The Father will show his power to the Gentiles that they may repent and be baptized.

   4. The Gentiles may know of the true points of doctrine, and be numbered with Israel.

  c. The Nephites may know that the work of the Father has already commenced. v. 7

➢ 21:8–10 When that day comes, kings shall shut their mouths because they see and consider great things.

  a. The great and marvelous work shall commence, and some will not believe it. v. 9

  b. The life of my servant shall be in my hand. v. 10

   1. They shall not hurt him although he shall be marred by them.

   2. I will heal him, and show that my wisdom is greater than the cunning of the devil.

➢ 21:11–29 Those who will not believe in the words of Jesus Christ, brought forth among the Gentiles, shall be cut off from my covenant people.

  a. My people, the remnant of Jacob, shall tread them down. vv. 12–13

   1. They shall be as a lion among beasts, or a flock of sheep.

   2. Their adversaries and enemies shall be cut off.

  b. Wo unto the Gentiles except they repent. vv. 14–18

   1. The Father will cut off their horses and their chariots.

   2. He will cut off their cities and destroy their strongholds.

   3. He will cut off witchcrafts and soothsayers.

      4.   Graven images and works of their hands shall no longer be worshipped.

      5.   Groves will be plucked up and cities destroyed.

  c. All lyings, deceivings, envyings, strifes, priestcrafts, and whoredoms shall be done away. vv. 19–21

      1.   Those who will not repent and come to Christ will be cut off from my people.

      2.   I will execute vengeance and fury upon them.

  d. If they repent and hearken to my words, I will establish my church among them, and they will be numbered among the remnant of Joseph to whom I have given this land. vv. 22–29

      1.   They shall assist in building the New Jerusalem.

      2.   They shall assist my people in gathering unto the New Jerusalem.

      3.   Then shall the power of heaven come down among them, and I shall be in their midst.

      4.   Then shall the work of the Father commence to preach the gospel among the remnant of this people.

      5.   Then shall the work of the Father commence among the lost tribes.

      6.   Then shall the work commence among all the dispersed of my people.

      7.   Then shall the work commence among all nations to gather his people to their land of inheritance.

      8.   They shall not go in haste or by flight, the Father shall go before them, and I will be their rearward.

➤ 22:1–17   The prophecy of Isaiah shall then be fulfilled.

  a. The barren shall cry, for more are the children of the desolate than the children of the married wife.

      1.   The tent of Israel shall be enlarged, and the stakes strengthened.

      2.   Their seed shall inherit the desolate cities of the Gentiles.

    b. The shame of thy youth shall not be remembered, nor the reproach of widowhood.

       1. The Holy One of Israel shall be thy husband.

       2. He forgot you for a small moment, but will gather you with great mercies.

    c. As the waters of Noah was promised to go no more over the earth, so has the Lord promised to not be wroth with Israel. vv. 9–12

       1. The mountains and hills shall be removed, but my covenant of peace shall not.

       2. I will lay stones of fair colors, and foundations and buildings of jewels.

    d. Thy children shall be taught of the Lord, and established in righteousness. vv. 13–17

       1. Those who gather against thee shall fall.

       2. I am the creator and the destroyer.

       3. No weapon against thee shall prosper.

       4. The heritage of the servants of the Lord shall be fulfilled.

NOTES AND COMMENTARY

Isaiah 52 was the basis of Jesus' explanation that the fulfillment of Isaiah's prophecies would be the fulfillment of the covenants made to the house of Israel (Abraham's covenant). He quoted the entire chapter, except verses four and five, although not in the same verse sequence as in the Bible. The last five verses (vv. 11–15) were quoted in sequence. We continue our analysis of Jesus' teachings on the second day.

43 Behold, my servant shall deal prudently; he shall be exalted and extolled and be very high.

44 As many were astonished at thee—his visage was so marred, more than any man, and his form more than the sons of men—

45 So shall he sprinkle many nations; the kings shall shut their mouths at him, for that which had not been told them shall they see; and that

which they had not heard shall they consider. [3 Nephi 20:43–45; Isaiah 52:13–15]

These last three verses of Isaiah 52 are considered by most Christians to be a prophecy of the suffering servant, Jesus Christ during his early ministry, and it is. However, after he had been through his suffering and was resurrected, Jesus quotes it to the Nephites in A.D. 34 as a future prophecy. Therefore, these verses must be considered as a dual prophecy. The second fulfillment of these verses is interpreted by the Savior. He gave the Nephites a sign that their seed may know when the covenant made to the house of Israel of the gathering of dispersed Israel, and the establishment of Zion, had commenced.

The Sign of the Covenant

1 And verily I say unto you, I give unto you a sign, that ye may know the time when these things shall be about to take place—that I shall gather in, from their long dispersion, my people, O house of Israel, and shall establish again among them my Zion;

2 And behold, this is the thing which I will give unto you for a sign—for verily I say unto you that when these things which I declare unto you, and which I shall declare unto you hereafter of myself, and by the power of the Holy Ghost which shall be given unto you of the Father, shall be made known unto the Gentiles that they may know concerning this people who are a remnant of the house of Jacob, and concerning this my people who shall be scattered by them;

3 Verily, verily, I say unto you, when these things shall be made known unto them of the Father, and shall come forth of the Father, from them unto you;

4 For it is wisdom in the Father that they should be established in this land, and be set up as a free people by the power of the Father, that these things might come forth from them unto a remnant of your seed, that the covenant of the Father may be fulfilled which he hath covenanted with his people, O house of Israel;

5 Therefore, when these works and the works which shall be wrought among you hereafter shall come forth from the Gentiles, unto your seed which shall dwindle in unbelief because of iniquity;

> 6 For thus it behooveth the Father that it should come forth from the Gentiles, that he may show forth his power unto the Gentiles, for this cause that the Gentiles, if they will not harden their hearts, that they may repent and come unto me and be baptized in my name and know of the true points of my doctrine, that they may be numbered among my people, O house of Israel;
>
> 7 And when these things come to pass that thy seed shall begin to know these things—it shall be a sign unto them, that they may know that the work of the Father hath already commenced unto the fulfilling of the covenant which he hath made unto the people who are of the house of Israel. [3 Nephi 21:1–7]

The sign given by Jesus to the Nephites of the covenant to Israel having commenced was the coming forth of the Book of Mormon. It is a record of the things he declared, and others declared by the power of the Holy Ghost. It has been "made known unto the Gentiles that they may know concerning this people who are a remnant of the house of Jacob" (v. 2). The Gentiles have been established in this land (America) and "set up as a free people by the power of the Father" (v. 4). President Ezra Taft Benson has confirmed that this is a prophecy of the establishment of the United States of America under the power of the Father.

> Our Father in Heaven planned the coming forth of the Founding Fathers and their form of government as the necessary great prologue leading to the restoration of the gospel. Recall what our Savior Jesus Christ said nearly two thousand years ago when He visited this promised land: (quotes 3 Nephi 21:4). America, the land of liberty, was to be the Lord's latter-day base of operations for His restored church. [CR, October 1987, 3]

President Brigham Young added this comment concerning the United States:

> There is not another nation under heaven, in whose midst the Book of Mormon could have been brought forth. The Lord has been operating for centuries to prepare the way for the coming forth of the contents of that Book from the bowels of the earth, to be published to the world, to show to the inhabitants thereof that he still lives, and that he will, in the latter days, gather his elect from the four corners of the earth. [JD 11:17]

Nephi saw in vision "the Spirit of the Lord, that it was upon the Gentiles, and they did prosper and obtain the land for their inheritance" (1 Nephi 13:15), about six hundred years prior to the Savior's declaration above. The setting up of a free people was through the establishment of the United States Constitution as a divinely inspired document. This was confirmed by revelation to the Prophet Joseph Smith.

> 77 According to the laws and constitution of the people, which I have suffered to be established, and should be maintained for the rights and protection of all flesh, according to just and holy principles;
>
> 78 That every man may act in doctrine and principle pertaining to futurity, according to the moral agency which I have given unto him, that every man may be accountable for his own sins in the day of judgment.
>
> 79 Therefore, it is not right that any man should be in bondage one to another.
>
> 80 And for this purpose have I established the Constitution of this land, by the hands of wise men whom I raised up unto this very purpose, and redeemed the land by the shedding of blood. [D&C 101:77–80]

The Gentiles who received the Book of Mormon were to take it to the remnants, or seed, of the Nephite people. The Gentiles spoken of in these verses are cultural Gentiles, but are really Israelites "who are identified with the Gentiles" (D&C 109:60).[1] Part of their mission is to take the gospel, contained in the Book of Mormon, to the seed of the Nephites who have dwindled "in unbelief because of iniquity" (3 Nephi 21:5). Another part of the mission of the Israelites, who have been identified with the Gentiles, is for the Father to "show forth his power unto the Gentiles . . . that they may repent and come unto me and be baptized in my name and know of the true points of my doctrine, that they may be numbered among my people, O house of Israel" (v. 6). Taking the gospel to the Gentiles is a part of the covenant made to Abraham that "all the kindreds of the earth be blessed" (3 Nephi 20:25). As before stated, the commencement of the

---

[1] See footnote 5, chapter 1.

covenant to the Nephite people will be known when the Book of Mormon is taken to them (v. 7).

Other Prophecies Fulfilled

Having firmly established the sign of the Gentiles bringing the gospel to the seed of the Nephites, Jesus gave other prophecies that would come to pass. These prophecies may be considered as other signs of the day when the Book of Mormon would be restored upon the earth. They are also the dual fulfillment of Isaiah 52:13–15, as interpreted by the Savior.

> 8 And when that day shall come, it shall come to pass that kings shall shut their mouths; for that which had not been told them shall they see; and that which they had not heard shall they consider.
>
> 9 For in that day, for my sake shall the Father work a work, which shall be a great and a marvelous work among them; and there shall be among them those who will not believe it, although a man shall declare it unto them. [3 Nephi 21:8–9]

The first additional prophecy and interpretation of the Savior was that in the day of the bringing forth of the Book of Mormon "kings shall shut their mouths" (v. 8). A glance back at 3 Nephi 20:45 will show that Jesus is again quoting Isaiah 52:15 without the introductory phrase, "So shall he sprinkle many nations." Thus, he is now interpreting or telling of the fulfillment of that passage. When the prophecy is fulfilled, "the last days, or in the days of the Gentiles" will be at hand (2 Nephi 26:14–27:1). The Gentiles of this time period had been the ruling nations, or the powerful nations of the world. They had been ruled by kings, but following the coming forth of the Book of Mormon these kings were going to become silent in government. Although they would still hold office, they would become mere figureheads as parliaments, or other political bodies, governed the various nations. This change in the function of government would come in a period of new discoveries and events that the kings had not seen or heard before.

"So shall he sprinkle many nations," the introductory phrase of Isaiah 52:15 that was not quoted by the Savior in his interpretive commentary, has reference to the Israelites being sprinkled or scattered among the Gentile nations. This interpretation is based on the Prophet Joseph's changing of the word "sprinkle" to "gather" in the JST of Isaiah 52:15. The JST change was to clarify the meaning, and not necessarily to restore the text. Therefore, the Prophet seems to be showing that this entire passage would be fulfilled after the gathering of Israel has commenced. This would explain why the Savior did not quote the introductory phrase. The fact that the gospel had been restored among the Gentiles before they were to take it to the seed of the Nephites meant that the gathering had already commenced. The kings shutting their mouths was the next step following the commencement of the gathering. It might also be concluded that the word "sprinkle" was the original meaning, because with the first fulfillment of the prophecy, the scattering had not been completed, but with the second or dual fulfillment, the scattering was over and the time of the gathering had come. Thus, the JST updates the prophecy.

Jesus continued to prophesy of "that day, for my sake shall the Father work . . . a great and a marvelous work among them" (v. 9). The great and marvelous work commenced, but was not limited to bringing forth the Book of Mormon. The Book of Mormon is shown to be the marvelous work by the verses that follow as well as by an interpretation given to Nephi, son of Lehi, by the Lord.

> 1 But behold, there shall be many—at that day when I shall proceed to do a marvelous work among them, that I may remember my covenants which I have made unto the children of men, that I may set my hand again the second time to recover my people, which are of the house of Israel;
>
> 2 And also, that I may remember the promises which I have made unto thee, Nephi, and also unto thy father, that I would remember your seed; and that the words of your seed should proceed forth out of my mouth unto your seed; and my words shall hiss forth unto the ends of the earth, for a standard unto my people, which are of the house of Israel; [2 Nephi 29:1–2]

That some "will not believe it, although a man shall declare it unto them" foretells that many of the Gentiles unto whom the Book of Mormon is taken will reject it. This same reaction by the Gentiles was also foretold by the Old Testament prophet Habakkuk (Habakkuk 1:5).[2] Possibly the Savior was here quoting Habakkuk without acknowledging it, or perhaps the prophecy made by Habakkuk was also originally made by Isaiah, and is now a part of "the many plain and precious things which have been taken out of the book" (1 Nephi 13:23–29).[3] Nonetheless, "but few of [the Gentiles] will be gathered with the chosen family" (TPJS, 15; see also D&C 45:28–29; Isaiah 41:12). This rejection by the Gentiles would be another sign of the day when the Book of Mormon was restored.

The Lord's Servant

> 10 But behold, the life of my servant shall be in my hand; therefore they shall not hurt him, although he shall be marred because of them. Yet I will heal him, for I will show unto them that my wisdom is greater than the cunning of the devil.
>
> 11 Therefore it shall come to pass that whosoever will not believe in my words, who am Jesus Christ, which the Father shall cause him to bring forth unto the Gentiles, and shall give unto him power that he shall bring them forth unto the Gentiles, (it shall be done even as Moses said) they shall be cut off from among my people who are of the covenant. [3 Nephi 21:10–11]

The first sentence of the above verse should be recognized as a paraphrase of Isaiah 52:13–14, which was quoted by Jesus in 3 Nephi 20:43–44. These verses are almost universally accepted in the Christian world as a prophecy of Jesus Christ's suffering in his mortal

---

[2] For a more complete analysis of the Habakkuk prophecy, see Monte S. Nyman and Farres H. Nyman, The *Words of the Twelve Prophets* (Salt Lake City: Deseret Book, 1990), 101–103.

[3] Jesus' quoting of Micah in 3 Nephi 20:16–19 was also suggested to be originally a part of Isaiah's writings (see the previous chapter).

ministry. This interpretation is certainly valid. However, the dual nature of these verses is again verified by Jesus' quoting it here among the Nephites in A.D. 34. He quoted it in the context of "all these things shall surely come," in fulfillment of the Father's covenant to Israel (3 Nephi 20:46). The context of the interpretation further verifies a latter-day fulfillment.

The Lord would protect his servant from the Gentiles who would reject the marvelous work. The marring of the servant would probably bring to mind the physical abuse that was heaped upon the Prophet Joseph, but the reference here is to a spiritual marring, the loss of the first 116 pages of manuscript that were first translated from the plates delivered to Joseph by Moroni. In a revelation to Joseph regarding this loss, the Lord explained that there was another record upon the [small] plates of Nephi that gave "a more particular account" and would replace the lost manuscript. When published, this other record would "confound those who have altered my words" (D&C 10:38–42). The Lord then said, "I will not suffer that they shall destroy my work; yea, I will show unto them that my wisdom is greater than the cunning of the devil" (D&C 10:43). The last phrase of this verse echoes exactly the last phrase of 3 Nephi 21:10. This certainly confirms the fulfillment of Jesus' prophecy as the loss of the 116 pages of manuscript, and the healing of that loss through the translation of the small plates of Nephi. The fulfillment of this prophecy is another sign of the fulfillment of the covenant to Israel.

While many of the Gentiles have, and will yet reject the Book of Mormon, the time will come when those who reject it will be rejected by the Lord. Jesus again refers to Moses' prophecy of being cut off from the covenant people (v. 11; referring to Deuteronomy 18:19; Acts 3:22–23; 3 Nephi 20:23; see also 3 Nephi 11). The words of Christ that were "brought forth unto the Gentiles" are, of course, the Book of Mormon. The one given power to bring forth the Book of Mormon was Joseph Smith. The Gentiles, and even Church members who do not believe the Book of Mormon, will be cut off from among the people of Israel. "The gathering together [of the church members] upon the land of Zion, and upon her stakes," or to their designated areas, will be "for a defense, and for a refuge from the storm, and from wrath when it shall be poured out without mixture upon the whole earth" (D&C 115:6; quoting Isaiah 4:5–6). Those who do not gather will be cut off. This interpretation is based on Jesus quoting from Micah 5:8–15 to teach what will happen to the unrepentant Gentiles after they have been cut off from the gathered places of the remnant of Jacob.[4]

The Gentiles Trodden Down

> 12 And my people who are a remnant of Jacob shall be among the Gentiles, yea, in the midst of them as a lion among the beasts of the forest, as a young lion among the flocks of sheep, who, if he go through both treadeth down and teareth in pieces, and none can deliver.
>
> 13 Their hand shall be lifted up upon their adversaries, and all their enemies shall be cut off.
>
> 14 Yea, wo be unto the Gentiles except they repent; for it shall come to pass in that day, saith the Father, that I will cut off thy horses out of the midst of thee, and I will destroy thy chariots;
>
> 15 And I will cut off the cities of thy land, and throw down all thy strongholds;
>
> 16 And I will cut off witchcrafts out of thy land, and thou shalt have no more soothsayers;
>
> 17 Thy graven images I will also cut off, and thy standing images out of the midst of thee, and thou shalt no more worship the works of thy hands;
>
> 18 And I will pluck up thy groves out of the midst of thee; so will I destroy thy cities.
>
> 19 And it shall come to pass that all lyings, and deceivings, and envyings, and strifes, and priestcrafts, and whoredoms, shall be done away. [3 Nephi 21:12–19; Micah 5:8–14]

---

[4] As stated before, the words of Micah quoted by the Savior to the Nephites may have also been in the book of Isaiah.

If the converted of Israel are gathered to her stakes, those who tread down the Gentiles must be Israelites who are not yet taught the gospel. Therefore, the native Lamanites in the Americas who are not as yet members of the Church will probably fulfill this prophecy. The remnant of Jacob is prophesied to go forth as a lion among a flock of sheep and tread down the Gentiles who will be their enemies at this time (vv. 12–13; quoting Micah 5:8–9). The concept of the remnant of Jacob being the Lamanites is sustained by the modern-day prophecy on war revealed through the Prophet Joseph Smith: "And it shall come to pass also that the remnants who are left of the land will marshal themselves, and shall become exceedingly angry, and shall vex the Gentiles with a sore vexation" (D&C 87:5).

Micah symbolically represented the conditions that will bring about the treading down of the Gentiles by the house of Israel. Recognizing that there are other possible interpretations, the following are offered. The Father will cut off from the Gentiles their horses and destroy their chariots (v. 14; quoting Micah 5:10). This may have reference to the transportation system among the Gentiles. Such things as gasoline shortages or truckers' strikes could certainly cripple a nation that relies heavily upon the transportation system.

The cutting off of the cities and throwing down of strongholds suggests a possible breakdown of law enforcement (v. 15; quoting Micah 5:11). Such a condition could be brought on by cities not having help from state or federal sources. The lawless conditions that flourish within areas of some of the larger cities in the Americas today may be the result of these breakdowns.

The Lord will also cut off witchcrafts and soothsayers from the Gentile lands (v. 16; quoting Micah 5:12). This could suggest the reliance of the Gentiles upon their philosophers, economists, educators, and scientists instead of relying upon the Lord, as well as the literal practice of witchcraft. These factions are certainly among the Gentiles today.

The Lord will cut off the graven images and other images, the worship of the work of the Gentile hands (v. 17; quoting Micah 5:13). While the literalness of this type of image worship does exist, only a small percentage of the Gentile population so worship. Therefore, this could more fully refer to the clothes, money, positions, and other worldly things worshipped in our society today.

Last of all, the Lord will pluck up the groves out of their midst and destroy their cities (v. 18; quoting Micah 5:14). Worshiping the pagan god Baal included gathering together in groves to participate in temple prostitution, child sacrifice, and other degenerative rituals. In our societies today, the communes, especially in large cities, where various immoral practices are conducted, certainly fit this symbolism

The Savior adds a general description of "all lyings and deceivings, and envyings, and strifes, and priestcrafts, and whoredoms, [that] shall be done away" (v. 19). Perhaps this was originally a part of the text; regardless, it shows that the Lord will cleanse from the Gentiles those things the Gentiles would not cleanse from themselves through repenting and accepting the gospel when it was restored among them.

Continuing the additional comment, Jesus returned to verify Moses' original prophecy concerning the unbelieving Gentiles being cut off, which had been the foundation of Micah's prophecy. He then quoted another verse of Micah before continuing his prophecy.

> 20 For it shall come to pass, saith the Father, that at that day whosoever will not repent and come unto my Beloved Son, them will I cut off from among my people, O house of Israel;
>
> 21 And I will execute vengeance and fury upon them, even as upon the heathen, such as they have not heard.
>
> 22 But if they will repent and hearken unto my words, and harden not their hearts, I will establish my church among them, and they shall come in unto the covenant and be numbered among this the remnant of Jacob, unto whom I have given this land for their inheritance;
>
> 23 And they shall assist my people, the remnant of Jacob, and also as many of the house of Israel as shall come, that they may build a city, which shall be called the New Jerusalem. [3 Nephi 21:20–23; v. 21 is Micah 5:15]

Not all of the Gentiles will be subject to the Lord's vengeance. Those who hearken to the Lord's word (the Book of Mormon) will have the Church established among them and be numbered among the remnant of Jacob [Joseph] (v. 22). Some would suppose this has reference to the present-day Lamanites, but it should be remembered that the land of America was given to both "branches" of Joseph's descendants, Ephraim and Manasseh (Genesis 49:22). Therefore, members of the Church, as descendants of Ephraim, are also given the land of America. In June 1831, the Lord designated the elders of the restored Church "whom he [had] called and chosen in these last days, by the voice of his Spirit . . . a remnant of Jacob, and those who are heirs according to the covenant" (D&C 52:1–2). Other Doctrine and Covenants revelations verify that the Church members gathered from among the Gentiles were literal descendants of Joseph, and thus heirs to the land of Zion, or America (D&C 58:44–45; cp. Deuteronomy 33:17; see also D&C 86:8–11; 96:7, and footnote #1). President Joseph Fielding Smith has declared that "it is Ephraim who will stand at the head and direct the work," as the birthright holder.[5] The Gentiles, those who do not have the blood of Israel, that are converted to the gospel, will be adopted into Israel. "For as many as receive this gospel shall be called after thy name, and shall be accounted thy seed" (Abraham 2:10), and will assist Ephraim and other Israelites who will gather to build the New Jerusalem (v. 23).

The New Jerusalem

24 And then shall they assist my people that they may be gathered in, who are scattered upon all the face of the land, in unto the New Jerusalem.

25 And then shall the power of heaven come down among them; and I also will be in the midst.

26 And then shall the work of the Father commence at that day, even when this gospel shall be preached among the remnant of this people.

---

[5] McConkie, Bruce R. *Doctrines of Salvation,* 2:250–251, Bookcraft, Inc., Salt Lake City, 1956.

Verily I say unto you, at that day shall the work of the Father commence among all the dispersed of my people, yea, even the tribes which have been lost, which the Father hath led away out of Jerusalem.

27 Yea, the work shall commence among all the dispersed of my people, with the Father to prepare the way whereby they may come unto me, that they may call on the Father in my name.

28 Yea, and then shall the work commence, with the Father among all nations in preparing the way whereby his people may be gathered home to the land of their inheritance.

29 And they shall go out from all nations; and they shall not go out in haste, nor go by flight, for I will go before them, saith the Father, and I will be their rearward. [3 Nephi 21:24–29]

Building the New Jerusalem is a focal point for many events to follow. This is shown in the Savior's teachings that follow his prophecy of Zion being built. He gives a series of four things that will happen after the New Jerusalem is built. These four things are each introduced with "and then," which also suggests a sequential order to the events.

The first thing to follow the building of the New Jerusalem is the gathering of the Father's people, the whole house of Israel, "who are scattered upon all the face of the land, in unto the New Jerusalem" (v. 24). This group constitutes Church members who have been gathered out from the Gentiles. It must be remembered that Jesus is still quoting the Father (v. 20), and therefore, "my people" has reference to the Father's people, all the house of Israel, and not to Jesus' people, the Jews (3 Nephi 20:46). It should also be remembered that not all of the house of Israel, or all the members of the Church will be gathered to the New Jerusalem.

35 There has been a day of calling, but the time has come for a day of choosing; and let those be chosen that are worthy.

36 And it shall be manifest unto my servant, by the voice of the Spirit, those that are chosen; and they shall be sanctified; [D&C 105: 35–36]

As will be explained later, the stakes of Israel will also continue to be populated and maintained after the Zion city is built.[6]

The second event outlined by Jesus to follow the building of the New Jerusalem is "the power of heaven [coming] down among them; and [Jesus] will also be in their midst" (v. 25). Some may suggest that this verse implies that the Millennium will have been ushered in by this time. However, as discussed in the previous chapter, it may have reference to the power of the priesthood being manifest, and the frequent visiting of the Savior to his house, the temple. Those who build up Zion will be a holy people of "one heart and one mind" (Moses 7:18), and will have such manifestations among them.

The third event to follow the building of Zion is the preaching of the gospel among the remnants of the house of Israel (v. 26). These remnants are not the ones who have been scattered among the Gentiles, but the posterity of the branches of Israel that were hidden "in the nethermost parts of the vineyard" (Jacob 5:14). There were three of these branches dispersed into the world: the ten tribes in 721 B.C., the Jews in about 607 B.C., and Lehi's group in 600 B.C. These three groups were to be brought back to their mother tree of Israel in the reverse order of their dispersion. "Graft in the branches: begin at the last that they may be first, and that the first may be last" (Jacob 5:63). Jesus mentions only two of the branches specifically at this time, the seed of the Nephites and the lost tribes, although the designation of "among all the dispersed of my people" may have reference to the Jewish people also since he stated they had been led out of Jerusalem. Nevertheless, the times for Israel to receive their opportunity for the gospel will be fully ushered in after the building of the

---

[6] The Doctrine and Covenants outlines the events to happen before the redemption of Zion or the New Jerusalem (D&C 105). The final event is the choosing of those from the army of Israel who are to go to Missouri and build the New Jerusalem. It will be manifest to the Lord's servant who is to go (see D&C 105:35–36). These who remain will maintain the stakes of Zion.

New Jerusalem, even though there has been and will continue to be the preaching of the gospel among a few of them before this time (v. 27).

The fourth and last event to follow the building of the New Jerusalem, as taught by Jesus, is the work among all nations in gathering the Lord's people "home to the land of their inheritance" (v. 28). Three of the events deal with the gathering. The sequence suggests that there will be a large number of each of the branches of Israel brought in (the third event), and then the work of rounding up those of the branches who have not been living with their own people will commence. This broader sense of gathering is supported by their not going "out in haste, nor by flight, for I will go before them, saith the Father, and I will be their rearward" (v. 29). The three sequences of the gathering among all of the groups of Israel suggests that there will be a few converted at first, then large numbers, and then the gathering of those who remain. This seems to follow a natural process. Following this explanation, Jesus quoted the prophet Isaiah's prophecy as coming to pass when the gathering of Israel in this sequence had taken place.

Isaiah Fulfilled

Throughout the Book of Mormon, the prophets have quoted Isaiah to teach of Christ, and of the covenant of Israel. They have usually quoted entire chapters, and then given extensive commentary to illustrate Isaiah's prophecies. Jesus also relied heavily upon Isaiah, but in this instance, and others, he followed a different pattern than the prophets. He taught what was going to happen, and then quoted Isaiah as evidence that what he was teaching had previously been taught (i.e. 3 Nephi 16:17; 20:11). Since he was the source of Isaiah's prophecies, this is certainly to be expected.

> 1 And then shall that which is written come to pass: Sing, O barren, thou that didst not bear; break forth into singing, and cry aloud, thou that didst not travail with child; for more are the children of the desolate than the children of the married wife, saith the Lord.

2 Enlarge the place of thy tent, and let them stretch forth the curtains of thy habitations; spare not, lengthen thy cords and strengthen thy stakes; [Isaiah 54:1–2]

The house of Israel had not been producing children unto the Lord in their state of apostasy. Although their numbers were large, they were not partakers of the covenant. With the conversion of millions following the building of the New Jerusalem, they would then far outnumber the children of the married wife, or the house of Israel who had entered into the covenant of Israel as members of the restored Church. Using the figures of A.D. 2000 to illustrate, there are now about eleven million members of the Church. However, there are probably some twenty million Jewish people, some seventy million Lamanites, and untold millions of the lost tribes.[7] Thus, less than ten percent of Israel has been gathered.

The great influx of Israelite converts will require an enlarging of the symbolic tent of Israel to bring these new members under the Lord's protective coverage (v. 2; Isaiah 54:2). The building of the New Jerusalem represents the "center place" of Zion, or the center pole of a large tent (D&C 57:3). A large tent requiring a center pole could not be pitched without having stakes all around that pole. Cords would also be required to stretch from the center pole to the stakes in order to maintain the uprightness of the tent. The stakes must be strong to hold the cords reaching from the central pole. When the stakes are in place, the center pole will be raised. However, with millions of new members, the stakes will need strengthening, even new ones added, and the cords of gospel correlation and communication will need to be lengthened. When this happens, the children of Israel who are converted will be housed in their tent. Therefore, Isaiah 54:1–2 is fulfilled through the establishment of the stakes of Zion by the early remnants of Israel as a preparation to raise the central pole,

---

[7] These figures are conservative estimates since exact censuses are not taken or known.

or to build the New Jerusalem. The converted Gentiles from whom the early remnants have been gathered are invited to "assist my people, the remnant of Jacob, and also as many of the people as shall come, that they may build the city, which shall be called the New Jerusalem," and in gathering those "who are scattered upon all the face of the land" (3 Nephi 21:23–24). After Zion is built, the millions of converted Israelites will require the tent's enlargement.

> 3 For thou shalt break forth on the right hand and on the left, and thy seed shall inherit the Gentiles and make the desolate cities to be inhabited.
>
> 4 Fear not, for thou shalt not be ashamed; neither be thou confounded, for thou shalt not be put to shame; for thou shalt forget the shame of thy youth, and shalt not remember the reproach of thy youth, and shalt not remember the reproach of thy widowhood any more.
>
> 5 For thy maker, thy husband, the Lord of Hosts is his name; and thy Redeemer, the Holy One of Israel—the God of the whole earth shall he be called.
>
> 6 For the Lord hath called thee as a woman forsaken and grieved in spirit, and a wife of youth, when thou wast refused, saith thy God. [3 Nephi 22:3–6]

As the tent of Israel is enlarged, the new converts will inherit the Gentiles' desolate cities (v. 3; Isaiah 54:3). The Gentiles' cities will have become desolate and uninhabited by their having been trodden down by the unconverted remnants of Jacob "as a lion among the beasts of the forest" (3 Nephi 21:12). As the Israelites are converted, they will "forget the shame of [their] youth . . . and shalt not remember the reproach of [their] widowhood any more" (v. 4; Isaiah 54:4). They will no longer be desolate or cast off by the Lord, and he will remember his covenant with them. He is their "maker, [their] husband . . . and [their] Redeemer, the Holy One of Israel—the God of the whole earth. . . . For the Lord hath called [Israel] as a woman forsaken and grieved in spirit, and a wife of youth," (vv. 5–6). The marriage of the Lamb will come at this time because the "wife [Israel] hath made herself ready" (Revelation 19:7).

7 For a small moment have I forsaken thee, but with great mercies will I gather thee.

8 In a little wrath I hid my face from thee for a moment, but with everlasting kindness will I have mercy on thee, saith the Lord thy Redeemer.

9 For this, the waters of Noah unto me, for as I have sworn that the waters of Noah should no more go over the earth, so have I sworn that I would not be wroth with thee.

10 For the mountains shall depart and the hills be removed, but my kindness shall not depart from thee, neither shall the covenant of my peace be removed, saith the Lord that hath mercy on thee. [3 Nephi 22:7–10]

In the Lord's time is, "one thousand years according to the time appointed unto that whereon thou standest. This is the reckoning of the Lord's time" (Abraham 3:4). Peter says, "one day is with the Lord as a thousand years" (2 Peter 3:8). In this time frame, the apostasy is defined: "for a small moment" he forsook them, "but with great mercies" he will have gathered them (v. 7; Isaiah 54:7). The fulfillment of the Lord's covenant to gather Israel is as sure as is his covenant made to Noah to not flood the earth with water again. Their covenant of peace will not be removed when it is reestablished (vv. 9–10; Isaiah 54:9–10).

11 O thou afflicted, tossed with tempest, and not comforted! Behold, I will lay thy stones with fair colors, and lay thy foundations with sapphires.

12 And I will make thy windows of agates, and thy gates of carbuncles, and all thy borders of pleasant stones.

13 And all thy children shall be taught of the Lord; and great shall be the peace of thy children.

14 In righteousness shalt thou be established; thou shalt be far from oppression for thou shalt not fear, and from terror for it shall not come near thee.

15 Behold, they shall surely gather together against thee, not by me; whosoever shall gather together against thee shall fall for thy sake. [3 Nephi 22:11–15]

Isaiah next describes the beauty of the New Jerusalem to those who had previously been afflicted and not comforted (Israel). The precious stones represent the beauty of the magnificent city of Zion, the New Jerusalem (3 Nephi 21:23; 20:22). Isaiah later described how her beauty would come: "the forces [wealth] of the Gentiles shall come unto thee . . . they shall bring gold and incense . . . and [the Lord] will glorify the house of his glory" (Isaiah 60:5–7; see also vv. 8–9 and footnotes in the LDS Bible for all verses).

The Lord verified the above interpretation in a revelation to Joseph Smith. In a proclamation to be written to all political leaders of the world, he said: "Awake, O kings of the earth! Come ye, O, come ye, with your gold and your silver, to the help of my people, to the house of the daughters of Zion" (D&C 124:11).

The Prophet Joseph also said: "The city of Zion spoken of by David, in the one hundred and second Psalm, will be built in the land of America" (TPJS 17). Part of the Psalm states:

> 14 For thy servants take pleasure in her stones, and favour the dust thereof.
>
> 15 So the heathen shall fear the name of the LORD, and all the kings of the earth thy glory.
>
> 16 When the LORD shall build up Zion, he shall appear in his glory. [Psalm 102:14–16]

With Zion established, all of Israel's "children shall be taught of the Lord; and great shall be the peace of thy children" (v. 13; Isaiah 54:13). Another scripture verifies this condition. As the Savior taught his people on the Mount of Olives in Jerusalem, he taught that "their children shall grow up without sin unto salvation. For the Lord shall be in their midst, and his glory shall be upon them, and he will be their king and their lawgiver" (D&C 45: 58–59). That the Lord was in their midst suggests the Millennium once more, but the following verses foretell that there will be those who gather against Zion who are not of the Lord (Isaiah 54:15). Therefore, the time element seems more logical to be prior to the Millennium, as the New Jerusalem is being built. The previous verse also suggests the same time period (Isaiah 54:14). Although there will be terror and oppression, the Lord will protect his people. It will be the only place for safety. The Prophet Joseph Smith saw this day and admonished us as to what was needed for our safety:

> Look to the Presidency and receive instruction. Every man who is afraid, covetous, will be taken in a snare. The time is soon coming, when no man will have any peace but in Zion and her stakes.
>
> I saw men hunting the lives of their own sons, and brother murdering brother, women killing their own daughters, and daughters seeking the lives of their mothers. I saw armies arrayed against armies. I saw blood, desolation, fires. The Son of Man has said that the mother shall be against the daughter, and the daughter against the mother. These things are at our doors. They will follow the Saints of God from city to city. Satan will rage, and the spirit of the devil is now enraged. I know not how soon these things will take place; but with a view of them, shall I cry peace? No; I will lift up my voice and testify of them. How long you will have good crops, and the famine be kept off, I do not know; when the fig tree leaves, know then that the summer is nigh at hand. [TPJS, 161; see also D&C 45:63–75]

The Prophet's instruction to look to "the [First] Presidency" is sustained in the next verses of Isaiah.

> 16 Behold, I have created the smith that bloweth the coals in the fire, and that bringeth forth an instrument for his work; and I have created the waster to destroy.
>
> 17 No weapon that is formed against thee shall prosper; and every tongue that shall revile against thee in judgment thou shalt condemn. This is the heritage of the servants of the Lord, and their righteousness is of me, saith the Lord. [Isaiah 54: 16–17; 3 Nephi 22:16–17]

The Lord is the creator of all things, including the instruments of creation. He has also created those whom he will use to destroy the wicked (v. 16; Isaiah 54:16; see also Mormon 4:5). "No weapon that is formed against [the covenant people of Israel] shall prosper." The members of the First Presidency (and the Twelve) are the servants of the Lord, and their righteous instruction comes from the Lord (v. 17;

Isaiah 54:17). The Lord reaffirmed Isaiah's promise to his Church in December 1831.

> 9 Verily, thus saith the Lord unto you—there is no weapon that is formed against you shall prosper;
>
> 10 And if any man lift his voice against you he shall be confounded in mine own due time. [D&C 71:9–10]

The Saints are entitled to this blessing and assurance.

Israel's servant of the latter days, Joseph Smith, has brought forth the marvelous work of the Lord. The signs given by the Savior have been or will be fulfilled. Zion will be established. Israel will be fully gathered. The covenants of the Lord will be fulfilled to Abraham and Israel. They are his children. The Lord will defend his people.

Chapter 13

Search the Prophets

3 Nephi 23:1–26:12

In Jesus' mortal ministry, he chastised the Jews and admonished them to "search the scriptures; for in them ye think ye have eternal life: and they are they which testify of me" (John 5:39). The Jews prided themselves in being the covenant people of the Lord, yet they failed to use the scriptures as they were intended, thinking that their covenant lineage and their possession of the scriptures would obtain the kingdom of God for them. Had they carefully read and analyzed the scriptures, they would have recognized that Jesus was the fulfillment of the prophets' testimonies of a coming Messiah.

Jesus' divine ministry among the Nephites was a teaching ministry. He had used the prophet Isaiah's teachings to testify of Israel's future gathering, and the fulfillment of the covenant to Israel. He now comments on Isaiah and the other prophets, and quotes two chapters of Malachi. Mormon then records his own comments about his abridgment. An outline of all these comments, as an overview to prepare for a deeper study, follows.

Outline • 3 Nephi 23:1–26:12

➤ 23:1–5   I command you to search the prophecies of Isaiah for great are his words.

      a. He spake all things concerning the house of Israel. vv. 2–3

           1. He must speak also to the Gentiles (Israel is scattered among them).

           2. All things he spake have been and shall be fulfilled.

      b. Give heed to my words for they shall go to the Gentiles. vv. 4–5

           1. Those who repent and are baptized shall be saved.

           2. Search the prophets for many testify of these things.

➤ 23:6–14   Jesus commanded that other scriptures be written.

      a. He commanded Nephi to bring forth the records he had kept. vv. 7–13

           1. He asked if many saints had not risen from the dead as Samuel the Lamanite had testified?

           2. He asked why it had not been written that they did arise?

           3. Nephi remembered that it had not been written and Jesus commanded that it be written.

      b. Jesus expounded on all the written scriptures, and commanded to teach them to the people. v. 14

➤ 24:1–18; 25:1–6   Jesus commanded that the words given to Malachi by the Father be written.

      a. My messenger shall prepare the way, and the Lord shall suddenly come to his temple. 24:1–4

           1. Who will abide the day of his coming; he is as a refiner and purifier of silver.

           2. He will purify the sons of Levi that they may make an offering in righteousness.

           3. The offering of Judah and Jerusalem shall be pleasant unto the Lord.

      b. I will come in judgment against the wicked. 24:5–7

           1. The Lord does not change; thus the sons of Jacob are not consumed.

2. They have gone away from my ordinances.

3. If they return to me I will return to them; they ask how they shall return?

c. The sons of Jacob have robbed God in tithes and offerings and are cursed. 24:8–12

1. Bring your tithes and offerings, and I will open the windows of heaven and bless you.

2. I will rebuke the devourer that he not destroy your crops and fruits.

3. All nations shall call you blessed.

d. The sons of Jacob have spoken stout things against the Lord. 24:13–15

1. They say it is vain to serve God and keep his ordinances.

2. They say that those that work wickedness and tempt God are delivered.

e. Those that feared the Lord are written in the Lord's book of remembrance. 24:16–18

1. They shall be his in the day the Lord makes up his jewels.

2. Then shall you discern between the righteous and the wicked.

f. The day comes when the proud and wicked shall be burned leaving neither root nor branches. 25:1–4

1. Those who feared the Lord shall be healed by the Son of Righteousness.

2. They shall grow up as calves in a stall.

3. The law originally given to Moses in Mount Horeb shall return.

g. I will send Elijah before the great and dreadful day of the Lord. 25:5–6

1. He will turn the hearts of the fathers to the children, and the children to the fathers.

2. Otherwise the earth will be smitten with a curse.

➤ 26:1–5   Jesus expounded all things to the multitude, both small and great.

   a.   The Father commanded Malachi be given so future generations would have it. 26:2

   b.   He expounded all things from the beginning until he should come again. 26:3–5

        1.   The elements shall melt with fervent heat, the earth be wrapped together as a scroll, and the heavens and earth pass away.

        2.   All people, kindreds, nations, and tongues shall stand before God and be judged.

        3.   The good will be resurrected to everlasting life, and the evil to the resurrection of damnation.

➤ 26:6–12   Mormon's abridgment does not include a hundredeth part of what Jesus taught.

   a.   The plates of Nephi contain the more part of what he taught. 26:7–10

        1.   Mormon wrote the lesser part that the Gentiles may bring them to the Lamanites.

        2.   If they believe what Mormon wrote, greater things shall be manifest.

        3.   If they do not believe, the greater things will be withheld to their condemnation.

   b.   Mormon was about to write all that was on the plates, but the Lord forbad him saying he would try the faith of my people. 26:11–12

        1.   He wrote the things the Lord commanded.

        2.   He concludes his sayings, and writes as commanded.

Notes and Commentary

1 And now, behold, I say unto you, that ye ought to search these things. Yea, a commandment I give unto you that ye search these things diligently; for great are the words of Isaiah.

2 For surely he spake as touching all things concerning my people which are of the house of Israel; therefore it must needs be that he must speak also to the Gentiles.

3 And all things that he spake have been and shall be, even according to the words which he spake.

4 Therefore give heed to my words; write the things which I have told you; and according to the time and the will of the Father they shall go forth unto the Gentiles.

5 And whosoever will hearken unto my words and repenteth and is baptized, the same shall be saved. Search the prophets, for many there be that testify of these things. [3 Nephi 23:1–5]

Isaiah is the only book of the sixty-six books in the Bible that has been singled out with a commandment to search it. Isaiah's words were great because in his prophecies he had touched "all things concerning . . . the house of Israel." Because the house of Israel had been scattered among the Gentiles, it was expedient for Isaiah to "speak also to the Gentiles" (v. 2) in order that the scattered Israelites among them would be able to know of the covenants that had been made to their fathers. At the same time, the Gentiles would have the opportunity to accept the gospel and be numbered with Israel. Jesus said further that all of Isaiah's words had or would be fulfilled (v. 3). Elder Wilford Woodruff stated: "three fourths of [Isaiah's] predictions relate to the establishment of the kingdom of God in the latter days" (JD 14:6). Thus, Jesus admonished the Nephites to "give heed to [his] words" and to write them so that "according to the will of the Father, they shall go forth unto the Gentiles" (v. 4). Those who would hearken to Jesus' words (spoken to and recorded by the Nephites), and repent and be baptized, would obtain salvation (v. 5), whether they be of the house of Israel or Gentile.

Having stated the reasons why Isaiah was to be searched, Jesus expanded the admonition to "search the prophets for many there be that testify of these things" (v. 5). Although, as suggested earlier, the Micah and Habakkuk quotes that Jesus had previously used were probably part of the original text of Isaiah, their words illustrate Jesus' point that many had so testified. Amos and Joel, cited in the previous chapter, are other examples, and of course many others could be quoted. The Lord does establish his word "at the mouth of two witnesses, or at the mouth of three witnesses" (Deuteronomy 19:15; see also Matthew 18:16).

A Second Witness of the Resurrection

6 And now it came to pass that when Jesus had said these words he said unto them again, after he had expounded all the scriptures unto them which they had received, he said unto them: Behold, other scriptures I would that ye should write, that ye have not.

7 And it came to pass that he said unto Nephi: Bring forth the record which ye have kept.

8 And when Nephi had brought forth the records, and laid them before him, he cast his eyes upon them and said:

9 Verily I say unto you, I commanded my servant Samuel, the Lamanite, that he should testify unto this people, that at the day that the Father should glorify his name in me that there were many saints who should arise from the dead, and should appear unto many, and should minister unto them. And he said unto them: Was it not so?

10 And his disciples answered him and said: Yea, Lord, Samuel did prophesy according to thy words, and they were all fulfilled.

11 And Jesus said unto them: How be it that ye have not written this thing, that many saints did arise and appear unto many and did minister unto them?

12 And it came to pass that Nephi remembered that this thing had not been written.

13 And it came to pass that Jesus commanded that it should be written; therefore it was written according as he commanded. [3 Nephi 23:6–13]

Samuel the Lamanite's prophecy "to bring to pass the resurrection of the dead, that thereby men may be brought into the presence of the Lord" had been recorded (Helaman 14:25), but not its fulfillment of the coming forth from the dead. Jesus commanded its fulfillment to be written, and it was (v. 13).

The Gospel of Matthew records a similar arising in Jerusalem at the time of Jesus' resurrection. "And the graves were opened; and many bodies of the saints which slept arose, and came out of the graves after his resurrection, and went into the holy city, and appeared unto many" (Matthew 27:52–53). Apparently, Jesus desired another witness of the resurrection so that his law of witnesses would be met. Although Christ was "the firstfruits" of the resurrection (1 Corinthians 15:23), many people on both sides of the world were also resurrected immediately after him. The bands of death had been broken. "Death [was] swallowed up in victory" (1 Corinthians 15:54–55).

> 14 And now it came to pass that when Jesus had expounded all the scriptures in one, which they had written, he commanded them that they should teach the things which he had expounded unto them. [3 Nephi 23:14]

Jesus further expounded the scriptures to the Nephites, but his words were not recorded by Mormon. He did, however, command them to teach the things that were written to the Nephite people (v. 14). Someday these records will be available.

A Second Witness of Malachi

The Old Testament prophet Malachi lived around 400 B.C. His words, therefore, had not been recorded upon the plates of brass that Nephi had obtained from Laban and brought out of Jerusalem in 600 B.C. The last two chapters of Malachi are significant to the people of Israel in the latter days. For this cause, Jesus commanded Nephi to record the last two chapters that the Father had revealed to Malachi. Jesus then quoted and expounded upon these words. The two accounts in the Bible and the Book of Mormon are another example of the law of witnesses. A third witness of the importance of Malachi' s words was given by the angel Moroni when he appeared to Joseph Smith in September 1823. Moroni "quoted part of the third chapter of Malachi, and he quoted also the fourth or last chapter of the same prophecy, though with a little variation from the way it reads in our Bibles" (JS–H 1:36). The subject of these two chapters is the preparation for the Second Coming of the Lord. The message follows.[1]

> 1 And it came to pass that he commanded them that they should write the words which the Father had given unto Malachi, which he should tell unto them. And it came to pass that after they were written he expounded them. And these are the words which he did tell unto them, saying: Thus said the Father unto Malachi—Behold, I will send my messenger, and he shall prepare the way before me, and the Lord whom ye seek shall suddenly come to his temple, even the messenger of the covenant, whom ye delight in; behold, he shall come, saith the Lord of Hosts.
>
> 2 But who may abide the day of his coming, and who shall stand when he appeareth? For he is like a refiner's fire, and like fuller's soap. [3 Nephi 24:1–2; Malachi 3:1–2]

The Lord promises to send his messenger to prepare the way before his coming (v. 1). A surface reading and cross-reference to the New Testament suggest this prophecy to be fulfilled through the mission of John the Baptist because Matthew records: "for this is he of whom it is written, Behold, I send my messenger before thy face, which shall prepare thy way before thee" (11:10). Although we are dealing with dual prophecy, the ultimate fulfillment will be in the latter days. This is obvious because the Savior is quoting this passage to the Nephites in the context of future fulfillment, and the angel Moroni quoted it to Joseph Smith among other prophecies soon to be fulfilled. Also, the Savior revealed this passage to Joseph Smith in March 1831, this time in the past tense: "And even so I have sent mine

---

[1] The analysis of these chapters was published with slight modification in The *Message of the Twelve Prophets* by Monte S. Nyman and Farres H. Nyman, Deseret Book, Salt Lake City, 1990. Textual differences and their significance are discussed therein.

everlasting covenant into the world, to be a light to the world, and to be a standard for my people, and for the Gentiles to seek to it, and to be a messenger before my face to prepare the way before me" (D&C 45:9). The messenger to prepare the way before the Second Coming of the Lord is therefore the restoration of the everlasting covenant, or the fulness of the gospel. The rest of Malachi 3:1 further confirms the latter-day fulfillment.

Malachi prophesied that the Lord "shall suddenly come to his temple even the messenger of the covenant" (v. 1; Malachi 3:1). Following the restoration of the new and everlasting covenant, December 1830, the Lord reaffirmed that in the future "I will suddenly come to my temple" (D&C 36:8). In November 1831 he identified himself as "The Lord who shall suddenly come to his temple" (D&C 133:2). He could not make this appearance until a temple had been built. The first temple was the Kirtland Temple, completed and dedicated on April 3, 1836. He came to the Kirtland Temple suddenly. Following the prayer of Joseph Smith and Oliver Cowdery, "The veil was taken from our minds, and the eyes of our understanding were opened. We saw the Lord standing upon the breastwork of the pulpit, before us" (D&C 110:1). He was the messenger of the covenant. Through his atoning "blood of the everlasting covenant" (Hebrews 13:20), his work was "to bring to pass the immortality and eternal life of man" (Moses 1:39). His appearance fulfilled the promise made through Malachi, and established that covenant again in preparation for his Second Coming.

That Malachi's prophecy is about the Second Coming of Christ and not his first ministry is further attested to by the declaration, "But who may abide the day of his coming, and who shall stand when he appeareth? For he is like a refiner's fire and like fuller's soap" (v. 2). There is no evidence that people could not abide his mortal ministry. His Second Coming, however, will constitute a cleansing of the earth; thus the analogy of a refiner's fire, where the impurities are cleansed from ores to make metals, is applicable. In latter-day revelation, the Lord has declared that "every corruptible thing, both of man, or of the beasts of the field, or of the fowls of the heavens, or of the fish of the sea, that dwells upon all the face of the earth, shall be consumed" (D&C 101:24). The fuller's soap of ancient days was also a purifier, often used to whiten cloth.

> 3 And he shall sit as a refiner and purifier of silver; and he shall purify the sons of Levi, and purge them as gold and silver, that they may offer unto the Lord an offering in righteousness.
>
> 4 Then shall the offering of Judah and Jerusalem be pleasant unto the Lord, as in the days of old, and as in former years.
>
> 5 And I will come near to you to judgment; and I will be a swift witness against the sorcerers, and against the adulterers, and against false swearers, and against those that oppress the hireling in his wages, the widow and the fatherless, and that turn aside the stranger, and fear not me, saith the Lord of Hosts.
>
> 6 For I am the Lord, I change not; therefore ye sons of Jacob are not consumed. [3 Nephi 24:3–6; Malachi 3:3–6]

Malachi's prophecy of the purifying of the sons of Levi so that they may "offer unto the Lord an offering in righteousness" (v. 3) was also a promise given by John the Baptist when the Aaronic Priesthood was restored to Joseph Smith and Oliver Cowdery on May 15, 1829 (D&C 13). This prophecy has a dual fulfillment. First, after Moses had descended the mount and found his people worshiping the golden calf, "all the sons of Levi gathered themselves together unto him (Exodus 32:26). They were to "bear the iniquity [responsibility] of your [the Aaronic] priesthood" for all of the tribes of Israel (Numbers 18:1–8). This assignment continued until the ten tribes were taken away and probably persisted after they were taken into the North. It was also among the people of Judah until their apostasy. When the ten tribes return, as a part of the gathering "together in one all things in Christ" or the restoration of all things "in the dispensation of the fulness of times" (Ephesians 1:10), they will again offer a literal sacrifice in righteousness. The Prophet Joseph Smith explained:

> These sacrifices, as well as every ordinance belonging to the Priesthood, will, when the Temple of the Lord shall be built, and the sons of Levi be purified, be fully restored and attended to in all their powers,

ramifications, and blessings. This ever did and ever will exist when the powers of the Melchizedek Priesthood are sufficiently manifest; else how can the restitution of all things spoken of by the Holy Prophets be brought to pass. It is not to be understood that the law of Moses will be established again with all its rites and variety of ceremonies; this has never been spoken of by the prophets; but those things which existed prior to Moses' day, namely, sacrifice, will be continued.

It may be asked by some, what necessity for sacrifice, since the Great Sacrifice was offered? In answer to which, if repentance, baptism, and faith existed prior to the days of Christ, what necessity for them since that time? The Priesthood has descended in a regular line from father to son, through their succeeding generations [TPJS, 173].

A second fulfillment of this prophecy of Malachi is established through the latter-day temple work for the dead. In an epistle to the Saints upon this subject on September 6, 1842, the Prophet Joseph Smith wrote that the great day of the Lord was at hand and, after quoting Malachi 3:2–3, declared, "Let us therefore as a church and a people, and as Latter-day Saints, offer unto the Lord an offering in righteousness; and let us present in his holy temple, when it is finished, a book containing the records of our dead, which shall be worthy of all acceptation" (D&C 128:24). This spiritual interpretation is probably based upon the fact that genealogical research must be done at the sacrifice of time and personal interests. It is not something that is scheduled in the Church, but rather must be done on our own initiative.

The offering of Judah and Jerusalem is to be pleasant to the Lord at this time (v. 4). Judah rejected the higher law of Christ, and continued in the law of Moses.[2] Therefore, her sacrifices through the years have not been pleasant to the Lord. As the ten tribes return, the Jewish people, having been taken away after the ten tribes, will already have begun to accept the gospel, "begin at the last that they may be first, and that the first may be last" (Jacob 5:63), and thus the Lord will accept their sacrifices. The judgments of God will come upon the wicked at this time also (v. 5). Since the Lord is unchanging, he will not consume the sons of Jacob (v. 6). He has covenanted to gather them and he will do so.

> 7 Even from the days of your fathers ye are gone away from mine ordinances, and have not kept them. Return unto me and I will return unto you, saith the Lord of Hosts. But ye say: Wherein shall we return?
>
> 8 Will a man rob God? Yet ye have robbed me. But ye say: Wherein have we robbed thee? In tithes and offerings.
>
> 9 Ye are cursed with a curse, for ye have robbed me, even this whole nation.
>
> 10 Bring ye all the tithes into the storehouse, that there may be meat in my house; and prove me now herewith, saith the Lord of Hosts, if I will not open you the windows of heaven, and pour you out a blessing that there shall not be room enough to receive it.
>
> 11 And I will rebuke the devourer for your sakes, and he shall not destroy the fruits of your ground; neither shall your vine cast her fruit before the time in the fields, saith the Lord of Hosts.
>
> 12 And all nations shall call you blessed, for ye shall be a delightsome land, saith the Lord of Hosts. [3 Nephi 24:7–12; Malachi 3:7–12]

---

[2] Woe to Ariel, to Ariel, the city [Jerusalem] *where* David dwelt! add ye year to year; let them kill sacrifices. Yet I will distress Ariel, and there shall be heaviness and sorrow: (Isaiah 29:1–2)

Elder Orson Pratt interpreted this passage thus: "After the Messiah came and was sacrificed for the sins of the world, the Jews continued to "kill sacrifices," when they should have been done away; they added "year to year" to the Law of Moses, until they brought down "heaviness and sorrow," and "great distress upon their beloved city" (Orson Pratt's Works The Desert News Press, Salt Lake City, Utah 1945 p. 270).

The modern-day sons of Jacob must repent of several things before their salvation can be obtained. Like their fathers of old, they have strayed. In the typical style of the previous chapters of Malachi (1:2, 6; 2:13–14, 17), the Lord through Malachi states the problem, the sons of Jacob ask how they are guilty, and the Lord gives the answer. The first problem in chapter three is the robbing of God through withholding tithes and offerings (v. 8). This refers to latter-day sons of Jacob, members of The Church of Jesus Christ of Latter-day Saints. Those of the Church who do not pay tithing will not survive the judgment to come upon the world (D&C 64:23–24; quoted later). Failure to comply has brought a curse upon the whole nation (v. 9).

The Lord then challenges the sons of Jacob to bring all their tithes to him, not just some of them, or by some of the people, and test him to see if he "will not open you the windows of heaven, and pour you out a blessing that there shall not be room enough to receive it" (v. 10). This oft-quoted scripture has been equated with rain coming upon the crops, becoming rich through tithe paying, and undoubtedly several other blessings. While these are sometimes the fulfillment, the principle involved was taught by President Harold B. Lee in this way:

> The promise following obedience to this principle is that the windows of heaven would be open and blessings would be poured out that we would hardly be able to contain. The opening of the windows of heaven, of course, means revelations from God to him who is willing thus to sacrifice. [Ensign, November 1971, 16]

Also, President Gordon B. Hinckley reminded the Church: *"The Lord will open the windows of heaven according to our need, and not according to our greed"* (CR, April 1982 p. 60).

A second promise to the tithe payer was that the Lord would rebuke the devourer, and not cause the fruits to be destroyed or to be unproductive (v. 11). This problem relates more to the weather. The elements that destroy crops include such things as frost, drought, insects, and hail. The Lord promises to control such for his people if they are faithful. Such blessings upon the sons of Jacob will bring the recognition of surrounding nations upon them (v. 12).

> 13 Your words have been stout against me, saith the Lord. Yet ye say: What have we spoken against thee?
>
> 14 Ye have said: It is vain to serve God, and what doth it profit that we have kept his ordinances and that we have walked mournfully before the Lord of Hosts?
>
> 15 And now we call the proud happy; yea, they that work wickedness are set up; yea, they that tempt God are even delivered.
>
> 16 Then they that feared the Lord spake often one to another, and the Lord hearkened and heard; and a book of remembrance was written before him for them that feared the Lord, and that thought upon his name.
>
> 17 And they shall be mine, saith the Lord of Hosts, in that day when I make up my jewels; and I will spare them as a man spareth his own son that serveth him.
>
> 18 Then shall ye return and discern between the righteous and the wicked, between him that serveth God and him that serveth him not. [3 Nephi 24:13–18; Malachi 3:13–18]

A second sin that the latter-day sons of Jacob must repent of is speaking against the Lord. Again they say they are not guilty, but the Lord specifies that they say it is vain to serve God (vv. 13–15). How many members of the latter-day Church fail to recognize the Lord's hand in the weather in spite of the many scriptures that proclaim that he does in fact use the weather to chasten or bless his people.[3]

Not all the sons of Jacob are guilty of these sins. Those who fear or love the Lord will have their names recorded in the Lord's book

---

[3] 7 And also I have withholden the rain from you, when *there were* yet three months to the harvest: and I caused it to rain upon one city, and caused it not to rain upon another city: one piece was rained upon, and the piece whereupon it rained not withered.

8 So two *or* three cities wandered unto one city, to drink water; but they were not satisfied: yet have ye not returned unto me, saith the LORD.

9 I have smitten you with blasting and mildew: when your gardens and your vineyards and your fig trees and your olive trees increased, the palmerworm devoured *them*: yet have ye not returned unto me, saith the LORD. (Amos 4:7–9; see also Helaman 12:1–3; D&C 43:25)

of remembrance. These will be the Lord's people in the day that he makes up his jewels; they will be spared the destructive judgment that comes upon the world (vv. 16–18). The Lord confirmed this promise to the Latter-day Saints in December 1833; "they shall be mine in that day when I shall come to make up my jewels" (D&C 101:3). A jewel reflects light, and the Lord's people will "hold up [Christ's] light" as they have been commanded (3 Nephi 18:24). These people will be prepared for the Lord's Second Coming.

In Malachi 4, the Lord speaks of the day when the proud and wicked would burn as stubble. In September 1830, the Lord quoted part of Malachi 4:1 when he revealed to Joseph Smith that "the hour is nigh and the day (in the Lord's time) was soon at hand" (D&C 29:9). The Book of Mormon prophets bore similar testimony long before the Lord quoted Malachi to the Nephites; "for the day soon cometh that all the proud and they who do wickedly shall be as stubble; and the day cometh that they must be burned" (1 Nephi 22:15; see also 2 Nephi 26:4).[4] The angel Moroni quoted this passage in Malachi a little differently than it is recorded in the Bible or the Book of Mormon. This was probably to clarify its meaning rather than to correct the text. As time passes, the usage and understanding of words and passages change. The three texts, referred to above, are duplicated here to illustrate the differences:

For, behold, the day cometh, that shall burn as an oven; and all the proud, yea, and all that do wickedly, shall be stubble: and the day that cometh shall burn them up saith the Lord of hosts, that it shall leave them neither root nor branch. (2 Nephi 25:1; Malachi 4:1)	For behold, the day cometh that shall burn as an oven, and all the proud, yea, and all that do wickedly shall burn as stubble; for they that come shall burn them, saith the Lord of Hosts, that it shall leave them neither root nor branch. JS–H 1:37; italics added)	For the hour is nigh and the day soon at hand when the earth is ripe; and all the proud and they that do wickedly shall be as stubble; and I will burn them up, saith the Lord of Hosts, that wickedness shall not be upon the earth; (D&C 29:9)

---

[4] The quotations in the Book of Mormon, being drawn from the plates of brass that did not include Malachi, show that other prophets had foretold of this burning, and that Malachi was quoting from an earlier source.

The message is the same, but Moroni stated it more clearly. The wicked shall burn, and the Lord, or those who come under the Lord's direction [destroying angels] shall supervise or cause the burning. Those who escape the burning will be the tithe payers.

> 23 Behold, now it is called today until the coming of the Son of Man, and verily it is a day of sacrifice, and a day for the tithing of my people; for he that is tithed shall not be burned at his coming.

> 24 For after today cometh the burning—this is speaking after the manner of the Lord—for verily I say, tomorrow all the proud and they that do wickedly shall be as stubble; and I will burn them up, for I am the Lord of Hosts; and I will not spare any that remain in Babylon. [D&C 64:23–24]

Note that the Lord used the words of Malachi 4:1 in the revelation, another evidence of the time frame of the original message.

Those who are burned will be left without root or branch. Elder Theodore M. Burton explains:

> What is meant by the expression "that it shall leave them neither root nor branch"? This expression simply means that wicked and indifferent persons who reject the gospel of Jesus Christ will have no family inheritance or patriarchal lineage— neither root (ancestors or progenitors) nor branch (children or posterity). Such persons cannot be received into the celestial kingdom of glory of resurrected beings, but must be content with a lesser blessing. [CR, September 1967, p. 81]

The Lord once more holds out hope to those who fear his name. The Son of Righteousness will arise with healing in his wings.

> 2 But unto you that fear my name, shall the Son of Righteousness arise with healing in his wings; and ye shall go forth and grow up as calves in the stall.

> 3 And ye shall tread down the wicked; for they shall be ashes under the soles of your feet in the day that I shall do this, saith the Lord of Hosts.

> 4 Remember ye the law of Moses, my servant, which I commanded unto him in Horeb for all Israel, with the statutes and judgments. [3 Nephi 25:2–4; Malachi 4:2–4]

The Book of Mormon text changes the word "Sun" to "Son," referring to the Son of God (v. 2). The same change is also in 2 Nephi 25:13 and 26:9. Those who are left after the judgment of the Second Coming will be able to raise up their children as calves are raised in a stall. The calf is protected from the elements, and his environment is controlled (v. 2). The children in the Millennium will similarly "grow up without sin unto salvation" (D&C 45:58). The telestial element will be removed, and with Satan being bound,[5] the environment will be more controlled. The wicked who are destroyed, the telestial people, will have their ashes walked upon by those who survive the burning (v. 3).

The law of Moses that was first given in Mount Horeb (Sinai) will by this time be restored to the earth (v. 4). This is sometimes confusing to the reader as it appears to be a return to the law of Moses, but when we remember that [the Lord] "took Moses out of their midst, and the Holy Priesthood also; And the lesser priesthood continued," it makes sense (D&C 84:25–27; see also JST Exodus 34:1–2; JST Deuteronomy 10:1–2). In support of the fuller law of Moses being restored, Joseph Smith said, "The law revealed to Moses in Horeb never was revealed to the children of Israel as a nation" (TPJS, 323).

The coming of Elijah before the great and dreadful day of the Lord, an event still looked forward to by the Jewish nation, was the last great doctrine taught by Malachi (vv. 5–6; see also D&C 138:46–47; D&C 35:4). The angel Moroni also quoted these last two

---

[5] 1 And I saw an angel come down from heaven, having the key of the bottomless pit and a great chain in his hand.

2 And he laid hold on the dragon, that old serpent, which is the Devil, and Satan, and bound him a thousand years,

3 And cast him into the bottomless pit, and shut him up, and set a seal upon him, that he should deceive the nations no more, till the thousand years should be fulfilled: and after that he must be loosed a little season. (Revelation 20: 1–3; see also 1 Nephi 22:15; D&C 101:28)

verses differently. Again, the differences were to clarify the meaning. After quoting these two verses in an epistle to the Saints in 1842, precisely as they are in the Book of Mormon and the Bible, Joseph commented: "I might have rendered a plainer translation to this, but it is sufficiently plain to suit my purpose as it stands" (D&C 128:17–18). A comparison of the two texts illustrates the difference:

Behold I will send you Elijah the prophet before the coming of the great and dreadful day of the Lord; And he shall turn the heart of the fathers to the children, and the heart of the children to the fathers, lest I come and smite the earth with a curse. (3 Nephi 25:5–6; Malachi 4:5–6)	And again, he quoted the fifth verse thus: *Behold, I will reveal unto you the Priesthood, by the hand of Elijah the prophet, before the coming of the great and dreadful day of the Lord.* He also quoted the next verse differently: And *he shall plant in the hearts of the children the promises made to the fathers, and the hearts of the children shall turn to their fathers. If it were not so, the whole earth would be utterly wasted at his coming.* (JS–H 1:38–30; see also D&C 2)

The priesthood that was to be revealed by Elijah was not the Aaronic or the Melchizedek, because they were both restored before Elijah's appearance on April 3, 1836. Insight into the priesthood that Elijah restored can be gained from the Prophet Joseph Smith:

> Elijah was the last Prophet that held the keys of the Priesthood, and who will, before the last dispensation, restore the authority and deliver the keys of the Priesthood, in order that all the ordinances may be attended to in righteousness. It is true that the Savior had authority and power to bestow this blessing: but the sons of Levi were too prejudiced. "And I will send Elijah the Prophet before the great and terrible day of the Lord," etc., etc. Why send Elijah? Because he holds the keys of the authority to administer in all the ordinances of the Priesthood; and without the authority . . . , the ordinances could not be administered in righteousness. [TPJS, 172]

Joseph Smith also taught that the whole purpose of the gathering of Israel in any age of the world "was to build unto the Lord a house whereby He could reveal unto His people the ordinances of His house and the glories of His kingdom, and teach the people the way of salvation" (TPJS, 307–8). This concept helps explain why Elijah did not come until the temple in Kirtland, the first in this dispensation, was completed.

Although all priesthood is Melchizedek, Joseph Smith later referred to the three grand orders of the priesthood: the Melchizedek, the Patriarchal, and the Levitical. He instructed the Saints to "go to and finish the temple, and God will fill it with power, and you will then receive more knowledge concerning this priesthood" (TPJS, 322–23). The priesthood restored by Elijah, as stated by the angel Moroni, was evidently the patriarchal order of the priesthood, the power to seal the living and the dead as eternal families.

The promises made to the fathers were the promises of the restoration and the work for the dead. Enos and his fathers were promised that the Lord "would preserve the records [Book of Mormon]; and he covenanted with me that he would bring them forth in his own due time" (Enos 1:16–18). "According to their faith in their prayers," it was brought forth (D&C 10:45–52). "Abraham rejoiced to see the [Christ's] day: and he saw it, and was glad" (John 8:56; see also Helaman 8:17). The founding fathers of the United States of America "laid the foundation you now enjoy, and we never apostatized from it, but we remained true to it and were faithful to God," and sought for and had their ordinances of the gospel done for them in the LDS temple in St George, Utah (JD 19:229). The ancestors of the present-day Latter-day Saints were also given promises, and these promises were planted "in the hearts of [their] children" who do the ordinance work for them in the LDS temples (v. 6; D&C 2). The keys of the power of turning the hearts of the fathers to the children, and the children to the fathers, were committed to Elijah.

> 9 And also Elijah, unto whom I have committed the keys of the power of turning the hearts of the fathers to the children, and the hearts of the children to the fathers, that the whole earth may not be smitten with a curse; [D&C 27:9]

Joseph Smith said that Elijah would "reveal the covenants of the fathers in relation to the children, and the covenants of the children in relation to the fathers" (TPJS, 321).

The hearts of the children were to turn to their fathers (v. 6); that is, the spirit of Elijah was to move upon them. The Saints were admonished to "seek diligently to turn the hearts of the children to the fathers" and to fulfill this commandment (D&C 98:16). Joseph Smith said regarding this:

> Now, the word *turn* here should be translated *bind*, or seal. But what is the object of this important mission? or how is it to be fulfilled? The keys are to be delivered, the spirit of Elijah is to come, the Gospel to be established, the Saints of God gathered, Zion built up, and the Saints to come up as saviors on Mount Zion.

> But how are they to become saviors on Mount Zion? By building their temples, erecting their baptismal fonts, and going forth and receiving all the ordinances, baptisms, confirmations, washings, anointings, ordinations and sealing powers upon their heads, in behalf of all their progenitors who are dead, and redeem them that they may come forth in the first resurrection and be exalted to thrones of glory with them; and herein is the chain that binds the hearts of the fathers to the children, and the children to the fathers, which fulfills the mission of Elijah. And I would to God that this temple was now done, that we might go into it, and go to work and improve our time, and make use of the seals while they are on earth. [TPJS, 330]

Joseph also said that God would "come to the rescue this generation" by sending Elijah the prophet to "reveal the covenants to seal the hearts of the fathers to the children, and the children to the fathers" (TPJS, 323). After testifying that the signs of the coming of the Son of Man had already commenced, Joseph declared that "the hearts of the children of men will have to be turned to the fathers, and the fathers to the children, living or dead, to prepare them for the coming of the Son of Man. If Elijah did not come, the whole earth would be smitten" (TPJS, 160). When the angel Moroni appeared to Joseph Smith, he reworded the ending statement of the book of Malachi to read: "If it were not so, the whole earth would be utterly wasted at his coming" (D&C 2:3). God is a just God, and through the work of Elijah, he has provided an opportunity for all to have an opportunity to receive saving ordinances. Anything short of complete justice would result in God being partial, and the earth would not fulfill the purpose of its creation, namely, for his "children that they should possess it" (1 Nephi 17:36), and "that they should keep his commandments and glorify him forever" (Jacob 2:21). Joseph Smith explained that the curse of the earth was removed when the Lord ushered in "the dispensation of the fullness of times that a whole and complete and perfect union, and welding together of dispensations, and keys, and powers, and glories . . . from the days of Adam even to the present time" would begin (D&C 128:18). This work was begun through baptism and other work for the dead.

Another statement of the Prophet Joseph is a good summary of Elijah's mission:

> Now for Elijah. The spirit, power, and calling of Elijah is that ye have power to hold the key of the revelations, ordinances, oracles, powers and endowments of the fulness of the Melchizedek Priesthood and of the kingdom of God on the earth; and to receive, obtain, and perform all the ordinances belonging to the kingdom of God, even unto the children, and the hearts of the children unto the fathers, even those who are in heaven. . . .

> Now comes the point. What is this office and work of Elijah? It is one of the greatest and most important subjects that God has revealed. He should send Elijah to seal the children to the fathers, and the fathers to the children. [TPJS, 337]

Joseph's summary statement helps us understand why he later said, "The greatest responsibility in this world that God has laid upon us is to seek after our dead" (TPJS, 356). The prophet Elijah has come; he restored the keys for his work in the Kirtland Temple on April 3, 1836. Elijah then announced: "the time has fully come, which was spoken of by the mouth of Malachi—testifying that he [Elijah] should be sent, before the great and dreadful day of the Lord come" (D&C 110:14–15). The work that he restored is under way, and the coming of the great and dreadful day of the Lord is much nearer.

1 And now it came to pass that when Jesus had told these things he expounded them unto the multitude; and he did expound all things unto them, both great and small.

2 And he saith: These scriptures, which ye had not with you, the Father commanded that I should give unto you; for it was wisdom in him that they should be given unto future generations.

3 And he did expound all things, even from the beginning until the time that he should come in his glory—yea, even all things which should come upon the face of the earth, even until the elements should melt with fervent heat, and the earth should be wrapt together as a scroll, and the heavens and the earth should pass away;

4 And even unto the great and last day, when all people, and all kindreds, and all nations and tongues shall stand before God, to be judged of their works, whether they be good or whether they be evil—

5 If they be good, to the resurrection of everlasting life; and if they be evil, to the resurrection of damnation; being on a parallel, the one on the one hand and the other on the other hand, according to the mercy, and the justice, and the holiness which is in Christ, who was before the world began. [3 Nephi 26:1–5]

We are some of the future generations to whom these words were to be given. The "great and small" things expounded upon included "from the beginning until the time that [Jesus] should come in his glory" (v. 3). The Lord confirmed the melting of the elements of the earth at his second coming in a revelation to Joseph Smith in December 1833.

23 And prepare for the revelation which is to come, when the veil of the covering of my temple, in my tabernacle, which hideth the earth, shall be taken off, and all flesh shall see me together.

24 And every corruptible thing, both of man, or of the beasts of the field, or of the fowls of the heavens, or of the fish of the sea, that dwells upon all the face of the earth, shall be consumed;

25 And also that of element shall melt with fervent heat; and all things shall become new, that my knowledge and glory may dwell upon all the earth. [D&C 101:23–25]

Isaiah also prophesied of the earth being "rolled together as a scroll," and "the heavens shall vanish away like smoke, and the earth shall wax old like a garment" (Isaiah 34:3; 51:6). Jesus also bore witness of "all nations and tongues" being "judged of their works": "if they be good, to the resurrection of everlasting life; and if they be evil, to the resurrection of damnation . . ." (vv. 4–5). Perhaps Jesus insisted on the recording of the resurrection among the Nephites in the meridian of time as a basis for his teachings of judgment and resurrection.

> 6 And now there cannot be written in this book even a hundredth part of the things which Jesus did truly teach unto the people;
>
> 7 But behold the plates of Nephi do contain the more part of the things which he taught the people.
>
> 8 And these things have I written, which are a lesser part of the things which he taught the people; and I have written them to the intent that they may be brought again unto this people, from the Gentiles, according to the words which Jesus hath spoken.
>
> 9 And when they shall have received this, which is expedient that they should have first, to try their faith, and if it shall so be that they shall believe these things then shall the greater things be made manifest unto them.
>
> 10 And if it so be that they will not believe these things, then shall the greater things be withheld from them, unto their condemnation.
>
> 11 Behold, I was about to write them, all which were engraven upon the plates of Nephi, but the Lord forbade it, saying: I will try the faith of my people.
>
> 12 Therefore I, Mormon, do write the things which have been commanded me of the Lord. And now I, Mormon, make an end of my sayings, and proceed to write the things which have been commanded me. [3 Nephi 26:6–12]

Mormon's brief summary statements certainly whet one's appetite for a much larger account of Jesus' teachings. Mormon's inclusion of less than a hundredth part to "be brought again unto this people, from the Gentiles" (vv. 6–8) reminds us of John's testimony as he concluded his New Testament record: "And there are also many other things which Jesus did, the which, if they should be written every one,

I suppose that even the world itself could not contain the books that should be written. Amen" (John 21:25).

We have received Mormon's abridgment as a second witness to the resurrection and to the prophets and their teachings. We must study and believe the record that we have received in order to receive the unabridged records. Our faith is being tried. Are we meeting the challenge?

PART 4

Day Three and the Ending
of the 34th Year

3 Nephi 26:13–30:2

After an explanation concerning the briefness of his record (3 Nephi 26:6–12), Mormon summarized the third day of Jesus' divine ministry, and what followed.

13 Therefore, I would that ye should behold that the Lord truly did teach the people, for the space of three days; and after that he did show himself unto them oft, and did break bread oft, and bless it, and give it unto them.

14 And it came to pass that he did teach and minister unto the children of the multitude of whom hath been spoken, and he did loose their tongues, and they did speak unto their fathers great and marvelous things, even greater than he had revealed unto the people; and he loosed their tongues that they could utter.

15 And it came to pass that after he had ascended into heaven the second time that he showed himself unto them, and had gone unto the Father, after having healed all their sick, and their lame, and opened the eyes of their blind and unstopped the ears of the deaf, and even had done all manner of cures among them, and raised a man from the dead, and had shown forth his power unto them, and had ascended unto the Father

16 Behold, it came to pass on the morrow that the multitude gathered themselves together, and they both saw and heard these children; yea, even babes did open their mouths and utter marvelous things; and the

things which they did utter were forbidden that there should not any man write them. [3 Nephi 26:13–16]

There is only one verse (v. 16) describing that entire third day as compared to seventeen pages comprising eight chapters (3 Nephi 11–18) describing the first day, and twelve and a half pages comprising four chapters (3 Nephi 19:1–26:11) about the second day of his ministry. Mormon concludes his record with a few events of the ministry of the twelve disciples, and one of the "oft" appearances of the Savior to the people during the ending of the thirty-fourth year. This one appearance to the Nephite Twelve is the basis of 3 Nephi 27–28, and is discussed in the next two chapters. The last chapter of this work (discussing 3 Nephi 29–30) is Mormon's concluding admonitions as he finished his record.

Chapter 14

This Is My Church and My Gospel

3 Nephi 26:17–27:33; Moroni 6

The ministry of the Twelve Nephite Disciples began as the three-day divine ministry of Jesus ended. Mormon's description of their ministry is summarized in the last five verses of 3 Nephi 26.

> 17 And it came to pass that the disciples whom Jesus had chosen began from that time forth to baptize and to teach as many as did come unto them; and as many as were baptized in the name of Jesus were filled with the Holy Ghost.
>
> 18 And many of them saw and heard unspeakable things, which are not lawful to be written.
>
> 19 And they taught, and did minister one to another; and they had all things common among them, every man dealing justly, one with another.
>
> 20 And it came to pass that they did do all things even as Jesus had commanded them.
>
> 21 And they who were baptized in the name of Jesus were called the church of Christ.

As stated before, we must be tested and thus wait for the "unspeakable things, which [were] not lawful to be written," to be revealed (v. 18; see also v. 10). Mormon further bore record that the members "had all things common among them, every man dealing justly, one with another" (v. 19). Following the forty-day ministry of the resurrected Christ in Jerusalem, those who believed also had "all things common" (Acts 2:44).

The New Testament gives only one brief description of having all things in common: "And the multitude of them that believed were of one heart and of one soul: neither said any of them that ought of the things which he possessed was his own; but they had all things common" (Acts 4:32). Some interpret this verse to mean they had communal property. Mormon does not explain the meaning of having "all things in common" among them, nor does he in Fourth Nephi when it is recorded again. The Lord apparently inspired him to leave the explanation for the Doctrine and Covenants. A full explanation will not be given here either. Suffice it to say that it was not a communal society, but was undoubtedly the law of consecration. Under this law, property was dedicated to the Lord by spiritual covenant and by a legal deed. The people were appointed a steward-ship to operate, and that was their source of earning a living. Their "dealing justly, one with another" implies individual ownership and operation (v. 19).[1]

The remainder of the Nephite Twelve's ministry was described as doing "all things even as Jesus had commanded them" and were organized into the "church of Christ" (vv. 20–21). Chapter twenty-seven gives details of one of the Savior's several times "he did show show himself unto them" following his three-day ministry (3 Nephi 26:13). An outline of this chapter, and the end of chapter twenty-six discussed above, and Moroni chapter six, as an overview to prepare for a deeper study, follows.

---

[1] For further details of the law of consecration see D&C 42:30–36; 51.

Outline • 3 Nephi 26:13–27:33; Moroni 6

➤ 26:13–21   The Lord taught his people for three days, and after that did appear oft, and did break bread oft and give to them.

   a. He did teach and minister to the children. v. 14

      1. He loosed their tongues and they spoke marvelous things to their fathers.

      2. They taught even greater things than Jesus had revealed to the people.

   b. He ascended to the Father the second time, after healing their sick and afflicted. vv. 15–16

      1. On the morrow (the third day?), the multitude saw and heard their children.

      2. The things they taught were forbidden to be written.

   c. From that time forth, the twelve disciples baptized and taught, and the baptized were filled with the Holy Ghost. vv. 17–21

      1. Many saw things that were not lawful to be written.

      2. They taught and ministered to one another.

      3. They had all things common, every man dealing justly one to another.

      4. They did all things Jesus commanded them.

      5. Those baptized were called the church of Christ.

➤ 27:1–32   As the disciples were preaching and baptizing, they gathered and united in fasting and prayer.

   a. Jesus came in their midst and asked what they willed. v. 2–6

      1. They asked what the name of the church should be.

      2. There were disputations among the people concerning the name.

      3. He asked if they had not read the scriptures that say you should take upon you the name of Christ.

      4.   Those who take the name of Christ, and endure to the end shall be saved.

  b. You shall call the church in my name, and call on the Father to bless the church for my sake. vv. 7–8

      1.   If it is called in Moses' name, or the name of a man, it is the church of a man.

      2.   If it is called in my name it is my church, if it is built upon my gospel.

  c. You are built upon my gospel, and if you call upon the Father he will hear you. vv. 9–12

      1.   The Father will show his own works in the church.

      2.   If the church is built upon the works of men, or the devil, there will be joy for a season, the end will come, and you will be cast into the fire.

      3.   Their works follow them, and cause them to be hewn down.

  d. The gospel is that I came into the world to do the will of the Father. vv. 13–17

      1.   I was to be lifted up on the cross that I might draw all men unto me.

      2.   Men shall be lifted up by the Father to be judged of their works by me.

      3.   Whoso repents and is baptized shall be filled.

      4.   If he endures to the end, I will hold him guiltless at the last day.

      5.   Those who do not endure shall be cast into the fire because of the Father's justice.

  e. This is the word of the Father, and he fulfills all his words. vv. 18–19

      1.   No unclean thing can enter into his kingdom.

      2.   Those who enter his rest have washed their garments in his blood because of their faith.

      3.   They have repented of all their sins and endured to the end.

f. The commandment is; Repent all ye ends of the earth, and come unto me and be baptized, that ye may be sanctified by the reception of the Holy Ghost, and stand spotless before me at the last day. vv. 20–22

    1. The works ye shall do in the church are those you have seen me do.

    2. Then you will be blessed and lifted up at the last day.

g. Write the things you have seen and heard save those that are forbidden. vv. 23–27

    1. Write the works of this people as the past works have been written.

    2. Out of the books written shall men be judged.

    3. You shall be judges of this people according to the judgment I shall give you.

    4. You shall be the manner of men that I am.

h. I go to the Father, and what you ask of the Father shall be given you. vv. 28–29

    1. Ask and you shall receive, knock and it shall be opened to you.

    2. He that asks receives, and he that shall knock shall have it opened.

i. My joy is full because of you and this generation. vv. 30–31

    1. The Father rejoices and all the holy angels for none of them are lost.

    2. None who are alive are lost, and in them I have fulness of joy.

j. I sorrow for the fourth generation for they are led captive as was the son of perdition. v. 32

    1. They shall sell me for silver and gold and things that will corrupt and be stolen.

    2. I will visit them and turn their works upon their own heads.

➢ 27:33   When Jesus had ended these sayings he told the disciples to enter in at the straight gate.

  a. Strait is the gate and narrow the way that leads to life and few find it.

  b. Wide is the gate and broad the way that leads to death and many travel therein.

➢Moroni 6:1–9   Moroni speaks concerning baptism and church meetings.

  a. Elders, priests, and teachers were baptized if worthy. vv. 1–4

    1. They came forth with a broken heart and a contrite spirit, witnessing they had repented of all sin.

    2. They took upon them the name of Christ, determined to serve him to the end.

    3. After baptism, they were cleansed by the Holy Ghost, and numbered with the church.

    4. Their names were taken that they might be nourished by the word of God.

  b. The church met oft to fast and pray, and speak to one another of the welfare of their souls. vv. 5–9

    1. They met oft to partake of bread and wine in remembrance of Jesus.

    2. There was to be no iniquity.

    3. Three witnesses to their iniquity caused them not to be numbered with the church.

    4. As often as they sought forgiveness with real intent they were forgiven.

    5. Meetings were conducted by the workings and power of the Holy Ghost.

Notes and Commentary

1 And it came to pass that as the disciples of Jesus were journeying and were preaching the things which they had both heard and seen, and were baptizing in the name of Jesus, it came to pass that the disciples were gathered together and were united in mighty prayer and fasting.

2 And Jesus again showed himself unto them, for they were praying unto the Father in his name; and Jesus came and stood in the midst of them, and said unto them: What will ye that I shall give unto you?

3 And they said unto him: Lord, we will that thou wouldst tell us the name whereby we shall call this church; for there are disputations among the people concerning this matter.

4 And the Lord said unto them: Verily, verily, I say unto you, why is it that the people should murmur and dispute because of this thing?

5 Have they not read the scriptures, which say ye must take upon you the name of Christ, which is my name? For by this name shall ye be called at the last day;

6 And whoso taketh upon him my name, and endureth to the end, the same shall be saved at the last day.

7 Therefore, whatsoever ye shall do, ye shall do it in my name; therefore ye shall call the church in my name; and ye shall call upon the Father in my name that he will bless the church for my sake.

8 And how be it my church save it be called in my name? For if a church be called in Moses' name then it be Moses' church; or if it be called in the name of a man then it be the church of a man; but if it be called in my name then it is my church, if it so be that they are built upon my gospel. [3 Nephi 27:1–8]

There are two requirements for a church to be the Church of Jesus Christ. First, it is to be called by his name, and second, it is to be built upon his gospel.

Regarding the name of the Church, in the Christian world today there are many churches; some are named or nicknamed after their founders, or who they claim to be their founder; some are named after an ordinance or a principle; and others have part or even all of the name of Christ. However, "The Church of Jesus Christ of Latter-day Saints" is the name that the Lord revealed for his restored church today. "The Church" designates it as "the only true and living church upon the face of the whole earth "as the Lord said on an earlier occasion (D&C 1:30). Nephi prophesied of the last days when there would be "two churches only; one is the church of the Lamb of God, and the other is the church of the devil" (1 Nephi 14:10). The same condition was true among the Nephites, and among the people of Jerusalem in the meridian of time. Jesus clearly taught the Pharisees the same concept when they accused him: "This fellow doth not cast out devils, but by Beelzebub, the prince of the devils" (Matthew 12:24).

> And Jesus knew their thoughts, and said unto them, every kingdom divided against itself is brought to desolation; and every city or house divided against itself shall not stand:
>
> And if Satan cast out Satan, he is divided against himself; how shall then his kingdom stand?
>
> And if Beelzebub cast out devils, by whom do your children cast them out? Therefore they shall be your judges.
>
> But if I cast out devils by the Spirit of God, then the kingdom of God is come unto you,
>
> Or else how can one enter into a strong man's house, and spoil his goods, except he first bind the strong man? And then he will spoil his house.
>
> *He that is not with me is against me; and he that gathereth not with me scattereth abroad.* [Matthew 12:25–30; italics added]

The kingdom of God had come to the people in Jerusalem. All other churches were not recognized by Christ in Jerusalem, and among the Nephites.

The term *Latter-day Saints* designates the difference between this dispensation and former dispensations when the true Church was upon the earth. As with other religions, the nickname "Mormons" has been attached by some because of the belief in the Book of Mormon, but the official name was declared by revelation. However, the true name is not sufficient for a church to be Christ's church.

> 9 Verily I say unto you, that ye are built upon my gospel; therefore ye shall call whatsoever things ye do call, in my name; therefore if ye call upon the Father, for the church, if it be in my name the Father will hear you;
>
> 10 And if it so be that the church is built upon my gospel then will the Father show forth his own works in it.

> 11 But if it be not built upon my gospel, and is built upon the works
> of men, or upon the works of the devil, verily I say unto you they have
> joy in their works for a season, and by and by the end cometh, and they
> are hewn down and cast into the fire, from whence there is no return.
>
> 12 For their works do follow them, for it is because of their works that
> they are hewn down; therefore remember the things that I have told you.
> [3 Nephi 27:9–12]

The second requirement designated by the Savior for recognizing the true church was its' being "built upon my gospel." Jesus reminded the Nephite disciples that they had been "built upon [his] gospel"; therefore, if they called upon the Father he would hear them and would "show forth his own works in [the Church]" (vv. 9–10). Jesus further declared that any church that was "built upon the works of men, or upon the works of the devil . . . have joy in their works for a season," but when the end cometh "they are hewn down and cast into the fire, from whence there is no return" (v. 11). The cause of the churches being eventually hewn down was the works that they produced (v. 12). The works of men or of the devil were certainly not of the Lord, and remind us of Jesus' prior teaching, "Wherefore, by their fruits [works] ye shall know them" (3 Nephi 14:20; see also vv. 15–19). After Peter declared to Jesus, "Thou are the Christ, the Son of the living God" (Matthew 16:16), Jesus proclaimed:

> Blessed art thou, Simon Bar-jona: for flesh and blood hath not
> revealed it unto thee, but my Father which is in heaven. And I say also
> unto thee, that thou art Peter, and upon this rock I will build my church;
> and the gates of hell shall not prevail against it. And I will give unto thee
> the keys of the kingdom of heaven: and whatsoever thou shalt bind on
> earth shall be bound in heaven: and whatsoever thou shalt loose on earth
> shall be loosed in heaven. [Matthew 16:17–19]

Some interpret this scripture to mean that the church would be built upon Peter. If this interpretation is correct, then the church would be built upon a man and should be called the Church of Peter. It is true that Peter and James and John were given the "power and the keys of this ministry until I [Christ] come," and that Peter was thus the president of the church (D&C 7:7), but as the head of the church he was

to receive revelation for the church and administer the gospel principles and ordinances. Joseph Smith gave two interpretations of Jesus'
statement to Peter that confirms this doctrine.

> Jesus in His teaching says, "Upon this rock I will build my Church,
> and the gates of hell shall not prevail against it." What rock? Revelation.
> [TPJS, 247]

> Christ was the head of the Church, the chief corner stone, the spiritual
> rock upon which the church was built, and the gates of hell shall not
> prevail against it. He built up the Kingdom, chose Apostles, and ordained
> them to the Melchizedek Priesthood, giving them power to administer
> in the ordinances of the Gospel. [TPJS, 318]

The Church is built upon Christ and the revelations of his gospel.
There is no contradiction in Joseph's two statements.

The Gospel Defined

> 13 Behold I have given unto you my gospel, and this is the gospel
> which I have given unto you—that I came into the world to do the will
> of my Father, because my Father sent me.

> 14 And my Father sent me that I might be lifted up upon the cross; and
> after that I had been lifted up upon the cross, that I might draw all men
> unto me, that as I have been lifted up by men even so should men be
> lifted up by the Father, to stand before me, to be judged of their works,
> whether they be good or whether they be evil—

> 15 And for this cause have I been lifted up; therefore, according to the
> power of the Father I will draw all men unto me, that they may be judged
> according to their works.

> 16 And it shall come to pass, that whoso repenteth and is baptized in
> my name shall be filled; and if he endureth to the end, behold, him will
> I hold guiltless before my Father at that day when I shall stand to judge
> the world.

> 17 And he that endureth not unto the end, the same is he that is also
> hewn down and cast into the fire, from whence they can no more return,
> because of the justice of the Father. [3 Nephi 27:13–17]

Many definitions of the gospel are used in the Christian world.
These definitions may even influence the thinking of some Church

members. But the definition given here is the most complete of any in the scriptures, and is the one that Church members should know and follow. To appreciate Jesus' definition, we shall first consider some of the other definitions.

One of the common definitions of the gospel comes from its meaning in Greek: "good news." This is a good definition if it is remembered that the gospel is the good news that there is a plan of salvation for mankind to come back into the presence of their Father in Heaven, the place they resided as spirits before they came into this earth as mortal beings. In the Book of Abraham we learn:

> 24 And there stood one among them that was like unto God, and he said unto those who were with him: We will go down, for there is space there, and we will take of these materials, and we will make an earth whereon these may dwell;
>
> 25 And we will prove them herewith, to see if they will do all things whatsoever the Lord their God shall command them;
>
> 26 And they who keep their first estate shall be added upon; and they who keep not their first estate shall not have glory in the same kingdom with those who keep their first estate; and they who keep their second estate shall have glory added upon their heads for ever and ever. [Abraham 3:24–26]

The Savior's teachings in 3 Nephi 27 outline this plan of salvation.

Another definition comes from the same meaning in Hebrew. The angel who appeared to King Benjamin said: "I am come to declare unto you the glad tidings of great joy" (Mosiah 3:3). The angel who appeared to the shepherds at the time of Christ's birth said: "I bring you good tidings of great joy, which shall be to all people" (Luke 2:10). The same comments above concerning the Greek definition apply here.

Within the Church membership, some have defined the gospel to include all truth. Again, this is a good definition if used in the proper context. However, Henry B. Eyring, as commissioner of the LDS Church Education System, gave this caution:

There are two views of the gospel— both true. They make a terrific difference in the power of your teaching. One view is that the gospel is all truth. It is. The gospel is truth. With that view I could teach pretty well anything true in a classroom, and I would be teaching the gospel. The other view is that the gospel is the principles, commandments, and ordinances which, if kept, conformed with, and accepted, will lead to eternal life. That is also true.

When I choose which of these views I will let dominate my teaching, I take a great step. If I take the view that the gospel is all truth, rather than that it is the ordinances and principles and commandments which, if kept, conformed with, and accepted, lead to eternal life, I have already nearly taken myself out of the contest to help a student withstand the sea of filth. Why? Because he needs to have his eyes focused on light, and that means not truth in some abstract sense but the joy of keeping the commandments and conforming with the principles and accepting the ordinances of the gospel of Jesus Christ. If I decide I will not make that my primary vision of the gospel, I am already out of the contest to help my student with his capacity to see good and to want and desire it in the midst of filth.[2]

Therefore, the gospel as defined by the Savior to the Nephite Twelve is the one that should be taught in the Church.

Jesus defined the gospel as his coming "into the world to do the will of my Father, because my Father sent me" (v. 13). This one-sentence definition is the overall or general definition of the gospel. Jesus then explained that his Father sent him: "that I might be lifted up upon the cross; and after that I had been lifted up upon the cross, that I might draw all men unto me, that as I have been lifted up by men even so should men be lifted up by the Father, to stand before me, to be judged of their works, whether they be good or whether they be evil" (v. 14). He had set the example for men to follow; both in Jerusalem and to the Nephites. To the Nephites he said: "for the works which ye have seen me do that shall ye also do" (3 Nephi 27:27). He had undoubtedly done and probably said the same to the

---

[2] Eyring, Henry B. The *Eighth Annual Church Educational System Religious Educators' Symposium, New Testament,* "Eyes to See, Ears to Hear," p. 11, 1984.

Jews, and yet they had judged him by their standards and crucified him. In a similar manner, after a person has lived on this earth and has had an opportunity to receive the teachings of Jesus Christ, he or she will be lifted up and judged by the standard that Christ established while upon the earth. The power of the Father granted unto Christ would enable him to make this judgment of men's works (v. 15). This is the gospel that Christ's church must be built upon. The Lord gave a second witness to the above Book of Mormon definition of the gospel to Joseph Smith and Sidney Rigdon.

> And this is the gospel, the glad tidings, which the voice out of the heavens bore record unto us That he came into the world, even Jesus, to be crucified for the world, and to bear the sins of the world, and to sanctify the world, and to cleanse it from all unrighteousness;
>
> That through him all might be saved whom the Father had put into his power and made by him. [D&C 76:40–42]

Jesus continued to outline the plan of salvation for the Nephites to follow in order to return to Heavenly Father's presence. Again, in a general or overall pattern, it was that "whoso repenteth and is baptized in my name shall be filled; and if he endureth to the end, behold, him will I hold guiltless before my Father at that day when I shall stand to judge the world" (v. 16). To be held guiltless is a recognition to the Father that the person being judged has met the requirements that Jesus gave in order that the demands of justice be paid by the mercy of Jesus' Atonement. Those who do not meet these requirements, or do not endure to the end, will be subject to the justice of the Father and be "hewn down and cast into the fire, from whence they can no more return" (v. 17). As he taught in Jerusalem, Jesus has been delegated the responsibility to judge. "For the Father judgeth no man, but hath committed all judgment unto the Son:" (John 5:22). Jacob also taught that Jesus was the sole judge. "Behold the way for man is narrow, but it lieth in a straight course before him, and the keeper of the gate is the Holy One of Israel; and he employeth no servant there; and there is none other way save it be by the gate; for he cannot be deceived, for the Lord God is his name" (2 Nephi 9:41).

> 18 And this is the word which he hath given unto the children of men. And for this cause he fulfilleth the words which he hath given, and he lieth not, but fulfilleth all his words.
>
> 19 And no unclean thing can enter into his kingdom; therefore nothing entereth into his rest save it be those who have washed their garments in my blood, because of their faith, and the repentance of all their sins, and their faithfulness unto the end. [3 Nephi 27:18–19]

The Father's words, or the plan revealed for the salvation of men, will thus be fulfilled through Jesus Christ, as are all his words (v. 18). The specific steps of the gospel plan are enlarged upon as Jesus continued to instruct the Nephite disciples.

As summarized in the fourth Article of Faith, the first step is to have faith in the Lord Jesus Christ. The term "Lord" designates him as the divine personage that he is. The term "Jesus" designates him as a historical being who literally lived upon the earth. His ministry among the Nephites is a second witness to his historicity.[3] The designation of "Christ" means an acceptance of him as the Messiah, the one who made the Atonement. The Atonement must be accepted and become efficacious in our lives because "no unclean thing can enter into [the Father's] kingdom; therefore nothing entereth into his rest save it be those who have washed their garments in [his] blood, because of their faith, and the repentance of all their sins, and their faithfulness unto the end" (v. 19). The rest of the Lord "is the fulness of his glory," or the celestial kingdom (D&C 84:24). To wash our garments in the blood of Christ is to have the Atonement pay for the sins we have committed. Our garments are cleansed as Christ takes our sins upon himself.

The second step of the plan of salvation for all mankind is to repent "of *all* their sins" (v. 19; italics added). Thus, repentance is an

---

[3] The historicity of Jesus is questioned by many in the world who look upon him as a mythical character who never existed or one who was embellished by his followers to be created as a Savior in their eyes. See "The Quest For the Historical Jesus" by Albert Sweitzer. Translated by W. Montgomery, New York; MacMillian, 1968.

ongoing process as one is faithful unto the end. However, it is not a principle of repeated repentance for the same problem. As the Prophet Joseph Smith taught, "Repentance is a thing that cannot be trifled with every day. Daily transgression and daily repentance is not that which is pleasing in the sight of God" (TPJS, 148). As people grow in gospel knowledge, they become aware of the finer points of the gospel or principles for living with their fellowmen. As they follow the knowledge they have gained, they must change their lives to conform to the higher plane of understanding. Repentance means to turn about or change, and so they are continually repenting. Repentance is what brings the Holy Ghost into their lives to bring "a remission of your sins" (2 Nephi 31:17). Moroni, in expanding upon the teachings of Christ's ministry, stated that those who were "received unto baptism, and were wrought upon and cleansed by the power of the Holy Ghost . . . were numbered among the people of the church of Christ" (Moroni 6:4). The principle of repentance must continue in people's lives after they enter into the Church. The specific steps of repentance will not be considered at this point. Suffice it to say that repentance is "the thing which will be of the most worth" (D&C 15:6) unto the people of the Church, as well as to those who are required to repent and be baptized (v. 16).

Moroni later recorded "And now I speak concerning baptism, Behold, elders, priests, and teachers were baptized; and they were not baptized save they brought forth fruit meet that they were worthy of it" (Moroni 6:1). As discussed in chapter 9, those holding the priesthood were baptized into "a new and an everlasting covenant' (D&C 22:2). "Neither did they receive any unto baptism save they came forth with a broken heart and a contrite spirit, and witnessed unto the church that they truly [had] repented of all their sins. And none were received unto baptism save they took upon them the name of Christ, having a determination to serve him to the end" (Moroni 6:2–3). To come unto Christ and be baptized in his name is the third step in the gospel plan of salvation (v. 16). The mode of baptism, the prerequisites for it, and the baptismal prayer were revealed earlier when Christ appeared to the Nephites (3 Nephi 11:21–27), and were discussed in chapter 4. The same requirements for entrance into the Church among the Nephites were revealed in this dispensation.

> 37 *And again, by way of commandment to the church concerning the manner of baptism*—All those who humble themselves before God, and desire to be baptized, and come forth with broken hearts and contrite spirits, and witness before the church that they have truly repented of all their sins, and are willing to take upon them the name of Jesus Christ, having a determination to serve him to the end, and truly manifest by their works that they have received of the Spirit of Christ unto the remission of their sins, shall be received by baptism into his church. [D&C 20:37]

The ordinance of baptism is an eternal principle: "As many as would believe and be baptized in his holy name, and endure in faith to the end, should be saved—Not only those who believed after he came in the meridian of time, in the flesh, but all those from the beginning" (D&C 20:25–26). It has undoubtedly had the same requirements for its administration in every dispensation as those outlined by Moroni.

> 20 Now this is the commandment: Repent, all ye ends of the earth, and come unto me and be baptized in my name, that ye may be sanctified by the reception of the Holy Ghost, that ye may stand spotless before me at the last day.
>
> 21 Verily, verily, I say unto you, this is my gospel; and ye know the things that ye must do in my church; for the works which ye have seen me do that shall ye also do; for that which ye have seen me do even that shall ye do;
>
> 22 Therefore, if ye do these things blessed are ye, for ye shall be lifted up at the last day. [3 Nephi 27:20–22]

Jesus had given the Father's requirements for coming into his presence, which was the law of justice (v. 16–19). He now gives a commandment, a requirement for his mercy in paying the demands of justice.

Through repentance, baptism, and "the reception of the Holy Ghost," a person is able to be sanctified and "stand spotless before [Christ] at the last day" (v. 20). This is the fourth step in the gospel plan. Sanctification is a process that makes people pure and holy "because of their yielding their hearts unto God" (Helaman 3:35). It is the condition of the soul that is brought about through the priesthood and the power of the Holy Ghost. "Their garments were washed white, through the blood of the Lamb. . . . Being pure and spotless before God, [they] could not look upon sin save it were with abhorrence" (Alma 13:11–12). Paul taught the Thessalonians that "God hath from the beginning chosen you to salvation through sanctification of the Spirit and belief of the truth:" (2 Thessalonians 2:13; see also 1 Peter 1:2; Romans 15:16). The visitation of the Holy Ghost fills one "with hope and perfect love, which love endureth by diligence unto prayer, until the end shall come, when all the saints shall dwell with God" (Moroni 8:26). Finally, sanctification is required for entrance into the celestial kingdom. Joseph Smith's description of man approaching God summarizes the sanctification process:

> We consider that God has created man with a mind capable of instruction, and a faculty which may be enlarged in proportion to the heed and diligence given to the light communicated from heaven to the intellect; and that the nearer man approaches perfection, the clearer are his views, and the greater his enjoyments, till he has overcome the evils of his life and lost every desire for sin; and like the ancients, arrives at that point of faith where he is wrapped in the power and glory of his Maker and is caught up to dwell with Him. But we consider that this is a station to which no man ever arrived in a moment: he must have been instructed in the government and laws of that kingdom by proper degrees, until his mind is capable in some measure of comprehending the propriety, justice, equality, and consistency of the same. [TPJS, 51]

This is the step-by-step plan of salvation, or the gospel plan, as defined by Jesus to the Nephite Twelve. He had taught them and set the example for them, and they knew their course of action (v. 21). The Savior has given the same definition of the gospel for us to follow in the latter days. In October 1830 he said:

> Yea, repent and be baptized, every one of you, for a remission of your sins; yea, be baptized even by water, and then cometh the baptism of fire and of the Holy Ghost. Behold, verily, verily, I say unto you, this is my

gospel; and remember that they shall have faith in me or they can in
nowise be saved. [D&C 33:11–12]

About three months later he gave a similar definition:

And verily, verily, I say unto you, he that receiveth my gospel
receiveth me; and he that receiveth not my gospel receiveth not me. And
this is my gospel repentance and baptism by water, and then cometh the
baptism of fire and the Holy Ghost, even the Comforter, which showeth
all things, and teacheth the peaceable things of the kingdom. [D&C
39:5–6]

Those who would "do these things" and endure to the end would be
lifted up at the last day (v. 22). This is the good news or the glad
tidings of great joy achieved through living the gospel of Jesus Christ.

The attaining of gospel blessings is possible in this life. The Book
of Mormon testifies of several who had become sanctified to the
degree that they were assured of being lifted up at the last day. Father
Lehi is the first one recorded in the sacred Nephite record: "But
behold, the Lord hath redeemed my soul from hell; I have beheld his
glory, and I am encircled about eternally in the arms of his love" (2
Nephi 1:15).

Nephi, son of Lehi also received the same promise: "I glory in
plainness; I glory in truth; I glory in my Jesus, for he hath redeemed
my soul from hell" (2 Nephi 33:6). Alma the elder was promised
eternal life: "Thou art my servant; and I covenant with thee that thou
shalt have eternal life; and thou shalt serve me and go forth in my
name, and shalt gather together my sheep" (Mosiah 26:20). Others
could be cited as probably having been "sealed up unto eternal life"
(D&C 131:5–6), or having given "diligence to make their calling and
election sure" (2 Peter 1:10), but the principle is established with these
three witnesses. Further discussion and examples will be cited in the
next chapter.

The Church In Action

The functioning of the Church was enlarged upon by Moroni as he added to the record after A.D. 400.

> 4 And after they had been received unto baptism, and were wrought upon and cleansed by the power of the Holy Ghost, they were numbered among the people of the church of Christ; and their names were taken, that they might be remembered and nourished by the good word of God, to keep them in the right way, to keep them continually watchful unto prayer, relying alone upon the merits of Christ, who was the author and the finisher of their faith.
>
> 5 And the church did meet together oft, to fast and to pray, and to speak one with another concerning the welfare of their souls.
>
> 6 And they did meet together oft to partake of bread and wine, in remembrance of the Lord Jesus.
>
> 7 And they were strict to observe that there should be no iniquity among them; and whoso was found to commit iniquity, and three witnesses of the church did condemn them before the elders, and if they repented not, and confessed not, their names were blotted out, and they were not numbered among the people of Christ.
>
> 8 But as oft as they repented and sought forgiveness, with real intent, they were forgiven.
>
> 9 And their meetings were conducted by the church after the manner of the workings of the Spirit, and by the power of the Holy Ghost; for as the power of the Holy Ghost led them whether to preach, or to exhort, or to pray, or to supplicate, or to sing, even so it was done. [Moroni 6:4–9]

Records were kept in order that the members "might be remembered and nourished by the good word of God, to keep them in the right way, to keep them continually watchful unto prayer, relying alone upon the merits of Christ" (v. 4). Thus, through the collective efforts of the Church, the members could work toward sanctification.

The Church met "together oft, to fast and to pray, and to speak one with another concerning the welfare of their souls" (v. 5). This reminds us of the present-day fast and testimony meetings. The sacrament was also partaken of often (v. 6). The Church had a disciplinary program to prevent "iniquity among them" and to help the members obtain a forgiveness of sin. Those who did not repent and were condemned by three witnesses of the Church before the elders had their names "blotted out, and they were not numbered among the people of Christ" (vv. 7–8). Jesus had given similar instructions to the disciples in Capernaum of Galilee.

> Moreover if thy brother shall trespass against thee, go and tell him his fault between thee and him alone: if he shall hear thee, thou hast gained thy brother. But if he will not hear thee, then take with thee one or two more, that in the mouth of two or three witnesses every word may be established. And if he shall neglect to hear them, tell it unto the church: but if he neglect to hear the church, let him be unto thee as an heathen man and a publican. [Matthew 18:15–17]

The instructions given during both ministries sound similar to the disciplinary process used in the Church today.

"Meetings were conducted by the church after the manner of the workings of the Spirit and by the power of the Holy Ghost" (v. 9). Paul gave similar instructions to the Corinthian Saints.

> 26 How is it then, brethren? when ye come together, every one of you hath a psalm, hath a doctrine, hath a tongue, hath a revelation, hath an interpretation. Let all things be done unto edifying. [1 Corinthians 14:26]

This procedure does not mean that the meetings were not organized. Certainly there was an order in their meetings, and the Holy Ghost was an external force in that organization as well as an internal influence as the meetings proceeded. The pattern followed in the Church today suggests how the Holy Ghost operates. The Lord instructed that: "the elders are to conduct the meetings as they are led by the Holy Ghost, according to the commandments and revelations of God" (D&C 20:45). The Church is administered as the Lord commands and reveals to his servants in any gospel dispensation.

Returning to Third Nephi, Mormon records Jesus' instructions to write what had happened.

23 Write the things which ye have seen and heard, save it be those which are forbidden.

24 Write the works of this people, which shall be, even as hath been written, of that which hath been.

25 For behold, out of the books which have been written, and which shall be written, shall this people be judged, for by them shall their works be known unto men.

26 And behold, all things are written by the Father; therefore out of the books which shall be written shall the world be judged.

27 And know ye that ye shall be judges of this people, according to the judgment which I shall give unto you, which shall be just. Therefore, what manner of men ought ye to be? Verily I say unto you, even as I am. [3 Nephi 27:23–27]

The writing was to include things of the future among the Nephite people, and was to follow the pattern of the records that had been written before. The past and future records were to be used in judgment upon the Nephite people collectively, They were also to make known their works unto men (vv. 24–25). The keeping of records to be used in judging is according to the plan of the Father: "out of the books which shall be written shall the world be judged" (v. 26).

In addition to the written scriptures that will be used in judging, the Savior tells the Nephite Twelve that they will also act as judges of the Nephite people. The judgment referred to is not one of passing sentence, but rather standing as special witnesses of Jesus Christ and his gospel.[4] The phrase "according to the judgment which [Christ] shall give unto you," referred to the words that Jesus would inspire them to speak. The people will be accountable for the words the Twelve speak, and will be judged by their actions or works as measured by the disciples' teachings. "Therefore, what manner of men

---

[4] See Nyman, Monte S. "The Judgment Seat of Christ" Chapter 16, p. 199 *The Book of Mormon, Fourth Nephi Through Moroni FROM ZION TO DESTRUCTION*, Edited by Monte S. Nyman and Charles D. Tate, Provo, Utah: Religious Study Center Brigham Young University, 1995.

ought [the Twelve] to be?" Their lives were to be "even as [Christ]" (v. 27), examples so that the people will be more willing to follow their teachings.

> 28 And now I go unto the Father. And verily I say unto you, whatsoever things ye shall ask the Father in my name shall be given unto you.
>
> 29 Therefore, ask, and ye shall receive; knock, and it shall be opened unto you; for he that asketh, receiveth; and unto him that knocketh, it shall be opened.
>
> 30 And now, behold, my joy is great, even unto fulness, because of you, and also this generation; yea, and even the Father rejoiceth, and also all the holy angels, because of you and this generation; for none of them are lost.
>
> 31 Behold, I would that ye should understand; for I mean them who are now alive of this generation; and none of them are lost; and in them I have fulness of joy.
>
> 32 But behold, it sorroweth me because of the fourth generation from this generation, for they are led away captive by him even as was the son of perdition; for they will sell me for silver and for gold, and for that which moth doth corrupt and which thieves can break through and steal. And in that day will I visit them, even in turning their works upon their own heads. [3 Nephi 27:28–32]

The prayers of the disciples had been answered. Jesus was going back to the Father, but he gave a promise to them before leaving: "whatsoever things ye shall ask the Father in my name shall be given unto you" (v. 28). The same promise was given to the Jerusalem Twelve. "Ye have not chosen me, but I have chosen you, and ordained you, that ye should go and bring forth fruit, and that your fruit should remain: that whatsoever ye shall ask of the Father in my name, he may give it you" (John 15:16). Because of this promise, if they would ask, they would receive. Because of being judges of this people, if they would knock or endeavor to live the example set by the Savior, the way would be opened for them to fulfill their ministry among the people (v. 29).

Jesus expressed his joy in the generation of people to whom he spoke. In doing so he showed his omniscience as well as the Father's and the holy angels. Their joy was full because they knew that none of the generation was lost (vv. 30–31). However, Jesus also sorrowed because "the fourth generation from this generation" would be "led away captive by [the devil] even as was the son of perdition" (v. 32; see also 3 Nephi 29:7). The reference to "the son of perdition" is undoubtedly Judas, one of the Jerusalem Twelve. In Jerusalem, Jesus stated that "none of them is lost, but the son of perdition; that the scripture might be fulfilled" (John 17:12). The designation of Judas as a "son of perdition" indicates his eternal status, but that interpretation is controversial.[5]

There was one final admonition given collectively to the disciples:

> 33 And it came to pass that when Jesus had ended these sayings he said unto his disciples: Enter ye in at the strait gate; for strait is the gate, and narrow is the way that leads to life, and few there be that find it; but wide is the gate, and broad the way which leads to death, and many there be that travel therein, until the night cometh, wherein no man can work. [3 Nephi 27:33]

During his mortal ministry, Jesus answered a question about how many would be saved. Jesus replied, "Strive to enter in at the strait gate: for many, I say unto you, will seek to enter in, and shall not be able" (Luke 13:24). Those in Jerusalem were admonished to enter the gate of baptism. The Nephite disciples had already been baptized and entered into the strait gate. Therefore, this last admonition to them seems to be a summary, or overall endorsement of the plan of salvation, or the gospel of the Church of Jesus Christ, that had been the subject of Christ's visit. They knew the name to call the Church, and the gospel that was to be taught and lived. It was now their responsibility to be an example to the rest of the members of the Church.

---

[5] President Joseph F. Smith said that his (Judas) being called a son of perdition may have been merely by association (*Gospel Doctrine*, 11th Edition pp. 434–35). Elder James E. Talmage wrote that he (Judas) was indeed a son perdition (*Jesus the Christ*, 19th Edition pp. 649–51).

Chapter 15

The Blessings to the Twelve Disciples

3 Nephi 28

In June of 1829, the Lord revealed that the modern day Twelve [Apostles] that were to be called "are they who shall desire to take upon them [Christ's] name with full purpose of heart" (D&C 18:27). The Nephite Twelve whom Jesus had called certainly had that qualification as exemplified by their works during the thirty-fourth year. Jesus promised both the Nephite Twelve and the Jerusalem Twelve: "whatsoever things ye shall ask the Father in my name shall be given unto you" (3 Nephi 27:28; John 15:16). Such a promise is made because he knew that they would "not ask that which is contrary to [Christ's] will" (Helaman 10:5). As an extension of that promise, before Jesus departed from the Nephite Twelve, he asked each one individually what "ye desire of me, after that I am gone to the Father" (3 Nephi 28:1). There is some indication that he had made a similar gesture to the Jerusalem Twelve, but it is not recorded.[1] Although the

---

[1] John 21:12–23 records a meeting with the Jerusalem Twelve where specific things were said to Peter and John. Doctrine and Covenants, section 7, shows that John was given an individual promise. The context of the discussion between Jesus and Peter suggests that promises had been made to others of the Twelve.

promise to the Twelve Nephites was extended to each individually, the requests from nine of them were identical, and the desire of the other three was apparently also the same. The unity of the Twelve seems to be demonstrated in their desires. They were certainly willing to take upon themselves the name of Christ and be his special witnesses. An outline of the conversation between them, as an overview for a deeper study, follows.

Outline • 3 Nephi 28

➤ 28:1–24   Jesus asked his disciples one by one what they desired of him after he was gone to the Father.

    a.   All but three desired to live to the age of man, fulfill their ministry, and then come unto him in his kingdom. vv. 2–3

        1.   They were blessed because of what they desired.

        2.   When they were seventy-two years old, they could come to him and find rest.

    b.   The other three sorrowed because they dared not ask what they desired.

        1.   He knew they desired the same thing that John the Beloved desired of him.

        2.   They shall never taste of death, but live to behold all things until he comes in his glory.

        3.   They shall be changed from mortality to immortality in the twinkling of an eye.

        4.   Then they will be blessed in the kingdom of the Father.

        5.   They will not have the pains of the flesh nor sorrow save for the sins of the world.

        6.   Their desire to bring souls to Christ as long as the world stands brought these blessings.

        7.   They shall have fulness of joy and sit down in the kingdom of the Father.

        8. They shall be even as Christ and the Father, who are one.

        9. The Holy Ghost bears witness of the Father and Christ.

     10. The Father gives the Holy Ghost unto the children of men because of Christ.

  c. Jesus touched all but the three with his hand and then departed. vv. 12–16

        1. The three were caught up to heaven, and saw and heard unspeakable things (v. 36).

        2. It was forbidden, nor did they have power to speak.

        3. They could not tell whether they were in or out of the body, it seemed to be a transfiguration from the body to an immortal state.

        4. They ministered on earth again, but not of the things they had seen and heard.

  d. Mormon does not know if they were mortal or immortal after their transfiguration. vv. 17–23

        1. They united to the church as many as believed and were baptized. These received the Holy Ghost.

        2. They were cast into prison and pits, but were delivered.

        3. Three times they were cast into a fiery furnace and received no harm.

        4. Twice they were cast into a den of wild beasts, but played with them as would a child.

        5. They preached the gospel, converted people to the Lord, and united them to the church.

  e. Mormon ends speaking of these things for a time. v. 24

➤ 28:25–35 Mormon was about to write the names of the three who never died, but the Lord forbade it.

  a. He has seen them, and they have ministered to him. vv. 26–28

        1. They will be among the Gentiles, and the Gentiles shall not know them.

      2.   They will be among the Jews and the Jews shall not know them.

  b. When the Lord sees fit, they will minister to all Israel, and to all nations and people. vv. 29–33

      1.   They will bring many souls to Jesus.

      2.   They are as angels of God; if they pray to the Father they can appear to anyone that it seems good.

      3.   Great and marvelous things shall be wrought even among the Gentiles before the judgment day.

      4.   All scriptures about the works of Christ say these things shall come.

  c. Wo to those who will not hearken to the words of Christ, and those chosen of him. vv. 34–35

      1.   He will not receive them at the last day.

      2.   It would be better for them had they not been born.

      3.   The justice of an offended God cannot be ignored.

➤ 28:36–40   Mormon inquired of the Lord concerning the three caught up to heaven.

  a. They had a change come over their bodies, or they would taste of death. vv. 37–39

      1.   The change was not equal to the change at the last day.

      2.   The change was such that Satan could have no power over them.

  b. They were sanctified in the flesh, and the powers of the earth could not hold them. vv. 39–40

      1.   They would remain in this state until the judgment day.

      2.   Then they would receive a greater change, and be received in the kingdom of God.

Notes and Commentary

1 And it came to pass when Jesus had said these words, he spake unto his disciples, one by one, saying unto them: What is it that ye desire of me, after that I am gone to the Father?

2 And they all spake, save it were three, saying: We desire that after we have lived unto the age of man, that our ministry, wherein thou hast called us, may have an end, that we may speedily come unto thee in thy kingdom.

3 And he said unto them: Blessed are ye because ye desired this thing of me; therefore, after that ye are seventy and two years old ye shall come unto me in my kingdom; and with me ye shall find rest. [3 Nephi 28:1–3]

Nine disciples had a simple but admirable request. Their desire was to live "unto the age of man," fulfill their ministry, and then "speedily come unto [Christ] in [his] kingdom" (v. 2). Their request was granted, and they were commended for their desire. Jesus promised that when they were "seventy and two years old ye shall come unto me in my kingdom; and with me ye shall find rest" (v. 3). The age of seventy-two was probably the average age of a man's life at that time, and in accordance with their request. Obviously, the Twelve were of different ages when called since "Nephi and his brother . . . and also his son, . . . and also Mathoni, and Mathonihah, his brother" were among them (3 Nephi 19:4). Ending their ministry at a set age would allow for replacements at various times, and allow for continuity in the quorum as "there were other disciples ordained in their stead" (4 Nephi 1:14). Other apostles were ordained periodically in Jerusalem as the original Twelve passed on. "The lot fell upon Matthias, and he was numbered with the eleven apostles" to replace Judas (Acts 1:26). "Paul, an apostle, (not by man, but by Jesus Christ)," and "James the Lord's brother," were called to be apostles (Gal. 1:1,19), although we do not know who of the original ones they replaced. Herod "killed James the brother of John with the sword," one of the first to be killed (Acts 12:2), and could have been replaced by Paul or James, the Lord's brother, or another not named.

It is commendable that the Nephite disciples desired to fulfill their ministry before returning to Christ. Each of us should have the same desire, whatever is our ministry. If we do fulfill our ministry as they did, we also will enter the rest of the Lord, which "is the fulness of his glory," or celestial glory (see D&C 84:24).

> 4 And when he had spoken unto them, he turned himself unto the three, and said unto them: What will ye that I should do unto you, when I am gone unto the Father?
>
> 5 And they sorrowed in their hearts, for they durst not speak unto him the thing which they desired.
>
> 6 And he said unto them: Behold, I know your thoughts, and ye have desired the thing which John, my beloved, who was with me in my ministry, before that I was lifted up by the Jews, desired of me.
>
> 7 Therefore, more blessed are ye, for ye shall never taste of death; but ye shall live to behold all the doings of the Father unto the children of men, even until all things shall be fulfilled according to the will of the Father, when I shall come in my glory with the powers of heaven.
>
> 8 And ye shall never endure the pains of death; but when I shall come in my glory ye shall be changed in the twinkling of an eye from mortality to immortality; and then shall ye be blessed in the kingdom of my Father.
>
> 9 And again, ye shall not have pain while ye shall dwell in the flesh, neither sorrow save it be for the sins of the world; and all this will I do because of the thing which ye have desired of me, for ye have desired that ye might bring the souls of men unto me, while the world shall stand. [3 Nephi 28:4–9]

The other three disciples were reluctant to make their desire known. Jesus perceived their thoughts and responded, "Ye have desired the thing which John, my beloved, . . . desired of me" (v. 6). Before analyzing what their blessing was, it is important to once more show the role of the Book of Mormon in "proving to the world that the holy scriptures are true" (D&C 20:11). The wording of the Gospel of John is indefinite as to what John's blessing was. There is much speculation still in the world about what happened to him. In April 1829, as Oliver Cowdery began his work as scribe to Joseph Smith in the translation of the Book of Mormon, a difference of opinion arose between them "about the account of John the Apostle, mentioned in the New Testament, as to whether he died or continued to live." They inquired of the Lord and received, through the Urim and Thummim, a revelation that was a translated version of the record made on parchment by John and hidden up by [John] (HC 1:35–36). Through this revelation, we learn what was said to John when he was promised to remain upon the earth. It is here compared to the biblical text:

Then Peter, turning about, seeth the disciple whom Jesus loved following; which also leaned on his breast at supper, and said, Lord, which is he that betrayeth thee?	And the Lord said unto me: John, my beloved, what desirest thou? For if you shall ask what you will, it shall be granted unto you.
Peter seeing him saith to Jesus, Lord, and what *shall* this man *do?*	And I said unto him: Lord, give unto me power over death, that I may live and bring souls unto thee.
Jesus saith unto him, If I will that he tarry till I come, what *is that* to thee? follow thou me.	And the Lord said unto me: Verily, verily, I say unto thee, because thou desirest this thou shalt tarry until I come in my glory, and shalt prophesy before nations, kindreds, tongues and people.
Then went this saying abroad among the brethren, that that disciple should not die: yet Jesus said not unto him, He shall not die; but, If I will that he tarry till I come, what is *that* to thee? (John 21:20–23)	And for this cause, the Lord said unto Peter: If I will that he tarry till I come, what is that to thee? For he desired of me that he might bring souls unto me, but thou desirest that thou mightest speedily come unto me in my kingdom.
	I say unto thee, Peter, this was a good desire; but my beloved his desired that he might do more, or a greater work yet among men than what he has before done. (D&C 7:1–5)

Thus, we have three witnesses to the promise that John the Beloved did not die, but was allowed instead to remain upon the earth. These witnesses are the Bible, the Book of Mormon, and the Doctrine and Covenants. The book of Revelation is even a fourth witness. An angel told John that he "must prophesy again before many peoples, and nations, and tongues, and kings" (Revelation 10:11). In June of 1831, at a conference of the Church, "the Spirit of the Lord fell upon Joseph (Smith) in an unusual manner, and he prophesied that John the Revelator was then among the ten tribes of Israel who had been led away by Shalmaneser, King of Assyria, to prepare them for their return from their long dispersion, to again posses the land of their fathers."[2] As we study the second witness, the Book of Mormon, the promises to the three Nephite disciples who were similarly blessed, give us further insight into the mission of John as well.

Initially, Mormon records that Jesus told the Three Nephites they would "never taste of death; but ye shall live to behold all the doings of the Father unto the children of men" until Christ shall come in his glory (v. 7). Their change from mortality to immortality was not to come until Christ's Second Coming, but there was a change to come upon them at this time (A.D. 34) that would not subject them to the pains of the body or to the pains of death. Their only experiences of sorrow would be "for the sins of the world" as they beheld the doings of the children men (vv. 8–9).

Later Mormon inquired of the Lord and learned more about the changes that had come upon the three (and also John):

> 36 And now behold, as I spake concerning those whom the Lord hath chosen, yea, even three who were caught up into the heavens, that I knew not whether they were cleansed from mortality to immortality—

> 37 But behold, since I wrote, I have inquired of the Lord, and he hath made it manifest unto me that there must needs be a change wrought upon their bodies, or else it needs be that they must taste of death;

> 38 Therefore, that they might not taste of death there was a change wrought upon their bodies, that they might not suffer pain nor sorrow save it were for the sins of the world.

> 39 Now this change was not equal to that which shall take place at the last day; but there was a change wrought upon them, insomuch that Satan could have no power over them, that he could not tempt them; and they were sanctified in the flesh, that they were holy, and that the powers of the earth could not hold them.

---

[2] John Whitmer's History of the Church (ch. v) as quoted in a footnote. HC 1:176.

> 40 And in this state they were to remain until the judgment day of Christ; and at that day they were to receive a greater change, and to be received into the kingdom of the Father to go no more out, but to dwell with God eternally in the heavens. [3 Nephi 28:36–40]

After repeating what had been stated earlier (vv. 36–38), Mormon stated that the change upon their bodies "was not equal to that which shall lake place at the last day; but . . . Satan could have no power over them . . . they were sanctified in the flesh . . . that the powers of the earth could not hold them. And in this state they were to remain until the judgment day of Christ; and at that day they were to receive a greater change, and . . . dwell with God eternally in the heavens" (vv. 39–40).

The change that came upon the Three Nephites' bodies was apparently the same, or similar to, the change that came upon translated beings such as Moses "whom the Lord took unto himself" (Alma 45:19), and Elijah who "went up by a whirlwind into heaven" (2 Kings 2:11). Concerning the doctrine of translation, Joseph Smith taught:

> Now the doctrine of translation is a power which belongs to this Priesthood. There are many things which belong to the powers of the Priesthood and the keys thereof, that have been kept hid from before the foundation of the world; they are hid from the wise and prudent to be revealed in the last times.
>
> Many have supposed that the doctrine of translation was a doctrine whereby men were taken immediately into the presence of God, and into an eternal fullness, but this is a mistaken idea. Their place of habitation is that of the terrestrial order, and a place prepared for such characters He held in reserve to be ministering angels unto many planets, and who as yet have not entered into so great a fullness as those who are resurrected from the dead. [TPJS, 170]

The terrestrial-type body received by translated beings was probably also given to the Three Nephites. However, there are some differences in the Three Nephites and the translated beings. While the translated beings are taken off the earth and minister to many planets (TPJS, 170 quoted above), the Nephites (and John) were to remain upon the earth and minister to the people of this earth. As revealed anew to Joseph Smith and Oliver Cowdery, John the Beloved was to be made "as flaming fire and a ministering angel; he shall minister for those who shall be heirs of salvation who dwell on the earth" (D&C 7:6). To be "as flaming fire and a ministering angel" seems to be equating his mission with those of spirits and angels. "Spirits can only be revealed in flaming fire and glory. Angels have advanced further, their light and glory being tabernacled; and hence they appear in bodily shape" (TPJS, 325). The Nephites and John would have the same mission: they would minister in the flesh, but would not have the light and glory of an angel or of a resurrected being. Therefore, they would not have to tabernacle their light and glory, but would be able to appear as mortal men. This will be discussed later. John's ministering to those "who shall be heirs of salvation" seems to be the equivalent of the Three Nephites' desire to "bring the souls of men unto [Christ], while the world shall stand" (v. 9).

> 10 And for this cause ye shall have fulness of joy; and ye shall sit down in the kingdom of my Father; yea, your joy shall be full, even as the Father hath given me fulness of joy; and ye shall be even as I am, and I am even as the Father; and the Father and I are one;
>
> 11 And the Holy Ghost beareth record of the Father and me; and the Father giveth the Holy Ghost unto the children of men, because of me.
> [3 Nephi 28:10–11]

The blessing of sitting "down in the kingdom of my Father; yea, your joy shall be full" (v. 10) was essentially the same promise given to the nine Nephite disciples to "come unto [Christ] in my kingdom; and with me ye shall find rest" (v. 3). Thus, for each of the Twelve Nephites to become "even as I am, and I even as the Father," is to become as God or to become a God. "Therefore, all that the Father hath shall be given him," which is the blessing of the oath and covenant of the Melchizedek Priesthood (D&C 84:35–39). The oneness of the Father and the Son can be confirmed by the Holy Ghost. Jesus concluded his promise to the Nephites with the declaration that "the Holy Ghost beareth record of the Father and me" (v. 11). The doctrine of the "Three Nephites" remaining upon the earth can, therefore, also be confirmed by the Holy Ghost.

The Three Disciples Caught up to Heaven

12 And it came to pass that when Jesus had spoken these words, he touched every one of them with his finger save it were the three who were to tarry, and then he departed.

13 And behold, the heavens were opened, and they were caught up into heaven, and saw and heard unspeakable things.

14 And it was forbidden them that they should utter; neither was it given unto them power that they could utter the things which they saw and heard;

15 And whether they were in the body or out of the body, they could not tell; for it did seem unto them like a transfiguration of them, that they were changed from this body of flesh into an immortal state, that they could behold the things of God. [3 Nephi 28:12–15]

Jesus touched each of the nine disciples who had requested to come unto him following his enumeration of their promised blessing. The three other disciples were then "caught up into heaven, and saw and heard unspeakable things"[3] (vv. 12–13). What the three of the Twelve saw and heard during their apparent transfiguration was forbidden to be told, nor were they granted power to tell of their experience. Also, they did not know whether they had been taken out of their body or remained in it (vv. 14–15). Paul had a similar experience " (whether in the body, I cannot tell; or whether out of the body, I cannot tell: God knoweth;) such an one caught up to the third

---

[3] A cross-reference to v. 36 shows that it was only the three who were caught up, not all twelve disciples.

heaven" (2 Corinthians 12:1–7).[4] Such experiences are too sacred, it seems, to be shared with mortal man. However, other experiences were shared.

Mormon knew about the early ministry of the three disciples from the record that he was abridging. He gave a brief synopsis of their experiences.

16 But it came to pass that they did again minister upon the face of the earth; nevertheless they did not minister of the things which they had heard and seen, because of the commandment which was given them in heaven.

17 And now, whether they were mortal or immortal, from the day of their transfiguration, I know not;

18 But this much I know, according to the record which hath been given—they did go forth upon the face of the land, and did minister unto all the people, uniting as many to the church as would believe in their preaching; baptizing them, and as many as were baptized did receive the Holy Ghost.

19 And they were cast into prison by them who did not belong to the church. And the prisons could not hold them, for they were rent in twain.

20 And they were cast down into the earth; but they did smite the earth with the word of God, insomuch that by his power they were delivered out of the depths of the earth; and therefore they could not dig pits sufficient to hold them.

21 And thrice they were cast into a furnace and received no harm.

22 And twice were they cast into a den of wild beasts; and behold they did play with the beasts as a child with a suckling lamb, and received no harm.

---

[4] Paul does not say that he was the man caught up into the third heaven, but a careful reading of the text shows that he is speaking about himself. It is also possible that Joseph Smith's vision of the Father and Son in the spring of 1820 was another similar experience. He records that he could not write all of the things he was told and then states: "When I came to myself again, I found myself lying on my back, looking up into heaven" (JS–H 1:20). It is possible that he did not know whether he had been in or out of his body.

> 23 And it came to pass that thus they did go forth among all the people of Nephi, and did preach the gospel of Christ unto all people upon the face of the land; and they were converted unto the Lord, and were united unto the church of Christ, and thus the people of that generation were blessed, according to the word of Jesus. [3 Nephi 28:16–23]

Their ministry was not easy; however, the change that had come upon their bodies prevented them from harm, even death, as opposition came. Mormon records that, when cast into prisons, the prisons could not hold them; when thrown into pits, the power of the word of God delivered them out; three times "they were cast into a furnace and received no harm. Twice were they cast into a den of wild beasts" but merely played with the beasts as would a child with a lamb" (vv. 19–22). However, the opposition to the Three Nephites, spoken of by Mormon, came between the years A.D. 211 and A.D. 230, as shown by his later testimony of that period.

> 30 Therefore they did exercise power and authority over the disciples of Jesus who did tarry with them, and they did cast them into prison; but by the power of the word of God, which was in them, the prisons were rent in twain, and they went forth doing mighty miracles among them.
>
> 31 Nevertheless, and notwithstanding all these miracles, the people did harden their hearts, and did seek to kill them, even as the Jews at Jerusalem sought to kill Jesus, according to his word.
>
> 32 And they did cast them into furnaces of fire, and they came forth receiving no harm.
>
> 33 And they also cast them into dens of wild beasts, and they did play with the wild beasts even as a child with a lamb; and they did come forth from among them, receiving no harm. [4 Nephi 1:30–33; the dates are given in vv. 27 & 35]

All of the people of the first generation "were converted unto the Lord, and were united unto the Church of Christ" (v. 23; see also 4 Nephi 1:1–2). During this generation the other nine disciples were taken into the paradise of God as they had been promised, and "other disciples were ordained in their stead" (4 Nephi 1:14). The ministry of the original twelve disciples, in the first generation, was the epitome of the gospel being preached.

24 And now I, Mormon, make an end of speaking concerning these things for a time.

25 Behold, I was about to write the names of those who were never to taste of death, but the Lord forbade; therefore I write them not, for they are hid from the world.

26 But behold, I have seen them, and they have ministered unto me.

27 And behold they will be among the Gentiles, and the Gentiles shall know them not.

28 They will also be among the Jews, and the Jews shall know them not.

29 And it shall come to pass, when the Lord seeth fit in his wisdom that they shall minister unto all the scattered tribes of Israel, and unto all nations, kindreds, tongues and people, and shall bring out of them unto Jesus many souls, that their desire may be fulfilled, and also because of the convincing power of God which is in them. [3 Nephi 28:24–29]

Mormon chose not to give more details of the ministry of the three transfigured disciples to future generations (v. 24). He just bore testimony of their continued existence among the Nephites. He was going to write the names of those three disciples, but for some reason the Lord forbade him (v. 25). However, they had ministered to Mormon, and also to his son several hundreds of years later "until the wickedness of the people was so great that the Lord would not suffer them to remain with the people" (3 Nephi 28:26; Mormon 8:10–11). Therefore, their ministry among the Nephite people lasted for between three and four hundred years.

The ministry of the three disciples continued into the duration of the mortal earth. We know nothing about their ministry between approximately A.D. 400 and the restoration of the gospel in A.D. 1830, but they have ministered in this dispensation as Mormon prophesied they would. He foretold of their being among the Gentiles and among the Jews, although they would not be known by either group (vv. 27–28). Therefore, much of their work would be unknown even by those to whom they ministered. He also said, "when the Lord seeth fit in his wisdom [the Three Nephites] shall minister unto all the scattered tribes of Israel, and unto all nations, kindreds, tongues and people, and shall bring . . . unto Jesus many souls" (v. 29). The basis of their appearances was, as stated before, to bring souls unto Jesus. A few instances that verify their ministry in these latter days are given below.

According to Lucy Mack Smith, the mother of the Prophet, as Joseph Smith was translating the Book of Mormon, he received a revelation to write a letter to a man named David Whitmer, and request his assistance in moving Joseph and Oliver to the Whitmer's area because of threats on Joseph's life. David Whitmer, under the advice of his father, Peter Whitmer, Sr., agreed to go as soon as he had sown his field with plaster of paris.

> The next morning, David took a wooden measure under his arm and went out to sow the plaster, which he had left, two days previous, in heaps near his sister's house, but, on coming to the place, he discovered that it was gone! He then ran to his sister, and inquired of her if she knew what had become of it. Being surprised she said, "Why do you ask me? was it not all sown yesterday?"
>
> "Not to my knowledge," answered David.
>
> "I am astonished at that," replied his sister, "for the children came to me in the forenoon, and begged of me to go out and see the men sow plaster in the field, saying, that they never saw anybody sow plaster so fast in their lives. I accordingly went, and saw three men at work in the field, as the children said, but, supposing that you had hired some help, on account of your hurry, I went immediately into the house, and gave the subject no further attention."
>
> David made considerable inquiry in regard to the matter, both among his relatives and neighbors, but was not able to learn who had done it. However, the family were convinced that there was an exertion of supernatural power connected with this strange occurrence. [Lucy Mack Smith, History of Joseph Smith, Preston Nibley, ed. (Salt Lake City: Bookcraft, 1956), 148–49].

Were these three men the Three Nephites? Certainly the "convincing power of God . . . [was] in them" (3 Nephi 29:29) as far as the Whitmers were concerned.

As a second incident, Golden R. Buchanan, while serving as the president of the Southwest Indian Mission (in Arizona) wrote an article entitled "Indian Traditions." Therein, he stated:

> Some months ago I spent a few days in the hinterlands of the reservation. Among others that I visited was an old medicine man. His home was remote, and up to this time he had never heard the gospel. As we sat in his home, I began the story of the gospel, using his lovely daughter as an interpreter. As the story progressed, I could see his interest rising, and by the time our story reached the part of the visit of the Savior to this continent and his choosing of the Twelve, he could contain his eagerness no longer.

> In his native tongue, for he could speak no English, he said, "I know of that," and putting up his hands he named the Twelve disciples chosen by the savior [sic]. He gave them all names and in order. As the story continued, more and more he entered into the discussion, supplying parts of it. He was so completely enthralled that he seemed not to notice that we were white people. He fitted in the stories of the people with the message of the restoration.

> Later on in the day, as we sat in the shade visiting, I asked him if he would let me have and write the names of the Twelve as he had given them. He thought a while and then cautioned that should I write, I must never give them to the world. They were sacred, and not to be used lightly. But, since I was a friend and knew the story anyway, he would give them to me and I might write them if I would keep them to myself. He then named them one by one, each in its place; there could be no variation. As we sat there visiting, I thought to try him on another point. "Which of these Twelve are the three that did not die?" I asked. His eyes flashed, he looked at me searchingly. I seemed to read the thoughts in his mind, which were something like this. "How could you white men know about such things?"

> I said further to him, "Yes, I know about it. It is here in your book, the Book of Mormon. It is no secret. Your forefathers wrote it, and we have it here. I just wanted to see if you could give me the names of the three."

> He sat for some time with his head bowed, and then finally looked up and said, "The names of the Twelve I have just given you, are not the Twelve that he chose on this continent, they are the Twelve that were with him across the waters before he came here. Their names are sacred and must not be used lightly." After some little time I asked him if he

could give me the names of the Twelve chosen here. He looked up at me with a twinkle in his eye and said, "My friend, you have had enough for one time. Come again some other time." He got up from the log and hurried away and busied himself with some sheep that were in the pen. As I sat there pondering, his wife came over and warned me again of the sacredness of what I had learned and suggested that they should only be used on rare occasions.

On other occasions I have been told the story of the three who never died. Some of the old patriarchs claim that they have seen the three, that they have sat with them in conference and have discussed the program of the Navajo people. But, said one, "They are not just like us although they look like it. They are not dead, but something has happened to their bodies because they can sit with us in council and then, quick as a flash, they are clear across the reservation with another group of Navajos. I do not know how they do it, but I know them and have talked with them many times." [Golden R. Buchanan, "Indian Traditions," *Improvement Era,* April, 1955, 286–87]

In still another incident, President Harold B. Lee recorded in his journal a story told him by a missionary in 1959:

I met a 75-year-old woman, who, when the first missionaries came to that area, told them she knew that their message was true because three elderly men had come to their community some time before, and had taught these same doctrines and had gone from there south into Central America. This story agrees with the report of natives in Guatemala, when the first Elders opened the work there. [L. Brent Goates, HAROLD B. LEE: Prophet and Seer (Salt Lake City: Bookcraft, 1985), 291]

There are many other accounts, both written and verbal, among the Latter-day Saints today.[5] Many of these are spurious and embellished, and have not been endorsed by the Church or its leaders. Each story should be tested by the purpose given in the Third Nephi account; does the incident bring souls unto Christ? However, the

---

[5] In 1949, Hector Lee, a professor at the University of New Mexico published a collection of stories about the Three Nephites. He titled it *"The Three Nephites: The Substance and Significance of the Legend in Folklore."* The University of New Mexico Press, 1949. This is only one example of such collections.

incidents quoted above certainly verify that the three transfigured beings do minister in the world today.

> 30 And they are as the angels of God, and if they shall pray unto the Father in the name of Jesus they can show themselves unto whatsoever man it seemeth them good.
>
> 31 Therefore, great and marvelous works shall be wrought by them, before the great and coming day when all people must surely stand before the judgment-seat of Christ;
>
> 32 Yea even among the Gentiles shall there be a great and marvelous work wrought by them, before that judgment day.
>
> 33 And if ye had all the scriptures which give an account of all the marvelous works of Christ, ye would, according to the words of Christ, know that these things must surely come.
>
> 34 And wo be unto him that will not hearken unto the words of Jesus, and also to them whom he hath chosen and sent among them; for whoso receiveth not the words of Jesus and the words of those whom he hath sent receiveth not him; and therefore he will not receive them at the last day; [3 Nephi 28:30–34]

Mormon described them as being "as the angels of God, and if they shall pray unto the Father in the name of Jesus they can show themselves unto whatsoever man it seemeth them good. Therefore, great and marvelous works shall be wrought by them . . . even among the Gentiles" (vv. 30–33). Some day we will know much more concerning their ministry at the time of the restoration of the gospel, and their work that followed, and will have the above testimony of Mormon verified in our hearts and minds. However, not all will be receptive of their existence and work among us.

Many people are reluctant to believe in an additional volume of scripture such as the Book of Mormon, or in the ministering of angels (people who have once lived upon the earth and died, but now return in the spirit body or as resurrected beings). It is probably even more difficult for an unbelieving person to accept the visitations of people such as John the Beloved and the Three Nephites. Perhaps that is why Mormon concluded his record of Jesus' ministry with a warning to those who would not believe Jesus' words, or the words of those whom he hath sent. Jesus will not receive these people at the last day (v. 34). He had taught the same concept to the Twelve during his Jerusalem mortal ministry.

> Whosoever therefore shall confess me before men, him will I confess also before my Father which is in heaven.
>
> But whosoever shall deny me before men, him will I also deny before my Father which is in heaven.
>
> He that receiveth you receiveth me, and he that receiveth me receiveth him that sent me. [Matthew 10:32–33; 40]

Mormon instructed us about another New Testament teaching as he concluded his account of Jesus' ministry. Those who offend God by trampling him under their feet, by rejecting or setting at naught his counsel, will be subjected to his justice. "And it would be better for them if they had not been born. For do ye suppose that ye can get rid of the justice of an offended God, who hath been trampled under feet of men, that thereby salvation might come?" (3 Nephi 28:35; see also 1 Nephi 19:7). Jesus said the same thing about the person (Judas) who would betray him. "The Son of man goeth as it is written of him: but woe unto that man by whom the Son of man is betrayed! it had been good for that man if he had not been born" (Matthew 26:24).

The same was revealed regarding "the sons of perdition" in Joseph Smith's vision of the various degrees of glory; "of whom I [Jesus Christ] say that it had been better for them never to have been born: (D&C 76:24). Mormon's injunction may imply that he also speaks of sons of perdition. Regardless, persons who knowingly reject the words of Jesus, when they are taught by the Spirit, are offending God; and if they do not repent have wasted their mortal probation. They could have attained much more.

The twelve Nephite disciples had all chosen an admirable desire. The Lord had honored that desire and had promised great blessings. Mormon verified the blessings to the three disciples and undoubtedly the blessings of the other nine disciples also. As members of the restored Church of Jesus Christ, there are also many conditional blessings extended to us.

> 20 There is a law, irrevocably decreed in heaven before the foundations of this world, upon which all blessings are predicated—
>
> 21 And when we obtain any blessing from God, it is by obedience to that law upon which it is predicated. [D&C 130:20–21]

These blessings will also be verified if the conditions are met. "I, the Lord, am bound When ye do what I say; but when ye do not what I say, ye have no promise" (Doctrine and Covenants 82:10).

Chapter 16

Mormon's Concluding Remarks

3 Nephi 29–30

Mormon stated that, in the ending of the thirty-fourth year, Jesus "did show himself unto [the Nephites] oft" (3 Nephi 26:13), but he only recorded one of those appearances in his abridgment (3 Nephi 27–28). He abruptly concluded that one event, and then added a few words concerning "when the Lord shall see fit, in his wisdom, that these sayings shall come unto the Gentiles according to his word" (3 Nephi 29:1). This may suggest that the last two chapters of 3 Nephi were done at a later time, perhaps after he was interrupted from his abridging to battle again with the Lamanites. Regardless, he now speaks of the future time when God shall bring forth the Book of Mormon. In other words, he is speaking of our day, the day of Joseph Smith and the Restoration and those events that follow. The divine ministry of Jesus was over. Mormon was coming to the end of the Nephite era, the time of their destruction. He looked forward to a better day, the day when his work would come forth. An outline of these last two chapters of Third Nephi, an overview to prepare for a deeper study, follows.

Outline • 3 Nephi 29–30

➤ 29:1–9   When the Lord brings these sayings to the Gentiles, the covenant with the children of Israel to restore them to their lands is beginning to be fulfilled.

a.   The words of the Lord spoken by the holy prophets shall all be fulfilled. vv. 2–3

1.   You need not say the Lord delays his coming to Israel.

2.   The Lord's words are not vain; he will remember his covenant.

b.   When these sayings come, do not spurn his doings; the sword of justice will overtake you. vv. 4–5

c.   Wo to those who deny the revelations, prophecy, or gifts by the power of the Holy Ghost. vv. 6–9

1.   Those who deny the miracles wrought by Christ to get gain shall be like the son of perdition.

2.   No longer hiss, nor spurn, nor make game of the Jew, or any of the house of Israel.

3.   You cannot turn to the right or left to avoid the execution of justice in fulfilling the covenant.

➤ 30:1–2   O ye Gentiles, hear the words that Jesus Christ commands to be written.

a.   Turn from your wicked ways and repent, be baptized and receive a remission of sins. v. 2

b.   Be filled with the Holy Ghost, and be numbered with Israel. v. 2

NOTES AND COMMENTARY

1 And now behold, I say unto you that when the Lord shall see fit, in his wisdom, that these sayings shall come unto the Gentiles according to his word, then ye may know that the covenant which the Father hath made with the children of Israel, concerning their restoration to the lands of their inheritance, is already beginning to be fulfilled.

2 And ye may know that the words of the Lord, which have been spoken by the holy prophets, shall all be fulfilled; and ye need not say that the Lord delays his coming unto the children of Israel.

3 And ye need not imagine in your hearts that the words which have been spoken are vain, for behold, the Lord will remember his covenant which he hath made unto his people of the house of Israel. [3 Nephi 29:1–3]

One of the signs Jesus gave to the Nephites, in fact the initial sign, to indicate when the covenants made to the house of Israel, their gathering and the building of Zion, had commenced, was "when these works and the works which shall be wrought among you hereafter [the Book of Mormon] shall come forth from the Gentiles, unto your seed" (3 Nephi 21:2–5). Mormon now gives the same sign to the Gentiles. He adds that they "may know that the words of the Lord, which have been spoken by the holy prophets, shall all be fulfilled" (v. 2). Jesus had used Isaiah's writings as the basis for teaching the Nephites about "the fulfilling of the covenant which the Father hath made unto his people, O house of Israel" (3 Nephi 20:12). He had commanded them to "search [Isaiah] diligently"and "Search the [other] prophets, for many there be that testify of these things" (3 Nephi 23:1, 5). Mormon knew this since he had abridged Jesus' teachings concerning the Nephites. The Gentiles of the latter days would be believers in the Bible; therefore, his declaration that the prophets would all be fulfilled is a plea for the Gentiles to search their Bibles as further verification for what the Book of Mormon would teach. He apparently knew that they would "say that the Lord delays his coming unto the children of Israel" (v. 2). He also testified that the words of the prophets were not in vain, and the Lord will remember the covenant made to the house of Israel (v. 3). Therefore, Mormon's plea is very timely, and his testimony that the covenant will be fulfilled is appropriate.

4 And when ye shall see these sayings coming forth among you, then ye need not any longer spurn at the doings of the Lord, for the sword of his justice is in his right hand; and behold, at that day, if ye shall spurn at his doings he will cause that it shall soon overtake you.

5 Wo unto him that spurneth at the doings of the Lord; yea, wo unto him that shall deny the Christ and his works!

6 Yea, wo unto him that shall deny the revelations of the Lord, and that shall say the Lord no longer worketh by revelation, or by prophecy, or by gifts, or by tongues, or by healings, or by the power of the Holy Ghost!

7 Yea, and wo unto him that shall say at that day, to get gain, that there can be no miracle wrought by Jesus Christ; for he that doeth this shall become like unto the son of perdition, for whom there was no mercy, according to the word of Christ!

8 Yea, and ye need not any longer hiss, nor spurn, nor make game of the Jews, nor any of the remnant of the house of Israel; for behold, the Lord remembereth his covenant unto them, and he will do unto them according to that which he hath sworn. [3 Nephi 29:4–8]

Mormon cautions the Gentiles to no "longer spurn at the doings of the Lord, for the sword of his justice is in his right hand" and it will overtake those who spurn his doings (v. 4). Spurning his doings is to ignore or ridicule the coming forth of the Book of Mormon, and the restoration of the gospel. Mormon warned the Gentiles of four specific ways to avoid spurning the Lord's doings. These four ways are each introduced with the word "yea." The first was a warning against denying "the Christ and his works" (v. 5). This seems to be a failure to acknowledge that the translation and coming forth of the Book of Mormon, and the restoration of the priesthood and the Church was the work of Christ. To label the restoration of these things as the works of men, a cultist group, or the devil would be denying Christ and his works.

The second warning was against denying the revelation of the Lord, and the gifts of the Spirit through the power of the Holy Ghost (v. 6). One purpose of the Book of Mormon is to prove "to the world that God does inspire men, and call them to his holy work in this age and generation, as well as in generations of old" (D&C 20:11). The divine ministry of Christ is a testimony to the inspiring and calling of men in the Americas as well as in Jerusalem. The work of the Restoration was done through revelation, and the gift and power of the Holy Ghost was once more established upon the earth. The Gentiles who deny the restoration of the gospel and the Church are denying the basic tenets of the Christian faith to which they claim allegiance.

The third warning was to those who say "that there can be no miracle wrought by Jesus Christ." Mormon warns that they do this "to get gain" (v. 7). This suggests that their denial of miracles is a knowing denial. Either they do not want to lose their present advantages, or else they see a way to obtain more worldly possessions or advantages through their rejection of the Restoration. Their knowingly denying is further affirmed by the consequences to which Mormon refers. Those who deny miracles for this reason "shall become like unto the son of perdition, for whom there was no mercy" (v. 7). To become a son of perdition, a person "must receive the Holy Ghost, have the heavens opened unto him, and know God, and then sin against him" (TPJS, 358). He must "deny the truth and defy [Christ's] power" (D&C 76:31). Note, however, that Mormon warns that they "shall become *like* unto the son of perdition" (italics added). It is not their denying of the miracles that makes them sons of perdition, but their doing so to get gain. They are thus linking themselves with Satan to fight against God. If they do not repent, they will be led into the devil's fold and eventually be of his kingdom. When this happens, "there [is] no mercy, according to the word of Christ" (v. 7).

The fourth and last warning is for the Gentile to no "longer hiss, nor spurn, nor make game of the Jews, nor any of the remnant of the house of Israel" (v. 8). Throughout the history of the world the house of Israel has been ridiculed. Around and after the time of the coming forth of the Book of Mormon, there was much anti-Semitism against the Jews, particularly among the Gentile nations of the world. The Lamanites were "driven and scattered by the Gentiles" as Mormon had prophesied (Mormon 5:20). Since that time they have suffered ridicule and persecution. Elder Spencer W. Kimball pleaded with the Saints in 1954 concerning the treatment of the Lamanites:

Mr. and Mrs. Anonymous: I present to you a people who, according to prophecies, have been scattered and driven, defrauded and deprived, who are a ' branch of the tree of Israel lost from its body wanderers in a strange land' their own land. I give you nations who have gone through the deep waters of the rivers of sorrow and anguish and pain; a people who have had visited upon their heads the sins of their fathers not unto the third and fourth generation but through a hundred generations. I bring to you a multitude who have asked for bread and have received a stone and who have asked for fish and have been given a serpent. [See 3 Nephi 14:9–10]

This people ask not for your distant, faraway sympathy, your haughty disdain, your despicable contempt, your supercilious scorn, your turned-up nose, your scathing snobbery, your arrogant scoffing, nor your cold, calculating tolerance. It is a people who, unable to raise themselves by their own bootstraps, call for assistance from those who can push and lift and open doors. It is a people who pray for mercy, ask forgiveness, beg for membership in the kingdom with its opportunities to learn and do. It is a good folk who ask for fraternity, a handclasp of friendship, a word of encouragement; it is a group of nations who cry for warm acceptance and sincere brotherhood. I give you a chosen race, an affectionate and warm-hearted people, a responsive but timid and frightened folk, a simple group with childlike faith. I point you to a people in whose veins flows the blood of prophets and martyrs; a people who have intelligence and capacity to climb to former heights but who need the vision and the opportunity and the assistance of the nursing parents.

These people can rise to the loftiness of their fathers when opportunity has knocked at their door a few generations. If we fully help them, they can eventually soar to greatness. The ungerminated seeds are waiting for the rains of kindness and opportunity; the sunshine of gospel truth; the cultivation through the Church program of training and activity, and the seeds will come to life, and the harvest will be fabulous, for the Lord has promised it repeatedly.

O ye, who hiss and spurn, despise and scoff, who condemn and reject, and who in your haughty pride place your selves above and superior to these Nephite-Lamanites: I pray you to not despise them until you are able to equal their faraway folk who had such faith and fortitude and strength until you have that faith to burn at the stake with the Prophet Abinadi. It is possible that the prophet's children may be among us. [CR, April 1960, 106–7]

Elder Kimball's address continued with several other comparisons to the great faith of the ancient Nephites. Mormon's warning is certainly applicable to the situations of the Jews and the Lamanites.

Mormon's warning was probably based upon his having seen the day when the gospel would be restored. Although he doesn't proclaim his having seen that day, the other major abridgers of the record did see it. Nephi was forbidden to "write the remainder of the things which [he] saw and heard," but "the remainder [to the end of the world] shalt thou see" (1 Nephi 14:22, 24–28). Jacob was shown the Jews from the time they left to "when they shall come to the knowledge of their Redeemer, [and] they shall be gathered together again to the lands of their inheritance," and shown the Gentiles of the same time period (2 Nephi 6:8–13). Moroni was shown "that day when [the Book of Mormon] shall come forth among you" (Mormon 8:34–35). Since Mormon was the major abridger, it is only logical that he would have seen the future as well. Further evidence of his having seen the future is given in the last statement he makes in 3 Nephi 29 to those who receive the Book of Mormon. As be bears testimony once again that the Lord will remember his covenant to Israel, he states: "Therefore ye need not suppose that ye can turn the right hand of the Lord unto the left, that he may not execute judgment unto the fulfilling of the covenant which he hath made unto the house of Israel" (3 Nephi 29:9). The course of the Lord was set and Mormon knew this, whether he knew by vision, by the Spirit, or through his faith. His final testimony to the Gentiles was that he knew the covenants to Israel would be fulfilled. Having concluded his cautions to the Gentiles who receive the Book of Mormon, Mormon speaks directly to all Gentiles by invitation and commandment.

> 1 Hearken, O ye Gentiles, and hear the words of Jesus Christ, the Son of the living God, which he hath commanded me that I should speak concerning you, for, behold he commandeth me that I should write, saying:
>
> 2 Turn, all ye Gentiles, from your wicked ways; and repent of your evil doings, of your lyings and deceivings, and of your whoredoms, and

of your secret abominations, and your idolatries, and of your murders,
and your priestcrafts, and your envyings, and your strifes, and from all
your wickedness and abominations, and come unto me, and be baptized
in my name, that ye may receive a remission of your sins, and be filled
with the Holy Ghost, that ye may be numbered with my people who are
of the house of Israel. [3 Nephi 30:1–2]

Mormon makes two very important points in his last chapter.
First, he testifies to the Gentiles of the divinity of Jesus Christ; and
second, he is speaking under commandment of him whom he bears
testimony. Those Gentiles who are honest in heart will know that his
testimony is true. President Brigham Young declared that "there is
not a man or woman that loves the truth, who has heard the report of
the Book of Mormon, but the Spirit of the Almighty has testified to
him or her of its truth; neither has any man heard the name of Joseph
Smith, but the Spirit has whispered to him 'He is a true Prophet.'"[1]
The witness of Jesus Christ will come to the honest in heart "because
of their belief in [Jesus Christ], in and of the Holy Ghost" and then
"the fullness of these things [the gospel] shall be made known to
them" (3 Nephi 16:6–7).

The words that Mormon was commanded to write to the Gentiles
were an invitation for them to repent and also a promise that would
be of eternal worth to them. The invitation to repent correlates with
Jesus' promise to take the gospel from among the Gentiles because
of their sinning against the gospel. The same kinds of sins are enumerated by Jesus and Mormon: lyings, deceivings, whoredoms, secret
abominations, idolatries, murders, and priestcrafts (v. 2; see also 3
Nephi 16:8–10). There is, however, one sin mentioned by Jesus and
Mormon that needs some clarification. The Gentiles are invited to
repent of their murders. The Book of Mormon declares: "the law
requireth the life of him who hath murdered" (Alma 34:11–12; see
also 1:13–14). The Doctrine and Covenants, as part of "the law of the
Church" states:

---

[1] *JD* 1:93

18 And now, behold, I speak unto the church. Thou shalt not kill; and he that kills shall not have forgiveness in this world, nor in the world to come.

19 And again, I say, thou shalt not kill; but he that killeth shall die. [D&C 42:18–19]

However, Alma equated murder with leading God's children "away unto destruction" (Alma 36:14). He also taught "that it is not easy for [whosoever murdereth against the light and knowledge of God] to obtain forgiveness," (Alma 39:5), suggesting that there is a possibility of obtaining forgiveness in some circumstances. Therefore, it seems that there is some hope for the Gentiles who, probably because of unique circumstances, may have been guilty of this heinous crime. The judgment, of course, will be with the Lord; and "the law of the Church" instructs: "that if any persons among you shall kill they shall be delivered up and dealt with according to the laws of the land; for remember that he hath no forgiveness; and it shall be proved according to the laws of the land" (D&C 42:70).

The promise of eternal worth to the Gentiles is one that was held out to them by Jesus in his ministry to the Nephites, and recorded earlier in Third Nephi. If they would repent and "come unto [Christ], and be baptized in [His] name, that ye may receive a remission of your sins, and be filled with the Holy Ghost . . . ye may be numbered with my people who are of the house of Israel" (v. 2; cp. 3 Nephi 21:20–22; 23:4–5). In being numbered with Israel, they may receive the blessings of salvation and eternal life promised to Israel. Part of the covenant made to Abraham was:

And I will bless them through thy name; for as many as receive this Gospel shall be called after thy name, and shall be accounted thy seed, and shall rise up and bless thee, as their father. [Abraham 2:10]

Since the gospel was to go first to the Gentiles in the latter days, this promise is a most fitting promise with which to conclude Jesus' divine ministry.

Jesus had completed his ministry among the Nephites. He had taught them the gospel, demonstrated his power, and given the disciples the authority to carry on his work. The book of Third Nephi is the First Gospel because of its contribution to our understanding of Jesus Christ and his teachings. It does not cover the same historical events of the mortal ministry in Jerusalem, nor all of the teachings that were associated with those incidents. However, like the Gospel or testimony of John, it does verify, clarify, and expound upon the gospel principles that are necessary for salvation. It further gives undeniable evidence of the historicity and divinity of our Lord and Savior. It is "Another Testament of Jesus Christ."

Scripture Index

OLD TESTAMENT

NEW TESTAMENT

JOSEPH SMITH TRANSLATION

BOOK OF MORMON

DOCTRINE AND COVENANTS

PEARL OF GREAT PRICE

Topical Index